THE USE OF THE OLD TESTAMENT IN ST. MATTHEW'S GOSPEL

SUPPLEMENTS
TO
NOVUM TESTAMENTUM

VOLUME XVIII

LEIDEN
E. J. BRILL
1967

THE USE OF THE OLD TESTAMENT IN ST. MATTHEW'S GOSPEL

WITH SPECIAL REFERENCE TO THE MESSIANIC HOPE

BY

ROBERT HORTON GUNDRY

LEIDEN
E. J. BRILL
1967

PRINTED IN THE NETHERLANDS

TO LOIS,
MY WIFE

TABLE OF CONTENTS

The Matthaean Argument from the Fulfilment of Messianic Prophecy

ACKNOWLEDGEMENTS

This book is a Ph.D. dissertation presented to and accepted by the University of Manchester in the spring of 1961 and brought up to date in the summer of 1964. I express my gratitude to Professor F. F. Bruce, who supervised my research, to Mr. P. R. Weis, who graciously allowed me to peruse photographs of the as yet unpublished Codex Neofiti I of the Old Palestinian Targum to the Pentateuch in the Vatican Library, to Dr. W. H. Chaloner, who counselled me in my course of study at the University of Manchester, to my former mentor Dr. Marchant King, and most of all to my wife, who first encouraged me to undertake this work and who typed the rough draft of the thesis. The time devoted to this study was made financially possible through the Laymen's Scholarship Fund, administered by the Los Angeles Baptist College and Seminary, and through the generosity of others. To them I give my thanks. I also express my appreciation for the assistance given me by the librarians and their assistants at the University of Manchester, The John Rylands Library, the University of Edinburgh, the National Library of Scotland, the University of Basel, the University of Tübingen, Westmont College, and Fuller Theological Seminary. Finally, I am indebted to E. J. Brill Publishers for their undertaking the publication of this volume, and to the editor of the *Journal of Biblical Literature* for permission to use material from my article which appeared in vol. 83 (1963), pp. 404ff., of that journal.

Robert H. Gundry

Westmont College

Santa Barbara, California

ABSTRACT

A re-examination of the OT quotations in Mt is needed because of the neglect in past examinations of the allusive quotations, because of our present knowledge from the Dead Sea Scrolls that allusive quotation of the OT was a conscious literary practice, and because of the bewildering variety of hypotheses advanced to account for the Matthaean quotations.

Formal quotations which Mt shares with Mk are almost purely Septuagintal. In all other strata of synoptic quotation material—formal and allusive, Marcan, Lucan, and peculiarly Matthaean—the text-form is very mixed, showing contacts with the Hebrew, the Targums, the LXX, the OT Peshitta, Theodotion (in Dan), rabbinic tradition, and apocryphal literature. This mixture stands in contrast to the prevailingly Septuagintal form of OT quotations throughout the rest of the NT. Thus, the inclusion of allusive quotations leads to two new and important discoveries: first, contrary to former opinion, the Matthaean formula-citations do not stand out from the other synoptic quotations in their mixed text-form; second, the formal quotations in the Marcan tradition stand out in their adherence to the LXX.

Redactional theories about the origin of Mt mistakenly treat the formula-citations as a textually distinctive group. The view of C. C. Torrey that the quotations in Aramaic Mt stood in metrical Hebrew stumbles against the non-Marcan Septuagintal quotations and parts of quotations. The liturgical-homiletical hypothesis of G. D. Kilpatrick does not explain the text-form of the Matthaean quotations, for if Septuagintal and non-Septuagintal quotations can derive from the homiletical tradition, they can equally well derive from the first evangelist himself and no need for the liturgical-homiletical hypothesis then exists. K. Stendahl's argument for a Matthaean school similar to the Qumran community again mistakenly regards the formula-citations as a textually distinctive group, largely through neglect of the allusive quotations. Lindars' treatment shares this neglect. The Testimony Book hypothesis has been partially confirmed by the discovery of Qumran *testimonia*, but offers no help in explaining the text-form of the quotations in Mt. The abundance of non-Septuagintal Greek Targums advocated by P. Kahle could not explain non-Septuagintal quotations unless it could be proved the NT author was incapable of translating the Hebrew and of utilizing other Semitic textual tradition. But the higher the number of Greek translations of the OT that can be proved, the greater the likelihood a NT author could and would translate for himself. Since the church emerged from the synagogue, in which the practice of targumizing prevailed, it is best to say that the first evangelist utilized a number of textual traditions in a targumic manner.

The mixture of Septuagintal, Hebrew, and Aramaic elements in synoptic quotations harmonizes perfectly with the trilingual milieu now known from archaeological data to have existed in first century Palestine. The Septuagintal form of formal Marcan quotations implies a Hellenistic strain, to which agrees the tradition that Mk was a Roman gospel. The taking over of these quotations by Mt confirms the dependence of Mt upon Mk. But the mixed text in other quotations throughout all three synoptics (including allusive Marcan quotations) points to a common tradition behind all three, not merely a Q behind Mt and Lk or Lucan dependence on Mt. An Aramaic Ur-Mt is excluded by the Septuagintal element as deeply embedded in the tradition as the Semitic elements. The only hypothesis with enough flexibility to meet the requirements is that a body of loose notes stands behind the bulk of the synoptic tradition. The wide use of shorthand and the carrying of notebooks in the Graeco-Roman world, the school practice of circulating lecture notes and utilizing them in published works, and the later transmission of rabbinic tradition through shorthand notes support this hypothesis. As a former publican, the Apostle Matthew would have been admirably fitted to fill a position of note-taker in the band of uneducated apostles. That the same peculiar mixed text occurs in the quotations obviously due to the first evangelist and in the other quotations throughout the synoptics suggests the same hand is behind both.

These suggestions support the early date and the historical worth of the synoptic tradition. An examination of the effect which the fulfilment-motif exercised on the tradition shows a conforming of descriptive phraseology to OT language, but not a creative influence. With some modification and extension, the text-plots indicated by C. H. Dodd as areas of the OT on which Christian exegesis concentrated fit not only formal, but also allusive quotations. This fact and the naturalness with which the Matthaean quotations fall under easily recognizable principles of interpretation demonstrate that Matthaean hermeneutics were not atomizing—in contrast to Qumran and rabbinical literature. That every principle of interpretation is exhibited in quotations occurring on the lips of Jesus suggests he himself was the author of this new and coherent method of OT exegesis.

An examination of the Messianic hope from the side of OT scholarship shows that that hope arose in pre-exilic times. The OT passages interpreted in Mt as directly Messianic are found to be so. Thus, specific fulfilments of individual Messianic prophecies provide a basis for the broader Christian view of the divine purpose guiding OT history toward Jesus Christ.

LIST OF ABBREVIATIONS

Anger	=	Anger, R. *Ratio, qua loci Veteris Testamenti in evangelio Matthaei laudantur, quid valeat ad illustrandam huius evangelii originem, quaeritur.* (Leipziger Programme I-III.) Leipzig, 1861-62.
A & G	=	Arndt, W. F., and Gingrich, F. W. *A Greek-English Lexicon of the New Testament and Other Early Christian Literature.* Chicago, 1957.
BA	=	*Biblical Archaeologist.*
BASOR	=	*Bulletin of the American Schools of Oriental Research.*
BDB	=	*A Hebrew and English Lexicon of the Old Testament with an Appendix containing the Biblical Aramaic.* Based on the lexicon of W. Gesenius as translated by E. Robinson and edited by F. Brown with the co-operation of S. R. Driver and C. Briggs. Oxford, 1929.
BibSac	=	*Bibliotheca Sacra.*
BJRL	=	*Bulletin of the John Rylands Library.*
Bl-D	=	Blass, F., and Debrunner, A. *Grammatik des neutestamentlichen Griechisch.* Göttingen, 1954.
BZ	=	*Biblische Zeitschrift.*
CBQ	=	*Catholic Biblical Quarterly.*
DLZ	=	*Deutsche Literaturzeitung.*
DSS	=	Dead Sea Scrolls.
esp.	=	especially.
ET	=	*Expository Times.*
HDB	=	*A Dictionary of the Bible.* Edited by J. Hastings. 5 vols. Edinburgh, 1898-1904.
HDCG	=	*Dictionary of Christ and the Gospels.* Edited by J. Hastings. 2 vols. Edinburgh, 1906.
HTR	=	*Harvard Theological Review.*
HUCA	=	*Hebrew Union College Annual.*
ICC	=	International Critical Commentary.
IDB	=	*Interpreter's Dictionary of the Bible.* New York, 1962.
IF	=	introductory formula(e).
JAOS	=	*Journal of the American Oriental Society.*
JBL	=	*Journal of Biblical Literature.*
JSS	=	*Journal of Semitic Studies.*
JTS	=	*Journal of Theological Studies.*
Karnetzki	=	Karnetzki, M. "Die alttestamentlichen Zitate in der synoptischen Tradition." Dissertation; Tübingen, 1955.
Lindars	=	Lindars, B. *New Testament Apologetic.* Philadelphia, 1961.
L & S	=	Liddell, H., and Scott, R. *A Greek-English Lexicon.* 2 vols. New edition revised and augmented throughout by H. S. Jones with the assistance of R. McKenzie. Oxford, 1940.
LXX	=	Septuagint.
MPG	=	*Patrologiae cursus completus .... Series Graeca ....* Accurante J.-P. Migne. Paris, 1858-88.
MPL	=	*Patrologiae cursus completus .... Series Latina ....* Accurante J.-P. Migne. Paris, 1844-1904.

MS(S)	= manuscript(s).
MT	= Massoretic Text.
n.	= note
NovTest	= *Novum Testamentum.*
NT	= New Testament.
NTS	= *New Testament Studies.*
OT	= Old Testament.
par	= parallel(s)
PEQ	= *Palestine Exploration Quarterly.*
RB	= *Revue Biblique.*
RGG	= *Die Religion in Geschichte und Gegenwart.* 2. Aufl. Tübingen, 1927-31. 3. Aufl. Tübingen, 1957.—.
RHR	= *Revue de l'histoire des religions.*
SJT	= *Scottish Journal of Theology.*
Stendahl	= Stendahl, K. *The School of St. Matthew and Its Use of the Old Testament.* (Acta Seminarii Neotestamentici Upsaliensis, XX.) Uppsala, 1954.
Theol. Stud. u. Krit.	= *Theologische Studien und Kritiken.*
TLZ	= *Theologische Literaturzeitung.*
TWNT	= *Theologisches Wörterbuch zum Neuen Testament.* Begründet von G. Kittel und herausgegeben von G. Friedrich. Stuttgart, 1933.—.
VT	= *Vetus Testamentum.*
ZAW	= *Zeitschrift für die alttestamentliche Wissenschaft.*
ZDMG	= *Zeitschrift der deutschen morgenländischen Gesellschaft.*
ZNW	= *Zeitschrift für die neutestamentliche Wissenschaft.*
ZTK	= *Zeitschrift für Theologie und Kirche.*
ZWT	= *Zeitschrift für wissenschaftliche Theologie.*

N.B.: Commentaries are cited by the author and the abbreviation of the book of the Bible on which the commentary is based. Biblical references follow the book-titles of the English Bible and OT references follow the chapter and verse divisions in Kittel-Kahle, *Biblia Hebraica*, except where otherwise indicated. The generally accepted abbreviations for the books of the Bible are self-evident.

INTRODUCTION [1]

Within the last decade the quotations of the OT in Mt, particularly the "formula-quotations" (*Reflexionscitate*), have received such varied treatment as to be made the basis of a Matthaean "school" which practiced *pesher*-type exegesis similar to that displayed in the Qumran documents,[2] and minimized to the point of denial that Mt is a Jewish-Christian gospel.[3] Between these extremes, they have been regarded as one layer in multi-stage redactional theories concerning the composition of Mt,[4] translations into Greek of originally metrical Hebrew,[5] oral homiletical tradition,[6] traces of a Testimony Book, either incorporated into the first gospel [7] or constituting in large measure the format of the first gospel,[8] and remnants of Jewish Greek targums which were in use

[1] For a more detailed survey of studies in Mt outside the province of OT quotations, see P. Nepper-Christensen, *Das Matthäusevangelium, ein judenchristliches Evangelium?* (Aarhus, 1958), 13-36.

[2] K. Stendahl, *The School of St. Matthew* (Uppsala, 1954).

[3] Nepper-Christensen, *op. cit.*, esp. 136-162. For a critical review, see P. Benoit, *RB*, 66 (1959), 438-440. Since N.-Chr. simply ignores much of the OT and Jewish substratum of Mt, his thesis does not demand detailed refutation. His argument that Mt's use of the OT is exceeded in the Gospel of John (where N.-Chr. numbers fifteen fulfilment-citations) takes into account neither the penetration of OT language into the first gospel much deeper than the formula-citations nor the possibility that the fulfilment-citations in Jn reflect, if not a Jewish destination, at least a Jewish background (cf. the new light thrown upon the fourth gospel from the Dead Sea Scrolls).

[4] A. Resch, *Aussercanonische Paralleltexte zu den Evangelien* (Leipzig, 1897), II, 20-28; W. Soltau, *ZNW*, 1 (1900), 219-248, esp. 224; *idem, Unsere Evangelien* (Leipzig, 1901), 55 f.; B. W. Bacon, *Studies in Mt* (London, 1930), 156-164, 470, 475f.; W. L. Knox, *Sources of the Synoptic Gospels* (Cambridge, 1957), II, 121ff.; P. Parker, *The Gospel before Mark* (Chicago, 1953), 90ff.

[5] C. C. Torrey, *Documents of the Primitive Church* (New York, 1941), 41-90.

[6] G. D. Kilpatrick, *The Origins of the Gospel according to St. Mt* (Oxford, 1946), 56f.

[7] W. C. Allen, *ET*, 12 (1900/01), 284f.; F. C. Burkitt, *The Gospel History and Its Transmission* (Edinburgh, 1906), 124-128; V. H. Stanton, *The Gospels as Historical Documents* (Cambridge, 1909), II, 342ff.; A. H. McNeile, *Mt* (London, 1915), p. xi; J. R. Harris, *Testimonies* (Cambridge, 1916), I, 124ff.; T. W. Manson, *BJRL*, 34 (1951/52), 323; R. M. Grant, *The Letter and the Spirit* (London, 1957), 46; F. C. Grant, *The Gospels: Their Origin and Growth* (London, 1957), 65.

[8] J. B. Gregory, *The Oracles ascribed to Mt by Papias* (London, 1894); E. C. Selwyn, *The Oracles in the NT* (London, 1912), pp. vii, 396-427;

prior to Christian standardization of the LXX.[1] The traditional view that Mt directly translated and targumized the Hebrew text has recently been restated by M. Karnetzki.[2]

The very abundance of hypotheses attempting to account for the peculiarities of the Matthaean quotations requires a restudy of the whole matter. Yet another factor is of even greater importance: the neglect in previous studies of the *allusive* quotations and their text-form. There exists in the synoptic tradition, and pre-eminently in Mt, a large body of allusive quotations in which the language is only colored by the OT. These have been passed over as of little importance for two reasons:

It is felt that allusive quotations can have been made only from memory, so that textual variants cannot be considered significant.[3] However, the role of oral tradition in the textual history of the OT (and in the whole Semitic culture) was greater than we are sometimes prone to think,[4] so that the ancient mode of recitation produced "vivantes concordances de l'Ancien Testament." [5] Furthermore, easy access to synagogue scrolls as well as private possession of copies of individual OT books rendered complete reliance on memory unnecessary.[6] Many of even the minor divergences from

---

T. H. Bindley, *Church Quarterly Review*, 84 (1917), 41; J. A. Findlay, *The Expositor*, 20, 8th Series (1920), 388-400; *idem*, *Jesus in the First Gospel* (London, 1925), 7; B. P. W. Stather Hunt, *Primitive Gospel Sources* (London, 1951), 101f., 149f., 182-193, 319-322.

[1] P. E. Kahle, *The Cairo Genizah*[2] (Oxford, 1959), 165, 238, 249ff.; A. Sperber [with variations], *JBL*, 59 (1940), 193-293; cf. A. Baumstark, *Biblica*, 37 (1956), 296-313.

[2] Karnetzki, 255ff.

[3] Cf. F. Johnson, *The Quotations of the New Testament from the Old* (London, 1896), 2, 29ff., citing the unwieldiness of scrolls and their lack of chapter and verse divisions.

[4] See H. S. Nyberg, *ZAW*, 11 (1934), 243f. Cf. the oral transmission of Rabbinic law and the prohibition against reading the targums (B. J. Roberts, *The OT Text and Versions* [Cardiff, 1951], 19; E. Würthwein, *The Text of the OT* [Oxford, 1957], 57; J. F. Stenning, *The Targum of Is* [Oxford, 1949], p. vii). At the same time, the Dead Sea Scrolls have taught us not to exaggerate the influence of oral tradition on the OT text.

[5] J. Bonsirven, *Exégèse rabbinique et exégèse paulinienne* (Paris, 1939), 337. Recitation is relevant with relation to written documents inasmuch as readers in the ancient world pronounced aloud the words as they read them. See J. Balogh, *Philologus*, 82 (1926/27), 84-109, 202-240.

[6] See W. O. E. Oesterley, *The Jewish Background of the Christian Liturgy* (Oxford, 1925), 111ff.; C. W. Dugmore, *The Influence of the Synagogue upon the Divine Office* (Oxford, 1944), 71; Acts 17 : 11; Lk 2 : 46f.; Jn 5: 39; I Tim 4: 13; II Tim 4: 13.

the LXX in NT quotations of the OT appear to be deliberate.[1] Sometimes NT writers verbally agree against all known OT texts, a coincidence which cannot be accounted for by memory-quotation.[2] Key words in the LXX would hardly have been forgotten. Some of the words in the LXX hardly had adequate alternative renderings, yet even these are sometimes replaced. One remembers a quotation because of its attractiveness, yet this lies in the wording.[3] For these reasons memory-citation explains textual variants in allusive quotations no more than it does in formal quotations.

Again, it is felt that allusions are not based on any attempt to cite the OT accurately; i.e., the very allusiveness makes for a carelessness in text-form, this being so especially in the high-flown language of apocalyptic.[4] Apart from the uncertainty in judging isolated sayings as "apocalyptic" [5] and although allowance must be made for the working of an allusion into the context, with resultant changes in grammatical forms, *an allusive quotation rather reflects the language and phrase-forms with which the writer is most familiar and in which he habitually thinks*—all the more so in the case of Jewish authors, whose education from childhood was steeped in OT lore.[6] One might almost say that allusive quotations are more revealing than formal quotations, for "the least direct allusion testifies to the firmest grasp and appreciation of a subject." [7]

Above all, recent researches in the Qumran scrolls have shown that in the NT period the interweaving of scriptural phraseology and one's own words was a conscious literary method.[8] This mosaic

---

[1] This is, e.g., the central thesis of "The Use of the Septuagint in the Epistle to the Hebrews" by K. J. Thomas (unpublished thesis presented to the University of Manchester, 1959).

[2] Mt 11:10; Mk 1:2; Lk 7:27 with Mal 3:1; I Pet 2:6; Ro 9:33 with Is 28:16. See J. Scott, *Principles of NT Quotation* (Edinburgh, 1877), 93.

[3] See Hunt, *op. cit.*, 150f.

[4] So Stendahl, 143, 158f. Stendahl wishes to discount the allusive quotations which vary from the LXX in order to put the Matthaean formula-quotations, on which he bases his thesis, in a class by themselves. See below, 155ff.

[5] On the nebulousness of this term, see H. Gunkel, *Schöpfung u. Chaos* (Göttingen, 1895), 290; B. Vawter, *CBQ*, 22 (1960), 33f.

[6] See Tholuck, *BibSac*, 11 (1854), 583; E. C. S. Gibson, *The OT in the New* (London, 1907), 3ff.

[7] C. Taylor, *The Gospel in the Law* (Cambridge, 1869), p. xxi. For a remarkable illustration of an OT passage influencing the thought and vocabulary of a NT author, see E. G. King, *The Expositor*, 10, 3rd Series (1889), 233ff.—on I Cor 1:18f. Cf. W. Manson, *Jesus the Messiah* (London, 1948), 81f.

[8] In the non-Biblical texts "we rarely find a whole or even a half-verse,

style flourished in Jewish writings of the Middle Ages and of the eighteenth and nineteenth centuries.[1] M. Wallenstein has shown that in spite of the extremely allusive nature of such OT quotations, variant readings in the Piyyuṭ often go with the versions.[2] The work of Rabin,[3] M. H. Gottstein,[4] P. Wernberg-Møller,[5] and J. Carmignac [6] has now demonstrated that Biblical allusions in the Zadokite documents, the Manual of Discipline, the Hodayoth, and the War of the Sons of Light against the Sons of Darkness contain variant readings which agree with one or more against the others of the MT, Targum, LXX, OT Peshitta, Vulgate, and Old Latin. These variants cannot all be put down to the allusiveness of the quotations or to poor memory, for the same variant readings sometimes occur in different Qumran manuscripts and the same variant characteristics appear in explicit quotations.[7] We must therefore reckon with the text-form of the allusive quotations for a comprehensive view of the synoptic quotation material.

Several observations about OT allusions in Mt are pertinent. We can hardly think that a writer who introduces such out-of-the-way citations as, e.g., Hos 11:1 (2:6) would not have known the OT well enough to have recognized allusive quotations in the tradition upon which he worked. We are therefore justified in looking for his treatment of the OT text here as well as in formal citations. The far greater number of OT allusions in Mt, many of them introduced into the common synoptic tradition, confirms this judgment, as do also the frequently met circumstances in which repetition of the OT phraseology occurs within the OT itself or in the NT outside the gospels, showing a certain fixity of expression. In such cases we are usually safe in seeing conscious allusion to the OT.

Deciding whether an instance of verbal parallelism between OT and NT really constitutes an allusive quotation often presents a delicate task. There is no rule of thumb which will fit all cases.

---

but mostly only mere splinters of verses . . . it is natural to find not only single words but idioms and phrases from the O.T. used in them" (C. Rabin, *JTS*, 6 [1955], 174; cf. *idem*, *The Zadokite Documents*² [Oxford, 1958], p. ix).

[1] *Ibid.*

[2] *BJRL*, 34 (1952), 474ff.

[3] *JTS*, 6 (1955), 174ff.

[4] *VT*, 3 (1953), 79-82.

[5] *Studia Theologica*, 9 (1955), 40-66.

[6] *RB*, 63 (1956), 234-260, 375-390; *Revue de Qumran*, Tome 2, No. 7 (1960), 357-394.

[7] Rabin, *JTS*, *loc. cit.*

Certainly it is not adequate to require a certain number of parallel words or merely to follow the lists of OT quotations and the bold-faced type in critical editions of the Greek New Testament, commentaries, and other works on the subject, which differ among themselves anyway. In general, the procedure here followed has been not to require a certain number of words, but to require that recognizable thought-connection exist between the OT and NT passages. Some parallel phraseology has been discounted as being due to fortuitously similar circumstances, as, e.g., the flights to Egypt of the Holy Family and Jeroboam (Mt 2:13-15; I Kings 11:40). A Septuagintal text-form is not to be made a criterion for allusive quotations. Rid of the tacit assumption that it is, we are free to recognize many significant OT allusions. The inclusion or exclusion of some doubtful passages happily does not affect the thesis of this dissertation.[1]

The thesis is twofold: (1) contrary to former opinion, the Matthaean formula-citations do not stand out from other synoptic quotation material in their divergence from the LXX, but the formal quotations in the Marcan (and parallel) tradition stand out in their adherence to the LXX; (2) the OT-motif in Mt has led neither to radical alteration of the gospel tradition nor to atomizing exegesis of the OT. To substantiate this thesis we shall examine in order the text-form of the Matthaean quotations, problems of historicity, and Matthaean hermeneutics.

---

[1] For seizure upon every possible similarity of expression between NT and OT, see E. Hühn, *Die alttest. Citate u. Reminiscenzen im NT* (Tübingen, 1900), and Selwyn, *op. cit.* The inclusion of doubtful allusions would have but strengthened my argument.

PART ONE

THE TEXT-FORM OF THE MATTHAEAN QUOTATIONS OF THE OLD TESTAMENT

"The Use of the Old Testament in St. Matthew's Gospel . . ."

CHAPTER ONE

EXAMINATION OF THE TEXT-FORM

Formal Quotations in common with Mark

The formal quotations [1] in Mk are almost purely Septuagintal—often slavishly so, and even against the Hebrew text. Mt, however, tends to depart from Mk and the LXX.

Mt 3: 3; Mk 1: 3; Lk 3: 4-6: φωνὴ βοῶντος ἐν τῇ ἐρήμῳ· ἑτοιμάσατε τὴν ὁδὸν κυρίου, εὐθείας ποιεῖτε τὰς τρίβους αὐτοῦ.

Mt εὐθείας . . . αὐτοῦ] *om* syr^{sin} [2]

αὐτοῦ] τοῦ θεοῦ ἡμῶν b syr^{cur} Ir (= assimilation to LXX; strictly, syr^{cur} = αὐτοῦ + τοῦ θεοῦ ἡμῶν,[3] a conflate reading)

Lk extends the quotation through Is 40: 5 in abbreviated form.

Jn 1: 23: ἐγὼ φωνὴ βοῶντος ἐν τῇ ἐρήμῳ· εὐθύνατε τὴν ὁδὸν κυρίου, καθὼς εἶπεν Ἡσαΐας ὁ προφήτης.

Is 40: 3 LXX = Mt, except τοῦ θεοῦ ἡμῶν (= MT), instead of αὐτοῦ.

MT: קול קורא במדבר פנו דרך יהוה ישרו בערבה מסלה לאלהינו

The quotation is essentially Septuagintal in form, particularly in its construing במדבר with קול קורא rather than with פנו, in its omission of a phrase corresponding to בערבה, and in its possessive construction for לאלהינו.

That the syntax of the LXX suits the evangelists' desire to show

---

[1] The distinction between formal and allusive quotations is not always easily made. I have tried to judge by whether the quoted words flow from and into the context (allusive) or stand apart (formal). With this criterion, an allusive quotation may be of some length, i.e., more than a fleeting phrase or two.

[2] A. Merx prefers the shorter reading of syr^{sin} (*Die vier kanonischen Evangelien* [Berlin, 1897-1911], II, 32ff.). By its very brevity, however, this text appears to be an instance of Tatianic influence on the Old Syriac. Recent studies by A. Vööbus (*Studies in the History of the Gospel Text in Syriac* [Louvain, 1951]; *Early Versions of the NT* [Stockholm, 1954], 68ff., 77ff.) confirm the contention of H. J. Vogels (*Die altsyrischen Evangelien in ihrem Verhältnis zu Tatians Diatessaron* [Freiburg, 1911] and in *Synoptische Studien* [Wickenhauser *Festschrift*; München, 1953], 278-289) that the Diatessaron preceded the Syriac tetraevangelium and greatly influenced its text (against Zahn, Hjelt, Lewis, Mingana, Torrey, and M. Black). Cf. L. Vaganay, *An Introduction to the Textual Criticism of the NT* (London, 1937), 105f., 108; C. S. C. Williams, *ET*, 58 (1946/47), 251; A. Wikenhauser, *NT Introduction*[2] (London, 1958), 116.

[3] See M. Black, *An Aramaic Approach to the Gospels and Acts* (Oxford, 1946), 73.

that even the locality of John's preaching fulfilled prophecy has been unduly pressed.[1] John's call for preparation, the coming of the Lord, and the message of combined salvation and judgment are all leading themes in both the OT and NT passages. The syntax of the LXX is not necessary to the fulfilment-motif, for "if the command was uttered in the desert, it was in order to its being there obeyed or carried into execution. . . ." [2]

We must also consider the possibility that the MT is wrong in construing במדבר with פנו, since the LXX, Targum, OT Peshitta, Vulgate, and rabbinical expositors construe במדבר with קול קורא.[3] J. Ziegler has gathered a large number of agreements in syntax between the LXX and 1QIs[a] against the MT,[4] so that the accents in the MT must not be considered sacrosanct. Note further that במדבר *precedes* the verb פנו, whereas בערבה *follows* ישרו. This inexactness in the supposed parallelism suggests several possibilities: (1) the position of במדבר before פנו points to a connection with קול קורא; (2) בערבה was inserted to match במדבר when the latter was misconstrued with פנו (there was no compelling motive for the omission of בערבה by the LXX); (3) בערבה was a variant for במדבר and inserted as a conflate reading for its preservation, after which the present accents reworked the syntax of the verse (cf. the intentional preservation of variant readings in 1QIs[a] and the LXX [5]). The strange reading בערכה in 1QS viii. 12 ff. may possibly hint at the secondary nature of the word in the text of Is.

It is usually thought that the NT αὐτοῦ is a Christological adaptation designed to identify Jesus with Yahweh.[6] But since the identification has already been made by application of the verse to Jesus' forerunner, John, αὐτοῦ may be merely an abbreviation for τοῦ θεοῦ ἡμῶν.

---

[1] E.g., by A. Loisy, *Les évangiles synoptiques* (1907), I, 392; W. C. Allen, *Mt* (Edinburgh, 1907), 23; Stendahl, 48; W. Marxsen, *Der Evangelist Markus* (Göttingen, 1956), 20ff.; A. C. Sundberg, Jr., *NovTest*, 3 (1959), 275f.; J. A. Fitzmyer, *NTS*, 7 (1961), 318; S. L. Edgar, *NTS*, 9 (1962), 57.

[2] J. A. Alexander, *Mt* (London, 1861), 50, who also quotes Bengel: "ubi vox ibi auditores."

[3] See F. Delitzsch, *Is* (Edinburgh, 1884), II, 141; A. Edersheim, *The Life and Times of Jesus the Messiah* (Grand Rapids, 1953), II, 744; W. Michaelis, *Mt* (Zürich, 1948-49), I, 116.

[4] *JBL*, 78 (1959), 46-50.

[5] *Ibid.*, 57.

[6] Zahn, *Einleitung in das NT*[2] (Leipzig, 1899), II, 315; M.-J. Lagrange, *Mk*[4] (Paris, 1947), 4; Black, *loc. cit.*; Stendahl, *loc. cit.*

Mt 11: 10	Ex 23: 20 LXX	MT	Mal 3: 1 LXX	MT
ἰδοὺ ἐγὼ	ἰδοὺ ἐγὼ	הנה אנכי	ἰδοὺ ἐγὼ	הנני
ἀποστέλλω	ἀποστέλλω	שלח	ἐξαποστέλλω	שלח
τὸν ἄγγελόν μου	τὸν ἄγγελόν μου	מלאך	τὸν ἄγγελόν μου	מלאכי
πρὸ προσώπου σου,	πρὸ προσώπου σου,	לפניך	καὶ ἐπιβλέψεται	ופנה
ὅς κατασκευάσει	ἵνα φυλάξῃ σε	לשמרך	ὁδὸν	דרך
			πρὸ προσώπου	לפני
τὴν ὁδόν σου ἔμπροσθέν σου	ἐν τῇ ὁδῷ	בַּדרך	μου	

Mt 11: 10 ἔμπροσθέν σου] *om* D*pc* it (Mcion?) (= assimilation to Mk)
Ex 23: 20 MT מלאך] כי מלאך — Sam LXX Vg
Mal 3: 1 LXX ἐγώ AQW ℵ^{c}Luc] *om* Bℵ*C
MT מלאכי] מלאך K 597 Targ
Mk 1: 2[1] = Mt, except Mk omits ἔμπροσθέν σου. ℵAW*pl*vg^{s,cl}ς retain ἐγώ; BDΘ*pc*itvg^{codd}Ir omit ἐγώ.
Lk 7: 27 = Mt, except Lk omits ἐγώ. Cf. Jn 3: 28.

Here is a composite quotation in which the first half agrees with the LXX of Ex 23:20, and the second half shows a very slight influence from the Hebrew text of Mal 3:1. The combination of these two OT passages is probably pre-Christian, since it occurs in Jewish literature.[2]

Since the first clause derives from Ex 23:20, ὅς is not so much a divergence from the LXX as a grammatical link between the two OT passages. Κατασκευάσει in the gospels rests on the *piel* of פנה (= MT, as also the ἑτοιμάσει of Theodotion and the ἀποσκευάσει of Symmachus), against the LXX's ἐπιβλέψεται, which rests on the *kal*. The definite article with ὁδόν shows the lingering influence of Ex 23: 20, where the article is present with דרך and ὁδός,[3] as does

[1] Some commentators reject Mk 1: 2 as a copyist's gloss, partly because of the difficulty in the ascription to Is. See A. E. J. Rawlinson, *Mk* (London, 1925), 5, 250; M.-J. Lagrange, *Mt*^{7} (Paris, 1948), pp. cxx, cxxii; V. Taylor, *Mk* (London, 1952), 153; Stendahl, 50ff.

[2] *Ex*, R. 32. See E. Lohmeyer, *Mk* (Göttingen, 1937), 11; J. Jeremias, *TWNT*, II, 938. J. Mann shows that the synagogue sermon based on Ex 23: 20 was just as much taken from Mal 3: 1-8, 23f. (*The Bible as Read and Preached in the Old Synagogue* [Cincinnati, Ohio, 1940], I, 479). See also Stendahl, *loc. cit.* Why then should we see only a slight influence from Ex 23: 20, with many commentators, when the whole first clause agrees word for word with Ex 23: 20 LXX?

[3] Note also the possibility that the Hebrew text of Mal 3: 1 contained the article with דרך. Ziegler notes that 1QIs^a and the LXX often have the article where it is missing in the MT (*op. cit.*, 39). Parallel influence is very likely in two such traditionally associated passages. Cf. the parallel influence in the Samaritan Pentateuch (A. Geiger, *Nachgelassene Schriften* [Berlin, 1876], II, 60f.) and in the Hebrew *Vorlage* of the Is-LXX (J. Ziegler,

also the second personal pronoun σου. Ἔμπροσθεν is a purely stylistic change to avoid a second πρὸ προσώπου.

The quotation is Septuagintal in form, except for one contact with the Hebrew text and one stylistic change.

Mt 15: 4a (= 19: 19): τίμα τὸν πατέρα καὶ τὴν μητέρα
Mk 7: 10: τίμα τὸν πατέρα σου καὶ τὴν μητέρα σου
(Mk 10: 19 = 7: 10, except for omission of the second σου, retained by א* CWΘ*al.*)
Lk 18: 20: τίμα τὸν πατέρα σου καὶ τὴν μητέρα
μητέρα] + σου א*al*ς abc syr
Ex 20: 12; Dt 5: 16 LXX = Mk 7: 10. MT: כבד את אביך ואת אמך

The differences between the NT texts in the possessive pronouns may be due to the catechetical use of this commandment.[1] But the LXX often did not render the possessive pronoun,[2] so that Mt may merely have omitted them. Even the Hebrew text may sometimes have left suffixes to be implied.[3] Or Mt's omission may be stylistic, the definite articles half fulfilling the function of the possessives.[4] Influence from the emphatic state of nouns in Galilean Aramaic is also possible.[5] Whatever the reasons—and various influences may have combined—Mt has departed from Mk, the LXX, and the MT.

Mt 15: 4b; Mk 7: 10	Ex 21: 17 LXX	MT
ὁ κακολογῶν	ὁ κακολογῶν	ומקלל
πατέρα	πατέρα αὐτοῦ	אביו
ἢ μητέρα	ἢ μητέρα αὐτοῦ	ואמו
θανάτῳ τελευτάτω	τελευτήσει θανάτῳ	מות יומת

Ex 21: 17 LXX πατέρα αὐτοῦ] *om* αὐτοῦ Luc (75) | μητέρα αὐτοῦ] *om* αὐτοῦ bw (symbols of Brooke-McLean) | τελευτήσει θανάτῳ] θανάτῳ τελευτάτω AFLuc (75) (= NT)

Untersuchungen zur Septuaginta des Buches Is [Münster, 1934], 134ff.). An initial ה in הדרך could easily drop out by haplography after ופנה.

[1] So Stendahl, 54f.

[2] J. Ziegler (ed.), *Is* (Göttingen, 1939), 86.

[3] See I. L. Seeligman, *The Septuagint Version of Is* (Leiden, 1948), 65. R. D. Wilson is said to have suggested the same. One might even conjecture that in אמכ למען the כ was confused with the ל (as often happened when the top of the ל was unduly shortened or indistinct [J. Kennedy, *An Aid to the Textual Amendment of the OT* (Edinburgh, 1928), 82f.]) and omitted by haplography (note that Lk 18: 20 drops the possessive after μητέρα, but not after πατέρα), the first possessive subsequently being dropped through parallelism.

[4] A. T. Robertson, *A Grammar of the Greek NT in the Light of Historical Research*[3] (New York, 1919), 684.

[5] McNeile, *Mt*, 222; C. Schneider, *TWNT*, III, 469, n. 1, following Zahn, *Mt*[2] (Leipzig, 1905), *ad loc.*

The MT in Ex 21:15, 16, 17 contains the expression מוֹת יוּמָת, which LXX^B renders by θανάτῳ θανατούσθω (v. 15), τελευτήσει θανάτῳ (v. 17), and θανάτῳ τελευτάτω (v. 16). A, F, and Lucian have θανάτῳ θανατούσθω in verses 15, 16, but θανάτῳ τελευτάτω in verse 17. The interchange of verses 16 and 17 in the LXX may account for some of the confusion in the Greek MSS. The construing of θάνατος with τελευτᾶν is unusual, though occurring also in Ex 19:12. The usual rendering in the LXX is θανάτῳ θανατούσθω. Either the LXX has taken the infinitive absolute מוֹת as a noun (מָוֶת) or freely renders in order to preserve the assonance of the Hebrew. Since LXX^B has θανάτῳ τελευτάτω in verse 16, the same reading in LXX^AFLuc(75) may not be the result of assimilation to the NT.[1] Even were assimilation to the NT to be suspected, the presence of the same reading in the adjoining verse in LXX^B makes the NT reading essentially Septuagintal. Ὁ κακολογῶν shows dependence on the LXX, because the usual rendering for קלל is καταρᾶσθαι. The rendering ἤ for ו is legitimate,[2] but bears the Septuagintal stamp. The omission of the possessive pronouns does not necessarily show departure from the LXX (as it does by Mt alone in the first half of the verse)—and, in fact, may serve to show greater dependence on the Greek OT, since the first αὐτοῦ is omitted by Lucian (75) and the second by b w (Lagarde's Lucianic text [3]). In assimilation to the NT, *both* possessives would probably have dropped out, so that there is good evidence for a pre-Christian LXX text in which the possessives were absent, later inserted to conform with the Hebrew text.[4] We may safely assume this quotation is purely Septuagintal.

---

[1] Stendahl, *loc. cit.* I acknowledge indebtedness to Stendahl's admirable discussion of this quotation.

[2] See BDB, s.v. ו, 1, d.

[3] P. de Lagarde, *Librorum Veteris Testamenti Canonicorum pars prior Graece* (Göttingen, 1883). A. Rahlfs showed that these manuscripts did not contain a pure Lucianic text (*Mitteilungen des Septuaginta-Unternehmens der Gesellschaft der Wissenschaften zu Göttingen* [Berlin, 1928], Bd. 4, Heft 1, 76f.), but the possibility remains that the reading was Lucianic, Ur-Lucianic, and pre-Christian.

[4] On pre-hexaplaric and pre-Christian assimilation of the LXX to the Hebrew, see W. Staerk, *ZWT*, 36 (1893), 95f.; H. A. Sanders and C. Schmidt, *The Minor Prophets in the Freer Collection and the Berlin Fragment of Genesis* (New York, 1927), 25-29; J. Ziegler (ed.), *Duodecim Prophetae* (Göttingen, 1943), 33f.; *idem*, *ZAW*, 61 (1945/48), 93f.; P. Kahle, *TLZ*, 79 (1954), 88; P. W. Skehan, in *VT Supplement IV* (Leiden, 1957), 156-158.

Mt 15:8, 9	Is 29:13 LXXℵAQ	MT
ὁ λαὸς οὗτος	ἐγγίζει μοι	נגש
	ὁ λαὸς οὗτος	העם הזה
τοῖς χείλεσίν	τοῖς χείλεσιν αὐτῶν	בפיו ובשפתיו
με τιμᾷ	τιμῶσίν με	כבדוני
ἡ δὲ καρδία αὐτῶν	ἡ δὲ καρδία αὐτῶν	ולבו
πόρρω ἀπέχει ἀπ' ἐμοῦ·	πόρρω ἀπέχει ἀπ' ἐμοῦ·	רחק ממני
μάτην δὲ σέβονταί με	μάτην δὲ σέβονταί με	וַתְּהִי יראתם אתי
διδάσκοντες διδασκαλίας	διδάσκοντες ἐντάλματα	מצות אנשים מלמדה
ἐντάλματα ἀνθρώπων	ἀνθρώπων καὶ διδασκαλίας	

Mt 15:8, 9 ἀπέχει] ἐστιν D lat *similiter* syr Clpt
Is 29:13 LXX οὗτος] + (·※·) ἐν (*om* Luc) τῷ στόματι αὐτοῦ καὶ ἐν BLuc
MT רִחַק] רָחַק Targ it (= "be far away"); רחוק 1QIsa (= OT Pesh רחיק)
וַתְּהִי] וְתֹהוּ LXX it (μάτην)
יראתם] יראת 1QIsa
מצות] כמצות 1QIsa Targ
מלמדה] מלמדים Targ LXX

Mk 7:6, 7 = Mt, except Mk has οὗτος ὁ λαός] ὁ λαὸς οὗτος BD1071bcfilq r² vg syrsin,pesh Geo Bas
τιμᾷ] ἀγαπᾷ DWitClTert
ἀπέχει] ἔχει W; ἀφέστηκεν D; ἀπέστη Δ; ἀπεστιν Θ 565*pc*
Pap. Egerton 2: ὁ λαὸς οὗτος τοῖς χείλεσιν αὐτῶν τιμῶσίν με ματήν με σέβονται ἐντάλματα [ἀνθρώπων διδάσκοντες] [1]

The longer text of LXXB is hexaplaric.[2] The LXX reads וְתֹהוּ (μάτην) for וַתְּהִי (MT) (cf. Is 41:29).[3] In view of the variant readings in this clause in 1QIsa and the Targum, we may assume corruption of the Hebrew text and that the LXX has not rendered freely, but has reproduced a text which read ותהו יראו אתי. 1QIsa has dropped the suffix from יראתם. In the resultant יראת אתי, the ending את— in יראת may have been dropped by haplography (leaving ירא) or added (to ירא) by dittography. Whichever direction such a development may have taken, ירא stands very close to the LXX-*Vorlage*, יראו (the missing suffix of which is itself scribally close to the following [את]י). The LXX reads מצות as a plural, against the MT. The awkward Hebrew construction מצות אנשים מלמדה (= "a commandment of men taught" with "them" understood, or "learned" with "by rote" understood [4]) the LXX renders somewhat peri-

[1] See C. H. Dodd, *BJRL*, 20 (1936), 80f.

[2] F. Field, *Origenis Hexaplorum* (Oxford, 1875), *ad loc.*; E. Hatch, *Essays in Biblical Greek* (Oxford, 1889), 177f.; W. Staerk, *ZWT*, 40 (1897), 246; R. R. Ottley, *The Book of Is according to the Septuagint* (London, 1904-06), II, 249; Stendahl, 57.

[3] See esp. E. Nestle, *ET*, 11 (1899/1900), 330.

[4] It is said that in the Hebrew text God charges the people with fearing him only in obedience to human commandment; whereas in the LXX and

phrastically with a second form of διδασκ-, for which the Hebrew has no equivalent.[1,2] Like the Targum, the LXX (διδάσκοντες) presupposes a plural *piel* participle, מְלַמְּדִים, for the *pual* participle מְלֻמָּדָה (MT).[3] Either liberty was taken, or textual corruption had resulted from confusion of ם and ה.[4] The preposition כְּ in 1QIs[a] (כמצות) and the Targum (כתפקידת) is an attempt to smooth out the Hebrew text.

The text of Mt 15:8, 9; Mk 7:6,7 presents a very slight abridgement of the already short text of LXX[ℵAQ]. The order of the words οὗτος ὁ λαός is textually uncertain in Mk[5] and unimportant. With the omission of ἐγγίζει μοι and the dropping of the plural possessive αὐτῶν, it was only natural to treat λαός as a collective singular and so to change from τιμῶσιν (LXX) to τιμᾷ.[6] In the final participial phrase, the gospels have dropped the καί of the LXX and transposed ἐντάλματα ἀνθρώπων and διδασκαλίας, perhaps to bring the latter near its cognate verb.[7] Despite these minor stylistic departures from the LXX, the NT text remains Septuagintal throughout, particularly in πόρρω ἀπέχει,[8] μάτην, διδάσκοντες, the

---

NT they are charged with substituting human commandments for divine law (E. Gould, *Mk* [Edinburgh, 1896], 128). However, the Hebrew text has a stronger sense than this, for "their fear of me" is a consciously hypocritical substitution of human commandment (the MT has no weakening כְּ, as do the Targum and 1QIs[a]) for heart-sincere worship (cf. V. Taylor, *op. cit.*, 337f.). The MT contains, not a comparison, but an absolute equation, to which sense the LXX and the NT are faithful (against Stendahl, 58).

[1] Cf. Col 2:22; Justin, *Dial.* lxxviii, cxl (MPG VI, 661, 796f.).

[2] Ottley thinks διδασκαλίας represents the Hebrew participle, διδάσκοντες having been added (*op. cit.*, 250).

[3] T. Randolph, *The Prophecies and Other Texts Cited in the NT* (Oxford, 1782), 29; Karnetzki, 218f.

[4] Kennedy, *op. cit.*, 62.

[5] Either reading could be the result of assimilation, the one to Mt, the other to the LXX.

[6] T. W. Manson favors ἀγαπᾷ as the original reading in Mk, supposing that Mt conformed Mk to the LXX and that Mt's text worked its way into the majority of Marcan MSS (*BJRL*, 34 [1951/52], 317f.). But we should then expect Mt to have replaced the αὐτῶν and retained the plural τιμῶσιν. Though ἀγαπᾷ is the more difficult reading, the Septuagintal character of the quotation is too pronounced for ἀγαπᾷ to be regarded as original.

[7] So C. H. Toy, *Quotations in the NT* (New York, 1884), 43.

[8] The variant readings for ἀπέχει are not sufficiently well attested and appear to be Semitic avoidances of the Hellenistic word, as is evident in Mt, where the ἐστιν of D 1424 lat is influenced by the Old Syriac. The adjectival forms in the OT text (1QIs[a] רחוק; OT Pesh רחיק) show the Semitic preference for the simple predicate adjective construction. The numerous other agreements between the gospel texts and the LXX against the MT outweigh the

unusual plural διδασκαλίας, [1] and the double use of the root διδασκ- for one Hebrew word—all, except the first, against the MT.

Mt 19: 4; Mk 10: 6; Gen 1: 27 LXX: ἄρσεν καὶ θῆλυ ἐποίησεν αὐτούς
Mk αὐτούς] *om* DWit Gen 1: 27 MT: זכר ונקבה ברא אתם [2]
Mt 19: 5: ἕνεκα τούτου καταλείψει ἄνθρωπος τὸν πατέρα καὶ τὴν μητέρα καὶ κολληθήσεται τῇ γυναικὶ αὐτοῦ, καὶ ἔσονται οἱ δύο εἰς σάρκα μίαν.
ἕνεκα ℵBLZ892] ἕνεκεν *Uncs rell, Minusc pler,* Or (= assimilation to Mk)
κολληθήσεται] προσκολληθήσεται ℵC f1 33 *al pler* (= assimilation to Mk)
Mk 10: 7: ἕνεκεν τούτου καταλείψει ἄνθρωπος τὸν πατέρα αὐτοῦ καὶ τὴν μητέρα αὐτοῦ, καὶ προσκολληθήσεται πρὸς τὴν γυναῖκα αὐτοῦ, καὶ ἔσονται οἱ δύο εἰς σάρκα μίαν
αὐτοῦ 1°] *om* D *al*
μητέρα αὐτοῦ ℵBD (ἑαυτοῦ) *al* it syr] *om* αὐτοῦ *Uncs pler, Minusc pler,* klqr^{1,2} vg(*pler*) syr^{hk} Arm Aug (Kilpatrick retains; Nestle omits)
καὶ προσκολληθήσεται πρὸς τὴν γυναῖκα αὐτοῦ ADWΘ(f1)f13 *pl*latς] *om* ℵB *pc*syr^{sin} (Kilpatrick retains; Nestle omits)
Gen 2: 24 LXX: ἕνεκεν τούτου καταλείψει ἄνθρωπος τὸν πατέρα αὐτοῦ καὶ τὴν μητέρα αὐτοῦ καὶ προσκολληθήσεται πρὸς τὴν γυναῖκα αὐτοῦ, καὶ ἔσονται οἱ δύο εἰς σάρκα μίαν
μητέρα αὐτοῦ] *om* αὐτοῦ bw (Lagarde)
πρὸς τὴν γυναῖκα 911 DE Rahlfs Lagarde] τῇ γυναικί A (= assimilation to Mt?)
MT: על כן יעזב איש את אבוי ואת אמו ודבק באשתו והיו לבשר אחד
Eph 5: 31: ἀντὶ τούτου καταλείψει ἄνθρωπος τὸν πατέρα καὶ τὴν μητέρα καὶ προσκολληθήσεται πρὸς τὴν γυναῖκα αὐτοῦ, καὶ ἔσονται οἱ δύο εἰς σάρκα μίαν
καὶ προσκολλ. πρὸς τ. γυν. αὐτοῦ B*pmς*] κ. πρ. τῇ γυναῖκι αὐτοῦ (*om* αὐτ. ℵ*) P^{46}ℵADG*pc*; *om* Tert Or

Mk stays by the LXX. Mt deviates from Mk and the LXX. The Attic ἕνεκα of Mt stands over against the Ionic and Hellenistic ἕνεκεν of Mk and the LXX.[3] Mt omits αὐτοῦ after πατέρα and μητέρα (cf. Mt 15:4).[4] Whatever the genuine readings in Mk and the LXX (and Eph) in the clause containing προσκολληθήσεται, Mt's κολληθήσεται τῇ γυναικὶ αὐτοῦ conforms neither to Mk nor to the LXX. Δύο represents a Hebrew variant attested by the LXX, Sam Pent, Sam Targ, Targ Jon, the Old Palestinian Targ,[5] OT

---

possible argument that the Semitic character of the variants speaks for genuineness.

[1] See K. H. Rengstorf, *TWNT,* II, 163f.

[2] For the use of Gen 1: 27 in the Damascus Document (iv. 21), see M. Burrows, *More Light on the Dead Sea Scrolls* (London, 1958), 98f.; F. F. Bruce, *Biblical Exegesis in the Qumran Texts* (Den Haag, 1959), 29; P. Winter, *ZAW,* 68 (1956), 71-84, 264; 70 (1958), 260f.; D. Daube, *ZNW,* 48 (1957), 119-126.

[3] See A & G, s.v.

[4] The second αὐτοῦ is somewhat uncertain in the LXX as well as in Mk, so that in no case is it necessary to see a deviation by Mk from the LXX. Mt may have consulted a Hebrew text in which the suffixes (יו- and ו-) were missing, inasmuch as both are followed by another *waw.*

[5] MS Neofiti 1 of the Vatican Library.

Pesh, Vg, and Philo. Εἰς σάρκα μίαν contains an overliteral rendering of לְ, but the construction meets us in the papyri.[1] The insertion of καὶ εἶπεν between the quotations in verses 4 and 5 is a further, targumic-like deviation of Mt from Mk.[2]

Mt 19: 18, 19	Mk 10: 19	Lk 18: 20	Ex 20: 13-16 LXX^{B}
οὐ φονεύσεις	μὴ φονεύσῃς (*om* Df1 [*pc*]kIr)	μὴ μοιχεύσῃς	οὐ μοιχεύσεις οὐ κλέψεις
οὐ μοιχεύσεις (*om* **א***)	μὴ μοιχεύσῃς (*om* **א***; + μὴ πορνεύσῃς D[*pc*] kIr) (μοιχ . . . . φον. AWΘ f13 28 latClς; text **א**^{c} B*pc*syr^{sin}cop)	μὴ φονεύσῃς	οὐ φονεύσεις (φον . . . . κλέψ. Luc [75]) (φον . . . . μοιχ. . . . κλεψ. AFM arm boh eth syh)
οὐ κλέψεις (*om* **א***)	μὴ κλέψῃς	μὴ κλέψῃς	
οὐ ψευδομαρτυρή-σεις	μὴ ψευδομαρτυρή-σῃς μὴ ἀποστερήσῃς (*om* B*W f1 28 *al* syr^{sin} Cl)	μὴ ψευδομαρ-τυρήσῃς	οὐ ψευδομαρτυρή-σεις

Ex 20: 13-16 MT: לא תרצח: לא תנאף: לא תגנב: לא תענה ברעך עד שקר

Dt 5: 17-20 LXX^{B}: οὐ μοιχεύσεις· οὐ φονεύσεις· οὐ κλέψεις· οὐ ψευδομαρτυρήσεις

μοιχ . . . . φον.] φον . . . . μοιχ. AFM

MT = Ex, except for insertion of *waw*-conjunctives, the insertion opposed, however, by some Hebrew MSS, Sam, LXX, OT Pesh

Nash Pap.:[3] לוא תנאף לוא תרצח לו‹א תג›נב לוא ‹תע›נה

This quotation presents almost insoluble textual problems, doubtless because of its catechetical use. Probably the Marcan text which could be the source of Lk is likely to be original, especially since Lk shares Mk's unusual μή with the subjunctive. With this criterion, the order of A W Θ f13 28 lat Cl ς, μοιχ. . . . φον., will be correct. Possible confirmation lies in the fact that Cod. A has this order *against* its own order in the OT. The usually adopted order in Mk may then be considered assimilation to Mt.

The strongly attested omission of μὴ ἀποστερήσῃς by B* K W Δ Π Σ Ψ f1 28 69 579 700 syr^{sin} geo arm Cl may be assimilation to

[1] J. H. Moulton, *A Grammar of NT Greek* (Edinburgh, 1908-29), I, 71f., 76.

[2] In Gen 2: 23, these words are ascribed, not to Adam, but to God —so most OT commentators; contra Merx, *op. cit.*, I, i, pp. 273f. On the similar use of Gen 1: 27 in CDC iv. 19—v. 2, see Fitzmyer, *op. cit.*, 319f.

[3] S. A. Cook, *Proceedings of the Society of Biblical Archaeology*, 25 (1903), 34-56. Cf. W. F. Albright, *JBL*, 56 (1937), 145-176.

Mt and the OT.[1] However, since Lk as well as Mt does not have μὴ ἀποστερήσῃς, the omission may be original in Mk, the insertion having been introduced from the unregulated tradition.[2] Merx cogently argues that this prohibition is not based on Ex 21:10 or Dt 24:14, but on Lev 19:13 (cf. v. 11) because only in Lev does it appear as a general precept. But in Lev only ἄλλος of the Hexapla has ἀποστερεῖν,[3] so that the prohibition in Mk may well be a later insertion.[4]

C. H. Turner favors D k Ir in their omission of μὴ φονεύσῃς and insertion of μὴ πορνεύσῃς.[5] The unexpectedness of the reading, the independence of the Marcan tradition as shown by the certainly genuine [sic] μὴ ἀποστερήσῃς, the listing of both "adulteries" and "fornications" in Mk 7:21, and the unlikelihood of murder coming into the question, says Turner, support this reading. Turner's arguments are forceful, but one hesitates to adopt a "Western" reading unsupported by "Eastern" allies. Could not μὴ πορνεύσῃς be a doublet for μὴ μοιχεύσῃς, perhaps suggested by Mk 7:21, for which room has been made by the omission of μὴ φονεύσῃς? Note that "murder" is not omitted in Mk 7:21.

Mk's certain deviation from the LXX in μή with the subjunctive constitutes an exception to his close adherence to the LXX in formal quotations of the OT. But the same construction meets us in Jas 2:11, and the exception is understandable in view of the varying forms which the decalogue took in catechetical use, as illustrated in the following table:[6]

a)	Ex (MT, LXX^{AF}), Dt (MT, LXX^{AF}), Josephus (*Ant.* III. v. 5), *Did.* 2:2	6	7	8	9	10
	Mt 19:18, 19; Mk 10:19, 20 (ℵ^{c}B*pc*syr^{sin}cop)	6	7	8	9	
	Mt 19:18, 19 (ℵ*)	6			9	
	Mk 10:19, 20 (ℵ*)	6		8	9	
	Mk 10:19, 20 (Df1[*pc*]kIr)		7	8	9	
	I Tim 1:9, 10 (apparently)	6	7	8	9	

---

[1] So, e.g., B. Weiss, *Das Matthäusevangelium u. seine Lucas-Parallelen* (Halle, 1876), 578.

[2] Cf. V. Taylor, *op. cit.*, 428. Kilpatrick adopts the omission.

[3] See Field, *op. cit.*, *ad loc.*

[4] Merx, *op. cit.*, II, ii, p. 120.

[5] *JTS*, 29 (1928), 5; *idem*, in *A New Commentary on Holy Scripture* (London, 1929), 87f.

[6] This table is a complete revision and an expansion of that by A. H. McNeile, *The Book of Exodus* (London, 1908), 119. I have left out of account the fifth commandment, which the gospels reserve till last, possibly to emphasize its importance as a practical abrogation of the oral law (see H. B. Swete, *Mk* [London, 1898], 211).

b) Ex (LXX^{B})	7 8 6 9 10
c) Ex and Dt (some Hebrew MSS), Ex (LXX$^{\mathrm{Luc[75]}}$), Dt (LXX^{B}), Nash Pap., Philo (*De Decal.* xxiv, xxxii), Tert (*De Pud.* v), Theophilus (*Ad Autol.* ii. 35; iii. 9), Cl (*Strom.* vi. 146f.)	7 6 8 9 10
Mk 10: 19, 20 (AWΘ f13 28 lat Cl ϛ); Lk 18: 20	7 6 8 9
Ro 13: 9	7 6 8 10
Jas 2: 11	7 6

The probability is that Mt has deviated from both Mk and the LXX in following the order of the MT. LXX^{A} has always been suspected of assimilation to the NT; [1] and the case for assimilation here is especially strong, since the Chester Beatty Pap. 963, *not* as usual, agrees with B against A F.[2] If then Mt has not followed the order of his Greek OT, his change to οὐ with the future indicative is a partial reminiscence of the LXX or a literal rendering of the Hebrew or both.

Mt 21: 13a; Mk 11: 17; Is 56: 7 LXX	Lk 19: 46	Is 56: 7 MT
ὁ [+ γὰρ LXX] οἶκός μου οἶκος προσευχῆς κληθήσεται [+ πᾶσιν τοῖς ἔθνεσιν Mk, LXX]	καὶ ἔσται ὁ οἶκός μου οἶκος προσευχῆς ἔσται] *post* προσευχῆς ACD it syr	כי ביתי בית תפלה יקרא לכל העמים

Lk has changed the Hebraism κληθήσεται into ἔσται. Mt and Mk adopt the rendering of the LXX, which is faithful to the Hebrew.[3] Mt omits πᾶσιν τοῖς ἔθνεσιν, probably to avoid diverting Jewish readers from the main point.[4] Lk's same omission may be due to his following an Ur-Matthaean tradition.[5]

Mt 21: 13b; Mk 11: 17; Lk 19: 46; Jer 7: 11 LXX: σπήλαιον λῃστῶν
Jer 7: 11 MT: המערת פרצים

---

[1] See esp. J. Hänel, *Der Schriftbegriff Jesu* (Gütersloh, 1919), 114ff.

[2] See S. E. Johnson, *HTR*, 36 (1943), 150f. Stendahl seeks to counter this argument by noting that both the Nash and Chester Beatty papyri are of Egyptian origin and that LXX^{A} often displays Palestinian readings (pp. 62f.). But why then does not Pap. 963 agree with B against A more often? That Josephus has the order of LXX^{A} means nothing, since this is the order of the MT and the Targums.

[3] On the slight touch of contemporization in προσευχῆς, which also denoted "synagogue", see Seeligmann, *op. cit.*, 101.

[4] So Zahn, *Einl.*, II, 318. Cf. Acts 22: 21ff.

[5] It has also been suggested that Mt and Lk took this saying as a prophecy, and so, writing after the destruction of the Temple, dropped the final phrase as incapable of fulfilment. So J. Weiss - W. Bousset, *Die Schriften des NT*^{3} (Göttingen, 1917), I, 180; J. M. Creed, *Lk* (London, 1930), 242; F. Hauck, *Lk* (Leipzig, 1934), 238; C. K. Barrett, *JTS*, 48 (1947), 160. This is doubtful,

The dependence on the LXX is noteworthy in λῃστῶν ("robbers") for פרצים ("violent men"; Targ כנישת רשיעין = "assembly of the wicked"). It is not as though λῃστῶν were unsuitable in the expression "den of פרצים" [1] (cf. Ezek 18:10 ff.). But only here does it occur in the LXX for פריץ. The connotation of robbery is necessary to the NT context.[2]

Mt 21:42; Mk 12:10, 11; Lk 20:17; Ps 118 (117):22, 23 LXX: λίθον ὃν ἀπεδοκίμασαν οἱ οἰκοδομοῦντες, οὗτος ἐγενήθη εἰς κεφαλὴν γωνίας [end of Lucan quotation]· παρὰ κυρίου ἐγένετο αὕτη, καὶ ἔστιν θαυμαστὴ ἐν ὀφθαλμοῖς ἡμῶν.
Ps 118:22 MT: אבן מאסו הבונים היתה לראש פנה: מאת יהוה היתה זאת היא נפלאת בעינינו

Special points of dependence on the LXX by the gospels are the slavishly literal renderings, εἰς κεφαλὴν γωνίας [3] for לראש פנה, παρά for מֵאֵת (= "from with"), αὕτη for זאת,[4] and θαυμαστή, which presupposes a pointing of נפלאת as a *niphal* participle (cf. Targ, OT Pesh, Vg, Aq), instead of as a *niphal* perfect (MT). The only deviation from the Hebrew consonantal text by the LXX is the insertion of καί before ἔστιν, almost a stylistic necessity after ἅυτη to avoid asyndeton.

Mt 22:32	Mk 12:26	Lk 20:37	Acts 7:32	Ex 3:6 LXX[B]
ἐγώ	ἐγὼ		ἐγὼ ὁ θεὸς	ἐγώ εἰμι
εἰμι			τῶν πατέρων	ὁ θεὸς τοῦ
			σου	πατρός σου
ὁ θεὸς	ὁ θεὸς	τὸν θεὸν	ὁ θεὸς	θεὸς
'Α. καὶ	'Α. καὶ	'Α. καὶ	'Α. καὶ	'Α. καὶ
ὁ θεὸς	θεὸς	θεὸν		θεὸς
'Ισ. καὶ	'Ισ. καὶ	'Ισ. καὶ	'Ισ. καὶ	'Ισ. καὶ
ὁ θεὸς 'Ι.	θεὸς 'Ι.	θεὸν 'Ι.	'Ι.	θεὸς 'Ι.

---

because the context does not suggest that the statement is prophetic in import. In view of Lk's omission, we can hardly suppose that Mt here reveals an anti-Gentile bias.

[1] See an excellent note by F. Field on the propriety of the comparison to a "den of robbers" (*Notes on the Translation of the NT* [Cambridge, 1899], 15).

[2] In Jer the people were committing flagrant sins and then coming to the Temple to insure themselves against the consequences, as if the Temple were a "den of robbers" to which they could flee for safety after engaging in banditry. Worse was the situation in the NT, for the banditry took place right within the precincts of the Temple.

[3] On this expression as meaning a capstone, see J. Jeremias, *TWNT*, I, 793; IV, 278; *idem*, *ZNW*, 29 (1930), 264-280; 36 (1937), 154-157; and specifically as a pyramidion, see E. E. LeBas, *PEQ* (1946), 103-115.

[4] Αὕτη (= זאת) = τοῦτο is a Hebraism. Cf. I Sam 4:7; I Kings 11:39. See Bl-D § 138:2. Against H. A. W. Meyer, *Mt*[6] (Edinburgh, 1877-79), II, 72, and Gould, *op. cit.*, 222, who take κεφαλήν as the antecedent of αὕτη.

ὁ 2°3°] *om* ℵ	ὁ] *om* DW579 θεός 2°3° BD WOr^{semel}] *pr* ὁ ℵACLΘf1 f13 543 33 565 579 1071 *al pler* Or^{semel}	θεόν 2°3°] *pr* ὅν A	καί 1°2°]+ θεός D; +ὁ θεός E33 *pmς*	θεός 2°] *pr* ὁ ALuc (75) θεός 3°4°] *om* Luc (75)

Ex 3:6 MT: אנכי אלהי אביך אלהי אברהם אלהי יצחק ואלהי יעקב

Mk may omit εἰμι simply as a part of the larger omission which extends to πατρός σου. Alternatively, since Mk and Acts agree in the omission of εἰμι, their LXX text may not have contained the verb *to be,* its having been inserted into the original text for stylistic improvement or omitted from the original text in conformity with the Hebrew.[1]

That Lk lacks the articles before the second θεόν and the third θεόν (A being assimilated to Mt) favors their omission in Mk (the mass of Marcan MSS being assimilated to Mt). The Marcan text, then, is the same as LXX^{A}. Cod. A is probably not assimilated to the NT, since its OT reading disagrees with its own Marcan reading.[2]

Mt's thrice-repeated article stands alone against Mk and the LXX. His insertion of εἰμι may be a stylistic improvement or a reminiscence of a Septuagintal text.

The argument from the OT text for the resurrection has several facets:

a) The present tense, whether expressed or understood, is necessary to the argument. Otherwise, the text would have shown only that at one time Abraham, Isaac, and Jacob were alive. When no verb *to be* is present in the Hebrew or Aramaic, the present tense is implied.[3]

b) The idea of a continuing relationship with the patriarchs is emphasized in the OT context, both by Yahweh's faithfulness to the promise he gave them and by the name with which he designates himself, I AM THAT I AM.

c) This continuing relationship embraces the patriarchs' continuing existence by virtue of the connotation of protection and salvation in the title "God of Abraham. . . ." [4]

---

[1] The omission of εἰμι is Hebraic or Aramaic (see Zahn, *Einl.*, II, 318), but this does not tell us whether the omission is original to Mk or to a text of the LXX.

[2] LXX$^{\text{Luc(75)}}$ = Acts in the omissions of θεός is interesting.

[3] H. H. B. Ayles, *The Expositor*, 11, 6th Series (1905), 441ff.

[4] See F. Dreyfus, *RB*, 66 (1959), 213-224.

d) That the patriarchs' continuing existence implies resurrection of the body follows from the unity of the human personality.[1]

Mt 22: 37: ἀγαπήσεις κύριον τὸν θεόν σου ἐν ὅλῃ τῇ καρδίᾳ σου καὶ ἐν ὅλῃ τῇ ψυχῇ σου καὶ ἐν ὅλῃ τῇ διανοίᾳ σου
Mk 12: 29, 30: ἄκουε, Ἰσραήλ, κύριος ὁ θεὸς ἡμῶν κύριος εἷς ἐστιν, καὶ ἀγαπήσεις κύριον τὸν θεόν σου ἐξ ὅλης τῆς καρδίας σου καὶ ἐξ ὅλης τῆς ψυχῆς σου καὶ ἐξ ὅλης τῆς διανοίας σου καὶ ἐξ ὅλης τῆς ἰσχύος σου
Mk 12: 33: καὶ τὸ ἀγαπᾶν αὐτὸν ἐξ ὅλης τῆς καρδίας καὶ ἐξ ὅλης τῆς συνέσεως καὶ ἐξ ὅλης τῆς ἰσχύος
Lk 10: 27: ἀγαπήσεις κύριον τὸν θεόν σου ἐξ ὅλης τῆς καρδίας σου καὶ ἐν ὅλῃ τῇ ψυχῇ σου καὶ ἐν ὅλῃ τῇ ἰσχύϊ σου καὶ ἐν ὅλῃ τῇ διανοίᾳ σου
ἐν 1° 2° 3°] ἐξ ACWΘΦς (= assimilation to Mk)
Dt 6: 4, 5 LXX: ἄκουε, Ἰσραήλ, κύριος ὁ θεὸς ἡμῶν κύριος εἷς ἐστιν· καὶ ἀγαπήσεις κύριον τὸν θεόν σου ἐξ ὅλης τῆς καρδίας σου καὶ ἐξ ὅλης τῆς ψυχῆς σου καὶ ἐξ ὅλης τῆς δυνάμεώς σου
MT: שמע ישראל יהוה אלהינו יהוה אחד: ואהבת את יהוה אלהיך בכל לבבך ובכל נפשך ובכל מאדך :

Cf. II Kings 23: 25.

The following table sets forth the textual situation concerning the three (or four) "tones":

Dt	καρδία	ψυχή	δύναμις	AFM
	διάνοια	ψυχή	δύναμις	B^{r}Pap. 963
			ἰσχύς	ἄλλος (Hexapla)
	καρδία	ψυχή	ἰσχύς	δύναμις Luc (75)
IIK	καρδία	ψυχή	ἰσχύς	A
	καρδία	ἰσχύς	ψυχή	B
Mt	καρδία	ψυχή	διάνοια	
	καρδία	ἰσχύς	διάνοια	33 (Ἰσχύς, a doublet for διάνοια, has displaced ψυχή.)
	καρδία	ψυχή	ἰσχύς	c syr$^{sin, cur}$ (Ἰσχύς displaces the un-Semitic and difficult διάνοια.)
	καρδία	ψυχή	ἰσχύς	διάνοια Θ f13 *al*syr^{pesh} (= assimilation to Mk, the gloss ἰσχύς inserted wrongly)
Mk	καρδία	ψυχή	διάνοια	ἰσχύς
12:	καρδία	ψυχή		ἰσχύς D*pc*it
30	καρδία	διάνοια	ψυχή	ἰσχύς A
12:	καρδία	σύνεσις	ἰσχύς	
33	καρδία	σύνεσις	ψυχή	ἰσχύς A f13 700 *al* ς (The unique σύνεσις has been provided with a doublet, ψυχή.)
	καρδία	δύναμις	ἰσχύς	Θ 565 it (The unique σύνεσις has been suppressed by a synonym for ἰσχύς, the LXX's δύναμις.)
	καρδία	δύναμις	ψυχή	ἰσχύς D (The two preceding phenomena concerning σύνεσις are combined.)
Lk	καρδία	ψυχή	ἰσχύς	διάνοια
	καρδία	ψυχή	ἰσχύς	D1241 *pc* it Mcion

[1] On the Hebrew concept of man as a psychical whole, see H. W. Robinson, in *The People and the Book* (Oxford, 1925), 353ff.; J. Pedersen, *Israel* (Oxford, 1926-40), I-II, 99ff.; C. Guignebert, *The Jewish World in the Time of Jesus*

The Marcan ἐκ against the Hebrew ב displays dependence on the LXX, as also in the first part of the *shema'*, missing in Mt and Lk. Mk's ἰσχύς does not show divergence from the LXX, for the occurrence of this word in Dt Luc ἄλλος and in II Kings and the total disappearance of δύναμις in the NT[1] demonstrate that ἰσχύς had been accepted into the Greek form of the *shema'*.

Contrastingly, Mt's ἐν and his reversion to the three tones show his independence from Mk, who has four tones, and from the LXX, which has δύναμις or ἰσχύς, but never διάνοια in the third tone. Had Mt wanted to retain the three tones and yet maintain dependence on Mk, he would have needed only to adopt or revise the second Marcan form (v. 33). Matthaean independence from Mk is further seen in his omission of ἄκουε, . . . καί, surely remarkable in view of Mt's Jewish bent and his tendency to expand quotation material.

Concerning διάνοια, ἰσχύς, and the third tone, numerous possibilities exist:

a) Mt has dropped Mk's ἰσχύς, not thinking that he now has no equivalent for מאד.[2] But since we know Mt had in mind the Hebrew text (ἐν-ב), which was no doubt second nature to him, this seems improbable. Nor is Mk's διάνοια beyond suspicion: it could be a doublet for καρδία or ψυχή, or assimilation to Mt—note its omission in D *pc* it and its different placement in A and the majority of Lucan MSS, both of which are often tell-tale signs of a gloss inserted into the text.

b, c) Mt's διάνοια represents a doublet alongside καρδία or ψυχή for לבב or נפש, the equivalent for מאד having been suppressed for

---

(London, 1939), 117f.; G. E. Whitlock, *Interpretation*, 14 (1960), 9ff. E. E. Ellis objects that the above interpretation rests on an unbiblical body/soul dualism and really implies that bodily resurrection is unnecessary ("If Abraham is now personally 'living', no resurrection would be necessary for God to be 'his God' ") (*NTS*, 10 [1964], 274f.). The first objection fails to recognize that there is a subdued Biblical dualism of spirit and body, and the second strangely fails to recognize the body-soul unity. Jesus' statement, "He is not the God of the dead, but of the living," supports the traditional view that there is a present spiritual existence which necessitates the raising of the body to be reunited with the spirit for a *whole* existence, eternal half-existence in spirit form being ruled out because God created man a body-soul unity.

[1] Except in D Θ 565 it of Mk 12: 33, perhaps because of assimilation to the LXX.

[2] Swete, *op. cit.*, 268; Allen, *Mt*, 241; B. F. C. Atkinson, *Journal of the Transactions of the Victoria Institute*, 79 (1947), 49; Stendahl, 75; J. Jeremias, *ZNW*, 50 (1959), 271.

the sake of the three tones. Again, Mt's dependence on the Hebrew presents a stumbling-block to this view.

d) Mt's διάνοια is meant to convey the intensifying force of מאד—note that διάνοια stands last in Lk—ἰσχύς (and δύναμις) rejected as having an improper connotation of physical might or material wealth. Διάνοια would then mean "mental might." [1] The rendering of מאד by διάνοια would be unique.

e) Ἰσχύς, a doublet with διάνοια for מאד, was a marginal gloss which made its way into the texts of Mk and Lk. All three synoptists originally had καρδία—ψυχή—διάνοια.[2]

f) Mk's διάνοια may be rejected. See above a).

g) Mk's διάνοια is a doublet with καρδία for לבב.[3] Διάνοια usually stands for לבב in the LXX. But why is it inserted after ψυχή?

h) Mk's διάνοια is a doublet alongside ψυχή for נפש. Then, with σύνεσις, Mk gives three alternative renderings for נפש! Also, διάνοια never renders נפש in the LXX.

i-k) The same possibilities as in Mk, f)-h), exist for Lk's διάνοια.[4] The striking combination of ἐκ and ἐν in Lk reveals knowledge of more than one text-tradition.[5]

The confusion, arising out of the fact none of the synoptists or copyists used the Greek *shema'* in their youth,[6] defies disentangling. Three general conclusions are certain: Mk stands close to the LXX; Mt goes directly to the Hebrew text; Lk conflates his sources.

Mt 22: 39 (= 19: 19b); Mk 12: 31 (cf. v. 33); Lev 19: 18 LXX: ἀγαπήσεις τὸν πλησίον σου ὡς σεαυτόν

Lk 10: 27b: (καὶ) τὸν πλησίον σου ὡς σεαυτόν

Some unimportant variation between σεαυτόν and ἑαυτόν exists in both the OT and the NT texts. Cf. Bl-D § 64: 1.

Lev 19: 18 MT: ואהבת לרעך כמוך

NT = LXX = MT.[7] The combination of this and the preceding

---

[1] So S. Davidson, *Sacred Hermeneutics* (Edinburgh, 1843), 353; D. M. Turpie, *The OT in the New* (Edinburgh, 1868), 19f., 166f.

[2] So A. Sperber, *op. cit.*, 223.

[3] Jeremias, *ZNW*, 50 (1959), 271.

[4] A. R. C. Leaney writes favorably of the omission of διάνοια in Lk (*Lk* [London, 1958], 182).

[5] Lk is working with a different tradition, probably concerning a different incident. See T. W. Manson, *The Sayings of Jesus* (in *The Mission and Message of Jesus*; London, 1937), 551f.; C. E. B. Cranfield, *Mk* (Cambridge, 1959), 376.

[6] Jeremias, *ZNW*, 50 (1959), 272f.

[7] Note that saying 25 in the Gospel of Thomas commands to love your brother "as your soul," a Semitism also occurring in the Biblical Syriac

OT text may be pre-Christian, inasmuch as it occurs in the *Testaments of the Twelve Patriarchs* (*Issachar* v. 2; vii. 6; *Dan* v. 3).[1]

Mt 22: 44; Mk 12: 36; Lk 20: 42, 43; Acts 2: 34; Heb 1: 13; Ps 110 (109) : 1
LXX: εἶπεν κύριος τῷ κυρίῳ μου· κάθου ἐκ δεξιῶν μου ἕως ἂν θῶ τοὺς ἐχθρούς σου ὑποκάτω τῶν ποδῶν σου.

Mt	κύριος **ℵ**BDZ] ὁ κύριος *rell* ς
Mk	κύριος BD] ὁ κύριος **ℵ**AΘ *pl* ς
Lk	ὑποκάτω D it syr (= assimilation to Mt and Mk)] ὑποπόδιον *rell* (= the usually adopted text)
	κύριος BD 579] ὁ κύριος *rell*
Acts	κύριος B*ℵ*D] ὁ κύριος *rell*
	ὑποκάτω] Acts = ὑποπόδιον
Heb	*om* εἶπεν . . . μου
	ὑποκάτω] Heb = ὑποπόδιον Cf. Heb 2: 8—ὑποκάτω; 10: 13—ὑποπόδιον; I Cor 15: 25, 26—ὑπέταξεν ὑπὸ τοὺς πόδας αὐτοῦ
Ps	κύριος] Ps = ὁ κύριος
	ὑποκάτω] Ps = ὑποπόδιον

Ps 110: 1 MT: נאם יהוה לאדני שב לימיני עד אשית איביך הדם לרגליך
Ps 8: 7 LXX: πάντα ὑπέταξας ὑποκάτω τῶν ποδῶν αὐτοῦ
MT: כל שתה תחת רגליו

This quotation is Septuagintal. The textual evidence on the definite article with κύριος is uncertain. Moreover, feelings of Greek style [2] and influence of Aramaic,[3] especially in connection with the title κύριος, may have worked upon copyists. Ὑποκάτω is parallel influence, but still Septuagintal, from Ps 8:7. The quotations in Heb and I Cor illustrate the freedom with which the similar expressions in Ps 110 and Ps 8 were interchanged.

Mt 26: 31	Mk 14: 27	Zech 13:7 LXX^{A}	Zech 13:7 LXX^{B}	Zech 13:7 MT
πατάξω	πατάξω	πάταξον	πατάξατε	הַךְ את
τὸν ποιμένα	τὸν ποιμένα	τὸν ποιμένα	τοὺς ποιμένας	הרעה
κ. διασκορ-	κ. τὰ	κ. διασκορ-	καὶ	
πισθήσονται	πρόβατα	πισθήσονται	ἐκσπάσατε	ותפוצין
τὰ πρόβατα	διασκορπισ-	τὰ πρόβατα	τὰ πρόβατα	הצאן
τῆς ποίμνης	θήσονται	τῆς ποίμνης		
		(κ. ἐπάξω . . .)	(κ. ἐπάξω . . .)	

---

versions (OT Pesh, syr$^{cur, pesh}$). See A. Guillaumont, *Journal Asiatique*, 246 (1958), 113-123; G. MacRae, *CBQ*, 22 (1960), 68.

[1] G. F. Moore, *Judaism* (Harvard, 1927), II, 86. But on the possibility of NT influence upon the *Testaments*, see below, p. 143, n. 1.

[2] See Foerster, *TWNT*, III, 1057, 1085f.

[3] See Black, *op. cit.*, 68, 70. In Aramaic proper names are *ipso facto* definite and are generally given in the *status absolutus*. Cod. D often reflects the Aramaic omission; therefore, D's support of B may be discounted here.

-ονται P^{53} ℵAB f13 700 *al*] -εται P^{37,45} DWΘ f1 28 565 *pm* ς	διασκορπ.] *pr* τὰ πρ. A f1 *al pler* it (exc. dik q) vg syr$^{sin, pesh, hk}$	πάταξον Aℵ^{cb} Q τὸν ποιμένα Aℵ$^{ca\ cb}$QΓ -ονται] -σθήτω ℵ^{ca} LucC; -σθήτωσαν ℵ^{cb}Γ	πατάξατε WBℵ*] πατάξω V Arab Arm

LXX^{A} appears to have been assimilated to Mt in τῆς ποίμνης, but not in other respects. In τῆς ποίμνης, LXX^{A} stands alone with Mt, in contrast with the support it receives from other MSS in its two other similarities to the NT, τὸν ποιμένα and διασκορπισθήσονται.[1] That Q, the correcting hands of ℵ, and Lucian do not share τῆς ποίμνης with A and Mt, have different forms of διασκορπίζειν, and disagree among themselves (e.g., Lucian has a form of διασκορπ., but not τὸν ποιμένα) is the strongest possible evidence that they are bearers of independent textual traditions. The correcting hands of ℵ must have worked from exemplars which had τὸν ποιμένα and two forms of διασκορπίζειν, but not τῆς ποίμνης. Therefore, the probability is that the Marcan quotation rests on an "Ur-LXX^{A}" form which lacked τῆς ποίμνης.[2, 3]

LXX^{Q} may indeed represent this Septuagintal text of Mk, unless it be thought LXX^{Q} is assimilated to Mk. If the latter, however, it is strange πάταξον was not likewise assimilated and the word order changed to agree with Mk. The transposition of διασκορπισθήσονται and τὰ πρόβατα belongs to an emphatic style and is not to be considered a genuine deviation by Mk from his *Vorlage*.[4]

---

[1] Διασκορπισθήσονται formally agrees with the Targum, יתבדרון (= "be dispersed"), and essentially agrees with the Hebrew, תפוצון (= "to scatter" [intransitive]), against LXX^{B}, ἐκσπάσατε (= "save, redeem"—a tendentious interpretation here). See Baumstark, *op. cit.*, 300; Stendahl, 82.

[2] This is not to say that Mk's OT text represented the original text of the LXX. On Lagarde's well-known second canon, prefer LXX^{B} because of its freedom from the Hebrew text. See P. de Lagarde, *Mittheilungen* (Göttingen, 1884), 21. But LXX^{AQ} seems to represent a pre-Christian assimilation to the Hebrew text. Cf. above, p. 13, n. 4.

[3] Stendahl attempts further to support the pre-hexaplaric, pre-Christian character of the LXX^{A} text by noting that in the latter part of the same verse in Zech, the Lucianic recension has been corrected from the MT, which makes a correction from the NT less probable (p. 81). However, the argument loses force when one notes that in yet another reading in this part of the verse, B ℵ* Syh have been corrected from the MT, the Lucianic text presenting a conflation of the original and the correction.

[4] See Stendahl, 80f.

The only significant difference between Mk and what must have been his Septuagintal text is πατάξω versus πάταξον. A number of emendations of the Hebrew text have been suggested: אך (Randolph, Owen),[1] הכיתי (Owen),[2] אַכֶּה (Wellhausen, Nowack, Marti, R. Kittel, C. C. Torrey),[3] הֹכֵי (Kahle, Sellin), הכות<הך את (Mitchell), and הֹכֵה אַכֶּה (Th. Robinson).[4] However, although 1QIs[a] supports the possibility of change of person in verb-forms,[5] the Damascus Document confirms the MT (CDCb 9:3; col. xix, 8). Stendahl thinks the first person in the NT is a Christian adaptation emphasizing the activity of God.[6] But such an adaptation is not necessary to the Christian use of this quotation, nor does it especially harmonize with anything in the NT context.[7] It is simplest to regard πατάξω as parallel influence from the immediately following verb in the LXX, ἐπάξω. Note also the series of first person singular verbs with Yahweh as subject in the following context of Zech. Whether such influence first occurred in the NT texts or had already slipped into the LXX cannot be ascertained; but either way, the quotation remains essentially Septuagintal, even in πατάξω.

In taking over the Marcan quotation Mt has made the addition τῆς ποίμνης, perhaps to underscore the antithesis between shepherd and sheep (Zahn),[8] or to emphasize the breaking up of a unit (Torrey).[9] Or perhaps the addition is a reminiscence of Ezek 34:31[10] and shows a targumic love for expansion.[11] Mt then reverts to the word order of the LXX. Thus, the emphasis on τὰ πρόβατα (Mk) shifts to διασκορπισθήσονται and the added τῆς ποίμνης, a point in favor of Torrey's suggestion. Mt's reversion to the word order of the LXX may therefore not be motivated by a desire to

---

[1] Randolph, *op. cit.*, 30; H. Owen, *The Modes of Quotation Used by the Evangelical Writers* (London, 1789), 54.

[2] *Ibid.*

[3] Cited by H. G. Mitchell, *Zech* (ICC; Edinburgh, 1912), 319; Torrey, *op. cit.*, 84.

[4] See the note by Stendahl, 81.

[5] See J. Ziegler, *JBL*, 78 (1959), 49.

[6] Stendahl, 82.

[7] Stendahl strains to get a point of harmonization by taking the instrumental use of ἐν in the statement σκανδαλισθήσεσθε ἐν ἐμοί (Mt 26:31a), forgetting that ἐν ἐμοί does not occur in Mk (*ibid.*).

[8] *Einl.*, II, 318.

[9] *Loc. cit.*

[10] Ezek 34:31: צאן מרעיתי MT; πρόβατα ποιμνίου μου LXX. Anger, I, 39, II, 28.

[11] For examples in the Targums, see Baumstark, *op. cit.*, 308f.

conform to the LXX, but by a desire to stress the dispersal of the flock.[1]

Allusive Quotations in common with Mark

We now pass to allusive quotations common to Mt and Mk (and Lk, where present). In strongest contrast with the almost purely Septuagintal character of the formal quotations in Mt and Mk, the allusive quotations present almost all possible permutations of text-forms, and these often within single quotations. We shall note agreements with the LXX where the LXX correctly renders the MT and where it does not, disagreements with the LXX where it correctly renders the MT and where it does not, agreements with the MT against the LXX, agreements with one or more of the Targums against all other known texts, with the OT Peshitta, with 1QIs[a], with variant readings in other Hebrew MSS, with the Samaritan Pentateuch. In quotations from Daniel, Mt and Mk may agree with the LXX against Theodotion or with Theodotion against the LXX, or may present an independent rendering of the MT—within the same quotation. We shall see contacts with rabbinical tradition, apocryphal literature, and Jewish liturgical usage. Mt will be seen to exhibit a tendency to expand quotation material and to add targumic embellishments. Occasionally Mt conforms Mk in minor details to the LXX, but in every instance he may be motivated by stylistic considerations. These numerous variations in text-form cover matters of vocabulary and grammatical structure, including word order, punctuation, and syntax.

Mt 3:16	Ezek 1:1 LXX	MT	Mk 1:10	Is 63:19 LXX	MT
καὶ ἰδοὺ	καὶ		εἶδεν	ἐὰν	
ἠνεῴχθησαν	ἠνοίχθησαν	נפתחו	σχιζομένους	ἀνοίξῃς	קרעת
οἱ οὐρανοὶ	οἱ οὐρανοὶ	השמים	τοὺς	τὸν	
καὶ εἶδεν	καὶ εἶδον	ואראה	οὐρανούς	οὐρανόν	שמים

Lk 3:21, 22: ἀνεῳχθῆναι τὸν οὐρανόν
Cf. *Test. Levi* xviii. 6f.; *Judah* xxiv. 2f.

Mk's vivid σχιζομένους must go back to the Hebrew text of Is 63:19. "Spirit" and "descend" occur together in the NT only in the

[1] I hesitatingly suggest there is something to be said for the reading in Mt διασκορπισθήσεται, which is well-supported by the papyri and Western and Caesarean representatives. *Prima facie,* it appears to be a grammatical correction. But one then asks, why do we not meet the same correction in Mk? Could not the usually adopted reading in Mt be assimilation to Mk and the LXX? If so, Mt again deviates from Mk and the LXX.

baptismal narratives, and in the OT very infrequently, the closest parallel to Mk being Is 63:14 according to the punctuation and rendering of the LXX: κατέβη πνεῦμα παρὰ κυρίου (MT: רוח יהוה תניחנו = "the Spirit of Yahweh caused them to rest").[1] In the whole Is passage (vv. 10 ff.) the Holy Spirit figures prominently. Even Mk's peculiar (καταβαῖνον) εἰς αὐτόν may go back to Is 63:11 (LXX: ἐν αὐτοῖς τὸ πνεῦμα τὸ ἅγιον; MT: בקרבו את רוח קדשו).[2] Therefore, σχιζομένους alludes to קרע ("rend," against the LXX, "open") in Is 63:19. Note that the following word in Is expresses the thought of God "coming down" (ירד, omitted by the LXX).

Mt assimilates the narrative to Ezek 1:1 (LXX= MT). The circumstances of the two passages are very similar: Ezekiel by the river Chebar, John and Jesus in the river Jordan, opened heavens, inaugural prophetic visions.[3] Lk has moved away from the OT phraseology in his complicated sentence structure.

Mt 3: 17: οὗτός ἐστιν ὁ υἱός μου ὁ ἀγαπητός, ἐν ᾧ εὐδόκησα
οὗτός ἐστιν] σὺ εἶ Dasyr$^{sin, cur}$Ir (= assimilation to Mk, Lk, and Ps 2: 7 [4])
Mk 1: 11: σὺ εἶ ὁ υἱός μου ὁ ἀγαπητός, ἐν σοὶ εὐδόκησα
Lk 3: 22 = Mk (The Western text in Lk = Ps 2: 7 LXX.)
Ps 2: 7 LXX: υἱός μου εἶ σύ MT: בני אתה
Is 42: 1 LXX: Ἰακὼβ ὁ παῖς μου, ἀντιλήψομαι αὐτοῦ· Ἰσραὴλ ὁ ἐκλεκτός μου, προσεδέξατο αὐτὸν ἡ ψυχή μου· ἔδωκα τὸ πνεῦμά μου ἐπ' αὐτόν
MT: הן עבדי אתמך בו בחירי רצתה נפשי נתתי רוחי עליו
Cf. Gen 22: 2; Is 41: 8f.; 44: 2.

This quotation presents a combination of Ps 2:7 and Is 42:1. The reference to Ps 2:7 has been opposed by various scholars who

---

[1] See Lohmeyer, *op. cit.*, 21.

[2] See I. Buse, *JTS*, 7 (1956), 74f.; A. Feuillet, *CBQ*, 21 (1959), 468-490.

[3] See F. Gils, *Jésus prophète d' après les évangiles synoptiques* (Louvain, 1957), 49f.; M. Traub, *TWNT*, V, 529f.

[4] F. C. Burkitt (*Evangelion da-Mepharreshe* [Cambridge, 1904], II, 266f.; cf. C. E. B. Cranfield, *SJT*, 8 [1955], 56) defends the Western reading here, saying the tendency for assimilation to οὗτος in the Transfiguration narrative (17: 5 and par) would have been at least as strong as that for assimilation to Mk and Lk—a doubtful argument in view of the known inter-gospel harmonistic element in D. See J. R. Harris, in *Texts and Studies* (Cambridge, 1891), II, 188ff.; F. H. Chase, *The Syro-Latin Text of the Gospels* (London, 1895), 76-100; H. J. Vogels, in *Texte u. Untersuchungen* (Leipzig, 1910), 3. Reihe, Bd. VI, 1-119. The πρὸς αὐτόν after λέγουσα in Dasyr$^{sin, cur}$ shows the Western text has been worked over, perhaps in view of Ps 2: 7 LXX: Κύριος εἶπεν πρός μέ, υἱός μου εἶ συ. Cf. the total assimilation to Ps 2: 7 in the Western text of Lk 3: 22. If my suggestion that the Western text in Mt shows partial assimilation to Ps 2: 7 be accepted, the strongest argument in favor of the Western text in Lk, viz., the absence of assimilation in Mt and Mk, is blunted.

feel that υἱός goes back to an ambiguous παῖς for עבד and that ἀγαπητός stands for בחיר, both derived from Is 42:1.[1] However, the close connection with the Temptation narratives in Mt and Lk, where εἰ υἱὸς εἶ τοῦ θεοῦ is twice repeated, presumes a reference to sonship in the baptismal voice.[2] It is argued that the variant reading, ἐκλεκτός, in Jn 1:34 (P5vidא*e ff2* syrsin, cur) is original and that it shows recognition of a reference to Is 42:1. But this variant looks like assimilation to the LXX of Is 42:1 (and perhaps to ἐκλελεγμένος in Lk 9:35), for one would not expect John to have written anything but υἱός.[3] Although Greek-speaking Christians may have thought παῖς too humble a term and so changed to υἱός, עבד may equally have been too humble for the baptismal occasion, so that the original reference was to Ps 2:7 with בני.[4] 'Αγαπητός is a poor rendering for בחיר, never occurring in the LXX.[5] Mt's ἀγαπητός in 12:18 is readily explained as an echo of the present passage. Finally, the demonstration by M.-A. Chevallier of the very close link between Ps 2 and Is 11 and the Servant-songs throughout the Messianic tradition of Judaism[6] makes practically certain the conflation of Ps 2 and Is 42 here.

'Ο ἀγαπητός stems from the Targum of Ps 2:7 (חביב),[7] perhaps

---

[1] J. Jeremias, *The Servant of God* (London, 1957), 80ff. (same in *TWNT*, V, 699); O. Cullmann, *Baptism in the NT* (London, 1950), 17f.; *idem, Christology of the NT* (London, 1959), 66; C. Maurer, *ZTK*, 50 (1953), 31f.; F. Gils, *op. cit.*, 56ff. Lindars asks for other examples of υἱός replacing παῖς for עבד (pp. 139f.).

[2] See Cranfield, *SJT*, 8 (1955), 60; *idem, Mk*, 54f., although Cranfield rejects a reference to Ps 2:7 because of the difference in word order between the LXX and the gospels. This poses no real difficulty, however, since it represents only a slight shift of emphasis, from that of sonship in the psalm (υἱός first) to one of assurance or identification in the gospels (σύ or οὗτος first).

[3] Cf. N. Clark, *An Approach to the Theology of the Sacraments* (London, 1956), 15.

[4] See L. Reinke, *Die messianischen Weissagungen* (Giessen, 1859-62), II, 9, n. 1, who notes that in the Transfiguration, "Son" stands in opposition to the mere servants, Moses and Elijah.

[5] See Morna D. Hooker, *Jesus and the Servant* (London, 1959), 70ff.

[6] *L'esprit et le messie dans le bas-judaïsme et le NT* (Paris, 1958), 1-67.

[7] So J. Hänel, *op. cit.*, 139; Plooij, in *Amicitiae Corolla* (J. R. Harris Volume; London, 1933), 248f. It has also been held that οὗτος . . . ὁ ἀγαπητός stems from Gen 22:2 (LXX: τὸν υἱόν σου τὸν ἀγαπητόν [MT: יחידך] ὃν ἠγάπησας) (so H. B. Swete, *Mk*, 9; C. H. Turner, *JTS*, 27 [1926], 113-129; F. C. Fenton, in *Studies in the Gospels* [R. H. Lightfoot Volume; Oxford, 1955], 106). However, the much closer verbal similarity to Ps 2:7 outweighs the admitted fact that ἀγαπητός in the LXX came to be an incorrect rendering

helped by the ἀγαπητός-motif in the Messianic expectation of the Jews[1] and by the occurrence of ἀγαπᾶν in two Servant-contexts very close in wording and location to Is 42, viz., Is 41:8f.; 44:2.[2]

Mt's οὗτος . . . ἐν ᾧ is an adaptation patterned after the voice at the Transfiguration with a view to the readers of the gospel.[3] After verses 14f., there is no need to see the οὗτος as addressed to John; [4] and οὗτος cannot have been intended for the bystanders, for none are in view in Mt.[5]

'Εν ᾧ εὐδόκησα refers to Is 42:1. Hooker doubts a conscious quotation of Is here, arguing that it is strange Mt did not conform to his rendering of Is 42:1 in 12:18: ὃν εὐδόκησεν.[6] But this should occasion no surprise if we keep in mind that Mt is here working with or conforming to Marcan tradition and that in the formula-citations he often blazes his own trail. The bestowing of the Spirit, spoken of in both Is and the gospels, confirms the bond between the passages. The assimilation in Mt and Lk to ἐπ' αὐτόν in Is 42:1 against εἰς αὐτόν in Mk points to the consciousness of the allusion. Nor should the variance with the LXX (προσεδέξατο αὐτόν) cause difficulty, for we must not demand a purely Septuagintal form in the double and triple tradition. That εὐδοκεῖν with ἐν is a perfectly natural rendering of רצה is shown by its being the usual rendering in the LXX for רצה ב and חפץ ב [7] and by the use of εὐδοκεῖν (though with the accusative) in Is 42:1 by Theodotion and Symmachus.

---

for יחיד, alongside μονογενής (see A. Souter, *JTS*, 28 [1927], 59f.; Hooker, *op. cit.*, 71f.). Even further afield is J. A. E. van Dodewaard's view that the reference is to Ex 4: 22f., based on the Son of God = Israel = Christ typology (*Biblica*, 36 [1955], 487f.), though the Ex passage may provide a broad base for the Messianic use of Ps 2: 7 (see T. W. Manson, *BJRL*, 34 [1951/52], 323f., who notes the Midrash on the psalm connects v. 7 with Ex 4: 22).

[1] See J. A. Robinson, *HDB*, II, 501; *idem*, *Eph* (London, 1903), 230f.; B. W. Bacon, *JBL*, 20 (1901), 28-30.

[2] Cf. F. Leenhardt, *Le baptême chrétien* (Paris, 1946), 27, n. 2.

[3] So J. Schniewind, *Mt* (Göttingen, 1937), 25; W. E. Bundy, *Jesus and the First Three Gospels* (Harvard, 1955), 55. Cf. E. Norden, *Agnostos Theos* (Stuttgart, 1956), 188, on the frequency of οὗτός ἐστιν.

[4] Against Zahn, *Mt*² (Leipzig, 1905), 142; E. Klostermann, *Mt*² (Tübingen, 1927), 25.

[5] See Bundy, *loc. cit.*; against Plooij, *op. cit.*, 245.

[6] *Loc. cit.*

[7] II Sam 22: 20; Is 62: 4; Mal 2: 17; Ps 44 (43): 4. See A. Schlatter, *Mt*² (Stuttgart, 1948), 94.

The aorist εὐδόκησα is probably intended to indicate the prehistoric election of the Messiah.[1]

This allusion differs from the word order of the LXX in Ps 2:7 and from the vocabulary and grammatical construction of the LXX in Is 42:1. There is one point of contact with the Targum, and Mt displays a targumic adaptation in his change of person.

Mt 8: 4; Mk 1: 44; Lk 5: 14: σεαυτὸν δεῖξον τῷ ἱερεῖ
(Lk transposes the first two words.)
Lev 13: 49 LXX: καὶ δείξει τῷ ἱερεῖ MT: והראה את הכהן

The OT context concerns garments and skins, so that the NT adaptation to human beings requires the reflexive pronoun.

Mt 9: 36: ὅτι ἦσαν ἐσκυλμένοι καὶ ἐρριμμένοι ὡσεὶ πρόβατα μὴ ἔχοντα ποιμένα
Mk 6: 34: ὅτι ἦσαν ὡς πρόβατα μὴ ἔχοντα ποιμένα
Num 27: 17 LXX: ὡσεὶ (ὡς AM) πρόβατα οἷς οὐκ ἔστιν ποιμήν
MT: כצאן אשר אין להם רעה
Cf. I Kings 22: 17 LXX: ἑώρακα πάντα τὸν Ἰσραὴλ διεσπαρμένον ἐν τοῖς ὄρεσιν ὡς ποίμνιον ᾧ οὐκ ἔστιν ποιμήν
MT: ראיתי את כל ישראל נפצים אל ההרים כצאן אשר אין להם רעה
II Chron 18: 16 LXX: εἶδον τὸν Ἰσραὴλ διεσπαρμένους ἐν τοῖς ὄρεσιν ὡς πρόβατα οἷς οὐκ ἔστιν ποιμήν
MT: ראיתי את כל ישראל נפוצים על ההרים כצאן אשר אין להן רעה
Ezek 34: 5 LXX: καὶ διεσπάρη τὰ πρόβατά μου διὰ τὸ μὴ εἶναι ποιμένας καὶ ἐγενήθη εἰς κατάβρωμα πᾶσι τοῖς θηρίοις
MT: ותפוצינה מבלי רעה ותהיינה לאכלה לכל חית השדה

The form of the statement as a comparison introduced by ὡσεί (or ὡς) stands closest to Num 27:17; I Kings 22:17; II Chron 18:16. Mt and Mk differ noticeably from the LXX in rendering the Hebrew by μὴ ἔχοντα rather than by the more literal dative of possession.

The first part of Mt's description, missing in Mk, is another characteristic expansion based on OT phraseology. Ezek 34:5 provides the background for the picture of a scattered flock huddling on the ground and exposed to the harrassing and preying of wild beasts. Ἐσκυλμένοι signifies the rending and mangling by wild beasts (= לאכלה לכל חית השדה),[2] while ἐρριμμένοι signifies their scattering and exposure (= ותפוצינה).[3] In favor of these terms Mt

[1] See B. W. Bacon, *JBL*, 16 (1897), 136-139; 20 (1901), 28-30; *idem*, *American Journal of Theology*, 9 (1905), 454f., who develops the parallel with Eph 1: 4-9. Cf. Allen, *Mt*, 29.

[2] On σκύλλειν, see A. T. Robertson, *Word Pictures in the NT* (Nashville, 1930), I, 76.

[3] Ῥίπτειν was also used of the exposure of new-born infants. See A & G, s.v. The correspondence to the OT text is not lessened if one adopts the view

by-passes the perfectly useable διασπείρειν of the LXX, and indeed shows no trace of Septuagintal terminology.

Mt 10: 21; Mk 13: 12: καὶ ἐπαναστήσονται τέκνα ἐπὶ γονεῖς
Mic 7: 6 LXX: διότι υἱὸς ἀτιμάζει πατέρα, θυγάτηρ ἐπαναστήσεται ἐπὶ τὴν μητέρα αὐτῆς
MT: כי בן מנבל אב בת קמה באמה

The two clauses in Mic are compressed into one with the use of τέκνα to include "son" and "daughter" and γονεῖς to include "father" and "mother." The verb and the preposition are chosen from the second clause and agree with the LXX. Notably, when in 10:35 Mt quotes Mic 7:6 independently from Mk, he departs from the LXX in the use of κατά and at other points.

Mt 12: 4; Mk 2: 26; Lk 6: 4; I Sam 21: 6 LXX: τοὺς ἄρτους τῆς προθέσεως
I Sam 21: 6 MT: קדש (and לחם הפנים, for which the LXX has ἄρτοι τοῦ προσώπου [v. 7])

The synoptists follow the LXX.

Mt 13: 13	Mk 4: 12	Is 6: 9 LXX	MT
ὅτι βλέποντες	ἵνα βλέποντες	ἀκοῇ ἀκούσετε	שמעו שמוע
οὐ βλέπουσιν	βλέπωσιν καὶ	καὶ οὐ μὴ	ואל תבינו
	μὴ ἴδωσιν		
καὶ ἀκούοντες	καὶ ἀκούοντες	συνῆτε	וראו ראו
οὐκ ἀκούουσιν	ἀκούωσιν καὶ	καὶ βλέποντες	
οὐδὲ συνιοῦσιν	μὴ συνιῶσιν	βλέψετε	ואל תדעו
	(μήποτε	καὶ οὐ μὴ	
	ἐπιστρέψωσιν	ἴδητε	
	καὶ ἀφεθῇ		
	αὐτοῖς)		

Mt 13: 13 ἵνα βλ. μὴ βλέπωσιν κ. α. μὴ ἀκούσωσιν καὶ μὴ συνῶσιν D(Θ) 1 *al* it syr$^{sin, cur}$ Ir; + μήποτε ἐπιστρέψωσιν D(Θ)f13 1 *pc* it syr$^{sin, cur}$ (= assimilation to Mk)
Lk 8: 10: ἵνα βλέποντες μὴ βλέπωσιν καὶ ἀκούοντες μὴ συνιῶσιν
βλέπωσιν] ἴδωσιν DW*pc* (= assimilation to Mk)
Cf. Jn 9: 39; 12: 40.

Mt changes Mk's ἵνα to ὅτι, a change which at first glance looks like the softening of a harsh doctrine.[1] However, the expansion of

---

of A. Pallis that the original reading in Mt was ἐρρηγμένοι ("mauled"; so Cod. M). See his *Notes on St Mk and St Mt* (Oxford, 1932), 77.

[1] For a survey of the literature on this problem, see M. Hermaniuk, *La parabole evangélique* (Louvain, 1947), 1-32. Although in Jewish thought the ideas of consequence and purpose became partially fused—so that Mt's ὅτι is justified—yet the telic idea was not lost (see K. L. Schmidt, *TZ*, 1 [1945], 1-17; C. F. D. Moule, *An Idiom Book of NT Greek* [Cambridge, 1953], 143; E. F. Sutcliffe, *Biblica*, 35 [1954], 320-327; F. Hesse, *Das Verstockungsproblem*

the allusion to Is into a further direct quotation in which the hardness of the people's hearts fulfils the divine decree hardly softens the thought. According to Mt, God's decree and human guilt are a unity![1] Furthermore, Mt retains the thought of purpose in verse 11b: ἐκείνοις δὲ οὐ δέδοται.[2] And ὅστις δὲ οὐκ ἔχει, καὶ ὃ ἔχει ἀρθήσεται ἀπ' αὐτοῦ. διὰ τοῦτο ἐν παραβολαῖς αὐτοῖς λαλῶ, . . . (vv. 12b, 13a) is fully as strong as Mk's ἵνα, for in this statement the judicial hardening is deepened and made irrevocable.[3] The Matthaean form brings into clearer relief the guilt of the people, but in no such way as to mitigate the divine activity of judgment on the whole and salvation for the remnant. Rather, in the Matthaean form the judicial sentence of blindness is seen as already beginning to work itself out.[4] Mt has correctly perceived that the parables veiled the truth to give room for the exercise of faith and to make final the obduracy of the unbelieving.[5]

---

im AT [Berlin, 1955], 64f.). Especially with μήποτε, ἵνα must keep much of its telic force. Conversely, with ἵνα, μήποτε cannot be weakened into a cautious assertion ("if perhaps"—see J. H. Moulton, *op. cit.*, I, 188) or into an exceptive clause, which would result in a "Satz . . . zum wildesten Ja-Nein" (A. Jülicher, *Die Gleichnisreden Jesu*[2] [Tübingen, 1910], 131). The same must be said concerning J. Jeremias' attempt on the basis of rabbinic interpretation to soften דלמא in the Targum into the meaning "unless" (*The Parables of Jesus* [London, 1954], 15). Only if this latter view is adopted can Mk's agreement with the Targum (and OT Pesh) be utilized to soften the Marcan statement.

T. W. Manson's view that Mk has misinterpreted an Aramaic relative ד as a final ד (*The Teaching of Jesus*[2] [Cambridge, 1951], 76ff.) would have Jesus describing those who did not understand the parables, rather than answering the question why he spoke in parables (see T. A. Burkill, *NovTest*, 1 [1956], 260f.). A mistranslation of ד is not likely (see D. K. Andrews, *JBL*, 66 [1947], 26, 33, 39, 41; E. Ullendorff, *NTS*, 2 [1955/56], 50f.), nor is a deliberate misinterpretation, unless one is prepared to deny the authenticity of the many passages in the gospels where Jesus appears as the divider of men. With a dependent דלמא (μήποτε), ד is quite unambiguous (Black, *op. cit.*, 154). All such softening interpretations also run up against the Biblical connotation of παραβολή as an "enigma" (see E. Hoskyns and N. Davey, *The Riddle of the NT* [London, 1958], 133) and J. A. Baird's analysis of the explained und unexplained parables, in which he shows that Jesus did use parables to conceal the truth from outsiders and regularly explained the parables to his disciples (*JBL*, 76 [1957], 201-207). Much of the difficulty is removed if we recognize that the parables had a double function because of two classes of hearers. They were designed to puzzle and blind the unbelieving and, with explanatory help, to illuminate the disciples.

[1] Schniewind, *Mt*, 162.

[2] H. Windisch, *ZNW*, 26 (1927), 208f.

[3] Michaelis, *op. cit.*, II, 193f.

[4] Swete, *Mk*, 73.

[5] E. Stauffer, *TWNT*, III, 328f.; T. F. Torrance, *SJT*, 3 (1950), 303ff.

Apart from the necessary change in mood after ὅτι, in which Mt is closer to the LXX and Mk to the Hebrew, Mt's only divergence from Mk is in abbreviating and smoothing out Mk's translation Greek, which is patterned after the LXX. The vocabulary is the same as in Mk, as is also the chiastic order, in relation to the OT text, of the expressions containing βλέπειν and ἀκούειν.[1]

Mt 13: 32	Lk 13: 19	Mk 4: 32	Ezek 17: 23 LXX	MT
		ὑπὸ τὴν σκιὰν αὐτου	ὑπὸ τὴν σκιὰν αὐτοῦ	בצל דליותיו
			LXX Dan 4: 9, 18	Theod
τὰ πετεινὰ τοῦ οὐρανοῦ καί	τὰ πετεινὰ τοῦ οὐρανοῦ	τὰ πετεινὰ τοῦ οὐρανοῦ	τὰ πετεινὰ τοῦ οὐρανοῦ	τὰ ὄρνεα τοῦ οὐρανοῦ
κατασκη-νοῦν	κατεσκήνω-σεν	κατασκη-νοῦν	ἐνόσσευον	κατῴκουν (v. 9) / κατεσκήνουν (v. 18)
ἐν τοῖς κλάδοις αὐτοῦ	ἐν τοῖς κλάδοις αὐτοῦ		ἐν αὐτῷ {*pr* τὰ πετ. in Dan}	ἐν τοῖς κλάδοις αὐτοῦ

Dan 4: 9, 18 MT: בענפוהי ידרון (ישכנן, v. 18) צפרי שמיא
Cf. Ps 104 (103): 12; Ezek 31: 6.

Mk presents a composite allusion [2] in which the first phrase ("under its shade") agrees with the abbreviated rendering of the LXX against the MT ("in the shade of its branches"); and, as also in Mt and Lk, the latter part of the statement shows a mixture of the LXX (against Theodotion) and Theodotion [3] (against the LXX).[4] Mt and Lk carry on the quotation in accordance with Theodotion, against the LXX.

---

[1] Only v. 13 is parallel to Mk. For vv. 14f., see below, pp. 116ff.

[2] See Lohmeyer, *op. cit.*, 88, on Mk's combining of Ezek and Dan.

[3] I am assuming an Ur-Theodotionic translation of Daniel antedating the Christian era. See A. Bludau, *Die alexandrische Übersetzung des Buches Daniel* (Freiburg i.B., 1897), 22f.; F. G. Kenyon, *The Chester Beatty Biblical Papyri* (London, 1933), 15, and Fasc. VII, *Ezekiel, Daniel, Esther* (London, 1937), p. x; H. B. Swete, *An Introduction to the OT in Greek* (Cambridge, 1914), 423; Karnetzki, 272ff.

[4] To explain Mt's agreement with Mk (κατασκηνοῦν) against Lk (κατεσκή-νωσεν), S. E. Johnson says Mt conflated Mk with the pure Q form of Lk (*op. cit.*, 148).

Mt 14:16; Mk 6:37; Lk 9:13	II Kings 4:42 LXX	MT
δότε	δότε	תן
αὐτοῖς	τῷ λαῷ	לעם
ὑμεῖς	καὶ	ויאכלו
φαγεῖν	ἐσθιέτωσαν	

Lk ὑμεῖς φαγεῖν] *trsp* B; text *rell*

The striking coincidence of the circumstances under which the commands of Jesus and Elisha were uttered—the hungry crowd, the small supply of food, the surprised question of the servant and the disciples, the multiplication of the loaves, and the superabundance with some left over—suggests that Jesus' choice of these particular words was a conscious allusion to this OT passage.[1] In his mouth the expression is somewhat abridged, in αὐτοῖς for τῷ λαῷ and in the omission of καί. The NT goes against the LXX in the emphatic ὑμεῖς and in its telic infinitive φαγεῖν for the final *waw* with אכל. In this latter construction the NT may be influenced by extra-Biblical usage, for Schlatter cites three rabbinical passages where the same terminology, "Give to . . . to eat," occurs.[2]

Mt 17:5	Mk 9:7	Lk 9:35	II Pet 1:17	
οὗτός ἐστιν	οὗτός ἐστιν	οὗτός ἐστιν	ὁ υἱός μου	
ὁ υἱός μου	ὁ υἱός μου	ὁ υἱός μου	ὁ ἀγαπητός μου	
ὁ ἀγαπητός	ὁ ἀγαπητός	ὁ ἐκλελεγμένος	οὗτός ἐστιν	
ἐν ᾧ			εἰς ὃν ἐγὼ	
εὐδόκησα			εὐδόκησα	
			LXX Dt 18:15	MT
ἀκούετε	ἀκούετε	αὐτοῦ	αὐτοῦ	אליו
αὐτοῦ	αὐτοῦ	ἀκούετε	ἀκούσεσθε	תשמעון
Some MSS in Mt and Mk have transposed ἀκούετε and αὐτοῦ in conformity to the LXX.		ἐκλελεγμένος P^{45}אB*pc*] ἐκλεκτός Θ f1 it; ἀγαπητός ADW f13 28 *pl* lat Mcion Cl ς; + ἐν ᾧ ηὐδόκησα DΨ544*pc*d (These variants are parallel influence from Is 42:1 LXX [ἐκλεκτός] and the baptismal narrative.)	II Pet υἱός . . . ἐστιν B] οὗτός ἐστιν ὁ υἱός κτλ. אA*pl*lat ς	

For texts of Ps 2:7 and Is 42:1, see above, p. 29.

The omission of ἐν ᾧ εὐδόκησα by Mk means he alludes only to

[1] Cf. McNeile, *Mt*, 214.

[2] *Op. cit.*, 464: הבון ליה דליכול (*Jer. Berak.* 11b); יהבון ליה מיכלא ומשתיא (*R. to Pred.* 10.19); תנו לו לאכול כל מה שהוא מבקש (*Tanch.* שמיני 10.28).

Ps 2:7 and Dt 18:15. Though Lk shares this omission, his ἐκλελεγμένος betrays influence from ἐκλεκτός in Is 42:1 LXX. Thus, the versions of Mt and Lk independently and differently allude to Is 42:1, Lk in (partial [1]) agreement with the rendering of the LXX, Mt in disagreement.

The present tense of ἀκούετε in the gospels departs from the LXX, as does also the chiastic order of the last two words (except Lk, who conforms to the LXX[2]). Lk has followed throughout a different, more Hellenized tradition. Mt has expanded the shorter Marcan form with a phrase from the baptismal voice, just as he had altered the baptismal voice with the οὗτος of the declaration here. But note that II Pet supports Mt in the insertion—as an independent witness, for εἰς ὅν and ἐγώ rule out dependence on the Matthaean account. Οὗτος is directed to the disciples. The word order is changed from that of Ps 2:7 LXX. Ὁ ἀγαπητός stems from the Targum to Ps 2:7, and Mt's ἐν ᾧ εὐδόκησα renders the Hebrew of Is 42:1 independently from the LXX. See above, pp. 31f.

Mt 17:11: Ἠλίας μὲν ἔρχεται καὶ ἀποκαταστήσει πάντα
Mk 9:12: Ἠλίας μὲν ἐλθὼν πρῶτον ἀποκαθιστάνει πάντα
Mal 3:23, 24 LXX: καὶ ἰδοὺ ἐγὼ ἀποστέλλω ὑμῖν Ἠλίαν . . . ὃς ἀποκαταστήσει καρδίαν πατρὸς κτλ.
MT: הנה אנכי שלח לכם את אליה ··· והשיב לב אבות ····

Mk's choice of ἀποκαθιστάνει for השיב shows dependence on the LXX, but the form itself deviates from the LXX. Mt's ἀποκαταστήσει conforms to the LXX exactly, but may be motivated more by a desire to make clear the futurity of Elijah's ministry of restoration.

Mt 19:7	Mk 10:4	Dt 24:1 LXX	MT
δοῦναι	βιβλίον	γράψει αὐτῇ	כתב לה
βιβλίον	ἀποστασίου	βιβλίον	ספר
ἀποστασίου	γράψαι	ἀποστασίου	כריתת
		καὶ δώσει	ונתן
		εἰς τὰς χεῖρας αὐτῆς	בידה
καὶ ἀπολῦσαι αὐτήν	καὶ ἀπολῦσαι	καὶ ἐξαποστελεῖ αὐτὴν	ושלחה
αὐτήν BC*pm* ς] *om* ℵDΘ*al*		ἐκ τῆς οἰκίας αὐτοῦ	מביתו

[1] Why Lk should not have written ὁ ἐκλεκτός is puzzling. Is he unconscious of the allusion to Is 42? Or is an emphasis on the thought of the perfect participle intended?

[2] So Creed, *op. cit.*, 135.

By placing δοῦναι before βιβλίον ἀποστασίου, Mt has smoothed out the emphatic order of Mk and conformed to the order in the OT text. On the other hand, whereas Mk drew on the verb "write," with which βιβλίον ἀποστασίου is construed in Dt, Mt has reached into the next clause in Dt for the verb "give." In both gospels the more technical ἀπολῦσαι replaces ἐξαποστελεῖ of the LXX. Although the reading αὐτήν in Mt may be suspected of assimilation to the OT text or may be a purely stylistic improvement, the lack of important evidence for αὐτήν as a variant reading in Mk [1] makes it more probable that the omission is due to harmonization with Mk. (Note the presence of the harmonistically corrupted Cod. D among supporters of the omission.) Otherwise, we should have expected the same stylistic improvement or assimilation to the OT in many more Marcan MSS of importance. If then αὐτήν be accepted as genuine, Mt has carried the quotation one word further than Mk.

Mt 19: 26	Mk 10: 27	Lk 18: 27	Gen 18: 14 LXX	MT
παρὰ	πάντα	τὰ (ἀδύνατα		
δὲ	γὰρ	παρὰ		
θεῷ		ἀνθρώποις)		
	δυνατὰ	δυνατὰ	μὴ ἀδυνατεῖ	היפלא
πάντα	παρὰ	παρὰ	παρὰ	
δυνατά	τῷ θεῷ	τῷ θεῷ	τῷ θεῷ	מיהוה
		ἐστιν	ῥῆμα;	דבר
π. δυν. *trsp* ℵ*pc*	τῷ *om* BΘ*pc* πάντα. . . θεῷ] (ἐστιν) παρὰ δὲ τῷ θεῷ δυνατόν DitCl		παρὰ] *om* Luc (75) τῷ θεῷ] κυρίῳ 911bw ῥῆμα] *pr* πᾶν Luc (75)C	

Some MSS in Mt and Mk add ἐστιν as a stylistic improvement.

Lk 1: 37: οὐκ ἀδυνατήσει παρὰ τοῦ θεοῦ πᾶν ῥῆμα
τοῦ θεοῦ Bℵ*D*pc*] τῷ θεῷ CΘ*pl* ς
Cf. Job 42: 2; Zech 8: 6.

At first glance the Western reading in Mk looks attractive because of its distinctiveness and brevity.[2] However, the unusualness of παρά with the dative in the sense required here [3] demands a clearer allusion to the LXX of Gen 18: 14 than the Western text would give. The Lucan word order and use of the definite article with θεῷ point to dependence on Mk [4] rather than on a Q or Ur-

---

[1] Only N and syr^{sin} have αὐτήν in Mk.
[2] J. Wellhausen favors this reading (*Mk* [Berlin, 1903], 87).
[3] See A. Fridrichsen, *Symbolae Osloenses*, 14 (1935), 44-46.
[4] The omission of τῷ by BΘ*pc* in Mk must be considered a stylistic change

Matthaean form. Yet Lucan dependence on Mk precludes the originality of the Western text in Mk, from which the Lucan word order and plural δυνατά could not derive. The similarity of the Western text to Mt suggests harmonistic (Tatianic?) influence. Mk, then, as well as Mt and Lk, contains a clear verbal reminiscence of Gen 18:14.

Παρά with the dative in the sense "for" or "with" is unique, so that dependence on the LXX is slavish at this point.[1] But in opposition to the LXX, Mt and Mk use the neuter form πάντα in place of the awkward ῥῆμα to render the indefinite דבר.[2] This understanding of דבר as a thing or matter rather than as a spoken word agrees with the OT Pesh (צבותא) and may draw on a common exegetical tradition.

By blending the two statements regarding the impossible and the possible Lk sacrifices πάντα and close verbal resemblance to Gen 18:14. To compensate for the loss of emphasis on παρὰ θεῷ by his dropping the Marcan ἀλλ' οὐ παρὰ θεῷ Mt places the phrase in the emphatic first position. Mt also omits the definite article with θεῷ in opposition to Mk and the LXX.

Mt 20:28; Mk 10:45	Is 53:10 MT			LXX
καὶ δοῦναι		אם תשים	I[3]	ἐὰν δῶτε
τὴν ψυχὴν αὐτοῦ		נפשו	III	ἡ ψυχὴ ὑμῶν (ὄψεται σπέρμα μακρόβιον)
λύτρον		אשם	II	περὶ ἁμαρτίας
ἀντὶ πολλῶν	(vv. 11f.)	רבים		πολλῶν (v. 12)

The thrice-repeated "his soul" in Is 53:10-12 and the peculiar designation πολλῶν-רבים demonstrate that Mt and Mk do indeed allude to Is 53:10.[4] The NT δοῦναι for שים shows reminiscence of

---

or assimilation to Mt. The presence of the article in Lk justifies its inclusion in the Marcan text.

[1] Fridrichsen thinks the LXX, although it does not substitute "heaven" for the divine name, goes a step in that direction by using παρὰ τῷ θεῷ for the divine sphere (= ἐν οὐρανῷ) as opposed to the earthly, human sphere (*loc. cit.*; cf. Field, *Notes*, 46f.). Contrast the Hebraistic παρὰ τοῦ θεοῦ in Lk 1:37, where otherwise the correspondence with the LXX (esp. Luc—πᾶν ῥῆμα) is close. Cf. P. Winter, *NTS*, 1 (1954/55), 115; D. Tabachovitz, *Die Septuaginta u. das NT* (Lund, 1956), 88f.

[2] Cf. Torrey, *op. cit.*, 73. On the uses and renderings of דבר, see G. Bertram, *Theologische Rundschau*, 10 (1938), 153.

[3] Roman numerals indicate the order in the OT text.

[4] See H. W. Wolff, *Jesaja 53 im Urchristentum*[3] (Berlin, 1952), 62, and R. H. Fuller, *The Mission and Achievement of Jesus* (London, 1954), 56f., who notes in Mk 8:31; 9:12 further allusions to Is 53, based on non-Septua-

the LXX; but the NT saying is based on an entirely different understanding of the OT passage, as is evident from the LXX's ἐάν with the subjunctive and the second person plural of the verb and of the possessive pronoun. Λύτρον may or may not be considered a loose rendering of אשם.[1] Even if not, the non-Septuagintal character of this allusive quotation is beyond doubt.

Mt 21:9, *etc.*

The only constant is εὐλογημένος . . . κυρίου, in which NT = LXX = MT.[2] Mt omits all reference to a "king" or "kingdom"—very noteworthily in view of the kingdom-motif throughout the first gospel—and refers rather to τῷ υἱῷ Δαυίδ. Mk repeats εὐλογημένος and refers to ἡ ἐρχομένη βασιλεία τοῦ πατρὸς ἡμῶν Δαυίδ.

Lk, as might be expected, stands farthest from the circle of Jewish thought in rejecting ὡσαννά and any reference to David (Mt, Mk) or Israel (Jn). Instead, he inserts ὁ βασιλεύς after ὁ ἐρχόμενος as an explanatory gloss (omitted, however, in Lk 13:35). Jn adds to the blessing a reference to ὁ βασιλεὺς τοῦ Ἰσραήλ, which stands between Lk's complete rejection of Jewish terminology and the typically Jewish terminology of Mt and Mk.

Mt and Mk agree in a final ὡσαννά ἐν τοῖς ὑψίστοις. But Lk, having rejected ὡσαννά as unintelligible to a Gentile reader, falls back on the words of the angelic song in the Nativity, δόξα ἐν ὑψίστοις θεῷ καὶ ἐπὶ γῆς εἰρήνη (Lk 2:14); only he has transposed δόξα and εἰρήνη and supplied the latter with a phrase parallel to ἐν ὑψίστοις,

---

gintal renderings of the Hebrew. Against Hooker (*op. cit.*, 74ff.) and C. K. Barrett (in *NT Essays* [T. W. Manson Memorial Volume; Manchester, 1959], 4ff.), who are able to minimize the individual points of verbal parallelism, but cannot account for the whole. Barrett's argument is further blunted by his confining his criticisms largely to the parallel with verse 12 in Is 53.

[1] See Karnetzki, 223; Wolff, *op. cit.*, 62. There is weight in the objection of Hooker and Barrett that אשם means sacrificial repayment, but that λύτρον means redemption by purchase. Nevertheless, the idea of payment is inherent in both words; and by virtue of its being applied to Jesus' redemptive death, the root λυτρ- gains a sacrificial connotation in the NT.

[2] Swete (*Mk*, 236) and Cranfield (*Mk*, 351) claim that the Hebrew accents show בשם יהוה to be connected with ברוך, not with הבא as in the LXX and the NT. However, most OT scholars render in accordance with the syntax of the LXX. So F. Delitzsch, *Ps* (London, 1887-89), III, 207; H. Schmidt, *ZAW*, 40 (1922), 3; W. O. E. Oesterley, *Ps* (London, 1939), II, 482; A. Weiser, *Ps* (Göttingen, 1950), 480; W. F. Albright, in *Interpretationes ad Vetus Testamentum Pertinentes* (Mowinckel *Festschrift*; Oslo, 1955), 9; H.-J. Kraus, *Ps* (Neukirchen Kreis Moers, 1958-), 801.

Mt 21:9	Mk 11:9, 10	Lk 19:38	Mt 23:39; Lk 13:35	Jn 12:13
ὡσαννὰ	ὡσαννά			ὡσαννά
τῷ υἱῷ Δαυίδ				
εὐλογημένος ὁ ἐρχόμενος	εὐλογημένος ὁ ἐρχόμενος	εὐλογημένος ὁ ἐρχόμενος ὁ βασιλεὺς	εὐλογημένος ὁ ἐρχόμενος	εὐλογημένος ὁ ἐρχόμενος
ἐν ὀνόματι κυρίου	ἐν ὀνόματι κυρίου	ἐν ὀνόματι κυρίου	ἐν ὀνόματι κυρίου	ἐν ὀνόματι κυρίου καὶ ὁ βασιλεὺς τοῦ Ἰσραήλ
	εὐλογημένη ἡ ἐρχομένη βασιλεία τοῦ πατρὸς ἡμῶν Δαυίδ			
ὡσαννὰ ἐν τοῖς ὑψίστοις	ὡσαννὰ ἐν τοῖς ὑψίστοις	ἐν οὐρανῷ εἰρήνη καὶ δόξα ἐν ὑψίστοις		

Variant readings in Mk and Lk show parallel influence and influence from liturgical usage.

Ps 118 (117): 25, 26 LXX: σῶσον δή . . . εὐλογημένος ὁ ἐρχόμενος ἐν ὀνόματι κυρίου
MT: הושיעה נא ··· ברוך הבא בשם יהוה

viz., ἐν οὐρανῷ—again as an explanatory gloss for the benefit of Gentile readers who might not understand ὑψίστοις.

The main questions concern ὡσαννά,[1] in which, of course, the NT departs from the LXX and from the original petitionary sense of the Hebrew. Specifically, had ὡσαννά become a cry of praise before the Triumphal Entry, or does the NT present a misunderstanding and Christian adaptation of an original cry for help? On one side it is argued that the Matthaean dative following ὡσαννά mistakes ὡσαννά as a shout of praise; [2] whereas ὡσαννά alone or in

[1] On the shortened form הושע נא, see G. Dalman, *The Words of Jesus* (Edinburgh, 1902), 221.

[2] *Ibid.* Torrey charges Mt with mistaking an Aramaic ל of direct object before "Son of David" for a ל of indirect object (*op. cit.*, 77 f.; cf. also C. T. Wood, *ET*, 52 [1940/41], 357). However, J. Jeremias has shown from Mt 22: 37 that Mt had a Semitic mother-tongue and therefore could not have misunderstood ὡσαννά in this way (*ZNW*, 50 [1959], 270-274). (Jeremias' argument need not rest on 22: 37 alone!) The intransitive use of הושיעה נא in the Ps lends itself to use with an indirect object, once the word has changed to an exclamation of praise. לבן would be a direct object *only if* Hosanna had not yet taken the exclamatory meaning. A further possibility exists

construction with ἐν τοῖς ὑψίστοις really was a suppliant cry to [1] or for [2] Jesus as Messiah, or a challenge for Jesus to reveal himself in an act of Messianic power and glory,[3] or a prayer to God [ὁ] ἐν τοῖς ὑψίστοις.[4] Other conjectures have also been made.[5]

On the other side, good evidence exists that ὡσαννά from before NT times had an exclamatory and laudatory signification. The Matthaean tradition is not to be rejected out of hand. By bringing into connection the Song of the Nativity, δόξα ἐν ὑψίστοις (θεῷ . . .), Lk independently attests the Matthaean understanding as very primitive.[6] If the construing of ὡσαννά with ἐν τοῖς ὑψίστοις be original—and Mk has it—it is probable that the prepositional phrase stems from Ps 148:1,[7] where the connotation of praise is clear (הללוהו במרומים—αἰνετε αὐτὸν ἐν τοῖς ὑψίστοις). The ascription of σωτηρία to God and to the Lamb (Rev 7:10) shows how easily the idea of salvation can become associated with praise.[8] The absence of the root ישע in Aramaic,[9] Jewish liturgical use of

---

that the crowd consisted of Greek-speaking Galilean pilgrims who shouted just as recorded in Mt—in Greek. Cf. below, pp. 174ff.

Stendahl sees the influx of a Christian liturgical hymn (p. 65). Cf. H. Köster, who thinks the evangelists lifted ὡσαννά out of the *Did.* 10:6 (*Synoptische Überlieferung bei dem apostolischen Vätern* [*Texte u. Untersuchungen*, 5. Reihe, Bd. 10; Berlin, 1957], 196ff.). Cf. also Swete, *Mk*, 236; C. Schmidt, *ZNW*, 24 (1923), 97f.; F. Herklotz, *BZ*, 18 (1929), 39; J.-P. Audet, *La Didachè* (Paris, 1958), 62-67, 420-425.

[1] So Merx, *op. cit.*, II, 132f.; E. Werner, *JBL*, 65 (1946), 112ff.

[2] Gould, *op. cit.*, 208f.

[3] K. Schubert, *The Dead Sea Community* (London, 1959), 133f.; J. S. Kennard, Jr., *JBL*, 67 (1948), 175f.

[4] So *Acta Pilati* i. 3, 4 (σῶσον δή, ὁ ἐν τοῖς ὑψίστοις); also some older commentators, cited in Meyer, *op. cit.*, 61.

[5] F. C. Burkitt conjectures the original words behind the gospel tradition were הושענא לעילא, "Hosanna upwards!" or "Up with your wands!" (*JTS*, 17 [1916], 144). E. F. F. Bishop thinks Hosanna originally was חֹסֶנ נו = "Our strength (is in the Son of David)" (*ET*, 53 [1941/42], 212-214). G. Klein supposes ἐν τοῖς ὑψίστοις arose from reading ברום for ברוך in Ps 118:25 (*ZNW*, 2 [1901], 345f.). T. K. Cheyne derives Hosanna from עוּשְׁנָא ("our strength"), shouted by the children in connection with Ps 8:3 (Hebrew, עֹז), which was quoted by Jesus (Mt 21:16) (*Encyclopaedia Biblica*, II, 2117ff.).

[6] A later witness to this tradition is Clement of Alexandria, who explains Hosanna as φῶς καὶ δόξα καὶ αἶνος μεθ' ἱκετηρίας τῷ κυρίῳ (*Paed.* i. 5 [MPG VIII, 264]).

[7] Cf. Dalman, *loc. cit.* Dalman thinks the evangelists added this phrase. But if they could add it, why not the crowd?

[8] Cf. J. Cooper, *HDCG*, I, 750.

[9] P. Joüon, *L'évangile de notre-seigneur Jésus Christ* (Paris, 1930), 128; J. Jeremias, *ZNW*, 50 (1959), 274.

הושע נא,[1] and the use of the word to designate the seventh day of the Feast of Tabernacles [2] deprived it of the original supplicatory intent and facilitated its festive use. That the Hallel had come not to be restricted to the Feast of Tabernacles [3] confirms that this is exactly what happened. The Targum II to Esther 3:8 puts in Haman's mouth the observation that at the Feast of Tabernacles the Jews "rejoice and go around with the Hosannas [lulabs] and jump and spring like kids." I Macc 13:50 ff. tells of a joyful feast celebrated under Simon with ritual borrowed from the Feast of Tabernacles: μετὰ αἰνέσεως καὶ βαΐων καὶ ἐν κινύραις καὶ ἐν κυμβάλοις καὶ ἐν νάβλαις καὶ ἐν ὕμνοις καὶ ἐν ᾠδαῖς . . . μετ' εὐφροσύνης.[4] No reason exists, then, to deny that the change from a cry for help to a cry of praise took place before the Christian era.[5]

Lk's assimilation to the Song of the Nativity favors the view that ἐν τοῖς ὑψίστοις has reference to the praise of heavenly beings. The idea that angels echo the praise of human beings is not unfamiliar in Judaism.[6]

Mt 21:33	Mk 12:1	Lk 20:9	Is 5:2 LXX		MT
ἐμφύτευσεν	ἀμπελῶνα. . .	ἐφύτευσεν	κ. ἐφύτευσα	II	ויטעהו
ἀμπελῶνα κ.	ἐφύτευσεν κ.	ἀμπελῶνα	ἄμπελον . . .		שרק
φραγμὸν αὐτῷ	περιέθηκεν		κ. φραγμὸν	I	ויסקלהו
περιέθηκεν	φραγμὸν		περιέθηκα . . .		
κ. ὤρυξεν	κ. ὤρυξεν		κ. προλήνιον	IV	וגם יקב
ἐν αὐτῷ ληνὸν	ὑπολήνιον		ὤρυξα ἐν αὐτῷ		חצב בו
κ. ᾠκοδόμησεν	κ. ᾠκοδόμησεν		κ. ᾠκοδόμησα	III	ויבן
πύργον[7]	πύργον		πύργον . . .		מגדל

[1] On the impressive ceremony in which Ps 118 and Hosanna figured, see A. Edersheim, *The Temple: Its Ministry and Services* (London, n.d.), 191-193; J. Jeremias, ΑΓΓΕΛΟΣ, 2 (1926), 100-105; *idem, ZNW*, 50 (1959), 273.

[2] *Lev.*, R. 27.2; *Sukka* 4, 5.

[3] Strack-Billerbeck, *Kommentar zum NT* (München, 1922-28), I, 845ff.; H. Bornhäuser (ed.), *Sukka* (Berlin, 1935), 106. See further E. Lohse, *NovTest*, 6 (1963), 114-116.

[4] Cf. Kennard, *loc. cit.*

[5] E. Werner's argument that Mt's dative requires in the Hebrew a vocative for the person addressed and an accusative for the person to be helped completely misses that the dative implies a new meaning for Hosanna (*op. cit.*, 100).

[6] See the Targum to Ps 148: 1f.; and Bab. *Chullin* 91b, quoted by Werner, *ibid.*, 110f.

[7] According to Pallis, πύργον denotes a country villa with an upper story, underneath which is a winepress (*op. cit.*, 41). If so, Mt and Mk may transpose the clauses in order to put the digging of the press before the building of the superstructure.

Since Jesus speaks this parable upon entering the Temple, it is probable he had in mind the Targumic interpretation of the tower as the Temple.

Lk shows little concern with the OT parallel. The difference between ἀμπελῶνα ("vineyard") in the NT and ἄμπελον ("vine") in the LXX is not significant, for in Is the "vine" is planted in the "vineyard." [1] The NT compresses the parable, so that the owner plants the vineyard. The clauses have been chosen from the OT passage without regard to order.[2]

NT, LXX, OT Peshitta, and Vulgate agree in understanding יסקלהו (*piel*: "to gather out stones") as meaning "to build a (stone) fence" around the vineyard. This does not anticipate the משוכה of verse 5, for that word means "a hedge of thorns." Rather, it is supposed that the stones gathered from the field the farmer would use for a fence.[3]

Mt	Mk	LXX	MT
ληνόν [4] (winepress)	ὑπολήνιον [5] (vat below the winepress—so Aq, Sym)	προλήνιον (ambiguous)	יקב (vat; secondarily, the winepress)

Προλήνιον (only here in the LXX) would have been suitable. Ὑπολήνιον (Mk) stands closest to יקב. But Mt's ληνόν is not necessarily incorrect, because the words were sometimes used by metonymy for the whole press.[6] Though Mt does not conform Mk's ὑπολήνιον to the LXX, he does carry the quotation a single phrase further with ἐν αὐτῷ. The differences in word order have to do with emphatic style.

Thus, in its text-form this quotation is primarily Septuagintal. But the occasion of its use makes probable a contact with the Targum.

---

[1] Seeligman rejects ἄμπελον in the LXX as secondary, because no fewer than seven times in these verses the entire textual tradition uses ἀμπελῶν (*op. cit.*, 33).

[2] For Targumic precedent in changing the order of phrases and clauses, see Baumstark, *op. cit.*, 312f.

[3] On the influx of Egyptian agricultural methods into the LXX's translation, see J. Ziegler, *Untersuchungen zur Septuaginta des Buches Is*, 179.

[4] In the LXX chiefly for גת, less correctly, for יקב.

[5] Always for יקב in the LXX.

[6] See A. R. S. Kennedy, *Encyclopaedia Biblica*, IV, 5311ff.

[M]t 22:24	Mk 12:19	Lk 20:28	Dt 25:5 LXX	MT	Gen 38:8 LXX	MT
ὰν τις	ἐάν τινος ἀδελφὸς	ἐάν τινος ἀδελφὸς	ἐὰν δὲ κατοικῶσιν ἀδελφοὶ ἐπὶ τὸ αὐτό,	כי ישבו אחים יחדו		
ποθάνη	ἀποθάνη καὶ καταλίπη γυναῖκα καὶ	ἀποθάνη ἔχων γυναῖκα καὶ οὗτος	καὶ ἀποθάνη εἷς ἐξ αὐτῶν σπέρμα δὲ	ומת אחד מהם		
ὴ ἔχων κνα	μὴ ἀφῇ τέκνον	ἄτεκνος ᾖ	μὴ ᾖ αὐτῷ. . . ὁ ἀδελφὸς τοῦ ἀνδρὸς. . .	ובן אין לו … יבמה …		
ιγαμβρεύσει ἀδελφὸς ὐτοῦ τὴν υναῖκα αὐτοῦ	ἵνα λάβῃ ὁ ἀδελφὸς αὐτοῦ τὴν γυναῖκα καὶ	ἵνα λάβῃ ὁ ἀδελφὸς αὐτοῦ τὴν γυναῖκα καὶ	λήμψεται αὐτὴν ἑαυτῷ γυναῖκα	ולקחה לו לאשה	γαμβρεῦσαι αὐτὴν	ויבם …
αὶ ἀναστήσει πέρμα ῷ ἀδελφῷ ὐτοῦ	ἐξαναστήσῃ σπέρμα τῷ ἀδελφῷ αὐτοῦ	ἐξαναστήσῃ σπέρμα τῷ ἀδελφῷ αὐτοῦ			κ. ἀνάστησον σπέρμα τῷ ἀδελφῷ σου	והקם זרע לאחיך
					γαμβρ. A] ἐπιγαμβρ. Luc (75)	

The use of τέκνον by the synoptists avoids the inexact σπέρμα of the LXX and correctly renders the Hebrew בן.[1] Mk's collective singular is closer to the MT than Mt's somewhat freer plural. All three synoptists differ from one another and from the LXX in the rendering of (בן) אין לו, ἀφῇ (Mk) being foreign to the OT text,[2] but μὴ ἔχων (Mt) and ἄτεκνος ᾖ (Lk) being very idiomatic translations.

By introducing ἐπιγαμβρεύσει, Mt crosses over to Gen 38:8 one step before Mk and Lk. Note Mt's agreement with Lucian in the compound form of the verb. On the other hand, Mt rejects the compound form ἐξαναστήσῃ in Mk and Lk for the simplex form of the LXX (though Mt may be motivated more by stylistic preference [3]).

---

1 OT commentators differ on the force of בן in Dt 25:5. S. R. Driver maintains the word means a male son (*Dt* [ICC; Edinburgh, 1895], 282). C. F. Keil has the better of the argument, however, for he points out that according to Num 27:4ff. the perpetuation of the house and name could be ensured through a daughter. Thus, the LXX, Vg, Josephus (*Ant.* IV. viii. 23), NT, and rabbis correctly interpret בן to mean a child of either sex (Keil and Delitzsch, *Biblical Commentary on the OT* [Edinburgh, 1865], III, 422).

2 The Hebrew construction is possessive, containing no thought of "leaving," though Mk's may be considered a loose translation.

3 Cf. J. H. Moulton, *The Expositor*, 7, 7th Series (1909), 411f.

Mt 24: 6a: μελλήσετε δὲ ἀκούειν πολέμους καὶ ἀκοὰς πολέμων· ὁρᾶτε μὴ θροεῖσθε
Mk 13: 7: ὅταν δὲ ἀκούσητε πολέμους καὶ ἀκοὰς πολέμων, μὴ θροεῖσθε.
Lk 21: 9: ὅταν δὲ ἀκούσητε πολέμους καὶ ἀκαταστασίας, μὴ πτοηθῆτε
πτοηθῆτε] φοβηθῆτε Ddq
Dan 11: 44 Theod: καὶ ἀκοαὶ καὶ σπουδαὶ ταράξουσιν αὐτόν
LXX: καὶ ἀκοὴ ταράξει αὐτόν
MT: ושמעות יבהלהו

The whole context in Dan has to do with wars. The plural of ἀκοή in the sense of "rumors" is rare.[1] Lk rejects the word and consequently moves away from the OT phraseology. In this word, therefore, and in the compound form of the expression the Theodotionic text is reflected (but not the LXX). However, the synoptics reject the other member of the doublet-rendering in Theodotion, σπουδαί, in favor of πολέμους. The exhortation μὴ θροεῖσθε stands in contrast with the troubling of the king of the north. Here the NT renders בהל independently from the LXX and Theodotion.[2]

Mt 24: 6b; Mk 13: 7; Rev 1: 1; 4: 1; 22: 6: ἃ [*om* Mt, Mk] δεῖ γὰρ [*om* Mk, Rev] γενέσθαι
Lk 21: 9: δεῖ γὰρ ταῦτα γενέσθαι πρῶτον
Dan 2: 28 Theod, LXX: ἃ δεῖ γενέσθαι (ἐπ' ἐσχάτων τῶν ἡμερῶν)
MT: מה די להוא (באחרית יומיא)

The idea of necessity (δεῖ) is an advance on the simple future of the MT, so that there is close dependence on the Greek OT text.[3]

Mt 24: 7; Mk 13: 8 | Lk 21: 10	Is 19: 2 LXX	MT	II Chron 15: 6 LXX	MT
ἐγερθήσεται	καὶ	וסכסכתי ...		
γὰρ	ἐπεγερθήσονται . . .	ונלחמו ...		
	καὶ πολεμήσει . . .		καὶ πολεμήσει	וכתתו
ἔθνος	πόλις	עיר	ἔθνος	גוי
ἐπὶ ἔθνος	ἐπὶ πόλιν	בעיר	πρὸς ἔθνος	בגוי
καὶ	καὶ		καὶ	
βασιλεία	νομὸς	ממלכה	πόλις	ועיר
ἐπὶ	ἐπὶ		πρὸς	
βασιλείαν	νομόν	בממלכה	πόλιν	בעיר
	-ονται] -εται א*		(ὅτι ὁ θεὸς	(כי אלהים
	πόλις] *pr* ἐπεγερθή-		ἐξέστησεν	הממם
	σεται AB^c (-ονται)		αὐτοὺς ἐν πάσῃ	בכל
			θλίψει)	צרה)

'Εγερθήσεται in the NT echoes ἐπεγερθήσονται of the LXX (Is 19:2), a very free, even incorrect translation of סכך (*pilpel*: "to

[1] See J. C. Hawkins, *Horae Synopticae*[2] (Oxford, 1909), 61.
[2] The Lucan πτοηθῆτε is probably due to a special liking for the word. Among NT writers only Lk uses it, here and in Lk 12: 4 (P^{45} 700); 24: 37.
[3] T. F. Glasson, *ET*, 69 (1957/58), 214.

cover with armour, to arm [for warfare]").[1] The synoptics' retention of the two ἐπί's in the LXX compensates for their discarding the prefix ἐπ-. Parallel influence from II Chron 15:6 enters with ἔθνος ἐπὶ ἔθνος.[2] In βασιλεία ἐπὶ βασιλείαν the NT gives an independent rendering of the Hebrew against the LXX.[3]

Mt 24:13 (= 10:22); Mk 13:13	Dan 12:12, 13 Theod	LXX	MT
	μακάριος	μακάριος	אשרי
ὁ δὲ ὑπομείνας	ὁ ὑπομένων	ὁ ἐμμένων	המחכה
	καὶ φθάσας . . .	καὶ συνάψει . . .	ויגיע ···
εἰς τέλος	εἰς συντέλειαν	εἰς συντέλειαν	לקץ
οὗτος σωθήσεται	(ἡμερῶν)	(ἡμερῶν)	(הימין)

Lk 21:19: ἐν τῇ ὑπομονῇ ὑμῶν κτήσεσθε τὰς ψυχὰς ὑμῶν

The synoptists follow Theodotion against the LXX in ὑπομένειν, a good rendering of חכה in this context.[4] But Mt and Mk reject εἰς συντέλειαν (Theod, LXX) in favor of εἰς τέλος in spite of the fact συντέλεια occurs in the introductory question to the Olivet Discourse (Mt 24:3; Mk 13:14).

The OT context does not settle the perplexing question whether we should punctuate with a comma after τέλος and translate "unto the end," or after ὑπομείνας and translate "at the end"; for in Dan 12:13 לקץ occurs twice, once in the sense of coming "to the end" and once in the sense of standing in one's lot "at the end."

Mt 24:15a	Mk 13:14	Dan 12:11 LXX	MT
τὸ βδέλυγμα	τὸ βδέλυγμα	τὸ βδέλυγμα	שִׁקּוּץ
τῆς ἐρημώσεως	τῆς ἐρημώσεως	τῆς ἐρημώσεως	שֹׁמֵם
		Dan 9:27 LXX Theod	MT
. . . ἑστὸς ἐν	ἑστηκότα	ἐπὶ τὸ ἱερόν	על כנף
τόπῳ ἁγίῳ	ὅπου οὐ δεῖ		
			9:27]
ἑστός] ἑστώς DΘ *pm* ς (Attic form of nt. ptcp.)			בהיכל יהוה 1 MS Ken

Dan 12:11 Theod: βδέλυγμα ἐρημώσεως (Cod. A assimilates to the LXX.)
Dan 9:27 LXX Theod: βδέλυγμα τῶν ἐρημώσεων MT: שִׁקּוּצִים מְשֹׁמֵם
Dan 11:31 LXX: βδέλυγμα ἐρημώσεως MT: הַשִּׁקּוּץ מְשׁוֹמֵם
Theod: βδέλυγμα ἠφανισμένον

---

[1] See Ottley, *op. cit.*, II, 198.

[2] The bringing in of II Chron 15: 6 was facilitated by the reference in that verse to θλίψει, a major theme in the Olivet Discourse. But note also that the passages are combined in *IV Esdras* 13: 31.

[3] Νομός (LXX) reflects the administrative districts in Ptolemaic Egypt. See A. Deissmann, *Bible Studies* (Edinburgh, 1901), 145.

[4] Glasson pits חכה ("to wait") against ὑπομένειν ("to endure") (*op. cit.*,

In τὸ βδέλυγμα τῆς ἐρημώσεως Mt and Mk agree only with the LXX of Dan 12:11, and this against the masculine participle(s) of שמם.[1] Dan 12:11 alone is grammatically correct in the MT.[2] Despite the primary importance of Dan 9:27 for the meaning of the expression, 12:11 is contextually the more suitable reference so far as the gospels are concerned, because allusions to Dan 11:40-12:13 surround this reference to the abomination of desolation.

Although Mk adopts ἐρημώσεως from the LXX, the masculine participle ἑστηκότα shows that his interpretation stems from the Hebrew text, specifically, from the masculine participles of שמם and possibly from the definite article in Dan 11:31.[3]

Mt brings the vague ὅπου οὐ δεῖ of Mk into closer conformity with the text of Dan 9:27. His ἐν τόπῳ ἁγίῳ (= Temple) [4] is verbally dissimilar from the LXX and Theodotion, but reveals the same understanding of כנף as an elliptical expression referring to a part

---

215). However, only the context gives ὑπομένειν the special connotation of endurance (missing, e.g., in Lk 2:43; Acts 17:14), and the Danielic context gives חכה just this connotation of patient, trusting endurance.

[1] The agreement with the LXX and disagreement with the MT may be greater yet, if the original sense was "the appalling abomination." On this expression as a contemptuous equivalent of בעל שמם (= Zeus Ouranios), see E. Nestle, *ZAW*, 4 (1884), 248; G. R. Beasley-Murray, *A Commentary on Mark Thirteen* (London, 1957), 54f.

[2] In 9:27 a plural noun is construed with a singular participle. But the singular noun of the LXX and Theod casts doubt on the MT. In 11:31 the article in השקוץ is very odd. See D. Daube, *The NT and Rabbinic Judaism* (London, 1956), 419; B. Rigaux, *Biblica*, 40 (1959), 675ff.

[3] *Ibid.*; Daube, *loc. cit.* So also the OT Pesh: חבלא, "destroyer." Cf. II Thess 2:4 and the concept of a personal Antichrist.

[4] Τόπος ἅγιος = Temple in the papyri and Josephus. Cf. Is 60:13; II Macc 1:29; 2:18; 8:17; Acts 6:13; 21:28. See A & G, s.v. τόπος, 1b. B. H. Streeter accepts the omission of ἑστὸς ἐν τόπῳ ἁγίῳ in syr^sin fam 1424, arguing that syr^sin best represents Mt, the Antiochean gospel (*The Four Gospels* [London, 1951], 519f.). However, syr^sin is defective in Mt, not even having an equivalent for ἐρημώσεως. Nor does Streeter reckon with the Tatianic influence in syr^sin (see above, p. 9, n. 2). Streeter's further argument that the lack of a definite article with τόπῳ indicates a careless marginal note has come into the text precariously rests on the delicate question of the use of the article in Greek. Especially in expressions which have almost gained the force of proper nouns, as here, the article is easily omitted (see above, p. 25). In view of the verbal differences between Mt and Dan (LXX, Theod) and Mk, Streeter's suggestion of parallel influence does not seem probable. S. G. F. Brandon defends the genuineness of the phrase by arguing that Mt is not an Antiochean, but an Egyptian gospel, and that the omission of the article may indicate Mt, like Josephus, knew the Roman standards were not placed in the sanctuary, but in the Temple area (*The Fall of Jerusalem*² [London, 1957], 173f., 245f.).

of the Temple, and, by metonymy, to the whole Temple—so also one MS of Kennicott. Cf. Mt 4: 5 (ἐπὶ τὸ πτερύγιον τοῦ ἱεροῦ).[1]

Mt 24:15b; Mk 13:14: ὁ ἀναγινώσκων νοείτω
Dan 12:10 Theod: καὶ οἱ νοήμονες συνήσουσι
LXX: καὶ οἱ διανοούμενοι προσέξουσιν
MT: והמשכלים יבינו

Νοείτω ("to understand"—Mt, Mk) alludes to יבינו ("to discern"), for which the LXX and Theodotion have different words. Nevertheless, the NT may reflect the use of (δια)νοεῖν in the participial forms of the LXX and Theodotion.

The abundance in the NT contexts of other allusions to this section of Dan and the prominence of the *maskilim* in Qumran texts [2] favor that this is indeed an allusion to Dan 12 and that the exhortation is original to the Olivet Discourse, referring to the reader of Dan, not to the reader of the gospel or of a pre-synoptic "Little Apocalypse." [3] Thus the Matthaean insertion τὸ ῥηθὲν διὰ Δανιὴλ τοῦ προφήτου is not incorrect.[4]

Mt 24:21	Mk 13:19	Dan 12:1 LXX	Theod	MT
ἔσται γὰρ τότε	ἔσονται γὰρ		καὶ ἔσται	והיתה
	αἱ ἡμέραι	ἐκείνη ἡ	καιρὸς	עת
	ἐκεῖναι	ἡμέρα		
θλῖψις μεγάλη	θλῖψις	θλίψεως	θλίψεως	צרה
οἵα οὐ γέγονεν	οἵα οὐ γέγονεν	οἵα οὐκ	οἵα οὐ γέγονεν	אשר לא
		ἐγενήθη		נהיתה
	τοιαύτη			
ἀπ' ἀρχῆς	ἀπ' ἀρχῆς	ἀφ' οὗ	ἀφ' οὗ	מהיות
		ἐγενήθησαν	γεγένηται	
κόσμου	κτίσεως ἣν		ἔθνος	גוי
	ἔκτισεν ὁ θεὸς			
ἕως τοῦ νῦν	ἕως τοῦ νῦν	ἕως τῆς	ἕως τοῦ	עד
		ἡμέρας	καιροῦ	העת
		ἐκείνης	ἐκείνου	ההיא
οὐδ' οὐ μὴ	καὶ οὐ μὴ			
γένηται	γένηται			
οὐ γέγονεν] οὐκ ἐγένετο ℵDΘIr	ἡν. . .θεός] *om* DΘ*al*it καὶ οὐ]οὐδέ D(Θ*al*)	(= assimilation to Mt)		

[1] On כנף as referring to the Temple, see E. Haupt, *Die alttestamentlichen Citate in den vier Evangelien* (Colberg, 1871), 138f.

[2] CDC 13:7; *Manual of Discipline* 3:13; 9:18; *Hodayoth* (*Meg. Gen.*) 2:50, 3. See Bruce, *op. cit.*, 55f.

[3] Ever since T. Colani (*Jésus Christ et les croyances messianiques de son temps* [Strasbourg, 1864]) this statement has been taken as proof that a document, not a speech, lies behind the Olivet Discourse.

[4] Cf. Marxsen, *op. cit.*, 110; Schlatter, *op. cit.*, 704.

I Macc 9:27: καὶ ἐγένετο θλῖψις μεγάλη ἐν τῷ Ἰσραήλ, ἥτις οὐκ ἐγένετο ἀφ᾽ ἧς ἡμέρας οὐκ ὤφθη προφήτης αὐτοῖς
Ex 9:18 LXX: ἥτις τοιαύτη οὐ γέγονεν ἐν Αἰγύπτῳ, ἀφ' ἧς ἡμέρας ἔκτισται ἕως τῆς ἡμέρας ταύτης
MT: אשר לא היה כמהו במצרים למן היום הוסדה ועד עתה
11:6 LXX: ἥτις τοιαύτη οὐ γέγονεν καὶ τοιαύτη οὐκ ἔτι προστεθήσεται
MT: אשר כמהו לא נהיתה וכמהו לא תסף
Cf. 9:24; 10:6, 14.
Joel 2:2 LXX: ὅμοιος αὐτῷ οὐ γέγονεν ἀπὸ τοῦ αἰῶνος καὶ μετ' αὐτὸν οὐ προστεθήσεται ἕως ἐτῶν εἰς γενεὰς γενεῶν
MT: כמהו לא נהיה מן העולם ואחריו לא יוסף עד שני דור ודור

Mt's μεγάλη after θλῖψις shows contact with I Macc 9:27 (cf. Rev 7:14). Mk's ἔσονται γὰρ αἱ ἡμέραι ἐκεῖναι θλῖψις recalls the LXX, ἐκείνη ἡ ἡμέρα θλίψεως, against Theodotion and the MT,[1] while Mt comes closer to the Hebrew והיתה עת צרה with ἔσται γὰρ τότε θλῖψις (μεγάλη), yet not in agreement with Theodotion. Οἵα οὐ γέγονεν (Mt, Mk) agrees with Theodotion (Dan 12:1) against the LXX.

In the circumlocutory ἀπ' ἀρχῆς κτίσεως ἣν ἔκτισεν ὁ θεός in Mk, the use of κτίζειν reveals an influx from the parallel passage Ex 9:18[2] in its Septuagintal form (against יסד, "to found"). Mt's shortened form, ἀπ' ἀρχῆς κόσμου, may be an idiomatic rendering of the Hebrew text in another parallel passage, Joel 2:2 (מן העולם),[3] or may show contact with the OT Peshitta of Dan 12:1 (מן יומת עלמא). Ἕως τοῦ νῦν (Mt, Mk) again recalls Ex 9:18, but this time is an exact rendering of the Hebrew text against the LXX. Οὐδ' (Mk: καὶ) οὐ μὴ γένηται (Mt, Mk) recalls the similar expressions in Ex 10:14; 11:6; Joel 2:2 in their Hebrew forms.

Mt 24:24; Mk 13:22	Dt 13:1-3 LXX	MT	Old Pal Targ Targ Jon
ἐγερθήσονται	ἐὰν δὲ ἀναστῇ	כי יקום	
γὰρ (Mk: δὲ)	ἐν σοὶ	בקרבך	
ψευδόχριστοι	προφήτης	נביא	נבי שקרא
καὶ	ἢ	או	
ψευδοπροφῆται	ἐνυπνιαζόμενος	חלם	
	ἐνύπνιον	חלום	
καὶ δώσουσιν	καὶ δῷ σοι	ונתן אליך	
σημεῖα	σημεῖον	אות	
μεγάλα (Mk: *om*)			
καὶ τέρατα	ἢ τέρας	או מופת	

Mk ψευδόχριστοι καί]
om D 124 1573 d i k
δώσουσιν] ποιήσουσιν DΘ*pc*a

[1] But Mk's Semitic idiom may reflect a pointing הָעֵת. See McNeile, *Mt*, 349.
[2] The assertions concerning the severity of the Egyptian plagues are the pattern for Dan 12:1. See Beasley-Murray, *op. cit.*, 78.
[3] ('Απ') ἀρχῆς stands for (מ)עולם in Josh 24:2; Prov 8:23; Is 63:16, 19 LXX.

Mt and Mk show independence from the LXX in ἐγερθήσονται. If the omission of ψευδόχριστοι καί in the Western text of Mk is to be preferred as a Western non-interpolation, Mt has inserted the words to correspond in chiastic order to the compound form of the OT text. Ψευδοπροφῆται (Mt, Mk) agrees with Targum Jonathan and the newly discovered Old Palestinian Targum against the LXX and the MT. The decision between δώσουσιν (= Mt and Dt LXX MT) and ποιήσουσιν in Mk is difficult. Δώσουσιν may be assimilation to Mt, Mt having conformed Mk to Dt,[1] or the Western text has replaced the Semitic "give" with "perform." [2] Μεγάλα, added by Mt, is a targumic embellishment.[3]

Mt 24:29; Mk 13:24	Is 13:10 LXX		MT	Lk 21:25, 26
ὁ ἥλιος	σκοτισθήσεται		חשך	καὶ ἔσονται
σκοτισθήσεται	τοῦ ἡλίου		השמש	σημεῖα ἐν
	ἀνατέλλοντος		בצאתו	ἡλίῳ καὶ
καὶ ἡ σελήνη	καὶ ἡ σελήνη		וירח	σελήνῃ καὶ
οὐ δώσει	οὐ δώσει		לא יגיה	ἄστροις καὶ
τὸ φέγγος	τὸ φῶς		אורו	ἐπὶ τῆς γῆς
αὐτῆς	αὐτῆς			συνοχὴ ἐθνῶν
	Is 34:4 LXX		MT	ἐν ἀπορίᾳ
καὶ οἱ	καὶ πάντα		וכל	ἤχους θαλάσσης
ἀστέρες	τὰ ἄστρα	II	צבאם	καὶ σάλου
πεσοῦνται ἀπὸ	πεσεῖται		יבול	[cf. Is 17:12]
[Mk: ἔσονται ἐκ]				. . .
τοῦ οὐρανοῦ				
[Mk: + πίπτοντες]			ונמקו	
καὶ αἱ δυνάμεις		I	כל צבא	αἱ γὰρ δυνάμεις
τῶν οὐρανῶν			השמים	τῶν οὐρανῶν
[Mk: αἱ ἐν τοῖς				σαλευθήσονται
οὐρανοῖς, exc.				
D*al* it syr]				
σαλευθήσονται	καὶ τακήσονται πάσαι αἱ δυνάμεις τῶν οὐρανῶν			
Cf. Joel 3:3, 4.	BLuc (in O sub ·※·) (= Hexaplaric addition [4])			

In the first clause Mt and Mk independently render the Hebrew ("the sun will be darkened [in its going forth]") against the LXX ("it will be dark when the sun rises," a legitimate translation). In the second clause the use of δώσει for נגה (instead of, e.g., λάμπειν)

[1] So B. Weiss, *Mt* (Meyer's Commentary[9]; Göttingen, 1898), 415; T. W. Manson, *BJRL*, 34 (1951/52), 318.

[2] So V. Taylor, *op. cit.*, 516.

[3] On the frequent combination of σημεῖα and τέρατα, see S. V. McCasland, *JBL*, 76 (1957), 149ff.

[4] See Ottley, *op. cit.*, II, 276.

points to dependence upon the LXX. Nevertheless, independence is still maintained in that the gospels have φέγγος where the LXX has φῶς.

In the first clause from Is 34:4, the NT agrees with the LXX ("stars," "fall") against the MT ("host," "fade away"). The idea of falling has been introduced from the comparison with the leaves of vines and fig trees, which immediately follows in Is 34:4, a comparison which may have suggested the parable of the fig tree immediately thereafter in the NT context.[1]

The second clause in Is 34:4 being omitted by the LXX (as well as the hexaplaric addition differing from the NT in τακήσονται), Mt and Mk present an independent rendering of the Hebrew. The idea of shaking (σαλευθήσονται, in place of מקק, "to melt away") may be another extension of the figure of the fig tree.

Mt 24:30	Mk 13:26; Lk 21:27	Jn 19:37		Rev 1:7	Zech 12:10 LXX		MT
κ. τότε κόψονται πᾶσαι αἱ φυλαὶ τῆς γῆς			III	κ. κόψονται ἐπ' αὐτὸν πᾶσαι αἱ φυλαὶ τῆς γῆς	κ. κόψονται ἐπ' αὐτὸν... ἡ γῆ κατὰ φυλὰς ...αἱ φυλαί	II	פדו ...יין ארץ שפחות משפחות כל המשפחות
καὶ ὄψονται	κ. τότε ὄψονται	ὄψονται εἰς ὃν ...	II	καὶ ὄψεται αὐτὸν πᾶς ὀφθαλμός...	κ. ἐπιβλέψονται πρός μέ...	I	ביטו ...י

Mt 24:30	Mk 13:26; Lk 21:27		Rev 1:7	Dan 7:13 Theod		LXX	MT
τὸν υἱὸν τοῦ ἀνθρώπου ἐρχόμενον	τὸν υἱὸν τοῦ ἀνθρώπου ἐρχόμενον			ὡς υἱὸς ἀνθρώπου ἐρχόμενος	II	ὡς υἱὸς ἀνθρώπου ἤρχετο	ר ש נה הוה
ἐπὶ τῶν νεφε- λῶν τοῦ οὐρανοῦ μετὰ δυνά- μεως καὶ δόξης πολλῆς	ἐν νεφέλαις [Lk: -ῃ] μετὰ δυνάμεως πολλῆς [Lk: *post* δόξης] καὶ δόξης	I	ἰδοὺ ἔρχεται μετὰ τῶν νεφελῶν	καὶ ἰδοὺ μετὰ τῶν νεφελῶν τοῦ οὐρανοῦ	I	καὶ ἰδοὺ ἐπὶ τῶν νεφελῶν τοῦ οὐρανοῦ	רו ז ני ויא

Mk ἐν] ἐπί Dsyr^{sin}
(= assimilation to Mt)

Zech 12:10 αἱ φυλαί AQW]
pr πᾶσαι BℵLucC

[1] So Gibson, *op. cit.*, 84.

Merx and Torrey reject καὶ τότε κόψονται . . . γῆς as an interpolation from Zech and Rev by a scribe whose eye was caught by the close resemblance between καὶ ὄψονται and καὶ κόψονται.[1] However, the MSS overwhelmingly support the insertion, and there is no reason why ἐπ' αὐτόν should have been omitted from the interpolation. That τότε has been shifted from ὄψονται (Mk, Lk) to κόψονται (Mt) speaks for the genuineness of the latter, for it is unlikely an interpolator would have taken such pains.

Πᾶσαι αἱ φυλαὶ τῆς γῆς [2] presents a conflation of כל המשפחות and הארץ. If the text represented in Zech 12:10 by BאLucC is hexaplaric, πᾶσαι in the NT shows direct recourse to the Hebrew. Ὄψονται shows independence from the LXX (ἐπιβλέψονται). Throughout the NT ὄψονται takes a third personal object, as also in many Hebrew MSS of Zech 12:10, the *Didache* (16:7), Justin (1 *Apol.* lii) and other early church fathers, the Talmud (*Sukka* v. 52), and early editions of the commentaries of Aben Ezra, Rashi, and Kimchi.[3] The MT, which reads the first person, is inherently difficult and probably corrupt. The remainder of the verse in Zech indicates a third personal object. The thought of God himself being pierced is strange, foreign to the context, and beyond the limits of legitimate anthropomorphism.[4] אלי might be favored as the more difficult reading. However, because of the scribal similarity between *yodh* and *waw* an original *waw* (אליו) could easily have dropped out by haplography.

While Jn and Rev continue to quote Zech, the synoptists transfer to Dan 7:13. The individualizing use of the article with "Son of man" is facilitated by the dropping of ὡς (כ) in the synoptics. Ἐρχόμενον agrees with Theodotion against the LXX. Mt's ἐπί agrees with the LXX and OT Peshitta (על) against Theodotion and Rev 1:7 (μετά), and the MT (עם).[5] Mt could have used ἐν

---

[1] Merx, *op. cit.*, I, i, pp. 347f.; Torrey, *op. cit.*, 83. Cf. Beasley-Murray, *op. cit.*, 92. Syr^{sin} Or omit.

[2] Mt = Rev. Cf. Atkinson, *op. cit.*, 53, concerning the apocalyptist's dependence on the Olivet Discourse.

[3] For the textual evidence, see T. Jansma, in *Oudtestamentische Studien* (Leiden, 1950), VII, 117f.; Mitchell, *op. cit.*, 334.

[4] *Ibid.*; T. W. Manson, *BJRL*, 34 (1951/52), 330.

[5] Dalman suggests that since it belongs to God alone to ride upon the clouds, עם was substituted for an original על (*op. cit.*, 242). But this appears to be an overrefinement of the distinction between the prepositions.

(Mk, Lk); but his rejection of μετά may be due to a stylistic consideration, viz., that μετά comes in his very next phrase. Ἐν is a free rendering,[1] consonant with the premature breaking off of the quotation in Mk and Lk; whereas Mt continues with the genitive τοῦ οὐρανοῦ (=LXX, Theod, MT). The singular νεφέλῃ (Lk) may be influenced by νεφέλη in the Lucan account of the ascension (Acts 1:9), in which a parallel is drawn between the ascension and the return of Christ. The final phrase in the synoptics is another targumic embellishment designed to paint the general picture given in Dan 7 of the power and glory of the Son of man.

Mt 24:31	Mk 13:27			
καὶ (τότε) ἀποστελεῖ				
τοὺς ἀγγέλους (αὐτοῦ)				
μετὰ		Is 27:13 LXX	MT	
σάλπιγγος		τῇ σάλπιγγα (*pr* ἐν		בשופר
μεγάλης		ALuc) τῇ μεγάλῃ		גדול
καὶ ἐπι-	καὶ ἐπι-	συνάξω		פרשתי
συνάξουσιν	συνάξει		II	
τοὺς	τοὺς	ὑμᾶς		אתכם
ἐκλεκτοὺς	ἐκλεκτοὺς	Zech 2:10 LXX	MT	
αὐτοῦ	αὐτοῦ	Cf. Ezek 37:9; Dan 8:8; 11:4		
ἐκ τῶν	ἐκ τῶν	ἐκ τῶν		
τεσσάρων	τεσσάρων	τεσσάρων	I	כארבע
ἀνέμων	ἀνέμων	ἀνέμων . . .		. . . רוחות
	ἀπ' ἄκρου	ἀπ' ἄκρου	Dt	מקצה
	γῆς	τῆς γῆς	13:8	הארץ
		ἕως ἄκρου	= Jer	ועד קצה
		τῆς γῆς	12:12	הארץ
ἀπ' ἄκρων		ἀπ' ἄκρου	Dt	בקצה
οὐρανῶν		τοῦ οὐρανοῦ	30:	השמים
ἕως ἄκρων	ἕως ἄκρου	ἕως ἄκρου	4	
αὐτῶν	οὐρανοῦ	τοῦ οὐρανοῦ		
		τ. οὐρ. 2°] αὐτοῦ Θ		

Mt alone contains a reference to the "great trumpet," an expression occurring only in Is 27:13.[2] His μετά with the genitive diverges from the LXX and shows a desire to produce an equivalent for ב, similar to that displayed in the literal rendering of LXX^{ALuc} (ἐν). Mt has also omitted the definite articles in conformity with the Hebrew.

---

[1] But ἐν may be justified by the interchange of עם and ב in Dan 2:43; 5:30 (cf. 7:2) and by Yahweh's coming in (ב) the cloud (Ex 19:9; 34:5; Num 11:25). See R. B. Y. Scott, *NTS*, 5 (1959), 128.

[2] See further T. F. Glasson, *The Second Advent*^{2} (London, 1947), 189ff.

Although Mt and Mk have added ἐπί to συνάξω, their dependence on the LXX is very obvious, for the MT means, "*As* [1] the four winds (of the heavens) I have *scattered* you." The Hebrew text has been suspected of corruption.[2] However, sense can be made of the MT, the reference being to the dispersion from which is the regathering (so the Targum) rather than to the regathering alone; and it is easier to account for the LXX's change from "scatter" to "gather" than vice versa.[3]

The Marcan ἀπ' ἄκρου γῆς stems from Dt 13:8,[4] with which is combined a phrase from Dt 30:4, where another συναξ- provides the link with Zech 2:10.[5] Mt brings the first phrase also into conformity with Dt 30:4. Both gospels depend on the LXX's expanded rendering of the MT in Dt 30:4, but Mt assimilates to the plural השמים and changes ἄκρου to ἄκρων in order to have four successive endings in -ων. But the reason is not only stylistic, for the plural ἄκρων agrees (against the MT, LXX, Mk) with the OT Pesh, the Old Palestinian Targum, Targum Jonathan, and Targum Onkelos (סיפי). Targum Jonathan refers this gathering to the activity of the King-Messiah and his forerunner, Elijah the great priest (כהנא רבא). It is further enlightening to note that סוף not only means "end," but also "remnant," i.e., those who survive to be gathered, and specifically the fruit remaining on a tree after harvest. Cf. the following parable of the fig tree and the foregoing quotation from Is 34:4. Mt's preference for αὐτῶν in place of a second οὐρανῶν may show contact with the text of LXX$^{\Theta}$ (αὐτοῦ).

Mt 24:34; Lk 21:32	Mk 13:30	Dan 12:7 LXX	Theod	MT
ἕως ἂν πάντα ταῦτα [Lk *om*] γένηται	μέχρις οὗ ταῦτα πάντα γένηται	ἡ συντέλεια χειρῶν ἀφέσεως λαοῦ ἁγίου καὶ συντελεσθήσεται πάντα ταῦτα	ἐν τῷ συντελεσθῆναι διασκορπισμὸν γνώσονται πάντα ταῦτα	תכלינה כל אלה

[1] Or "in." ב is read in twenty-three MSS and supported by the Vg and the OT Pesh. See Mitchell, *op. cit.*, 145.

[2] See Kittel-Kahle, *ad loc.*

[3] Cf. Glasson, *ET*, 69(1957/58), 214.

[4] Note this is the second quotation from Dt 13. See above, p. 50.

[5] Cf. the variant reading in *I Enoch* 57:2, cited by V. Taylor, *op. cit.*, 519; and Philo, *Cherub.* xcix, cited by Lohmeyer, *Mk*, 279, for similar combinations.

The synoptics are clearly far removed from the interpretative rendering of the LXX and Theodotion. The use of γίνεσθαι in fulfilment-formulae suits the word to render כלה.

Mt 26:3, 4	Mk 14:1	Lk 22:2	Ps 31 (30):14 LXX	MT
τότε			ἐν τῷ	בהוסדם
συνήχθησαν . . .			συναχθῆναι	יחד
			αὐτούς	
καὶ	καὶ	καὶ	ἅμα ἐπ' ἐμὲ	עלי
συνεβουλεύσαντο	ἐζήτουν . . .	ἐζήτουν. . .	τοῦ λαβεῖν	לקחת
ἵνα	πῶς	τὸ πῶς	τὴν ψυχήν μου	נפשי
τὸν Ἰησοῦν	αὐτὸν	ἀνέλωσιν	ἐβουλεύσαντο	זממו
		αὐτόν	Ex 21:14 LXX	MT
			ἐὰν δέ τις	וכי יזד
δόλῳ	ἐν δόλῳ		ἐπιθῆται	איש
κρατήσωσιν	κρατήσαντες		τῷ πλησίον	על רעהו
κ. ἀποκτείνωσιν	ἀποκτείνωσιν		ἀποκτεῖναι	להרגו
			αὐτὸν δόλῳ	בערמה
κ. ἀποκτ.] *om* B**pc*	ἐν δόλῳ] *om* Dair		Ps 31 συναχθ. BאR 1219 55] ἐπισυναχθ. ALuc	

The variant omissions in Mt and Mk appear to be slips of the pen, since the minor differences rule out insertion by parallel influence.

In the allusion to Ps 31:14, where Mt alone assimilates the language to the OT, the prefixing of συν-(βουλ.) by Mt is insignificant in view of the context and may be due to the parallelism with συνήχθησαν. This latter word may have prompted the allusion, for it links Ps 31:14 with Ps 2:2, a known early Christian proof-text (Acts 4:25 f.). Throughout both allusions the text-form is Septuagintal, Mt making a slight assimilation to the LXX by dropping Mk's ἐν (δόλῳ), which corresponds to the Hebrew ב.[1]

Mt 26:11; Mk 14:7: πάντοτε γὰρ τοὺς πτωχοὺς ἔχετε μεθ' ἑαυτῶν
Dt 15:11 LXX: οὐ γὰρ μὴ ἐκλίπῃ ἐνδεὴς ἀπὸ τῆς γῆς
MT: כי לא יחדל אביון מקרב הארץ
אביון] האביון 1 MS Ken, Sam

That there is an allusion to Dt 15:11 is evident, but it is so loose that comparison of text-form is possible only in the term "poor." Here Mt departs from the rendering of the LXX, and his collective plural with the article may reflect the textual tradition represented in the Samaritan Pentateuch and 1 MS Ken.

---

[1] I owe the notice of the allusion to Ex 21:14 to Lohmeyer-Schmauch, *Mt* (Göttingen, 1956), 348.

Mt 26:28	Mk 14:24	Ex 24:8 LXX	MT
τοῦτο γάρ	τοῦτό	ἰδού	הנה
ἐστιν	ἐστιν		
τὸ αἷμά μου	τὸ αἷμά μου	τὸ αἷμα	דם
τῆς διαθήκης	τῆς διαθήκης	τῆς διαθήκης	הברית
	τὸ	Is 53:12 LXX	MT
	ἐκχυννόμενον	παρεδόθη	הערה
		εἰς θάνατον	למות
		ἡ ψυχὴ αὐτοῦ	נפשו
		. . . καὶ αὐτὸς	··· והוא
τὸ περὶ	ὑπὲρ	ἁμαρτίας	חטא
πολλῶν	πολλῶν	πολλῶν	רבים
ἐκχυννόμενον		ἀνήνεγκεν	נשא
		Jer 31 (38): 34 LXX	MT
εἰς ἄφεσιν		ἵλεως ἔσομαι	אסלח
ἁμαρτιῶν		ταῖς ἀδικίαις	לעונם
		αὐτῶν καὶ	
διαθήκης P$^{37, 45}$ ℵB Θ*pc*] *pr* καινῆς AD W f1 f13 565 700 *pl* lat syr sah boh^{pm} ς; *pr* τό AC W f1 f13 *pl* syr^{hk}	τῆς διαθ.] τὸ τῆς καινῆς διαθ. A f1 f13 700 *pl* lat syr ς; πολλῶν] + εἰς ἄφεσιν ἁμαρτιῶν W f13 *pc* ag^2 sah(4) boh (= assimilation to Mt)	τῶν ἁμαρτιῶν αὐτῶν	ולחטאתם

Lk 22:20: τοῦτο τὸ ποτήριον ἡ καινὴ διαθήκη ἐν τῷ αἵματί μου τὸ ὑπὲρ ὑμῶν ἐκχυννόμενον
I Cor 11:25 = Lk, exc. διαθήκη] + ἐστιν; αἵματι μου] *pr* ἐμῷ, *om* μου (P^{46}AC*al* = Lk); τὸ ὑπὲρ ὑμῶν ἐκχυν. *om*
Heb 9:20: τοῦτο τὸ αἷμα τῆς διαθήκης ἧς ἐνετείλατο πρὸς ὑμᾶς ὁ θεός (= a quotation of Ex 24:8)
Jer 31 (38):31 LXX: διαθήκην καινήν MT: ברית חדשה
Cf. Zech 9:11.

All the NT texts have τοῦτο against "behold" (MT, LXX). We might suppose that τοῦτο replaced ἰδού through the parallelism with τοῦτό ἐστιν τὸ σῶμά μου (Mt 26:26 and parallels) and that no allusion to Ex 24:8 is here intended. But since Mt 26:28 presents a striking resemblance to Ex 24:8, we should rather think that an allusion is intended [1] and that parallel influence would have worked in the opposite direction, retaining ἰδού in Mt 26:28 (and par) and

[1] S. Aalen argues that since the sacrificial meal instituted by Jesus had to do with an offering *for sin* (against the Law of the Offerings), Jesus must have been alluding to Ex 24, the only place in the OT where blood-sprinkling for cleansing and a sacrificial meal are joined (*NovTest*, 6 [1963], 149ff.). Lindars' referring Mt 26:28 par to Zech 9:11 fails to recognize the redemptive nature of the Exodus context and rests on unwarranted denial of early typological exegesis (pp. 132f.).

conforming τοῦτο ... σῶμα to ἰδού ... σῶμα. This feeling is confirmed with the discovery that the OT Peshitta, Targum Jonathan, and Targum Onkelos to Ex 24:8 have the demonstrative pronoun (הנא—Pesh, הא דין—Targums) in agreement with the NT. Further confirmation comes from Heb 9:20, where Ex 24:8 is quoted with τοῦτο.[1] Perhaps this textual variant resulted from the close similarity between the Hebrew הנה ("behold") and the Syriac הנא ("this"), abetted by the fact that in Aramaic הא is both an interjection ("behold") and the feminine demonstrative pronoun.[2] Thus, it is very possible that the allusion shows contact with the OT Peshitta and the Targums.[3]

The insertion of καινῆς is better supported in Mt than in Mk and in view of the later allusion to Jer 31 (omitted in Mk) may be genuine. If so, Mt conforms more closely to the OT. Εἰς ἄφεσιν ἁμαρτιῶν (Mt) is an allusion to Jer 31:34, ἄφεσιν exactly corresponding to the meaning of סלח ("to forgive") against the free ἵλεως ἔσομαι of the LXX.

---

[1] Most commentators regard τοῦτο in Heb 9:20 as assimilation to the words of institution. See Thomas, *op. cit.*, 103ff.; F. H. Woods, *HDB*, IV, 187. However, the omission of ἐστιν and the lack of any distinct reference to the Eucharist in Heb reduces this possibility.

[2] Although דם is masculine, the double meaning of הא might have suggested the insertion of דין ("this"—masc.) after הא ("behold").

[3] At least since W. Wrede the difficulty of retranslating τὸ αἷμά μου τῆς διαθήκης into Aramaic or Hebrew has led to the conclusion that τῆς διαθήκης is an unauthentic addition to the original words (Wrede, *ZNW*, 1 [1900], 70f.; J. Jeremias, *The Eucharistic Words of Jesus* [Oxford, 1955], 133ff.; *idem*, *JTS*, 50 [1949], 7; E. Schweizer, *RGG*³, I, 13). Recent studies, however, have increasingly called in question the impossibility of a corresponding Semitic construction (G. Dalman, *Jesus-Jeshua* [London, 1929], 160f.; J. A. Emerton, *JTS*, 6 [1955], 238ff.; H. Gottlieb, *Studia Theologica*, 14 (1960), 115-118; Fuller, *op. cit.*, 69f.; cf. R. Deichgräber, *Revue de Qumran*, Tome 2, Num. 6 (1960), 279f.; Hooker, *op. cit.*, 81f.). Cf. the several expressions in which קֹדֶשׁ has a pronominal suffix which logically belongs to the preceding noun in the construct state (Lev 20:3; 22:2; Ps 2:6; 51:13; 89:21; Is 11:9; 63:11). A pertinent example is the Targum to Is 42:1, where רוח קודשי stands for רוחי. A contact with the Targums to Ex 24:8 would favor the authenticity of the quotation and the possibility of the construction in Aramaic, as well as obviate the objection that "the blood of the covenant" could only mean, as in late Judaism, "the blood of circumcision" (Jeremias, *Eucharistic Words*, *loc. cit.*; against which see Dalman, *Jesus-Jeshua*, 167f.). See further the *Auseinandersetzung* between Jeremias in the third edition of his book (Göttingen, 1960, pp. 186, 133ff.) and Emerton in *JTS*, 13 (1962), 111-117; 15 (1964), 58f. Emerton favors the more rare Aramaic construction in which the pronominal suffix is attached to the noun in the construct state, thinking Jesus wished to avoid being misunderstood to mean "the blood of my covenant." Postscript: Jeremias has now changed his mind.

In the allusion to Is 53:12, ἐκχυννόμενον (Mt, Mk, Lk) again exactly corresponds to the Hebrew, הערה,[1] against the loose rendering of the LXX, παρεδόθη. Πολλῶν agrees with both the LXX and the MT, the conjunction with ἐκχυννόμενον certifying an allusion to Is 53.[2]

Mt 26:38; Mk 14:34: περίλυπός ἐστιν ἡ ψυχή μου ἕως θανάτου

Ps 42 (41):6, 12; 43 (42):5 LXX: ἵνα τί περίλυπος εἶ, ψυχή
41:6 ψυχή 2013 *et* Or Rahlfs] *pr* ἡ B; ἡ ψ. μου *rell* (*etiam* א 1219)
41:12 ψυχή B[c] 2013] *pr* ἡ B* 1219; ἡ ψ. μου *rell*
42:5 ψυχή Bא boh 2013] ἡ ψ. μου *rell* (*etiam* 1219)
MT: מה תשתוחחי נפשי

Jonah 4:9 LXX: σφόδρα λελύπημαι ἐγὼ ἕως θανάτου
MT: היטב חרה לי עד מות

The singing of the Hallel toward the close of the Last Supper would have put the context of Jesus' thoughts in the Psalms. The rarity of περίλυπος strengthens the case for an allusive quotation here.[3] Dependence on the LXX in περίλυπος is close, since the Hebrew verb means "to be bowed (or cast) down." If ψυχή be the original reading in the LXX, as Rahlfs thinks, Mt and Mk may have assimilated to the Hebrew text by adding μου. But such assimilation might have taken place in pre-NT times.[4]

The root λυπ- provides the link between Ps 42-43 and Jon 4:9, and in both passages is an incorrect rendering (in Jon for חרה, "be angry"). Ἕως θανάτου = LXX = MT.

Mt 26:41; Mk 14:38	Ps 51 (50):14 LXX	MT
τὸ μὲν	πνεύματι	ורוח
πνεῦμα	ἡγεμονικῷ	נדיבה
πρόθυμον	στήρισόν με	תסמכני

The NT agrees with the Hebrew ("willing spirit") against the LXX ("governing spirit"). The OT context indicates the Holy

---

[1] Hooker objects that ἐκχυν. cannot render ערה, because the latter means "to lay bare" (*op. cit.*, 82). However, ערה also means "to pour out." See Is 32:15 and the lexicons.

[2] Cf. A. J. B. Higgins, *The Lord's Supper in the NT* (London, 1952), 32.

[3] Περίλυπος fails in the papyri, Philo, and Josephus and occurs but eight times in the LXX, only in Psalms 42 and 43 for שחח. See R. Bultmann, *TWNT*, IV, 325. In addition to Bultmann, E. Clapton (*Our Lord's Quotations from the OT* [London, 1922], 68), F. Hauck (*Mk* [Leipzig, 1931], *ad loc.*), L. Goppelt (*Typos* [Gütersloh, 1939], 120f.), P. Benoit (*Mt*[2] [Paris, 1953], 153), Karnetzki (p. 221), and T. Boman (*NTS*, 10 [1964], 271) recognize the allusion to the Ps and to Jon 4:9.

[4] See above, p. 13, n. 4.

Spirit is meant, so that the NT meaning is that the Holy Spirit is willing to help the disciples overcome the weakness of human nature.[1]

Mt 26:64	Mk 14:62	Lk 22:69	Zech 12:10 LXX		MT	
ἀπ' ἄρτι	καὶ	ἀπὸ τοῦ νῦν				
ὄψεσθε	ὄψεσθε	δὲ ἔσται	ἐπιβλέψονται		והביטו	
τὸν υἱὸν	τὸν υἱὸν	ὁ υἱὸς				
τοῦ ἀνθρώπου	τοῦ ἀνθρώπου	τοῦ ἀνθρώπου	Ps 110 (109):1			
καθήμενον	ἐκ δεξιῶν	καθήμενος	κάθου		שב	
ἐκ δεξιῶν	καθήμενον	ἐκ δεξιῶν	ἐκ δεξιῶν μου		לימיני	
τῆς δυνάμεως	τῆς δυνάμεως	τῆς δυνάμεως	Dan 7:13			
		τοῦ θεοῦ	Theod	LXX	MT	
καὶ ἐρχόμενον	καὶ ἐρχόμενον		ἐρχόμενος	ἤρχετο	אתה הוה	II
ἐπὶ	μετὰ		μετὰ	ἐπὶ	עם	
τῶν νεφελῶν	τῶν νεφελῶν		τῶν νεφελῶν		ענני	I
τοῦ οὐρανοῦ	τοῦ οὐρανοῦ		τοῦ οὐρανοῦ		שמיא	
	κ. ἐρχ.] *om* D					
	μετά] ἐπί G f1 33 *al*					

Ὄψεσθε is a faint reflection of Zech 12:10,[2] differing from the LXX (ἐπιβλέψ.; MT: והביטו).

In the allusion to Ps 110, Mt and Lk smooth Mk's chiastic, emphatic order, ἐκ δεξιῶν καθήμενον, into conformity with the OT text. Lk adds τοῦ θεοῦ as a genitive of apposition to explain to his Gentile readers τῆς δυνάμεως, a periphrasis for the divine name.[3]

In the phrase from Dan 7:13, Mt again has ἐπί in agreement with the LXX (as in 24:30). Mk's changing from his previous ἐν (13:26) to μετά, in agreement with Theodotion and the MT, shows a certain free interchange of these prepositions, as also, e.g., in Justin, who has both μετά and ἐπάνω.[4]

To explain the combination of these two OT passages, J. W. Doeve suggests that ἡ ἀρχή for נדבת and the reading of עַמְּךָ ("thy people") as עִמְּךָ ("with you") in the LXX of Ps 110:3 corresponds to the שלטן given to the Son of man in Dan 7:14. Ἐν ταῖς λαμπρό-

---

[1] So Cranfield, *Mk*, 434; against K. G. Kuhn, *Evangelische Theologie*, 12 (1952/53), 277f.; cf. E. Schweizer, *TWNT*, VI, 394.

[2] More fully alluded to in Mt 24:30 (and par).

[3] Ἡ δύναμις = הגבורה (Aramaic: גבורתא). See Strack-Billerbeck, I, 1006; Dalman, *Words*, 200-202; J. R. Harris, *ET*, 32 (1920/21), 375.

[4] *Dial.* xxxi (MPG VI, 541); 1 *Apol.* li (MPG VI, 404).

τησιν τῶν ἁγίων (Ps. 110:3 LXX) would also suggest the picture of myriad angels in Dan 7.[1]

Mt 26:67	Mk 14:65	Lk 22:63f.	Is 50:6 LXX
		καὶ οἱ ἄνδρες	δέδωκα . . . τὰς δὲ
		οἱ συνέχοντες	σιαγόνας μου εἰς
		αὐτὸν ἐνέπαιζον	ῥαπίσματα, τὸ δὲ
		αὐτῷ δέροντες	πρόσωπόν μου οὐκ
τότε ἐνέπτυσαν	καὶ ἤρξαντό		ἀπέστρεψα ἀπὸ
	τινες ἐμπτύειν		αἰσχύνης
εἰς τὸ πρόσωπον	αὐτῷ		ἐμπτυσμάτων
αὐτοῦ			
	κ. περικαλύπτειν	καὶ περικαλύψ-	
	αὐτοῦ	αντες	MT
	τὸ πρόσωπον	αὐτὸν	נתתי ··· ולחיי
καὶ ἐκολάφισαν	καὶ κολαφίζειν		למרטים
αὐτόν	αὐτὸν		(למטלים :1QIs^a)
οἱ δὲ			פני לא הסתרתי
ἐρράπισαν		ἐπηρώτων	(הסירותי :1QIs^a)
λέγοντες	καὶ λέγειν αὐτῷ	λέγοντες	מכלמות ורק
προφήτευσον	προφήτευσον	προφήτευσον	
ἡμῖν, χριστέ,	καὶ οἱ ὑπηρέται		
τίς ἐστιν	ῥαπίσμασιν	τίς ἐστιν	
ὁ παίσας σε;	αὐτὸν ἔλαβον	ὁ παίσας σε;	

αὐτῷ] τῷ προσώπῳ αὐτοῦ DΘ565 700 adf syr^{pesh} geo arm
καὶ περικαλ . . . . πρόσωπον] *om* Dafsyr^{sin}

The points of contact between the OT and NT texts are the thoughts of spitting (Mt, Mk= LXX= MT) in the face (Mt, Mk [Western, Caesarean texts [2]]= LXX= MT) and smiting (Mt, Mk= LXX [ῥαπίζω] against the MT [למרטים, "to the pluckers"], but possibly with 1QIs^a [למטלים, "to the smiters"?] [3]). Mt's use of εἰς (τὸ πρόσωπον) instead of a dative after ἐνέπτυσαν may reflect the εἰς in Is 50:6 (although in a different connection). Lk, following as usual in the passion narrative an independent tradition,[4] betrays no reminiscence of Is 50:6.

---

[1] *Jewish Hermeneutics in the Synoptic Gospels and Acts* (Assen, 1954), 152ff.

[2] In syr^{sin} and sah^{codd} τῷ προσώπῳ appears to have been displaced into a position after κολαφίζειν. See Streeter, *op. cit.*, 325ff. If so, we may add their support in favor of the originality of τῷ προσώπῳ after ἐμπτύειν. For a defence of the Western text in Mk, see R. H. Gundry, *Revue de Qumran*, Tome 2, Num. 8 (1960), 563ff.

[3] *Ibid.*, 559-567.

[4] Bundy, *op. cit.*, 480; J. B. Tyson, *NovTest*, 3(1959), 251ff.

Mt 27:35; Mk 15:24	Lk 23:34	Ps 22 (21):19 LXX	MT
διεμερίσαντο	διαμεριζόμενοι	διεμερίσαντο	יחלקו
[Mk: δια-ζονται]	δὲ		
τὰ ἱμάτια	τὰ ἱμάτια	τὰ ἱμάτιά	בגדַי
αὐτοῦ	αὐτοῦ	μου ἑαυτοῖς	להם
βάλλοντες	ἔβαλον	καὶ ἐπὶ τὸν	ועל לבושי
κλῆρον	κλήρους	ἱματισμόν μου	יפילו
[*Mk*: + ἐπ' αὐτά]	κλήρους Θ f1 33*al* lat] κλῆρον *rell*	ἔβαλον κλῆρον	גורל

Mt βάλοντες ℵADΘf1 *pm*; + Jn 19:24 (= LXX) (Θ) f1 (f13) *al*it vg^{cl}ς
Mk βάλοντες Θ*pc*

The aorist διεμερίσαντο in Mt agrees with the LXX and the OT Peshitta against the imperfect of the MT and the present tense of Mk. This could be assimilation of Mk to the LXX by Mt. However, Mk's present tense is dependent on parallelism with σταυροῦσιν in the first clause of his compound sentence. Therefore, Mt may avoid the vivid historical present of Mk and subordinate σταυροῦσιν into a participial form (σταυρώσαντες) purely as a matter of style. Cf. Lk's subordination of διαμερίζονται into a participle and raising of βάλλοντες into a main verb (= LXX). The allusion is Septuagintal in form, even in the plural τὰ ἱμάτια (בגדַי, plural, instead of בגדִי) and in the singular κλῆρον (except Lk, who agrees—probably by accident—with the Targum, עדבין). Mk's ἐπ' αὐτά carries the allusion a phrase farther than Mt and Lk.

Mt 27:39; Mk 15:29	Lk 23:35	Lam 2:15 LXX	MT
οἱ δὲ [Mk: καὶ οἱ]		πάντες οἱ παρα-	כל עברי
παραπορευόμενοι		πορευόμενοι ὁδὸν	דרך
ἐβλασφήμουν		ἐσύρισαν καὶ	שרקו
αὐτὸν		ἐκίνησαν κεφαλὴν	ויניעו
		αὐτῶν	ראשם
		Ps 22 (21):8 LXX	MT
	καὶ εἱστήκει	πάντες οἱ θεω-	כל
	ὁ λαὸς θεωρῶν	ροῦντές με	ראי
	ἐξεμυκτήριζον	ἐξεμυκτήρισάν	ילעגו
		με, . . .	לי ...
κινοῦντες τὰς		ἐκίνησαν	יניעו
κεφαλὰς αὐτῶν		κεφαλήν	ראש
Mk οἱ παραπορ.] *om* syr^{sin}; οἱ παράγοντες D		Cf. Lam 1:12.	

One would have expected a phrase like τινες τῶν παρεστηκότων (Mk 15:35), so that the peculiar οἱ παραπορευόμενοι must indicate an allusion to Lam 2:15.[1] 'Εβλασφήμουν may then be a loose rendering of שרקו ("to hiss" in mockery; the LXX correctly, ἐσύρισαν).[2] The reference to shaking the head was an obvious point of contact between Lam and Ps 22:8.

Lk inserts an allusion to the first part of Ps 22:8 in agreement with the LXX, omitting the allusion by Mt and Mk to the second part. Mt and Mk, omitting the Lucan allusion, agree with the LXX in κινοῦντες, where they could have used σαλεύειν.[3] But their plural form with the possessive pronoun, κεφαλὰς αὐτῶν, agrees with the OT Pesh, ברישיהון. The Targum has the plural possessive suffix but not the plural form of the noun, ברישהון. Perhaps an original plural noun in the Targum has been partially conformed to the MT.

Mt 27:46: ἠλὶ ἠλὶ λεμὰ σαβαχθάνι
  Bℵ ἐλωεὶ (ἐλωὶ ℵ) ἐλωεὶ (ἐλωὶ ℵ) λεμὰ σαβακτάνει (σαβαχθάνει ℵ)
  AW ἠλὶ (ἠλεὶ Θ f1) ἠλὶ (ἠλεὶ Θ f1) λιμὰ (μα W; λαμὰ Θ f1) σαβαχθάνει
  D ἠλεὶ ἠλεὶ λαμὰ ζαφθάνει

Mk 15:34: ἐλωΐ ἐλωΐ λαμὰ σαβαχθάνι
  B ἐλωΐ ἐλωΐ λαμὰ ζαβαφθάνει
  ℵA ἐλωΐ ἐλωΐ λεμὰ (λιμὰ A) σαβακτάνει (σαβακθάνει A)
  DΘ ἠλεὶ ἠλεὶ λαμὰ ζαφθάνει (Θ σαβαχθάνι)
    See Kilpatrick, *Origins*, 104f., for a table of the Latin transliterations, and Zahn, *Introduction to the NT* (Edinburgh, 1909), I, 15f., for the Syriac versions.

Mt 27:46: θεέ μου, θεέ μου, ἱνατί με ἐγκατέλιπες;

Mk 15:34: ὁ θεός μου, ὁ θεός μου, εἰς τί ἐγκατέλιπές με;
  μου 1°] *om* AΘf1 f13 sah
  ὁ θεός μου 2°] *om* B565boh (1 MS) Epiph[semel]
  ἐγκατέλιπες] ὠνείδισας DcikPorph

Ps 22 (21):2 LXX: ὁ θεός, ὁ θεός μου, πρόσχες μοι, ἵνα τί ἐγκατέλιπές με;
  πρόσχες μοι] *sub obelo* in Hexapla, but present in all major MSS.[4]
MT: אלי אלי למה עזבתני

A. Guillaume has shown from 1QIs[a] that *-iya*, the ancient Semitic suffix of the first person, was still occasionally used in the NT period. Thus, Jesus must have said *Eliya* ("my God"), which was mistaken for Elijah; and the Greek text of the NT has brought

---

[1] V. Taylor, *op. cit.*, 591; Lohmeyer-Schmauch, *op. cit.*, 391, n. 2.

[2] It might be thought the omission of οἱ παραπορ. in syr[sin] is original, or that an original παράγοντες (D) has been assimilated to Mt. Cf. Merx, *op. cit.*, II, ii, p. 167. However, Mk's special liking for παραπορεύεσθαι (2:23; 9:30; 11:20; 15:29) and the fact that the word is *hapax* in Mt and nowhere else in the NT speak in favor of the best-attested reading.

[3] Cf. Ps 109 (108):25 LXX: ἐσάλευσαν κεφαλὰς αὐτῶν.

[4] See Stendahl, 86.

the transliterations into line with the prevalent later pronunciation of Hebrew.[1]

Since Mk's Aramaic form ἐλωΐ cannot provide a basis for the confusion with Elijah, most commentators think Mt's ἠλί (אלי) is the original form and that Mk conformed to the Aramaic in accord with the Aramaic element throughout his gospel.[2] M. Rehm thinks that the remainder of the cry was in Aramaic; and so the crowd, more used to the Aramaic *elahi*, thought *eli* was an abbreviated form of Elijah or Elijjahu.[3] J. Gnilka thinks the whole was spoken in Hebrew and that the misunderstanding arose from the bystanders' ignorance of Hebrew.[4] But both explanations stumble against the facts that *eli* must have been familiar to Aramaic-speaking Jews (the Targum has אלי!) [5] and that recent studies and discoveries in the Dead Sea area show that Hebrew was understood and used by the Jews of that time.[6] At least the chief priests would have understood אלי.[7]

It is argued that the ὀνειδισμός-motif in the NT [8] favors the

---

[1] A. Guillaume, *PEQ* (1951), 78ff.

[2] So Zahn, *Mt*, 705, n. 86; P. Dausch, *Die drei älteren Evangelien* (Bonn, 1918), 343; E. Klostermann, *Mk*² (Tübingen, 1926), 185; Hauck, *Mk*, 189; Dalman, *Words*, 54; idem, *Jesus-Jeshua*, 205; J. Jeremias, *TWNT*, II, 937, n. 62; V. Taylor, *op. cit.*, 593.

[3] *BZ*, 2 (1958), 275-278.

[4] *BZ*, 3 (1959), 296.

[5] See Dalman, *Words*, 53.

[6] See below, pp. 174ff.

[7] A. B. Bruce would cut the Gordian knot by supposing the misunderstanding was only affected (*Expositor's Greek Testament* [Grand Rapids, 1951], I, 332). Other conjectures are ingenious, but unconvincing: (1) Jesus was thought to have said אֵלִיָּא תָּא ("Elia, come!"), but he really said אֵלִי אַתָּה ("My God you [are]"; cf. Ps 22:11), Mk originally having ἠλὶ ἀθά, ὅ ἐστιν μεθερμηνευόμενον· θεός μου εἶ συ. So H. Sahlin, *Biblica*, 33 (1952), 53-66; T. Boman, *Studia Theologica*, 17(1963), 103-119. (2) The original cry was עַל יָדָךְ לְעַמִּי אֲנָא אַשְׁבּוֹק אֲדֹנָי, Ἐλήδεκ λᾶμα [ἀνὰ] ἀσβῶκ ἀδοναί = "Into thy hands I commend my people, O my Lord." So F. W. Buckler, *American Journal of Semitic Languages and Literatures*, 55 (1938), 378-391. (3) Mt's שבקתני was originally שכחתני of Ps 42:10, a scribe having confused כ with ב and the Greek rendering having been conformed to Ps 22:2. So D. Sidersky, *Journal Asiatique*, 3 (1914), 232f. (4) The primitive reading in Mt was ζαβαχθάνι, a transliteration of זְבַחְתָּנִי. So D. Sidersky, *RHR*, 103 (1931), 154. Sidersky's conjectures are motivated by a desire to explain the transliteration by χ (usually for כ) instead of by κ (usually for ק) (see Swete, *An Introduction to the OT in Greek*, 67). But the irregular χ for ק is due to the immediately following θ. See Dalman, *Words*, 54, n. 2.

[8] Mt 5:11; Lk 6:22; I Pet 4:14; Acts 5:41; Ro 15:3; and esp. Heb 11:26; 13:13.

originality of the reading in Dcik in Mk and that a change from ἐγκατέλιπες against the double authority of the LXX and the gospels is unlikely, whereas that same double authority would present an overpowering temptation to harmonize with Mt and the LXX.[1] However, the argument can be turned around, so that the ὀνειδισμός-motif becomes the source of textual corruption in Cod. D.[2] Apparently ζαφθάνει (D), of which ζαβαφθάνει (B) is a corrupted form, rests on an original ἀζαφθάνει,[3] the initial α having fallen out after λαμά. Since both λαμά and ἀζαφθάνει transliterate the Hebrew text of Ps 22:2, the reading rests on a scribal attempt to conform to the Hebrew.[4] But the mutilated ζαφθάνει was associated with זעף[5] or זוף[6] and rendered by ὠνείδισας. It is possible that ὠνείδισας represents a desire to soften the offence of Jesus' desolation.[7] One may question, however, that the word

---

[1] A. Harnack, *Studien zur Geschichte des NT u. der alten Kirchen*. I. *Zur neutestamentlichen Textkritik* (Berlin, 1931), 98-103; C. H. Turner, *JTS*, 11 (1910), 19; cf. T. W. Manson, *BJRL*, 34 (1951/52), 318; F. C. Burkitt, *JTS*, 1 (1900), 278f.

[2] So C. S. C. Williams, *Alterations to the Text of the Synoptic Gospels and Acts* (Oxford, 1951), 40, who also suggests influence from Ps 78:12 or 88:51f. LXX. A closer source is Ps 22 (21):6 LXX.

[3] E. Nestle supposed (ἀ)ζαφθάνει represents the verb עצב, noting that in several passages עצב is rendered by ὀδυνᾶν (*ET*, 9 [1897/98], 521). Although transliteration of צ by ζ is possible, the required supposition that ὠνείδισας is a clerical error for ὠδύνησας is weak.

[4] J. H. Ropes notes that the Western text shows influence from the Hebrew OT (*The Beginnings of Christianity* [London, 1926], Part I, Vol. III, p. ccxlii).

[5] So Chase, *op. cit.*, 107. Nestle criticizes that זעף is construed with ב, not with the accusative. But Chase notes that זעף is followed by על in Prov 19:3 and by עם in II Chron 26:19, and thinks the abnormal construction here may be due to the intention that זעפתני be a rough transliteration of עזבתני, which has no corresponding root in Syriac. E. König criticizes that זעף means "to be violent (or) angry," but not "to rebuke (or) reproach" (ὠνειδ.) (*ET*, 11 [1899/1900], 237f.).

[6] *Ibid.* König notes זוף occurs in the Targum to Is 17:13; 54:9; Zech 3:2 in the sense "to rebuke."

[7] *Ibid.*; Stendahl, 85f. Stendahl likens the reading ἡ δύναμις μου in the Gospel of Peter 5:19, which rests on a theological adaptation of אלי as אילי, as did Aquila (ἰσχυρέ μου) (so W. Hasenzahl, *Die Gottverlassenheit des Christus* [Gütersloh, 1938], 77-94), or as חילי. But the latter may rest upon a simple confusion in the pronunciation of the gutterals א and ח (see L. Vaganay, *L'évangile de Pierre* [Paris, 1930], 255f.; J. Kennedy, *op. cit.*, 12; F. Zimmerman, *JBL*, 66 [1947], 465f.). Or ἡ δύναμις μου may be a mere avoidance of the divine name, as in Mt 26:64 and parallels (so an editorial note at the end of Zimmerman's article); however, Boman observes that the personal pronoun "my" militates against this view (*op. cit.*, 105f.). It is not necessary

really does lessen the offence. We conclude, then, that Cod. D is corrupt at this point and that the original reading in Mk is an Aramaized form of the original cry.

In the Greek translation Mt and Mk agree in omitting the LXX's πρόσχες μοι.[1] That the vocative θεέ (Mt)[2] diverges from Mk and the LXX makes it probable that Mt's ἱνατί is a stylistic correction of Mk's εἰς τί,[3] rather than a conforming to the LXX. Thus, both the Matthaean and the Marcan renderings of the Aramaic disagree with the LXX.

Mt 27:48: λαβὼν σπόγγον πλήσας τε ὄξους καὶ περιθεὶς καλάμῳ ἐπότιζεν αὐτόν
Mk 15:36: γεμίσας σπόγγον ὄξους περιθεὶς καλάμῳ ἐπότιζεν αὐτόν
Ps 69 (68):22 LXX: καὶ εἰς τὴν δίψαν μου ἐπότισάν με ὄξος
MT: ולצמאי ישקוני חמץ

In the use of ὄξος and ποτίζειν Mt and Mk agree with the LXX, but the Hebrew could hardly be translated otherwise.

Formal Quotations in common with Luke

The only formal quotations common to Mt and Lk and absent in Mk occur in the Temptation narrative. Two are Septuagintal, but whether or not the remaining two are so depends largely on the evaluation of variant readings in the NT and OT texts. The probability is that these latter two display independence from the LXX.

Mt 4:4; Dt 8:3 LXX: οὐκ ἐπ' ἄρτῳ μόνῳ ζήσεται ὁ ἄνθρωπος, ἀλλ' ἐπὶ παντὶ ῥήματι ἐκπορευομένῳ διὰ στόματος θεοῦ
Mt ἐπί] ἐν CD*al*
ἐκπορ. . . . στόματος] *om* Dabdg[1] Cl Tert Aug Ambrose[4] Epiph Arnobius Jr Firmicus Maternus Hil
LXX ὁ] *om* Luc (75)
ἐκπορ.] *pr* τῷ, exc. AF*Luc (75) Theod Ev Or-gr Cyr Thdt
θεοῦ] + ζήσεται ὁ (*om* Luc [75]) ἄνθρωπος

---

to see theological motivation either in Cod. D or in the Gospel of Peter. Notice should here be taken of L. R. Fisher's (and others') contention that the evangelists quoted the first line of Ps 22 as the ps-title and that therefore Jesus quoted the *whole* ps, including the confident last section (*Interpretation*, 18 [1964], 20-27).

[1] Πρόσχες μοι is probably a duplet, taking the second אלי as meaning "to me." See Toy, *op. cit.*, 73.

[2] An Attic form (Robertson, *Grammar*, 463; Bl-D § 44:2) and a late intruder into the text of the LXX (P. Katz, *Philo's Bible* [Cambridge, 1950], 152f.).

[3] See Black, *op. cit.*, 88.

[4] See R. W. Muncey, *The NT Text of Saint Ambrose* (Cambridge, 1959), pp. xxxviii, 4.

Lk 4:4 = Mt οὐκ . . . ἄνθρωπος BℵW*pc*
+ ἀλλ' ἐν (ἐπὶ Θ*pm* ς) παντὶ ῥήματι θεοῦ ADΘf1 f13*pl*lat ς
+ ἀλλ' ἐπὶ παντὶ ῥήματι ἐκπορευομένῳ διὰ στόματος θεοῦ *al* cop eth arm Thphyl
Dt 8:3 MT: לא על הלחם לבדו יחיה האדם כי על כל מוצא פי יהוה יחיה האדם

The usually adopted text in Mt is Septuagintal, most slavishly so in the use of ἐκπορευομένῳ with διά. ʽΡήματι, for which the Hebrew has no equivalent, is usually considered the clearest sign of dependence on the LXX. But the Targums (Old Palestinian, Jonathan, Onkelos) have מימרא ("word"), and any translation would almost have to expand the condensed form of the Hebrew expression כל מוצא פי. Θεός for יהוה is frequent in the LXX.

However, G. D. Kilpatrick has argued strongly in favor of the text represented in Mt by Cod. D.[1] As the shorter reading—and especially in view of the usually greater fulness of the Western text—it deserves preference. Also, the practice in the Western text of filling out according to the LXX increases the worth of the non-Septuagintal reading here. Aur., f, ff [1], l, vg have the long reading, "in omni uerbo quod procedit de ore dei." In h is an independent version of the long reading, "in omni uerbo procedenti ex ore dei." The shorter text has been corrected to the longer in c, but the correction has gone wrong: "in omni uerbo dei quod procedit de ore." Two Vulgate MSS, D and J, combine the longer and the shorter texts: "in omni uerbo dei quod procedit de ore dei." It appears, then, that the original text in Mt was ἐπὶ παντὶ ῥήματι, and this was expanded from the LXX. The unexpanded form was translated into Latin and later underwent two independent corrections from the Greek. The original text of Lk, ending at ἄνθρωπος, has been assimilated to the shorter text of Mt *even in MSS which do not have the shorter text in Mt.* This fact constitutes weighty evidence for the genuineness of the shorter text in Mt. Other MSS in Lk assimilate to the full Septuagintal form, showing that there was a tendency to assimilate this quotation to the LXX.

If then the text represented by Cod. D be accepted, the quotation is non-Septuagintal in form both in the omission of ἐκπορ. . . . στόματος and in ἐν for ἐπί.

Mt 4:6; Lk 4:10, 11; Ps 91 (90):11, 12 LXX: ὅτι τοῖς ἀγγέλοις αὐτοῦ ἐντελεῖται περὶ σοῦ τοῦ διαφυλάξαι σε ἐν πάσαις ταῖς ὁδοῖς σου· ἐπὶ χειρῶν ἀροῦσίν σε, μήποτε προσκόψῃς πρὸς λίθον τὸν πόδα σου

[1] *JTS*, 45 (1944), 176. J. Wellhausen also accepts the shorter reading (*Mt* [Berlin, 1904], 8f.).

Mt] *om* τοῦ διαφυλ . . . . ὁδοῖς σου; + καί after the omission.
Lk] *om* ἐν πάσαις ταῖς ὁδοῖς σου; + καὶ ὅτι
LXX πάσαις A] πᾶσιν R; *om* B
Ps 91:11, 12 MT: כי מלאכיו יצוה לך לשמרך בכל דרכיך: על כפים ישאונך פן תגף באבן רגלך

This quotation is Septuagintal; the LXX renders correctly. Ὅτι is probably part of the quotation in Mt and Lk, since it is not used to introduce the quotations in Mt 4:4, 7, 10.

Mt 4:7; Lk 4:12; Dt 6:16 LXX: οὐκ ἐκπειράσεις κύριον τὸν θεόν σου
Mt οὐκ ἐκπειράσεις] οὐ πειράσεις D
Dt 6:16 MT: לא תנסו את יהוה אלהיכם

Bacon argues that the reading of Cod. D may be a free rendering of the Hebrew.[1] But it probably represents a stylistic preference for the simplex form of the verb [2] or a harmonization with the simplex form used in Mt 4:1, 3.

The quotation is Septuagintal in form. The agreement with the singular verb of the LXX against the plural of the MT should not be stressed, for two reasons: (1) the singular in the NT depends on the circumstance that Jesus is applying the scripture to his own individual situation; (2) the LXX-*Vorlage* may have had the singular form,[3] since in Dt 6:2-16 there is a series of fifty-seven second personal pronouns in the singular, broken only by a first person plural in the *shema'* and a second person plural in verse 14.[4] Other than the difference in number, the LXX is faithful to the MT.

Mt 4:10; Lk 4:8: κύριον τὸν θεόν σου προσκυνήσεις καὶ αὐτῷ μόνῳ λατρεύσεις
Lk προσκυνήσεις] *pr* κύριον Θ *al* ς
Dt 6:13 LXX: κύριον τὸν θεόν σου φοβηθήσῃ καὶ αὐτῷ λατρεύσεις
φοβ.] προσκυνήσεις A Pap. 963 o Ev Clem Ath Cyr (*fere semper*) Cyp
αὐτῷ] + μόνῳ A Pap. 963 F[a mg] N Luc (75) arm-ed boh sah eth it Ev Clem Or-gr Ath CyrJulap-Cyr Thdt Cyp Spec
MT: את יהוה אלהיך תירא ואתו תעבד

Προσκυνήσεις emphasizes the antithesis with the Satanic temptation, ἐὰν πεσὼν προσκυνήσῃς μοι,[5] and therefore does not seem to be drawn from LXX[A].[6] Rather, LXX[A] has been assimilated to the

[1] *Studies in Mt*, 472.
[2] Cf. J. H. Moulton, *The Expositor*, 7, 7th Series (1909), 411f.
[3] Cf. the agreements in number between 1QIs[a] and the LXX in verb-forms. J. Ziegler, *JBL*, 78 (1959), 46.
[4] Cf. Torrey, *op. cit.*, 56.
[5] Schlatter thinks προσκυν. implies the Son worships God, but does not fear (φοβ.) him (*op. cit.*, 110).
[6] So Anger, I, 14; Turpie, *op. cit.*, 151; Hänel, *op. cit.*, 117f.; A. Clemen, *Der Gebrauch des A. T. in den neutest. Schriften* (Gütersloh, 1895), 22; McNeile, *Mt*, 42; Lagrange, *Mt*, 62.

NT.[1] S. E. Johnson argues that the support of Pap. 963 absolves LXX^A from this charge,[2] but he himself has noted that Pap. 963 usually goes with Cod. A against Cod. B.[3] Pap. 963 merely shows that the assimilation had taken place early in the second century.[4] Προσκυνεῖν nowhere else in the LXX renders ירא. And that parallel influence is at work in Cod. A is demonstrated by its reading προσκυνήσεις for φοβηθήσῃ and by its adding μόνῳ after αὐτῷ in the parallel passage Dt 10:20, against the MT and the rest of the Septuagintal text-tradition.[5]

The much weaker support that Cod. A receives in reading προσκυνήσεις than in μόνῳ suggests assimilation to the NT was progressive. Therefore, we must regard this quotation as independent from the LXX, προσκυνήσεις being a targumic adaptation to the circumstances in the narrative and μόνῳ possibly drawn from the parallel statement in I Sam 7:3 MT (ועבדהו לבדו).[6] Since the LXX uses δουλεύσατε in I Sam 7:3, parallel influence would have to be based on the Hebrew text.

Allusive Quotations in common with Luke

In the allusive quotations common to Mt and Lk (but absent from Mk) we shall find the same mixed text-form—Septuagintal, Hebrew, Targumic, etc.—that was prominent in the allusive quotations common to Mt and Mk. It is not always possible to tell whether Lk's phraseology when more distant from the OT than Mt's is due to his not recognizing the OT language or to a preference for his own literary style.

Mt 5:3: μακάριοι οἱ πτωχοὶ τῷ πνεύματι
Lk 6:20: μακάριοι οἱ πτωχοί
Is 61:1 LXX: εὐαγγελίσασθαι πτωχοῖς
MT: לבשר ענוים
Is 66:2 LXX: ἐπὶ τὸν ταπεινὸν καὶ ἡσύχιον
MT: אל עני ונכה רוח
1QM xiv. 7: עניי רוח
xiv. 10: נכאי רוח

---

[1] So even Staerk, *ZWT*, 40 (1897), 256f., who minimizes the harmonistic element in LXX^A.

[2] *Op. cit.*, 144.

[3] *Ibid.*, 150f.

[4] On the date of Pap. 963, see F. G. Kenyon, *Recent Developments in the Textual Criticism of the Greek Bible* (London, 1933), 108.

[5] Pap. 963 is not extant in Dt 10:20.

[6] Cf. Alexander, *op. cit.*, 86. Schlatter also points to several rabbinical

The use of πτωχός agrees with the LXX. ענוים properly means "the meek," but between עני ("poor") and ענו there exists no strict line of demarcation, the Massoretes having even pointed both words with the vowels of the other.[1] It may be that Mt adds τῷ πνεύματι to bring out the thought of meekness. If so, he works from the Hebrew text.

It has recently been suggested that "poor in spirit" shows contact with Qumran literature, particularly עניי רוח in the War Scroll xiv. 7 (cf. 1QpHab xii. 3, 6, 10). K. Schubert interprets the expression to mean "the voluntarily poor,"[2] citing Ex 35:21; Ps 51:12 as passages where רוח = "will." But in neither passage is "spirit" to be equated with "will." Rather, the "spirit" is "willing" or "makes willing," the thought of "willing" being expressed by another word, נדב. M. Burrows adds that "poor of will" could only signify weakness of will.[3] It is better to take the addition of רוח-τῷ πνεύματι as not altering the meaning, but only making patent the religious sense already latent in the word.[4] What the occurrence of עניי רוח in 1QM xiv. 7 does show is that the Matthaean form of the beatitude is not necessarily secondary, or if secondary to Lk is not an illegitimate spiritualizing interpretation.

C. Rabin has given the discussion a new turn by bringing into

---

passages where "only" occurs with reference to serving and worshipping God (*loc. cit.*).

[1] Mitchell, *op. cit.*, 276. Cf. G. A. F. Knight, *A Christian Theology of the OT* (London, 1959), 261.

[2] *Op. cit.*, 87, 137ff.; *idem*, in *The Scrolls and the NT*, 122. Cf. Lohmeyer-Schmauch, *op. cit.*, 82, n. 1, where Mt's expression is taken in the sense of willingness to endure poverty as Jesus' disciples.

[3] *Op. cit.*, 95f.

[4] See Tabachovitz, *op. cit.*, 65f. Ταπεινὸς τῷ πνεύματι in Ps 33:19 is equivalent to ταπεινός in, e.g., Ps 17:28. The dative τῇ καρδίᾳ is often added to adjectives like ταπεινός, πραΰς, and ὅσιος without affecting the sense. Cf. Mt 11:29; Dt 20:8; II Chron 13:7; Ex 35:10; Prov 10:8; Job 37:24; Ps 31:11; 36:14; 63:11; 72:1; 93:15; 96:11; 23:4; Mt 5:8. Also, Bammel, *TWNT*, VI, 903ff. The connotation of πτωχός, a beggar conscious of his need, as opposed to πένης, a poor man who works for a modest living, is suited to the religious idea. See V. Macchioro, *Journal of Religion*, 12 (1932), 40-49. Although the Lucan form has been viewed as sociologically orientated (J. Rezevskis, *Studia Theologica*, 1 [1935], 157-169, sees Ebionite influence; less radically, W. M. Macgregor, *ET*, 39 [1927/28], 294; C. H. Dodd, in *Mélanges bibliques rédigés en l'honneur de André Robert* [Paris, n.d.], 407f.), probably in Lk as well as in Mt primary emphasis lies on the ethical side. For a balanced discussion, see E. Percy, *Die Botschaft Jesu* (Lund, 1953), 40-108. E. Best takes "poor in spirit" as "faint-hearted" (*NTS*, 7 [1961], 255-258).

focus Is 66:2, עני ונכה רוח, and relating the two readings עניי רוח (1QM xiv. 7) and נכאי רוח (1 QM xi. 10). In addition D. Flusser parallels a passage from 1QH xviii. 14, 15, where the phrases לבשר ענוים, נכאי רוח, and ואבלים occur.[1] Rabin suggests the MT may present a conflate reading and that Mt 5:3 derives from a reading עני רוח in Is 66:2.[2] Because of the allusive quotation of Is 61:2 in the immediately following beatitude in Mt and because we know Is 61:1,2 constituted a leading OT text in Jesus' preaching (see Mt 11:5; Lk 4:18, 19; 7:22; Acts 10:38), Is 66:2 is probably not the primary reference in the first beatitude. But it does seem very possible that we have in the Matthaean τῷ πνεύματι parallel influence from Is 66:2—based on the Hebrew text, for the LXX does not even render רוח.

Mt 5:11	Lk 6:22	Is 51:7 LXX	MT
μακάριοί	μακάριοί	μὴ φοβεῖσθε	אל תיראו
ἐστε ὅταν	ἐστε ὅταν		
	μισήσωσιν ὑμᾶς		
	οἱ ἄνθρωποι		
	καὶ ὅταν		
	ἀφορίσωσιν ὑμᾶς		
ὀνειδίσωσιν ὑμᾶς	καὶ ὀνειδίσωσιν	ὀνειδισμὸν	חרפת
καὶ διώξωσιν		ἀνθρώπων	אנוש
καὶ εἴπωσιν	καὶ ἐκβάλωσιν	καὶ τῷ	ומגדפתם
πᾶν πονηρὸν	τὸ ὄνομα ὑμῶν	φαυλισμῷ αὐτῶν	
καθ' ὑμῶν	ὡς πονηρόν	μὴ ἡττᾶσθε	אל תחתו
ψευδόμενοι			

διώξωσιν] -ουσιν
ℵDWΘ
ψευδ.] *om* D it syr^{sin} Tert

The preceding beatitude pronounces blessing on οἱ δεδιωγμένοι ἕνεκεν δικαιοσύνης (Mt 5:10). The first clause of Is 51:7 addresses ידעי צדק ("you who know righteousness"), going on to encourage those who are persecuted for righteousness' sake. (The parallel between OT and NT depends on the Hebrew text, for the LXX renders Is 51:7a, οἱ εἰδότες κρίσιν.) The persecuted righteous are also addressed in this verse as "the people in whose heart is my law," a thought which forms the leading theme in the next section of the Sermon on the Mount, God's law in the heart as opposed to superficial righteousness (note esp. Mt 5:20; 28). It would therefore seem that Is 51:7 constitutes a keystone which binds together the

[1] *Israel Exploration Journal*, 10 (1960), 2-7.
[2] *JTS*, 6 (1955), 178.

beatitudes and the subsequent didactic portion of the sermon.

In the NT the form of the statement as a beatitude renders comparisons possible only in the terminology. Here—not as usual—Lk stands nearer to the OT text in οἱ ἄνθρωποι, which answers to אנוש, and possibly in ἀφορίσωσιν, which is strikingly close to the root meaning of גדף, "to cut off" and thence, "to cut off with opprobrious words." [1] Mt's periphrastic εἴπωσιν πᾶν πονηρὸν καθ' ὑμῶν ψευδόμενοι, however, conveys the meaning of the Hebrew exactly. And if ψευδόμενοι and διώξωσιν be omitted from the text of Mt, as J. H. Moulton suggests they should,[2] the resultant brevity increases resemblance to Is 51:7. Except in ὀνειδίζειν, a self-evident rendering for חרף, Mt and Lk betray no reminiscence of the LXX.

Mt 5:12: ὁ μισθὸς ὑμῶν πολὺς ἐν τοῖς οὐρανοῖς
Lk 6:23: ὁ μισθὸς ὑμῶν πολὺς ἐν τῷ οὐρανῷ
Gen 15:1 LXX: ὁ μισθός σου πολὺς ἔσται σφόδρα
MT: אנכי ··· שכרך הרבה מאד

Correspondence with the LXX is exact in ὁ μισθός and πολύς. The plural possessive ὑμῶν in Mt and Lk is necessitated by Jesus' address to his audience. The omission of the verb *to be* by Mt and Lk against the LXX conforms to the Hebrew. Ἐν τοῖς οὐρανοῖς (Lk avoids the Semitic plural) is a circumlocution for the divine name, suggested by construing the Hebrew, "I (am) . . . your exceedingly great reward," rather than as the LXX, "Your reward shall be exceedingly great." According to the NT, then, the great reward in heaven is God himself. The Targums (Old Palestinian, Jonathan, Jerusalem) present a haggadic expansion in which Abraham soliloquizes on the danger that he has already received his reward in this world (בעלמא הדין) and will have none in the coming world, to which Yahweh answers that his *Memra* is Abraham's great reward. It may well be that Jesus is adapting a piece of haggadic tradition.

Mt 5:39	Is 50:6 LXX	MT	Lk 6:29
ἀλλ' ὅστις	δέδωκα . . .	נתתי ···	
σε ῥαπίζει	τὰς σιαγόνας μου	לחיי	τῷ τύπτοντί σε
εἰς τὴν δεξιὰν	εἰς ῥαπίσματα	למרטים	ἐπὶ τὴν σιαγόνα
σιαγόνα σου	. . . οὐκ ἀπ-	פני לא	
στρέψον αὐτῷ	έστρεψα ἀπὸ	הסתרתי	πάρεχε καὶ
καὶ τὴν ἄλλην	αἰσχύνης	מכלמות ···	τὴν ἄλλην
		הסתרתי]	
		הסירותי 1QIs[a]	

[1] Otherwise, ἐκβάλωσιν . . . ὡς πονηρόν may be considered the Lucan clause parallel to מגדפתם.

[2] *The Expositor*, 2, 7th Series (1906), 107f.

W. Manson seems to be the first to have noticed this allusive quotation.[1] The further allusion to Is 50:6 in Mt 26:67 and parallels fortifies the case for an allusion here. We may also suppose that Jesus patterned his own conduct during his trial after this verse. The use of ῥαπίζειν, σιαγών, and στρέφειν by Mt are the points of contact with Is 50:6. In ῥαπίζειν Mt goes with the LXX against the MT, but possibly with 1QIs^a^ (למטלים).[2] Στρέφειν also agrees with the LXX and 1QIs^a^ (הסירותי, from סור, "to turn aside") against the MT. Lk has drifted away from the OT phraseology.

		Lev 19:2		Dt 18:13	
Mt 5:48	Lk 6:36	MT	LXX	MT	LXX
ἔσεσθε οὖν	γίνεσθε	קדשים	ἅγιοι	תמים	τέλειος
ὑμεῖς					
τέλειοι	οἰκτίρμονες	תהיו	ἔσεσθε	תהיה	ἔσῃ
ὡς	καθὼς	כי	ὅτι	עם	ἐναντίον
ὁ πατὴρ	ὁ πατὴρ	קדוש	ἐγὼ	יהוה	κυρίου
ὑμῶν ὁ	ὑμῶν	אני יהוה	ἅγιος	אלהיך	τοῦ θεοῦ
οὐράνιος		אלהיכם	κύριος		σου
τέλειός	οἰκτίρμων		ὁ θεὸς ὑμῶν		
ἐστιν	ἐστίν				

The form of the statement in Mt is patterned after Lev 19:2 in the future tense and plural form of the verb. The reference to Lev 19:2 finds confirmation in other quotations from Lev 19 in the preceding Matthaean context (5:33—Lev 19:12; 5:43—Lev 19:18; cf. also 5:38—Lev 24:20). But influx from Dt 18:13 is seen in τέλειοι (= תמים MT, OT Pesh; שלמין—Old Pal Targ, Targ Jon, Sam Targ, Targ Onk).[3] This influx is more easily understood in the light of the prominent תמים-motif in Qumran literature, קדש being a kind of subdivision under the more general concept.[4]

---

[1] *Op. cit.*, 31f. Cf. A. W. Argyle, *ET*, 67 (1955/56), 92f., 383; H. M. Draper, *ET*, 67 (1955/56), 317; R. M. Wilson, *ET*, 68 (1956/57), 121f. It may also be, as Manson believes, that ἀντιστῆναι in Mt 5:39a and κριθῆναι in Mt 5:40 reflect ἀντιστήτω and κρινόμενος in Is 50:8; but one cannot be certain, since Mt 5:39a and Is 50:8 are not parallel in thought.

[2] See above, p. 61.

[3] D. Daube decisively refuted C. C. Torrey's reconstruction of the Aramaic as גמרין in the sense of "all-including" (Torrey, *Our Translated Gospels* [London, n.d.], 93f.; *idem, The Four Gospels* [London, 1934], 291). גמר means "to complete," but not "to include" (Daube, *BJRL*, 29 [1945], 31ff.). Similarly, E. Fuchs' existential interpretation, "Be self-assured as your heavenly Father is self-assured," fails to comprehend the OT background of this verse (in *Neutestamentliche Studien für Rudolf Bultmann* [Berlin, 1954], 130-136).

[4] See W. D. Davies, *HTR*, 46 (1953), 115; P. J. Du Plessis, *ΤΕΛΕΙΟΣ*:

M. Black has pointed to the similarity between Targum Jonathan to Lev 22:28, "As our Father is merciful (*raḥman*) in heaven, so be ye merciful on earth," and Lk's οἰκτίρμονες.[1] The saying became well-known in the Palestinian Talmud,[2] so that the possibility of contact is increased. Targum Jerusalem I to the preceding verse in Lev (22:27) mentions "the virtue of the perfect man (*sh^elima*; cf. the Targum to Dt 18:13)." It would then seem that the double form of the injunction in Mt and Lk, the comparative words (ὡς and καθώς), and the designation ὁ πατὴρ (Mt, Lk) . . . ὁ οὐράνιος (Mt) derive from Targumic tradition.

Mt 6:11: τὸν ἄρτον ἡμῶν τὸν ἐπιούσιον δὸς ἡμῖν σήμερον
Lk 11:3: τὸν ἄρτον ἡμῶν τὸν ἐπιούσιον δίδου ἡμῖν τὸ καθ' ἡμέραν
Prov 30:8 LXX: σύνταξον δέ μοι (πάντα A) τὰ δέοντα καὶ τὰ αὐτάρκη
MT: הטריפני לחם חקי
Targ: זוניני לחמא מסתי

The etymology of ἐπιούσιος is not of direct concern.[3] The word appears in a papyrus account-book in the Fayum and edited by Sayce.[4] After A. Debrunner had noticed the word in the account-book,[5] F. Stiebitz related it to the Latin word *diaria*, which means the daily rations issued to slaves, soldiers, workmen, etc.[6] However, the matter still hangs in the air, because the papyrus has been lost, and B. M. Metzger has cast doubt on the reading by pointing to Sayce's shortcomings as a decipherer.[7]

The Idea of Perfection in the NT (Kampen, 1959), 104-115; F. Nötscher, *Revue de Qumran*, Tome 2, Num. 6 (1960), 163ff. Cf. H. J. Schoeps, *Aus frühchristlicher Zeit* (Tübingen, 1950), 290, and D. Daube, *BJRL*, 29 (1945), 31ff., who show that the τέλειος-תמים concept is not foreign to Judaism, against those who regard the Matthaean form as Hellenized and secondary to Lk (Weiss-Bousset, *op. cit.*, I, 272; Bundy, *op. cit.*, 194).

[1] *Op. cit.*, 138f.

[2] *Berach.* v. 3, f. 9c, l. 25; *Megilla* iv. 9, f. 75c, l. 14.

[3] Origen said the evangelists coined the word (*De Oratione* xxvii [MPG XI, 505ff.]). For the classic defence of derivation from ἐπί + οὐσία or the participle of εἶναι, see H. Cremer, *Biblico-Theological Lexicon of NT Greek*[3] (Edinburgh, 1883), 239ff. For derivation from ἐπιέναι or ἡ ἐπιοῦσα, see J. B. Lightfoot, *On a Fresh Revision of the English NT*[3] (London, 1891), 217-260; F. H. Chase, *Texts and Studies* (Cambridge, 1891), I, 45-53.

[4] F. Petrie, *Hawara, Biahmu, and Arsinoe* (London, 1889), 34, l. 20; also in Fr. Preisigke, *Sammelbuch griechischer Urkunden aus Aegypten* (Strassburg, 1915), I, 522, Nr. 5224.

[5] *TLZ*, 50 (1925), 119. A. Deissmann had already conjectured ἐπιούσιος belonged to the κοινή speech (*Light from the Ancient East* [London, 1927], 78).

[6] *Philologische Wochenschrift*, 47 (1927), 889-892.

[7] *ET*, 69 (1957/58), 52-54.

Even if the reading of the papyrus by Sayce be accepted, it is still not settled whether the word means "for the coming day," "necessary," "continual," "daily," etc. All explanations labor under the circumstance that other Greek words, e.g., αὔριον and αὐτάρκης, might have been chosen. Ever since A. Schweitzer wrote, it has been fashionable to take the meaning "of tomorrow" and to attach an eschatological significance, relating it to the future eschatological feast.[1] This is excluded, however, by the sequence of thought in the Lord's prayer, the coming of the kingdom having previously been mentioned.[2]

It is best to take the word—whatever its etymology—as denoting that which is required for daily sustenance. For this thought there are many rabbinical parallels, as well as the background of the manna in the wilderness.[3] And specifically, Prov 30:8 comes into view,[4] especially the Targumic version, "bread of my requirement (or) need" [5] (MT: "bread of my portion," for which the LXX gives a doublet-rendering, "the things needful and sufficient"). The use of δίδωμι in the NT may go back to נתן in the second, preceding member of the tristich.

Mt 7:23	Lk 13:27	Ps 6:9 MT	LXX
ἀποχωρεῖτε	ἀπόστητε	סורו	ἀπόστητε
ἀπ' ἐμοῦ	ἀπ' ἐμοῦ	ממני	ἀπ' ἐμοῦ
	πάντες	כל	πάντες
οἱ ἐργαζόμενοι	ἐργάται	פעלי	οἱ ἐργαζόμενοι
τὴν ἀνομίαν	ἀδικίας	און	τὴν ἀνομίαν

Mt diverges from the LXX in ἀποχωρεῖτε and the dropping of πάντες. Lk diverges from the LXX in ἐργάται in place of the literal participial rendering of the LXX and Mt and in ἀδικίας.[6] The latter

---

[1] A. Schweitzer, *The Mysticism of Paul the Apostle* (London, 1931), 239f., and recently J. Jeremias, *ET*, 71 (1960), 145.

[2] See W. G. Kümmel, *Promise and Fulfilment* (London, 1957), 52.

[3] Edersheim, *Life and Times*, II, 196; Strack-Billerbeck, *op. cit.*, I, 420f.

[4] So *ibid.*; B. Weiss, *Die vier Evangelien* (Leipzig, 1900), 41; J. Schmid, *Mt*[3] (Regensburg, 1956), 130; cf. Foerster, *TWNT*, II, 587-595.

[5] So A. Meyer, *Jesu Muttersprache* (Freiburg, 1896), 107f.

[6] J. S. Kennard, Jr., thinks Mt changes ἀδικίας to ἀνομίαν to combat Pauline antinomianism (*Anglican Theological Review*, 31 [1949], 245). Though it is true that ἀνομία presents the Jewish point of view and ἀδικία the Greek (A. Plummer, *Mt* [London, 1909], 117), Mt merely follows the LXX and Lk chooses a synonym. 'Ανομία is frequent in the LXX for עון and און; and in 1:21 Mt has ἁμαρτία, where he could have adopted, as Tit 2:14, the LXX's ἀνομία.

with its cognates appears frequently in Lucan (and Pauline) writings. Ἀφιστάναι also seems to be a favorite word with Lk. This may account for his retention of it in agreement with the LXX, while Mt renders independently.[1] Mt's omission of כל-πάντες suggests he worked from a Hebrew text in which כל was missing.[2] It is striking that in the context of Ps 6:9, it is the sufferer vindicated by Yahweh who tells the workers of iniquity to depart. Did Jesus have this in mind with regard to himself?

Mt 8:11	Lk 13:29	Ps 107 (106):3 LXX	MT	Is 49:12 LXX	MT
		ἐκ τῶν χωρῶν	מארצות	ἰδοὺ οὗτοι πόρρωθεν	הנה אלה מרחוק
	ἥξουσιν	συνήγαγεν αὐτούς	קבצם	ἔρχονται	יבאו
πολλοὶ					
ἀπὸ ἀνατολῶν	ἀπὸ ἀνατολῶν	ἀπὸ ἀνατολῶν	ממזרח		
καὶ δυσμῶν	καὶ δυσμῶν	καὶ δυσμῶν	וממערב		
ἥξουσιν					
	καὶ ἀπὸ βορρᾶ	καὶ βορρᾶ	מצפון	οὗτοι ἀπὸ βορρᾶ καὶ	והנה אלה מצפון
	καὶ νότου	καὶ θαλάσσης	ומים	οὗτοι ἀπὸ θαλάσσης	ומים
	ἀπό 2° B*alit*] *om* אDΘ*pm* ς			ἔρχ.] ἥξουσιν BאVLuc οἱ λ'	
Cf. Is 45:6; 59:19; Mal 1:11.				Cf. Is 60:6, 7	

The verb ἥξουσιν (Mt, Lk) comes from Is 49:12, probably as an independent rendering of the Hebrew since the group represented by BV is hexaplaric and the reading ἥξουσιν looks like a hexaplaric assimilation to the Hebrew.[3] The context in Is concerns the gathering of Israel for the eschatological kingdom and thus suits the verse for Jesus' use.[4]

The geographical expressions are drawn from the parallel passage

---

[1] Stendahl seeks to lessen the non-Septuagintal element by noting that ἀφιστάνει, though common in Lk, is lacking in Mt (p. 90). However, this fact means nothing, since ἀποχωρεῖν is *hapax* in Mt, but occurs several times in Lk (Lk 9:39; Acts 13:13; ἀποχωρίζεσθαι—Acts 15:39). That is, Mt shows no liking for ἀποχωρεῖν elsewhere, and Lk does—so that Mt's divergence from the LXX and Lk in ἀποχωρεῖτε is clear-cut.

[2] כל was often inserted into or deleted from the Hebrew text. See Würthwein, *op. cit.*, 74. Opening Kennicott and De-Rossi at random, I noticed this happening in I Kings 16:27. At least one OT commentator thinks כל is a gloss in the MT of Ps 6:9 (C. A. Briggs, *Ps* [ICC; Edinburgh, 1907], I, 51).

[3] See J. Ziegler (ed.), *Isaias, ad loc.*, 7, 23, 36-73; *idem, ZAW*, 61 (1945/48), 76-94; J. B. Payne, *JBL*, 68 (1949), 251-265; J. W. Wevers, *Theologische Rundschau*, 22 (1954), 97; Würthwein, *op. cit.*, 77.

[4] See J. Jeremias, *Jesus' Promise to the Nations* (London, 1958), 15ff.

Ps 107:3. Lk preserves the entire quotation, whereas Mt cuts off the statement after "east and west." Lk's νότου ("south") differs from the LXX and the MT ("from the sea"= west) and may be based either on a Hebrew text which read מימין ("from the south") or on the Targum, which preserves the reference to the sea but interprets with reference to the south (מן ימא סטר דרומא), as does also the Targum to Is 49:12. Since "west" has already been mentioned and the word stands in opposition to "north," the MT must be corrupt in מים.[1]

Mt 8:12; 13:42, 50; 22:13; 24:51; 25:30; Lk 13:28: ἐκεῖ ἔσται ὁ κλαυθμὸς καὶ ὁ βρυγμὸς τῶν ὀδόντων
Ps 112 (111):10 LXX: ἁμαρτωλὸς ὄψεται καὶ ὀργισθήσεται, τοὺς ὀδόντας αὐτοῦ βρύξει
MT: רשע יראה וכעס שניו יחרק

The NT differs from the LXX in taking כעס in the sense of grief[2] rather than anger.

Mt 10:32, 33	Lk 12:8, 9	I Sam 2:30 MT	LXX
πᾶς οὖν ὅστις	πᾶς ὃς ἂν		
ὁμολογήσει	ὁμολογήσῃ	מכבדי	τοὺς δοξάζοντάς
ἐν ἐμοὶ . . .	ἐν ἐμοὶ . . .		με
	ὁ υἱὸς τ. ἀνθρ.		
ὁμολογήσω	ὁμολογήσει	אכבד	δοξάσω
καγὼ ἐν αὐτῷ	ἐν αὐτῷ		
. . .	. . .		
ὅστις δ' ἂν	ὁ δὲ		καὶ
ἀρνήσηταί με	ἀρνησάμενός με	ובזי	ὁ ἐξουθενῶν με
. . . ἀρνήσομαι	. . . ἀπαρνηθήσεται	יקלו	ἀτιμωθήσεται
καγὼ αὐτόν . . .			
	ὁ δὲ ἀρν. κτλ.] *om* P45 245 e syr^{sin}		

The form of the declaration is patterned after I Sam 2:30, but in the first clause the thought of "confessing" or "praising"[3] adapts, if not renders, the cognate thought of "glorifying" in the OT text.[4] The Targum's קדמי probably suggested the four prepositional phrases in which ἔμπροσθεν is used (omitted above for brevity; Lk

[1] Kraus, *op. cit.*, 735.
[2] For this meaning, see Prov 17:25; Eccl 1:18; 2:23; 11:10; Ezek 32:9.
[3] Ὁμολογήσει ἐν . . . is usually taken as an Aramaism for אודה ב. See Moulton-Howard, *op. cit.*, I, 104, II, 463f.; F. C. Burkitt, *The Earliest Sources for the Life of Jesus*[2] (London, 1922), 23; Bl-D § 220:2.
[4] See O. Michel, *TWNT*, V, 204, on the close tie between ὁμολογεῖν in the meaning "to praise (God)" and the acknowledgment of sin.

uses ἐνώπιον in the last two). Ἀρνεῖσθαι ("to disdain, reject, deny" [1]) stands for בזה and קלל, both of which mean "to disdain, despise" and consequently "to reject." See especially Is 53:3, "despised (נבזה) and rejected (וחדל)." There is, obviously, no trace of Septuagintal terminology.

Mt 10:35, 36	Lk 12:53	Mic 7:6 LXX	MT
διχάσαι	διαμερισθήσονται		
	πατὴρ ἐπὶ υἱῷ		
ἄνθρωπον	καὶ υἱὸς	υἱὸς ἀτιμάζει	בן מנבל
κατὰ τοῦ	ἐπὶ πατρὶ	πατέρα	אב
πατρὸς αὐτοῦ			
	μήτηρ ἐπὶ θυγατέρα		
καὶ θυγατέρα	καὶ θυγάτηρ	θυγάτηρ	בת
		ἐπαναστήσεται	קמה
κατὰ τῆς	ἐπὶ τὴν	ἐπὶ τὴν	באמה
μητρὸς αὐτῆς	μητέρα	μητέρα αὐτῆς	
	πενθερὰ ἐπὶ τὴν νύμφην αὐτῆς		
καὶ νύμφην	καὶ νύμφη	νύμφη	כלה
κατὰ τῆς	ἐπὶ τὴν	ἐπὶ τὴν	בחמתה
πενθερᾶς αὐτῆς	πενθεράν	πενθερὰν αὐτῆς	
καὶ ἐχθροὶ		ἐχθροὶ	איבי
τοῦ ἀνθρώπου		ἀνδρὸς	איש
οἱ οἰκιακοὶ		οἱ ἄνδρες οἱ ἐν	אנשי
αὐτοῦ		τῷ οἴκῳ αὐτοῦ	ביתו
ἄνθρωπον] υἱόν D it syr sin, cur (= assimilation to Lk and Mic)	πατὴρ . . . πατρί] υἱὸς ἐπὶ πατρὶ καὶ πατὴρ ἐπὶ υἱῷ P45 157	ἀνδρός VOr(hex)Syh] πάντες WAQ; + πάντες Luc; *pr* πάντες B οἱ ἄνδρες] *om* B οἱ ἐν . . . αὐτοῦ] οἱ ἐκ τοῦ οἴκου V	

Mt's ἄνθρωπον is not so close to בן as υἱός (LXX, Lk) and may be drawn from the last part of the verse (איש; LXX—ἀνδρός). Similarly, Mt renders בְּ by κατά with the genitive independently from the LXX and Lk (ἐπί). Lk first writes the dative after ἐπί, and then the accusative in order to conform with the LXX. The paratactic καί's are sprinkled freely in Mt; but the first evangelist must have been working from a Semitic text in which the conjunctions were present, for the OT Peshitta has *waw*'s exactly where Mt has καί's. It is doubtful the Peshitta was influenced by the NT in such an insignificant detail and in so allusive a quotation. In the possessive pro-

[1] See H. Riesenfeld, *Coniectanea Neotestamentica*, 11 (1947), 207-219; Schlatter, *op. cit.*, 348, for the meaning "to disdain, refuse."

nouns after μητρός and πενθερᾶς Mt stands closer to the OT text than Lk. In the last clause Mt carries the quotation farther than Lk and renders independently from the LXX (where the textual tradition is hopelessly divided) with a very fine idiomatic rendering of the Hebrew, οἱ οἰκιακοὶ αὐτοῦ for אנשי ביתו.

For each prepositional phrase in Mt and Mic, Lk presents a doublet. Within the first member of each the nouns are in chiastic position. The emphasis intended can hardly be due to free-quotation. This is a detailed and conscious reworking of the OT text. G. Quispel has suggested that when rendered into Greek, Jesus' sayings which were cast in poetic parallelism may have been considerably abbreviated; i.e., only one of the two parallel *kola* may have been translated.[1] It would then seem that the expanded form of Lk is more primitive, that Mt has assimilated to the OT passage in its Semitic form(s), and that Lk conforms slightly to the LXX.

Mt 11:5; Lk 7:22	Is 35:5, 6 LXX		MT
τυφλοὶ ἀναβλέπουσιν	ἀνοιχθήσονται	I	תפקחנה
	ὀφθαλμοὶ τυφλῶν		עיני עורים
καὶ χωλοὶ περιπατοῦσιν	τότε ἁλεῖται ὡς	III	אז ידלג
	ἔλαφος ὁ χωλός		כאיל פסח
λεπροὶ καθαρίζονται			
καὶ κωφοὶ ἀκούουσιν	καὶ ὦτα κωφῶν	II	ואזני חרשים
	ἀκούσονται		תפתחנה
καὶ νεκροὶ ἐγείρονται	Is 61:1 LXX		MT
καὶ πτωχοὶ	εὐαγγελίσασθαι		לבשר
εὐαγγελίζονται	πτωχοῖς . . . καὶ		ענוים ···
	τυφλοῖς ἀνάβλεψιν		ולאסורים
			פקח קוח

Lk omits the καί's.
Mt κ. χωλοὶ περιπατ.] *om* D*pc*dCl
κ. νεκ. ἐγειρ. and κ. πτ. εὐαγγ.]
trsp Θf13 syr^{cur}
κ. πτ. εὐαγγ.] *om* k syr^{sin} Cl

Τυφλοὶ ἀναβλέπουσιν (Mt, Lk), although answering to the first clause in Is 35:5, draws on Is 61:1 in the use of ἀναβλέπειν. This fact favors the originality of καὶ πτ. εὐαγγ. in Mt. Souter[2] and Burkitt[3] accept the omission by k syr^{sin} Cl and (presumably) Tatian's Diatessaron, arguing that whereas εὐαγγελίζεσθαι never occurs elsewhere in Mt, Lk introduces it here because the word and the OT passage (Is 61:1,2) are favorites with him. It is better, however,

[1] G. Quispel, *Vigiliae Christianae*, 11 (1957), 199f., in relation to Logion 89 in the Gospel of Thomas, where such an explanation fits.

[2] In *Mansfield College Essays* (London, 1909), 363f.

[3] *Evangelion da-Mepharreshe*, II, 238f.

to regard the omission as a Tatianic shortening of the text, occasioned by the supposed difficulty that "preaching to the poor" is anticlimactic after "raising the dead." The transposition of the clauses in Θ f13 syr^{cur} shows that this really was felt to be a difficulty.[1] In τυφλοὶ ἀναβλέπουσιν dependence on the LXX is close, since the Hebrew probably means liberation of those who are bound in prison.

In the remaining clauses corresponding to Is 35 the highly figurative speech is made more prosaic, though dependence on the LXX is again seen in ἀκούειν for פתח. Jesus adds references to his cleansing the lepers and raising the dead to show that his ministry *surpasses* the prophetic expectation. In Mt 8 and 9 the giving of sight to the blind (9:27ff.) follows the healing of the paralytics (8:5 ff.; 9:2 ff.). Yet in summarizing his ministry Jesus inverts the order and modifies παραλυτικός to mean χωλός and the sense of κωφός as "dumb" into the sense "deaf" to conform to the OT text.[2]

This NT passage is paralleled in Mandaean literature.[3] R. Reitzenstein attempted to make the gospels, or rather Q, dependent on the Mandaean texts.[4] The Mandaean passages seem to be later, however, and dependent on NT tradition.[5] The OT lies much closer at hand.

Mt 11:19; Lk 7:34: ἰδοὺ ἄνθρωπος φάγος καὶ οἰνοπότης
Dt 21:20 LXX: συμβολοκοπῶν οἰνοφλυγεῖ ("reveller in drunkenness")
MT: זולל וסבא ("spendthrift and drunkard")
Old Pal Targ: אכל בבשרה ושתי בחמר ("an eater in flesh [= glutton] and drinker in wine [= drunkard]")
Targ Jon: גרגרן בבשרא ושתאי בחמרא ("glutton in flesh and drinker in wine")
Targ Onk: זליל בסר וסבי חמר ("spendthrift in flesh [= glutton; cf. Prov 23:20] and drinker of wine")

The LXX translates the compound terms by one phrase. Mt and Lk show no reminiscence of the LXX, retaining the compound form and rendering in accordance with the Targums. The ambiguous

---

[1] See Friedrich, *TWNT*, II, 715; Percy, *op. cit.*, 189; Schniewind, *op. cit.*, 136.

[2] Cf. B. Weiss, *Mt*, 213f.; A. B. Bruce, *op. cit.*, 170.

[3] M. Lidzbarski, *Ginza Rechter* (Göttingen, 1925), I, 201, p. 30, l. 3ff. = II, 1, 136, p. 48, l. 7ff.; *idem*, *Das Johannesbuch der Mandäer* (Giessen, 1915), II, p. 243, l. 10ff., 25ff.

[4] *ZNW*, 26 (1927), 55ff.; R. Reitzenstein and H. H. Schaeder, *Studien zum Antiken Synkretismus* (Leipzig, 1926), 333ff.

[5] H. Schlier, *Theologische Rundschau*, 5 (1933), 32f.; W. Brandt, in Hastings' *Encyclopaedia of Religion and Ethics* (Edinburgh, 1915), VIII, 380; C. H. Dodd, *The Interpretation of the Fourth Gospel* (Cambridge, 1953), 126f.

זולל is taken in the sense of "glutton" (= OT Pesh, אסוט, as well as the Targums); and οἰνοπότης answers quite literally to the Targumic renderings, all of which combine "drinker" and "wine."

Mt 11:23; Lk 10:15	Is 14:13, 15 LXX	MT
μὴ ἕως οὐρανοῦ	εἰς τὸν οὐρανὸν	השמים
ὑψωθήσῃ;	ἀναβήσομαι, . . .	אעלה ...
ἕως [Lk: + τοῦ] ᾅδου	εἰς ᾅδου	תל שאול
καταβήσῃ	καταβήσῃ	הורד
Mt μὴ . . . ὑψ. ℵBDWΘ1*al* lat syr^{cur} cop] ἢ . . . ὑψώθης f13 28 700*al*fq syr^{sin}; ἡ . . . ὑψωθεῖσα 33 565*al*h ς καταβήσῃ BDW*pc*lat syr$^{sin, cur}$Ir] καταβιβασθήσῃ *Uncs rell, Minusc pler* Lk μὴ . . . ὑψ. P^{45} ℵB*D700*pc*it (syr$^{sin, cur}$)] ἢ ἐ. οὐρ. ὑψώθης B^{c}; ἡ ε. οὐρ. ὑψωθεῖσα AWΘf1 f13*pl*lat ς καταβήσῃ BD579d syr$^{sin, cur}$ eth arm] καταβιβασθήσῃ *rell* ς	ᾅδου ℵALuc] ᾅδην BQC	

The NT readings adopted above have the best support from the MSS, answer to a Semitic background, and correspond to the OT text. The sense is not that Capernaum has been exalted to heaven (whether in pride or by virtue of Jesus' ministry), but that lest she be exalted to heaven she will "go down to Hades." [1] So also in Is 14 Babylon is plunged to Sheol to thwart her prideful intentions. In ἕως with the genitive Mt and Lk do not follow the LXX's εἰς with the accusative and genitive. Similarly ὑψωθήσῃ, which may reflect אָרִים ("exalt") in another clause and for which the LXX has a colorless θήσω, is foreign to the LXX. On the other hand, καταβήσῃ agrees with the LXX against the MT (*hophal*: "be brought down"). The variant reading καταβιβασθήσῃ must be considered an assimilation to ὑψωθήσῃ.[2]

Mt 12:42; Lk 11:31: τὴν σοφίαν Σολομῶνος
I Kings 10:4 LXX: πᾶσαν (τὴν) φρόνησιν Σαλωμών
6 LXX: περὶ τῆς φρονήσεώς σου
8 LXX: πᾶσαν τὴν φρόνησίν σου
4 MT: כל חכמת שלמה
6 MT: על חכמתך
8 MT: את חכמתך
Josephus, *Ant.* VIII. vi. 4: τὴν σοφίαν τοῦ Σολόμωνος

[1] On the Semitic negative parataxis, see Wellhausen, *Mt*, 57; followed by E. Klostermann, *Mt*, 101; Percy, *op. cit.*, 112f.
[2] McNeile, *Mt*, 161.

In the NT both the choice of σοφία and the transliteration of Solomon's name show independence from the LXX and a relation to Josephus or the Greek textual tradition represented by him.

Mt 17:2	Lk 9:29	Ex 34:29 LXX	MT	Sifre Num.
καὶ ἔλαμψεν		δεδόξασται	קרן	140
		ἡ ὄψις		
	τὸ εἶδος	τοῦ χρώματος	עור	
τὸ πρόσωπον	τοῦ προσώπου	τοῦ προσώπου	פניו	פני משה
αὐτοῦ	αὐτοῦ	αὐτοῦ		
ὡς ὁ ἥλιος	ἕτερον			כפני חמה

Inasmuch as Mk omits any reference to the shining of Jesus' face,[1] the above allusion is a deliberate assimilation to the shining of Moses' face on Mt. Sinai. With the exception of Ro 12:2, the only other NT use of μεταμορφοῦσθαι occurs in II Cor 3:18, where Paul explicitly draws the parallel between the shining of Moses' face and the glory of the new covenant. There are numerous indications that the whole narrative concerning the Transfiguration finds a pattern in the theophany to Moses at Sinai: the reference to "six days" (cf. Ex 24:16), the presence of Moses, the use of ἔξοδος by Lk, the reference to "tabernacles," the overshadowing cloud, the divine voice speaking out of the cloud, the injunction to "Hear him," which is a quotation from a passage taken as prophetic of a Moses-like Messiah (Dt 18:15), and the allusion in Mt 17:17 ("faithless and perverse generation") to Dt 32:5, spoken concerning Israel's apostasy during Moses' stay on the mountain.[2] This is reinforced by the general Moses-Jesus parallel in Mt, seen in the pentateuchal format of the gospel [3] and in the correspondences between the slaughters by Pharaoh and Herod, the flights and

---

[1] Streeter's conjecture that the Marcan text originally contained a reference to Jesus' face rests on a questionable retranslation of syr^{sin} into Greek, requires several doubtful guesses about what happened to the original text, and possesses not a shred of positive evidence from the MSS that τὸ πρόσωπον was ever in the text of Mk (*op. cit.*, 315f.).

[2] On the parallel between the theophany at Sinai and the Transfiguration, see E. Wendling, *Theol. Stud. u. Krit.*, 84 (1911), 116f.; H. M. Teeple, *The Mosaic Eschatological Prophet* (Philadelphia, 1957), 84; J. Manek, *NovTest*, 2 (1957/58), 8-23; A. Feuillet, *Biblica*, 39 (1958), 292ff.; M. Sabbe, *Collationes Brugenses et Gandavenses*, 4 (1958), 467-503; A.-M. Denis, *La vie spirituelle*, 41 (1959), 136-149.

[3] F. Godet, *Introduction to the NT* (Edinburgh, 1899), 182; Bacon, *Studies in Mt*, p. xv; Hawkins, *op. cit.*, 163f.; differently, F. Delitzsch, *Neue Untersuchungen über Entstehung u. Anlage der kanonischen Evangelien* (Leipzig, 1853), I, 55-109; A. M. Farrer, in *Studies in the Gospels*, 77ff.

returns of Moses and the Holy Family, the Red Sea and Jesus' baptism, the wilderness and the temptation, the law-givers on the mount, the ten plagues and the ten miracles, the twelve tribes and the choice of twelve disciples, the manna and the feeding of the multitudes, the dying Moses on Mt. Nebo and the risen Christ on a mountain in Galilee.[1]

Mt's phraseology stands closer to the OT text than Lk's. The Hebrew קרן ("to send forth horns, [i.e.] beams of light") cannot be literally rendered into Greek. However, the active voice and the meaning of ἔλαμψεν in Mt are much nearer the Hebrew than δεδόξασται in the LXX. Mt's added comparison to the brightness of the sun shows contact with rabbinic tradition ("the face of Moses as the face of the sun").[2]

Mt 17:17; Lk 9:41: ὦ γενεὰ ἄπιστος καὶ διεστραμμένη
Mt, Lk] *trps* ἄπιστος and διεστρ. syr$^{sin, cur}$
Lk κ. διεστρ.] *om* a e Mcion Tat (venetus)
Mk 9:19 omits κ. διεστρ., except P^{45} W f13 *pc.*
Dt 32:5 LXX: γενεὰ σκολιὰ καὶ διεστραμμένη (= Phil 2:15)
MT: דור עקש ופתלתל
Dt 32:20 LXX: ὅτι γενεὰ ἐξεστραμμένη ἐστίν, υἱοὶ οἷς οὐκ ἔστιν πίστις ἐν αὐτοῖς
MT: כי דור תהפכת המה בנים לא אמן בם

To explain the agreement of Mt and Lk against Mk, Streeter takes the transpositions in syr$^{sin, cur}$ as satisfactory evidence for the omission of κ. διεστρ. in Mt and Lk.[3] However, the transposition in the Old Syriac may be for the sake of rhythm, as Streeter himself suggests, and the weak direct support for omission looks like assimilation to Mk. P.-L. Couchoud accepts the insertion of the words in Mk by P^{45} W f13.[4] But this reading also appears to be harmonistic. It is quite in keeping with Matthaean style to conform to OT phraseology; and the agreement in this respect between

[1] On the Moses-Jesus typology in Mt, cf. *Midr. Koh.* f. 73, 3: כגואל ראשון גואל אחרון; and see an extensive literature: Edersheim, *Life and Times*, I, 527; Friedrich, *TWNT*, VI, 848; Findlay, *Jesus in the First Gospel*, 19; H. J. Schoeps, *Theologie u. Geschichte des Judenchristentums* (Tübingen, 1949), 93ff.; K. Thieme, *Judaica*, 5 (1949), 133ff.; J. Daniélou, *Sacramentum Futuri* (Paris, 1950), 135-138; van Dodewaard, *Biblica*, 36 (1955), 488ff.; J. Dupont, *NTS*, 3 (1956/57), 295-298; Hunt, *op. cit.*, 169ff.; Teeple, *op. cit.*, 74ff.; Gils, *op. cit.*, 39; E. E. Ellis, *Paul's Use of the OT* (Edinburgh, 1957), 132; R. Schnackenburg, in *Studia Evangelica* (= *Texte u. Untersuchungen*, 5. Reihe, Bd. 18; Berlin, 1959), 622-639.

[2] Schlatter, *op. cit.*, 527, notes this parallel.

[3] *Op. cit.*, 317; also Leaney, *op. cit.*, 169.

[4] *JTS*, 35 (1934); 12 followed by V. Taylor, *op. cit.*, 398.

Mt and Lk in the preceding OT allusion should have prepared us for the same phenomenon here.

The replacement of the LXX's σκολιά (Dt 32:5) by ἄπιστος may be influenced by the later verse in Dt.[1] The matter is rendered doubtful, however, because in Dt 32:20 the sense "faithfulness" is required, and the Pauline allusion in Phil 2:15 takes over the LXX of verse 5. Probably the evangelist intends a play on עקש, which at once means "perverse" and "deceitful, false," and ἄπιστος, which means both "untrustworthy, treacherous" and "unbelieving."[2] Even with an influx from Dt 32:20 essentially the same play is required, since there also the matter in question is trustworthiness, not belief.

Mt 18:15: ἐὰν δὲ ἁμαρτήσῃ ὁ ἀδελφός σου, ὕπαγε ἔλεγξον αὐτόν
Lk 17:3: ἐὰν ἁμάρτῃ ὁ ἀδελφός σου, ἐπιτίμησον αὐτῷ
Lev 19:17 LXX: οὐ μισήσεις τὸν ἀδελφόν σου τῇ διανοίᾳ σου· ἐλεγμῷ ἐλέγξεις τὸν πλησίον σου
MT: לא תשנא את אחיך בלבבך הוכח תוכיח את עמיתך

That this is an allusion to the OT is confirmed by the other quotations from Lev 19 in Mt 5:33, 43, 48 and by the exactly similar theme, harmony among brethren, in the OT and NT passages. Either Mt's ἔλεγξον is assimilation to the LXX (a good rendering of יכח) or Lk has missed or cared nothing for the allusion. (Ἐπιτιμᾶν is frequent in the synoptics, but slightly more so in Lk.)

Mt 21:44: καὶ ὁ πεσὼν ἐπὶ τὸν λίθον τοῦτον συνθλασθήσεται· ἐφ' ὃν δ' ἂν πέσῃ, λικμήσει αὐτόν
D 33 it syr^{sin} Ir Or omit the verse.
Lk 20:18: πᾶς ὁ πεσὼν ἐπ' ἐκεῖνον τὸν λίθον συνθλασθήσεται· ἐφ' ὃν δ' ἂν πέσῃ, λικμήσει αὐτόν

In view of the omission in the Western text of Mt, in Origen's copious commentary on this passage, and in Irenaeus and Eusebius, who copy verses 33-43 and would hardly have failed to include so striking a concluding sentence, the verse in Mt may be an interpolation from Lk. Nevertheless, the possibility of genuineness remains. The minor differences between Mt and Lk are not easily accounted for on the hypothesis of interpolation. B. Weiss and S. G. F. Brandon ask why the verse was not placed after verse 42 to

[1] So J. R. Harris, *ET*, 37 (1925/26), 9; Tabachovitz, *op. cit.*, 113f.
[2] So in classical Greek often. See R. Bultmann, *TWNT*, VI, 176. Cf. Mt 24:45; 25:21, 23; Lk 12:46; 16:10f.; Ro 3:3; I Cor 1:9; 10:13; I Thess 5:24; I Tim 3:11; II Tim 2:2; Heb 3:12; 10:23; III Jn 5.

preserve the Lucan sequence. As it is, verse 43 disrupts the natural connection between verses 42 and 44, and this may be the very reason for omission in the Western text.[1] R. Swaeles argues that the general thought of Mt 21:43 refers to the whole of Dan 2:44 and leads into the allusive quotation in Mt 21:44, which therefore must be original.[2]

The allusion is to Dan 2:34, 35, 44, 45. Mt and Lk agree with Theodotion in λικμᾶν against the LXX (ἀφανίζειν) and the MT (סוף—"to make an end of"). But συνθλᾶσθαι ("to break in pieces") shows direct recourse to the Aramaic (דקק—"to break in pieces"), as against λεπτύνειν ("to make thin, beat out"—LXX, Theod) and καταλεῖν ("to grind"—LXX).

Mt 23:12	Lk 14:11; 18:14	Ezek 21:31 LXX	MT
ὅστις δὲ	πᾶς	ἐταπείνωσας	השפלה
ὑψώσει ἑαυτὸν	ὁ ὑψῶν ἑαυτὸν	τὸ ὑψηλὸν	הגבה
ταπεινωθήσεται	ταπεινωθήσεται		
καὶ ὅστις	καὶ ὁ [18:14: ὁ δὲ]	καὶ ὕψωσας	והגבה
ταπεινώσει	ταπεινῶν	τὸ ταπεινόν	השפיל
ἑαυτὸν	ἑαυτὸν		
ὑψωθήσεται	ὑψωθήσεται		

Although this maxim is often voiced in Prov, the NT expression is patterned after the saying in Ezek.[3] In the LXX the wicked prince of Israel has abased that which was high by taking off the mitre and exalted that which was low by putting on the crown. In the MT the mitre and the crown are both taken from the wicked prince and he himself is abased. Obviously, the NT adaptation to persons is based on the Hebrew text.

The LXX renders the clauses in chiastic order, and with this the NT agrees. It may be that the LXX-translator wished an exact parallel: "taken off the mitre"—"abased the high," "put on the crown"—"exalted the low." However, the Hebrew *Vorlage* of the LXX and NT may have had the order of the LXX. The difference in the consonantal text would be very slight, requiring only the shifting of a final paragogic ה: השפל הגבה והגבה השפלה. (There is not even a need to shift the *yodh* in the MT, if we assume a *sere* vocalization, הַשְׁפֵּל.) Ὑψοῦν and ταπεινοῦν are natural renderings of the Hebrew words. Thus, there is no necessary point of contact between the NT and the LXX.

[1] B. Weiss, *Mt*, 371; Brandon, *op. cit.*, 244.
[2] *NTS*, 6 (1959), 310-313.
[3] See Lohmeyer-Schmauch, *op. cit.*, 341.

Mt 23:35, 36	Lk 11:50, 51	Lam 4:13 LXX	MT
		τῶν ἐκχεόντων	השפכים
πᾶν αἷμα	τὸ αἷμα	αἷμα	בקרבה
	πάντων τῶν		דם
δίκαιον	προφητῶν	δικαίον	צדיקים
ἐκχυννόμενον	τὸ ἐκκεχυμένον		
ἐπὶ τῆς γῆς		ἐν μέσῳ αὐτῆς	
. . .	. . .	II Chron 24:20-22 LXX	MT
ἕως τοῦ αἵματος	ἕως αἵματος		
Ζαχαρίου	Ζαχαρίου	τὸν 'Αζαρίαν	זכריה
υἱοῦ Βαραχίου		τὸν τοῦ 'Ιωδαὲ. . .	בן יהוידע
		ἐλιθοβόλησαν [v. 21]	ירגמהו אבן
ὃν ἐφονεύσατε	τοῦ ἀπολομένου	[ἐθανάτωσεν, v. 22]	[יהרג]
μεταξὺ τοῦ ναοῦ	μεταξὺ τοῦ	. . . ἐν αὐλῇ	בחצר
καὶ τοῦ	θυσιαστηρίου	οἴκου κυρίου	בית יהוה
θυσιαστηρίου	καὶ τοῦ οἴκου		
Βαρ.] Ioiadae	τοῦ ἀπολομ. . . .		
Gospel of the	οἴκου] υἱοῦ Βαραχίου		
Nazarenes	ὃν ἐφόνευσαν ἀνάμεσον		
	τ.θ.κ.τ.ναοῦ D (*pc*) syr^{cur}		
	(= assimilation to Mt via Tatian?)		

One might think that there is no definite allusion here. But a comparison of Mt and Lk shows that Mt stands closer to the OT texts. The usual OT expression is דם נקי (LXX: αἷμα ἀθῷον) (II Kings 21:16; 24:4; Jer 26:15 [33:15]). Therefore, Mt's addition of δίκαιον and the combination with ἐκχεῖν fairly well establish his allusion to Lam 4:13. 'Επὶ τῆς γῆς (Mt) is an adaptation to the story of Abel, where emphasis is laid on the ground (אדם; LXX, γῆ) which received Abel's blood (Gen 4:10, 11).

In the reference to II Chron, Mt agrees with the Hebrew against the LXX in reading "Zachariah" and "son of . . .," but goes his own way in Βαραχίου.[1] 'Εφονεύσατε (Mt) renders יהרג independently

[1] F. Blass considers υἱοῦ Βαραχίου an interpolation from Zech 1:1 LXX (*Textkritische Bemerkungen zu Mt* (Gütersloh, 1900], 43). The utmost confusion exists in Jewish and early Christian literature between the Zechariahs, both those in the OT and those outside the OT. In the Targum to Lam 2:20 we read of "Zechariah, son of Iddo, the high priest." In Is 8:2 there is "Zechariah, the son of Jeberechiah." But the LXX reads Βαραχίου, which is based on a misunderstanding of עדים as "martyr(s)" instead of "witness(es)" and so connected with II Chron (see Stendahl, 92). Since the LXX reads 'Αζαρίαν in II Chron, a double confusion already exists in the Septuagintal tradition, within the text of II Chron and between that text and Is 8:2. In Zech 1:1 the prophet is "the son of Berechiah, the son of Iddo," but in Ezra 6:14 he is merely "the son of Iddo" (this has led to the conjecture that the Zechariah in II Chron had Jehoiada as a grandfather—note Jehoiada died not until the age of 130 years, yet Zechariah's ministry followed Jehoia-

from the LXX. The final prepositional phrase (μεταξύ . . .) conforms

---

da's death—and an otherwise unmentioned "Berechiah" as father [see J. P. Lange, *Mt* (New York, 1870), 414f.; Broadus, *Mt* (Philadelphia, 1886), 477]). In the second Epiphanius recension of *The Lives of the Prophets* the biography of Zechariah the son of Jehoiada "forms the second half of the biography of Zechariah son of Berechiah!" (C. C. Torrey, *The Lives of the Prophets* [Philadelphia, 1946], 47, sub 78). Confusion is added to confusion in Zacharias the father of John the Baptist, with whom Zechariah son of Jehoiada is confused in some MSS of *The Lives of the Prophets* (see Schoeps, *Aus frühchristlicher Zeit*, 138f.) and whom Origen saw as Jesus' reference (*Prot. Jac.* xxiii). More than one form of legend concerning the murder of the Baptist's father in the Temple exists in early Christian literature (Epiphanius, *Haer.* xxvi. 12; *The Birth of Mary*, in *The Apocryphal NT* [translated by M. R. James; Oxford, 1924], 19; *Protevangelium* xxiiif. [*ibid.*, 48]; the Coptic conclusion to the *Apocalypse of Paul* [*ibid.*, 554]; *The Latin Infancy Gospels* [edited by M. R. James; Cambridge, 1927], 90ff.—see T. W. Manson, in *The Mission and Message of Jesus*, 396; H. Smith, *Ante-Nicene Exegesis of the Gospels* [London, 1925-29], IV, 75, V, 85-96; H. J. Schoeps, *Revue de Qumran*, Tome 2, Num. 5 [1959], 79; *idem*, *Zeitschrift für Religions- u. Geistesgeschichte*, 11 [1959], 72, who discusses the further possibility that John's father is the Qumran Teacher of Righteousness; J. Jeremias, ΑΓΓΕΛΟΣ, 2 [1926], 87f.; H. Freiherr von Campenhausen, *Historisches Jahrbuch*, 77 [1958], 383ff.; A. Berendts, *Studien über Zacharias-Apokryphen u. Zacharias-Legenden* [Leipzig, 1895]). If further confusion is possible, a Zecharias son of Baris or Baruch or Bariscaeus (the MSS vary!), who Josephus says was murdered by two Zealots in the Temple (*Bellum* IV. v. 4), has been taken as Jesus' reference (so Chrysostom and Grotius, to whom this is a prediction, and O. Pfleiderer, *Primitive Christianity* [London, 1906-11], II, 364, n. 1; J. Wellhausen, *Mt*, 119f.; *idem*, *Einleitung in die drei ersten Evangelien*[2] [Berlin, 1911], 118-123; Weiss-Bousset, *op. cit.*, I, 363f.; J. S. Kennard, Jr., *Anglican Theological Review*, 29 [1947], 176ff.; Bundy, *op. cit.*, 355, to whom this is a *vaticinium ex eventu* put into the mouth of Jesus by the evangelists, and E. E. Ellis, *ET*, 74 [1963], 157f., to whom this is a logion of Jesus which an early Christian prophet has "peshered" and applied to the martyrdom of Christians and the destruction of Jerusalem). Schoeps suggests the Nazarene Gospel preserves an original "Jehoiada" from the Ur-Matthaean tradition, Greek-Mt making Jesus prophesy of Josephus' Zechariah (*Theologie u. Geschichte des Judenchristentums* [Tübingen, 1949], 266; *idem*, *Aus frühchristlicher Zeit*, 139, n. 1). Against any reference to the Zecharias in Josephus, there is no suggestion that he was a prophet or a martyr. He was ἐν μέσῳ the Temple, but probably not between the porch and the altar, since he was not a priest. It is improbable that the NT tradition, usually assigned to Q, dates from after A.D. 67. Jesus' idea is that all the *past* guilt will come upon the generation he addresses. And why the invention of legends concerning the death of John's father if the reference was to the Zecharias in Josephus? The traditional view that Jesus refers to the first and last murders in the OT canon, about both of which it is stated a reckoning would be made, remains the best—despite the contention that the OT canon and the order of the Hagiographa were not fixed by Jesus' time. The present passage is itself evidence to the contrary. Because of the confusion, we cannot be sure about the origin of the reading Βαραχίου in Mt. On the whole question and for further references, esp. in rabbinical to rabbinic tradition concerning the location within the Temple precincts of Zachariah's death.[1]

Mt 23:38; Lk 13:35: ἰδοὺ ἀφίεται ὑμῖν ὁ οἶκος ὑμῶν
Mt BLff²syr^sin sah boh^pl arm] + ἔρημος *rell* ς
Lk P^45vid ℵABW f1 69 565 *pm* it vg^w syr^sin sah boh^pl] + ἔρημος DΘ28*al* it vg^s, cl syr^sin boh (7) ς
Jer 12:7 LXX: ἐγκαταλέλοιπα τὸν οἶκόν μου, ἀφῆκα τὴν κληρονομίαν μου
MT: עזבתי את ביתי נטשתי את נחלתי
22:5 LXX: εἰς ἐρήμωσιν ἔσται ὁ οἶκος οὗτος
MT: לחרבה יהיה הבית הזה

Either Mt has rendered עזב (Jer 12:7) independently from the LXX, or he has allowed ἀφῆκα in the next clause of the LXX to influence his wording. The change from first person (Jer) to second person (Mt, Lk) deepens the thought of desolation. It is possible that ἔρημος is genuine in Mt, where the omission is less well supported than in Lk.[2] If so, Mt has woven together the two verses in Jer.

Mt 24:28	Lk 17:37	Job 39:30 LXX	MT
ὅπου ἐὰν	ὅπου	οὗ δ' ἂν	ובאשר
τ		ὦσι	
ᾖὸ πτῶμα	τὸ σῶμα	τεθνεῶτες	חללים
ἐκεῖ	ἐκεῖ καὶ	παραχρῆμα	שם
συναχθήσονται	οἱ ἀετοὶ		הוא
οἱ ἀετοί	ἐπισυναχθήσονται	εὑρίσκονται	

Mt and Lk supply οἱ ἀετοί from the preceding context in Job. Their (ἐπι)συναχθήσονται supplies the missing verb in the Hebrew and completely disagrees with the LXX, according to which the carcasses are found by the vultures. Both the NT and the Hebrew mean that the vultures are present wherever the carcases may be.

Mt's πτῶμα (esp. of something "killed") is a more exact rendering of חללים ("the slain") than Lk's σῶμα, a more refined word (used of corpses especially in Homer), or the LXX's τεθνεῶτες (simply "the dead"). Mt and Lk use the singular against the MT and the LXX; but their Hebrew *Vorlage* may have read the singular, since the OT Peshitta also has the singular (ואיכא דמתקטל קטילא).

---

literature, see Edersheim, *Life and Times*, II, 413f.; Strack-Billerbeck, *op. cit.*, I, 940-942; S. H. Blank, *HUCA*, 12/13 (1937/38), 327-346; E. Nestle, *ZNW*, 6 (1905), 198-200; J. Chapman, *JTS*, 13 (1912), 398-410.

[1] Jerusalem Talmud, *Taanith* IV. 69a. See Schoeps, *Aus frühchristlicher Zeit*, 139f.; Schlatter, *op. cit.*, 688f.

[2] Zahn (*Lk* [Leipzig, 1913], 543) and Knox (*op. cit.*, II, 83) regard the omission in Mt as assimilation to Lk. However, both longer readings may be regarded as assimilations to Jer 22:5.

Παραχρῆμα in the LXX reveals a temporal understanding of שם, which is indeed possible. Ἐκεῖ (Mt, Lk) is based on the more usual locative sense of שם in accordance with the Targum (תמן). Similarly ὅπου (Mt, Lk) diverges in form, though not in meaning, from the LXX.

Mt 24:38; Lk 17:27: εἰσῆλθεν Νῶε εἰς τὴν κιβωτόν
Gen 7:7 LXX: εἰσῆλθεν δὲ Νῶε . . . εἰς τὴν κιβωτόν
MT: ויבא נח ··· אל התבה.

All the texts agree; there is little room for variation.

Mt 24:45: δοῦναι αὐτοῖς τὴν τροφὴν ἐν καιρῷ
Lk 12:42: τοῦ διδόναι ἐν καιρῷ τὸ σιτομέτριον
Ps 104(103):27 MT: לתת אכלם בעתו
LXX: δοῦναι τὴν τροφὴν αὐτοῖς εὔκαιρον
LXX δοῦναι] *pr* τοῦ R
τ. τρ. αὐτοῖς Bא boh sah He 1219] αὐτοῖς τροφὴν R; τὴν τρ. αὐτῶν Luc A (= MT)
εὔκαιρον] εἰς καιρόν A

In αὐτοῖς Mt stands closer to the OT text than Lk, who omits. The dative agrees with the LXX and the OT Peshitta (להון) against the possessive of the MT. Since LXX^A appears to be hexaplaric, the similarity between ἐν καιρῷ (Mt, Lk) and εἰς καιρόν is not significant. The NT gives an exact and independent rendering of בעתו (except for the dropping of the possessive pronoun).[1] In τὸ σιτομέτριον ("food-allowance") Lk uses a more concrete word.

Formal Quotations Peculiar to Matthew

The formal quotations peculiar to Mt, consisting mainly of the formula-citations, have always been noted for their divergence from the LXX. Two points, however, must receive emphasis: (1) the formula-citations are not a homogeneous group in text-form, because they range from the purely Septuagintal to the wholly non-Septuagintal; (2) the allusive quotations in all layers of the synoptic tradition show the same mixed text-form.

Mt 1:23; Is 7:14 LXX: ἰδοὺ ἡ παρθένος ἐν γαστρὶ ἕξει καὶ τέξεται υἱόν, καὶ καλέσουσιν τὸ ὄνομα αὐτοῦ Ἐμμανουήλ
Mt καλέσουσιν] καλέσεις D*pc*d^c (d* vocabit)
LXX ἕξει AQ] λήμψεται BאVSyh 88 Luc Just Eus Bas Chr Thdt Tert Cypr Ir^lat
καλέσουσιν (not in the LXX-tradition)] καλέσεις BAC; καλέσει א; καλέσετε Q*Luc sah Tert Cypr Ir^lat; καλέσουσιν Γ
Is 7:14 MT: הנה העלמה הרה וילדת בן וְקָרָאת שמו עמנו אל
וקראת] וקרא 1QIs^a; vocabitur OT Pesh, Vg

[1] Ἐν καιρῷ = "at the right time." See A & G, s.v. καιρός, 2.

This formula-quotation is almost purely Septuagintal and perhaps wholly so. Special points of dependence are ἕξει (=LXX[A] against LXX[B])—λαμβάνεσθαι is the usual rendering for הרה—and the transliteration Ἐμμανουήλ.[1]

The third person plural of καλέσουσιν has usually been considered as motivated by the circumstance that neither Joseph nor Mary gave the name "Emmanuel" to the child.[2] However, the reading in 1QIs[a] throws new light on the picture, for קרא can be pointed קֹרָא (*pual* perfect—"it [his name] shall be called"= OT Pesh, Vg) or קָרָא (*kal* perfect—"one shall call"= LXX[א]), both of which are equivalent to Mt's impersonal plural.[3] In view, then, of the inner-Hebrew variants[4] and the inner-Greek variants, Mt may be following the reading of his Greek OT text, a reading otherwise unknown to us. Note especially the reading καλέσετε, plural, in LXX[Q*Luc etc.]. Justin's καλέσουσι (*Dial.* lxvi. 2) may be influenced by Mt, but καλέσεται (*Dial.* xliii, 5) is not—and both readings occur in longer quotations from Is. Thus, also outside Mt we have Greek readings which do not occur in the extant MSS of the LXX and for which there is no equivalent in Hebrew MSS. Therefore, we may conjecture that 1QIs[a] represents the original reading, that the initial ש of the next word gave rise to the final ת of the MT by a kind of audible dittography as the scribe pronounced the words (ת was often pronounced as a slight sibilant—cf. the interchange of ש and ת in Aramaic), that the inner-Greek variants reflect the confusion in the Semitic textual tradition, and that the Matthaean text witnesses to yet another Septuagintal reading. (Confusion of ש and ת

---

[1] I omit ἡ παρθένος, as that is the only pre-Christian interpretation of עלמה in Is 7:14 known to us. See Torrey, *Documents*, 48f.

[2] So Zahn, *Einl.*, II, 315; Stendahl, 98; and Baumstark, *op. cit.*, 309, who compares the Targum Frgm. Kahle F to Dt 34:6, where the indefinite וקברו is substituted for ויקבר to escape the thought that God himself buried Moses' body. Of course, the meaning in Mt 1:23 is not that Jesus should bear the name in real life, but that he should be what the name signifies. See Alexander, *op. cit.*, 16; J. Neil, *Figurative Language of the Bible* (London, 1892), 2f.; K. L. Schmidt, *TWNT*, III, 490; A & G, s.v. καλέω, 1aδ.

[3] See M. Burrows, *The Dead Sea Scrolls* (New York, 1955), 312; cf. Torrey, *Documents*, *loc. cit.*

[4] 1QIs[a] can also be pointed as *kal* imperative, קְרָא; some MSS of the MT read וקראתָ (second masc. sing.) and some וקראתְ (second fem. sing.—also two MSS of the Targum). See De-Rossi, *ad loc.* The usual pointing in the MT can be either third fem. sing. (= most MSS of the Targ) or the fem. participle.

might also have worked in the opposite direction, ת dropping out in pronunciation.)

Mt 2:6	Mic 5:1 MT	LXX
καὶ σὺ Βηθλέεμ	ואתה בית לחם	καὶ σὺ Βηθλέεμ
γῆ Ἰούδα	אפרתה	οἶκος τοῦ Ἐφράθα
οὐδαμῶς ἐλαχίστη εἶ	צעיר להיות	ὀλιγοστὸς εἶ τοῦ εἶναι
ἐν τοῖς ἡγεμόσιν Ἰούδα	באלפי יהודה	ἐν χιλιάσιν Ἰούδα
ἐκ σοῦ γὰρ	ממך	ἐκ σοῦ
ἐξελεύσεται	לי יצא	μοι ἐξελεύσεται
ἡγούμενος	להיות מושל	τοῦ εἶναι εἰς ἄρχοντα
	II Sam 5:2; I Chron	11:2
ὅστις ποιμανεῖ	אתה תרעה	σὺ ποιμανεῖς
τὸν λαόν μου	את עמי	τὸν λαόν μου
τὸν Ἰσραήλ	את ישראל	τὸν Ἰσραήλ
γῆ Ἰούδα] τῆς Ἰουδαί Dit ἐκ σοῦ] ἐξ σοῦ B; ἐξ οὗ ℵCD		ὀλιγοστός] *pr* μή LucC La^{C} boh syp Arab ἐκ σοῦ] ἐξ οὗ B*C ἐξελεύσεται] + ἡγούμενος A boh syp Eus Cypr^{p} (*ex* Mt)

Mt's γῆ Ἰούδα is a contemporization of the antique אפרתה [1] similar to that found in one MS of De-Rossi (בית לחם יהודה) and often in the LXX.[2] "Bethlehem-Judah" was the common OT designation (Ruth 1:1; I Sam 17:12; etc.), and the insertion of γῆ [3] is similar to the LXX of I (III) Kings 19:3, εἰς Βηρσαβεε γῆν Ἰούδα for באר שבע אשר ליהודה (MT).

It is impossible to be certain whether the emphatic negative in Mt, οὐδαμῶς ἐλαχίστη εἶ, is a targumic interpretation whereby the small size of Bethlehem, affirmed in the MT,[4] is exchanged for the greatness of Bethlehem's destiny as birthplace of the Messianic King [5] (a greatness implied even in the Hebrew text, for otherwise

---

[1] As often in poetry, Mic used the old name.

[2] Seeligmann, *op. cit.*, 80f.

[3] Nestle adopts in his critical apparatus the conjecture of Drusius (d. 1616), γῆς.

[4] Bethlehem is not named among the cities of Judah in the MT of Josh 15:59, though inserted with ten others by the LXX.

[5] So Anger, I, 23, and others. Essentially the same is done in the Targum, but by a softening כְּ (כזעיר) rather than by a negative. The possibility of a relationship between Mt and the Targum is heightened by the agreement of εἶ (Mt) and הויתא (Targ) against the infinitives of the LXX and the MT. Baumstark compares the Targums Jonathan, Jerusalem, and the Kahle Fragment D to Gen 37:33, where according to the Hebrew text Jacob laments that a wild beast has killed Joseph, but according to the Targums he denies that a wild beast killed Joseph (*op. cit.*, 310ff.).

the emphasis on insignificance is without point [1]); whether the emphatic negative is an answer to a rhetorical question in a Semitic text of Mic; [2] or whether Mt's text actually had the negative.[3, 4]

'Εν τοῖς ἡγεμόσιν is based on the reading אַלְפֵי or אלופי and is a personification of the cities of Judah in the persons of the clan-heads. The personification is justified by the use of אֶלֶף for clans and tribes (Jdg 6:15; I Sam 10:19; 23:23; Is 60:22), particularly in the phrase ראשי אלפי ישראל (Num 1:16; 10:4; Josh 22:21, 30),[5] and by the already existing personification of Bethlehem in Mic;[6] and it is motivated by or suggests the link with II Sam 5:2, where the LXX has ἡγούμενον (נגיד). The LXX renders אלוף by ἡγεμών in Gen 36:15 ff.; Ex 15:15; I Chron 1:51 ff.

The omission of לי agrees with the OT Peshitta and the Hebrew concordance of Rabbi Nathan.[7] Along with Mt's ἡγούμενος, the reference to "shepherding" Israel in Mic 5:3 provides the link with

---

[1] E. W. Hengstenberg, *Christology of the OT*[2] (Edinburgh, 1854-58), I, 475f.; E. König, *Die messianischen Weissagungen des A. T.* (Stuttgart, 1923), 193f.

[2] So Randolph, *op. cit.*, 27; Owen, *op. cit.*, 17; Davidson, *op. cit.*, 338f.; Turpie, *op. cit.*, 190, following Grotius and Drusius. The OT Pesh reads interrogatively; and very possibly the final paragogic ה of אפרתה in the MT (missing in Gen 48:7) was an interrogative ה attached to צעיר in Mt's Semitic text. The wrong connection of ה is very common. See Friedrich Delitzsch, *Die Lese- u. Schreibfehler im A.T.* (Berlin, 1920), 2. J. Kennedy says that the interrogative ה may be omitted and inferred, in some cases the omission being due to the immediate precedence of a final ה, as would be the case here (*op. cit.*, 134).

[3] So the Arabic in Mic 5:2 and LXX[Luc]. C. Heller notes that the OT Pesh often translates a word beginning with ל as if it were preceded by לא (*A Critical Essay on the Palestinian Targum to the Pentateuch* [New York, 1921], 60). צ' להיות is difficult, perhaps poor Hebrew (better: צ' הי'—see J. M. P. Smith, *Mic* [ICC; Edinburgh, 1912], 102), and may have resulted from the identical form in the next clause. לא היית may be read (Hühn, *op. cit.*, 2; Lohmeyer-Schmauch, *op. cit.*, 23, and suggested as early as Cappellus), or לו הית, the *waw* in the defective לו (= לא; cf. I Sam 2:16; 20:2 [MT, LXX] and Job 6:21 [*Qere* Ec 4 MSS Ken]) having been transposed and the ל attached to form להיות (MT) (see H. Hodius, *De Bibliorum Textibus Originalibus* [Oxford, 1705], 257; I. Hoffmann, *Demonstratio Evangelica* [Tübingen, 1773], I, 16; Baumstark, *loc. cit.*).

[4] A suggestion less worthy of acceptance is that צעיר means "greatest" as well as "smallest." So Kidder, *A Demonstration of the Messias*[2] (London, 1726), 22f., following Pocock. Cf. words of medial signification, like ברך, "to bless" and "to curse."

[5] See esp. Edersheim, *Life and Times*, I, 206f.

[6] Reinke, *op. cit.*, III, 341, 371.

[7] See De-Rossi, *ad loc.* The Peshitta is not influenced by Mt, for elsewhere it differs radically, e.g., in דתהוין = "because you are (little)."

II Sam 5:2 (= I Chron 11:2), a verse regarding the throne-right of David. Mt attaches the latter quotation to Mic 5:1 by means of a relative pronoun with a consequent changing of the person of the verb; but otherwise he agrees with both the LXX and the MT.

Mt 2:15: ἐξ Αἰγύπτου ἐκάλεσα τὸν υἱόν μου
Hos 11:1 Aq: ἀπὸ Αἰγύπτου ἐκάλεσα τὸν υἱόν μου
MT: ממצרים קראתי לבני
LXX: ἐξ Αἰγύπτου μετεκάλεσα τὰ τέκνα αὐτοῦ
Targ: וממצרים קריתי להון בנין
Theod: ἐκάλεσα αὐτὸν υἱόν μου
Sym: ἐξ Αἰγύπτου κέκληται υἱός μου

Mt independently translates the MT.[1] Because the quotation is construed with the sojourn in Egypt and the account of the departure from Egypt is not taken up till verse 20, we may render, "Since Egypt" (i.e., from the time he dwelt there[2]). The meaning then becomes that the preservation of Jesus in Egypt showed that God was dealing with him as a father with a son.[3] In the Arabic Gospel of the Infancy this OT text is cited, not concerning Christ's egress from Egypt, but concerning his preservation there from the cruelty of Herod.[4] The OT text means the same for Israel: "When Israel was a child [i.e., during the Egypt-sojourn], then I loved him" (Hos 11:1a).[5]

This is not to say that a reference to egress from Egypt is wholly

---

[1] Allen (*Mt*, 15) and Stendahl (pp. 101, 200) think it possible Mt used an "Ur-Aquila" Greek OT text and stress that only the singular, "son," was useful to him. But Mt and Aquila are alike merely because they both render the MT exactly. And it is hardly significant that only the singular is useful to Mt, when time and again he independently renders the Hebrew apart from hermeneutical motives and where the LXX would suit his purpose. One may even question that the singular is necessary to Mt's use of this text in the light of the concept of corporate personality and the Israel-Christ typology.

[2] For ἐκ in this temporal sense, see A & G, s.v. ἐκ, 5a. Cf. ἐκ κοιλίας μητρός, ἐκ γενετῆς, ἐκ νεότητος, etc.

[3] Among modern commentators J. A. Bengel was the first to advocate this view (*Gnomon*[2] [Tübingen, 1855], 24). It is most cogently argued by C. Taylor, *op. cit.*, 61ff.

[4] B. H. Cowper, *The Apocryphal Gospels*[3] (London, 1870), 178-180.

[5] "From (the land of) Egypt" requires a temporal sense also in Hos 12:10; 13:4; Ezek 23:8; Num 14:19. The following OT commentators advocate the rendering "Since Egypt" in Hos 11:1: K. Marti, *Das Dodekapropheton* (Tübingen, 1904), 85f.; A. Van Hoonacker, *Les douze petits prophètes* (Paris, 1908), 104; J. Lindblom, *Hosea literarisch untersucht* (Åbo, 1928), 100f.; J. Vandervorst, *Introduction aux textes hébreu et grec de l'Ancien Testament* (Malines, 1935), 81.

excluded either in the NT or in the OT.[1] Rather, in both places there is a deliberate play on the double meaning, local and temporal, of the phrase "from Egypt." The emphasis, however, lies on the father-like love and concern which preserved them in Egypt and brought them out again, not upon the departure alone or as such.[2] (In Hos this is made the basis for divine summons away from idolatry).

Because of the following plurals in Hos 11, some commentators emend the text of verse 1 to read plural also.[3] But the singular deserves preference as the more difficult reading, and the singulars in the first part of the verse—"Israel," "child," "him"—require a parallel singular here. The ever-so-frequent בני ישראל facilitated assimilation to the following plurals in the LXX [4] and the Targum. The reference to Israel's infancy occasioned the idea of *naming* Israel God's son in the Targum, the OT Peshitta, and Theodotion. It is enough for our purpose to note that Mt correctly follows the MT.

Mt 2:18	Jer 31(38):15 LXX	MT
φωνὴ ἐν Ῥαμὰ	B φωνὴ ἐν Ῥαμὰ ἠκούσθη	קול ברמה
ἠκούσθη	A φωνὴ ἐν τῇ ὑψηλῇ ἠκούσθη	נשמע
κλαυθμὸς κ.	(also א*Aq Targ Pesh boh eth arab)	נהי בכי
ὀδυρμὸς πολύς·	θρήνου κ. κλαυθμοῦ κ. ὀδορμοῦ·	תמרורים
	B Ῥαχὴλ ἀποκλαιομένη	

---

[1] Cf. Hos 11:5: "They shall not return into the land of Egypt"; see E. Sellin, *Das Zwölfprophetenbuch*[3] (Leipzig, 1930), 112.

[2] Cf. Ex 4:22, 23; Acts 13:17, 18.

[3] So, e.g. Marti, *loc. cit.*; Sellin, *loc. cit.*

[4] It is possible the assimilation had already taken place in the LXX-*Vorlage*. לבניו (= LXX) could have arisen by a mere dittography of the *yodh* written for a *waw*. Ziegler notes many agreements in number between 1QIs^a and the LXX (*JBL*, 78 [1959], 46-50). A further possibility is influence from the parallel passages in Num, where wide disagreements exist: 23:22, singular—LXX^{AF}, plural—MT, LXX^B, OT Pesh, Targums (Old Pal, Jon, Jerus, Onk); 24:8, singular—MT, LXX, plural—OT Pesh, Targums (Old Pal, Jon, Jerus, Onk). Mt 2:15 was referred to Num 24:8 by Theodore of Heraclea and Photius of Constantinople (see J. Reuss [ed.], *Matthäus-Kommentare aus der griechischen Kirche* [= *Texte u. Untersuchungen*, 5. Reihe, Bd. 6; Berlin, 1957], 60, 272); and a scribe actually adds a note in Codex Sinaiticus that refers the reader to Num (see McNeile, *Mt*, 18). Therefore, the possibility of a traditional association of the OT passages and resultant parallel influence is heightened. On the attempt to relate Mt to Num, esp. by the old defenders of the LXX, see Hody, *op. cit.*, 246. Lindars suggests that αὐτόν in Num 24:8 (LXX) refers not to Jacob, but to ἄνθρωπος (= Messiah) in verse 7, and that Mt interpreted Hos 11:1 with this understanding and association in mind (Lindars, 217).

'Ραχὴλ κλαίουσα	AℵQV 'Ραχὴλ ἀποκλαιομένης	רחל מבכה
	Bℵ *om*	
τὰ τέκνα αὐτῆς	A ἐπὶ τῶν υἱῶν αὐτῆς	על בניה
	B οὐκ ἤθελεν	
καὶ οὐκ ἤθελεν	Aℵ*rell* καὶ οὐκ ἤθελεν	מאנה
	Bℵ παύσασθαι ἐπὶ τοῖς υἱοῖς αὐτῆς	להנחם
παρακληθῆναι	A παρακληθῆναι	על בניה
ὅτι οὐκ εἰσίν	ὅτι οὐκ εἰσίν	כי איננו
κλαυθμός ℵB1*pc*latt syr^{pesh}cop] *pr* θρῆνος καί DW f13 28 565 700 *pl* syr$^{sin, cur}$ (= assimilation to LXX)		

In understanding רמה as a place-name, Mt agrees with the MT and LXX^{B} against LXX^{A}.[1] By rendering the expressions of sorrow as nominative appositions to φωνή, Mt follows more literally the MT than does the LXX, with its genitives of apposition.[2] Furthermore, the LXX takes תמרורים ("bitterness") as another apposition, whereas it is really a noun in construct relationship with an adjectival force. Mt renders somewhat loosely, but correctly, with an intensifying πολύς.[3] Differing in simplex versus complex and active voice versus middle, Mt and LXX^{B} nevertheless agree in regarding the participle as in apposition to the nominative φωνή against LXX^{A}, which puts the participle in apposition to the genitives denoting sorrow. Against LXX^{B}, which omits, Mt renders the first על בניה, as does LXX^{A}, but not so literally as LXX^{A}, for Mt has no ἐπί for על, and his τέκνα, though very frequent in the LXX for בנים, is not so close as υἱῶν (LXX^{A}). Mt and LXX^{A} agree against the MT and LXX^{B} in the insertion of καί before οὐκ ἤθελεν. It is probable that the Semitic *Vorlage* of Mt and the LXX contained the *waw* [4] and that LXX^{B} was assimilated to the MT. Mt goes again

[1] Some would emend the MT from בְּרָמָה to בָּרָמָה. See J. Simons, *The Geographical and Topographical Texts of the OT* (Leiden, 1959), 446.

[2] Strictly speaking, it looks as if Mt transposes נהי and בכי, or works from a text in which they are transposed. Κλαυθμός and בכי = "weeping." 'Οδυρμός and נהי = "lamentation." (Θρῆνος [LXX = "dirge"] is even closer to נהי.) But perhaps Mt considered his two words as synonyms for Hebrew synonyms.

[3] Lohmeyer suggests Mt read רב before בכי, but then Mt has no equivalent for תמרורים (Lohmeyer-Schmauch, *op. cit.*, 29, n. 1). Πικρός would have answered more closely to the Hebrew.

[4] The OT Pesh contains the *waw*. Insertion and deletion of the *waw* is common in Hebrew MSS. See Friedrich Delitzsch, *op. cit.*, 85f.; Würthwein, *op. cit.*, 74; M. Burrows, *JBL*, 68 (1949), 209; M. Greenberg, *JAOS*, 76 (1956), 159; L. Delekat, *Biblica*, 38 (1957), 190f.; W. H. Brownlee, *The*

with LXX^A against LXX^B in omitting the second על בניה and in rendering by παρακληθῆναι. As in the insertion of the καί, the OT Peshitta agrees with LXX^A and Mt. Finally, Mt agrees with the LXX and the other versions in reading אֵינָם ("they are not") for the senseless אֵינֶנּוּ ("he is not") of the MT.[1] It may be that מ was confused with נו;[2] but another possibility shortly to be discussed also exists.

With the exceptions of καί, οὐκ εἰσίν, and the omission of the second על בניה, Mt appears to have rendered the MT independently. The first two exceptions doubtless represent variants in the Hebrew text, as noted above. The probability is the same in the third exception. The second על בניה is rejected by almost all modern OT commentators.[3] Certainly the fact that Septuagintal MSS differ on the position of the phrase but agree with the support of the OT Peshitta on its single occurrence favors omission in the original Hebrew; for in view of the clear signs of assimilation to the Hebrew in differing MSS of the LXX,[4] one would have expected the phrase to appear a second time had it been present in the Hebrew exemplars.

Streane suggests the phrase was accidentally omitted in a Hebrew MS and subsequently inserted from the margin in different places in two copies.[5] This would account for the different positions yet single occurrence in MSS of the LXX.[6] Torrey thinks a variant בנה ("her son") existed for בניה ("her sons"). This variant was accompanied by איננו ("he is not"), the present reading of the MT. To preserve the variant, the guardians of textual tradition inserted a

---

Text of Habakkuk in the Ancient Commentary from Qumran (Philadelphia, 1959), 4.

[1] P. Volz claims that the MT gives good sense, translating, "kein einziger ist mehr da!" (*Studien zum Text des Jeremia* [Leipzig, 1920], 232f.). But the translation is questionable.

[2] J. J. O'Rourke, *CBQ*, 24 (1962), 396.

[3] A. W. Streane, *The Double Text of Jer* (Cambridge, 1896), 214f.; B. Duhm, *Jer* (Tübingen, 1901), 248; C. H. Cornill, *Die metrischen Stücke des Buches Jer* (Leipzig, 1901), 29; *idem, Jer* (Leipzig, 1905), 337; H. Schmidt, *Die grossen Propheten* (Göttingen, 1915), 353. Again Volz defends the MT, suggesting the versions did not appreciate the meter (*loc. cit.*; *idem, Jer*² [Leipzig, 1928], 281). Others strike out the words on metrical grounds!

[4] Esp. ἐν τῇ ὑψηλῇ in LXX^Aℵ* (so also Aq).

[5] *Loc. cit.*

[6] Or the scribe of B might have omitted the phrase, caught his error, and inserted it after παύσασθαι—or put it in the margin, from which it was subsequently inserted in the wrong place.

second על בניה to prevent loss of בניה in the face of איננו. That is, lest the singular "he is not" suppress the plural "her sons," the plural was repeated to insure its preservation.[1]

The differences between LXX^A and LXX^B (ὑψηλῇ—Ῥαμά; ἀποκλαιομένης—ἀποκλαιομένη; ἐπὶ τῶν υἱῶν αὐτῆς—ἐπὶ τοῖς υἱοῖς αὐτῆς [*post* παύσ.]; καί—. . .; παρακληθῆναι—παύσασθαι) and the vacillation of Cod. א between A and B suggest we are dealing with distinct Greek textual traditions somewhat based on variants in the Hebrew, since neither A nor B nor א agrees with the MT. Yet it is difficult not to feel that A, B, and א stem from the same translation, because their common θρήνου καὶ κλαυθμοῦ καὶ ὀδυρμοῦ would hardly have been arrived at by independent translators. One is therefore compelled by the lack of pattern in the Septuagintal variants to see pre-hexaplaric assimilation of the LXX to Hebrew MSS which differed among themselves.

Mt is far closer to A than to B.[2] Nevertheless, he still is far distant from A: Ῥαμά (Mt)—ὑψηλῇ (A); the expressions of grief; κλαίουσα (Mt)—ἀποκλαιομένης (A); τὰ τέκνα (Mt)—ἐπὶ τῶν υἱῶν (A). Mt and LXX^A, therefore, represent independent renderings of the same Hebrew text.[3]

Mt 2:23: ὅπως πληρωθῇ τὸ ῥηθὲν διὰ τῶν προφητῶν ὅτι Ναζωραῖος κληθήσεται
Is 11:1 LXX: καὶ ἄνθος ἐκ τῆς ῥίζης ἀναβήσεται
MT: ונצר משרשיו יפרה
Jdg 13:5 LXX: ὅτι ναζὶρ θεοῦ ἔσται
MT: כי נזיר אלהים יהיה
ναζίρ B] ἡγιασμένον ναζιραίον A; ναζιραίον Luc
See also Jdg 13:7; 16:17.

This is a quotation of substance quite in accord with rabbinical and classical style.[4] But the exact OT reference, if such there be,[5] is a much-mooted question.

---

[1] Torrey, *Documents*, 51.

[2] Stendahl ascribes the coincidences of Mt and LXX^A to the latter's hexaplaric character (p. 102; cf. Lagrange, *Mt*, 35; Torrey, *Documents*, 51-53). This cannot be so, however, because none of Mt's agreements with A against B agree with the MT. Παρακληθῆναι in A is probably influence from the NT, since the usual Septuagintal rendering of "to comfort" is "to cease" and since παρακληθῆναι appears in the margin of B.

[3] Οὐκ εἰσίν is Greek style, so that no relationship between Mt and the LXX is here necessary. See Klostermann, *Mt*, 18, who cites Herodotus, iii. 65.

[4] Strack-Billerbeck, *op. cit.*, I, 92f.; F. Johnson, *op. cit.*, 103-110.

[5] Euthymius Zig., following Chrysostom, refers to a lost prophecy (MPG CXXIX, 156). J. A. Fitzmyer notes similarly indefinite citations in Qumran literature and improbably suggests references to non-canonical literature (*op. cit.*, 304).

The quotation has been referred to passages where נצר, "to keep, preserve," occurs: Ex 34:6 f.; Ps 31:24; Is 42:6; 49:6.[1] The first two passages are non-Messianic, non-prophetic general statements concerning divine preservation of the godly. In the verse from the Servant-song in Is 42 the form of the verb (ואצרך) contains no *nun* and consequently provides no phonetic contact with Ναζωραῖος. In Is 49:6 the term is plural (נצירי) and refers to the preserved remnant of Israel *as distinguished from* the Servant who restores them.[2] Besides, Mt has already emphasized the idea of preservation in the narrative of the flight to Egypt and in the quotation of Hos 11:1; the emphasis here lies on *residence* in Nazareth, not on preservation there.[3]

E. Zolli suggests a reference to the נצרים in Jer 31:6 f., the watchmen who shout glad tidings of Israel's salvation. Christ and Christians are bearers of glad tidings of salvation.[4] Again, no relationship with Jesus' residence in Nazareth exists. And the OT passage can hardly be stretched to refer to an individual Messiah, not even with an appeal to corporate personality.

H. Smith favors a reference to נזיר in Lam 4:7, the only place the word is used without the technical meaning "Nazirite." Here the LXX has Ναζειραῖοι, the Vulgate *Nazaraei*. Tertullian connects this verse with the name of Jesus.[5] Eusebius similarly connects Mt 2:23 with נזר in Lev 21:12.[6] Therefore, Mt's idea is that Jesus was holy and consecrated.[7] Yet again, one misses any connection with the NT context. And in Lam the word may mean "nobles" or "Nazirites" (note also the plural).

A more popular view is that Mt refers to נזיר in Jdg 13:5, 7; 16:17, concerning Samson.[8] Jesus is then the Consecrated or Holy

---

[1] Cf. H. A. W. Meyer, *op. cit.*, I, 98, who cites Riggenbach, *Stud. u. Krit.* (1885), 606f.; P. Benoit, *RB*, 66 (1959), 440f.; G. H. Box, *The Virgin Birth of Jesus* (London, 1916), 31; Lindars, 195.

[2] Doubtful is the syntax which would yield, "It is too light a thing that thou shouldst be my Servant to raise up the tribes of Jacob, and (shouldst be) the Nazarean to restore Israel."

[3] Also against N. Walker, *NTS*, 9 (1963), 392f.

[4] *ZNW*, 49 (1958), 135f.

[5] *Adv. Marc.* iv. 8.

[6] MPG XXII, 548f.

[7] H. Smith, *JTS*, 28 (1927), 60.

[8] See, e.g., Loisy, *op. cit.*, I, 376; C. Guignebert, *Jésus* (Paris, 1947), 88f.; S. Lyonnet, *Biblica*, 25 (1944), 196-206, who traces Jerome's shift to this view; J. S. Kennard, Jr., *JBL*, 65 (1946), 132f. Cf. the calling of Samuel a Nazirite in 4QSam (F. M. Cross, Jr., *BASOR*, 132 [1953], 18).

One (cf. Mk 1:24 f.; Lk 1:35; Jn 6:69; Acts 4:27).[1] H. H. Schaeder arrives at this view by arguing that since Mt writes for Greek readers, a play on Hebrew words would mean nothing. Hence, the reference must be to ναζιραῖον in Jdg LXX^{ALuc}.[2] But in Mt 1:21 the significance of Ἰησοῦς (from the root ישע) is not evident on the purely Greek level. That Mt's readers were limited to Greek cannot be demonstrated. In fact, the presumption is otherwise if they were Jews, as is generally thought. Even monoglottic Greek-speakers must have understood the significance of such outstanding Christian terms as Ἰησοῦς, Ἐμμανουήλ, Χριστός, and Ναζωραῖος. F. C. Burkitt arrives at this view on the basis of the usual transliteration of צ by σ and ז by ζ.[3] However, numerous exceptions to this rule exist in the LXX;[4] and the reverse process, צ for ζ, occurs in syr$^{sin, cur, pesh}$, substantiated by the Arabic writing of the name and the Talmud.[5]

E. Schweizer also argues that the conjunction of "Nazarene" and "Holy One of God" in Mk 1:24 betrays an association with the Samson story, where the LXX tradition has both ναζιραῖος and ἅγιος θεοῦ for נזיר אלהים (Jdg 13:5, 7; 16:17).[6] But "Holy One of God" is simply a variant for "Son of God" (cf. Jn 6:69 with Mt 16:16; Jn 10:36; Lk 1:32, 35) and forms a contrast with the "unclean spirit"; i.e., the designation is motivated by immediate context rather than by derivation from the double textual tradition of the LXX in Jdg. The term "Nazarene" is a slurring, perhaps contemptuous reference by the Capernaum demoniac to Jesus' coming from the neighboring rival village of Nazareth.

Under the above view one would have expected Ναζιραῖος, exactly as in LXX^{ALuc} of Jdg and in conformity with the Hebrew

---

[1] K. Furrer adds that Mt sees Jesus as one living apart in a secluded town (*Die Bedeutung der biblischen Geographie für die biblische Exegese* [Zürich, 1870], 15f.). This suggestion at least attempts to relate to the NT context, but it loses contact with the religious rather than geographical signification of נזיר.

[2] *TWNT*, IV, 883.

[3] *The Syriac Forms of NT Proper Names* (London, 1912), 16f., 28ff.

[4] For slightly differing lists, *ibid.*; Schaeder, *op. cit.*, 884; Burkitt succeeds in robbing some examples of their significance, but not all. G. F. Moore notes that Burkitt's list might be expanded by taking account of a greater variety of Septuagintal MSS and some striking instances in Josephus (in *The Beginnings of Christianity*, I, 427).

[5] *Ibid.*; Zahn, *Mt*, 12, n. 18.

[6] In *Judentum, Urchristentum, Kirche* (J. Jeremias *Festschrift*; Berlin, 1960), 90-93.

vowel sound. Nor does there appear to be any deeper connection with Jesus' residence in Nazareth than the similarity in sound between the words. But the most serious objection is that in conduct Jesus was anything but a Nazirite (Mt 11:19; Lk 7:34),[1] so that it is doubtful he would have become designated thus at an early date.

A view that has gained much favor is that the name came from a pre-Christian sect, probably to be equated with the Mandaeans (cf. the pre-Christian Νασαραῖοι in Epiphanius, *Haer.* xxix. 6 [2]), and that the name was mediated through John the Baptist and his sect, who were related to the Mandaeans. The philological argument is that the Mandaean self-designation נצוראייא cannot depend on the Syriac, which would come to נָצְרָיָא, and that Ναζωραιος cannot come from נֵצֶר or Ναζαρέθ. Therefore, Ναζωραιος stems from נצוראייא, and perhaps Mk's preference for the latinized Ναζαρηνός is motivated by a desire to dissociate Christianity from the sect of John the Baptist. But how then do we account for *reversion* to Ναζωρ- in later writing ,when the association with John the Baptist was still felt (cf. Jn 1-3)?

The use of "Nazareth" in formulae of exorcism (Acts 3:6; 4:10) has been pressed into service for this view. But the healing of the lame man in Acts 3 and 4 is the only incident in which Ναζωραῖος is so used, and there appears to be no exorcism as such, but a simple healing. Furthermore, in these rubrics the stress lies on "Jesus Christ." "Christ" emphasizes Jesus' office, and Ναζωραῖος is merely a place-name to distinguish Jesus from other bearers of that com-

---

[1] It is a weak answer to generalize the specific concept of "Nazirite" into the thought of holiness (so Guignebert, *loc. cit.*; Kennard, *op .cit.*, 133f.). Burkitt's suggestion that Jesus was nicknamed as an odd sort of Nazirite who called for repentance, yet ate and drank like other people, does not explain why such a nickname should have been attached to Jesus in the first place in spite of his conduct (*Syriac Forms*, 17).

[2] MPG XLI, 400. W. Bousset thinks Epiphanius' Νασαραῖοι were taken from a catalog of sects known in the second century to Justin and to Hegesippus and in the fourth century to Ephraem of Syria and to the *Apostolic Constitutions*. Bousset supposes that the list was of Jewish origin and that Νασαραῖοι was an exact transliteration of nāṣrājē, by which were meant the Christians—but in taking over the list the Christians did not realize they themselves were meant (*Theologische Rundschau*, 14 [1911], 373-385). M. Black presents the view that the Νασαραῖοι are merely the Samaritans or a group of them referred to by their Aramaic name (cf. נטר and שמר) and that the opprobrious use of Ναζωραῖος for Christians (whatever the derivation of the term) was intended to suggest Christians were in a class with the Samaritans (cf. Jn 8:48) (*BJRL*, 41 [1958/59], 285-303).

mon personal name, just as in other passages where exorcism is certainly not in view [1] and the meaning is equivalent to ἀπὸ Ναζαρέθ (and Ναζαρηνός).[2]

The Mandaean name is supposed to come from the root נצר or נטר ("to guard, observe") and to have been used of the sect because of their observance of certain rites and customs.[3] Recent enquiries have established the pre-Christian origin of Mandaeanism,[4] and the recent acquisition and publication by Lady E. S. Drower of a Mandaean document which contains a tradition that the Mandaeans migrated from Palestine to Mesopotamia under King Artabanus (the third, c. A.D. 12-38) will doubtless lend momentum to the above-outlined view.[5]

It must be pointed out, however, that a pre-Christian origin of the Mandaeans, their residence in or around Palestine about the time Christianity arose, and obvious contacts between Mandaean tradition and Christian tradition do not establish an organic relationship between the two movements or the precedence of the Mandaean in their points of contact. In the gospels neither the adherents of John the Baptist nor the disciples of Jesus are called "Nazarenes." Only later do we hear of a sect of "Nazarenes" (Acts 24:5).[6] Were there a connection between the Mandaeans and John the Baptist, we should have expected in Mandaean literature much more historical and legendary material about John than that about his birth and his baptizing Jesus, which is all we have and

---

[1] Mt 26:71; Mk 10:47; Lk 18:37; 24:19; Jn 18:5, 7; 19:19; Acts 2:22; 6:14; 22:8.

[2] Moore, in *Beginnings of Christianity*, I, 428, gives examples of the Jewish practice of putting place-names with personal names. See also Schlatter, *op. cit.*, 49.

[3] Or because they were "keepers of the mysteries." So H. Zimmern, *ZDMG*, 74 (1920), 429f., who relates this to Babylonian esotericism. Since early Christianity was not esoteric, this view has not gained general acceptance.

[4] For literature, see Cullmann, *Christology*, 27.

[5] E. S. Drower, *The Haran Gawaita and the Baptism of Hībil-Ziwa* (The Vatican, 1953); notice by R. Macuch, *TLZ*, 82 (1957), 401-408. In favor of this view generally, see Lidzbarski, *Ginza*, pp. ixf.; *idem, Mandäische Liturgien* (Göttingen, 1920), pp. xvif.; Reitzenstein-Schaeder, *op. cit.*, 308; R. Bultmann, *ZNW*, 24 (1925), 100ff.; *idem, Jesus and the Word* (London, 1935), 24; Black, *Aramaic Approach*, 144-146; O. Cullmann, *The Earliest Christian Confessions* (London, 1949), 24, n. 3; *idem, Christology*, 27; B. Gärtner, *Die rätselhaften Termini Nazoräer u. Iskariot* (Lund, 1957), 25ff.; Lohmeyer-Schmauch, *op. cit.*, 32f.

[6] See O. Michel, *RGG*², IV, 475.

which can easily derive from NT tradition.[1] The Arabic form of John's name in Mandaean literature points to the Islamic period.[2] That the oldest tractates in *Ginza* are polytheistic, that the eminent names in Judaism came to them orally as foreign words (evident from the fact the names are read incorrectly in Mandaean literature), and that they apparently did not observe the sabbath, circumcise, turn toward Jerusalem in prayer, or offer animal sacrifices militate against their being a Jewish sect out of which Christianity could have arisen.[3] Mandaeanism was very syncretistic; and it is possible that in order to secure status under the rule of Moslems, who regarded as pagans those who could not produce a sacred book and a prophet, the Mandaeans adopted the name by which Christians were known to Moslems.[4] One may also ask how the name "observers" came to be applied to Jesus and his followers, when throughout the gospels they are accused of flouting the law and the traditions —this in contrast with the disciples of John, as noticed by John's disciples themselves and by the Pharisees and as admitted publicly by Jesus (Mt 9:14; 11:18 f.; Mk 2:18; Lk 5:33; 7:33 f.). H. M. Shires notes that in Mandaean literature "Nazarene" is used variously for Mandaeans in good standing, apostates (including those who have accepted Christianity), and Christians. Thus, evidence exists that the Mandaeans themselves were conscious of the Christian derivation of the name.[5]

Nor is the philological obstacle to derivation of Ναζωραιος from Ναζαρεθ, Lidzbarski's strongest argument, insuperable. The accent does not lie on the syllable in question; and substitution of the o-sound for the a-sound was frequent in Talmudic literature and in the Greek OT, especially in proper names.[6]

[1] See Dodd, *The Interpretation of the Fourth Gospel*, 123.

[2] Brandt, in Hastings' *Encyclopaedia of Religion and Ethics*, VIII, 380.

[3] *Ibid.*, 380, 385.

[4] So S. A. Pallis, *Mandaean Studies* (London, from the Danish edition of 1919), 161. In the Book of John, XXII, 86, 4-6, the Moslems ask the Mandaeans, "Who is thy prophet?" Mandaeans were willing under pressure to profess themselves Christians with mental reservations (*Ginza*, I, 199, p. 29).

[5] *Anglican Theological Review*, 29 (1947), 24.

[6] See R. Payne Smith, *The Authenticity and Messianic Interpretation of the Prophecies of Is* (Oxford, 1862), 80f.; Schlatter, *op. cit.*, 50; Moore, *Beginnings of Christianity*, I, 427ff.; W. F. Albright, *JBL*, 65 (1946), 397-401; G. Dalman, *Grammatik des jüdisch-palästinischen Aramäisch*^{2} (Leipzig, 1905), 178; Schaeder, *TWNT*, IV, 882 (a list of examples in which *omega* stands for the vocal *shewa* in Greek transliteration in the LXX, Aq, Sym, and the Hexapla).

It is sometimes urged that a town Nazareth did not even exist in NT times, since the name does not occur in the OT, Josephus, or the Talmud and Midrash.[1] However, the rabbis remark on the fact that many of the chief cities in Galilee of the first and second centuries A.D. were not mentioned in the OT. Josephus names almost exclusively places which figured in the war of A.D. 66. The Talmuds and the Midrashim mention chiefly places where rabbinical schools after the war under Hadrian were located and home-towns of rabbis.[2] "Nazareth" does occur in two synagogue poems by Ḳalir, whose source seems to have been a list of the priestly courses with the places where the priests settled, probably after the Hadrianic war.[3] A good deal of NT tradition has to be rejected for no reason at all if the claim that Nazareth was non-existent is accepted. The matter now seems settled by the very recent discovery of an early Caesarean inscription in Hebrew mentioning Nazareth.[4]

We therefore fall back on the old view that Ναζωραῖος denotes one ἀπὸ Ναζαρέθ, that the designation came to be used contemptuously,[5] and that Mt related it to the honorific Messianic title נצר in Is 11:1 (perhaps in connection with Messianic צמח-passages—Is 4:2; Jer 23:5; 33:15; Zech 3:8; 6:12) with emphasis on the lowliness and contemptibility out of which Jesus appeared.[6] This lowliness is portrayed in the lowly stump of David and in various prophetic passages (Ps 22, Is 53, Zech 9, 11, 12)—hence the plural διὰ τῶν προφητῶν. That is, the various prophetic allusions to Messiah's humble appearance are, so to speak, concentrated in the thought of נצר, from which Mt derives נצרת.[7] The plural προφητῶν must point

---

[1] E.g., Burkitt, *The Syriac Forms of NT Proper Names*, 17.

[2] See Moore, in *Beginnings of Christianity*, I, 429.

[3] Moore, *Judaism*, III, 93.

[4] *Christian News from Israel*, 14 (July, 1963), 12. See also M. Avi-Yonah, *Bible et Terre Sainte*, 61 (1964), 2-5 (unavailable to me).

[5] Cf. Jn 7:52: Μὴ καὶ σὺ ἐκ τῆς Γαλιλαίας εἶ; ἐραύνησον καὶ ἴδε ὅτι ἐκ τῆς Γαλιλαίας (ὁ P^{66}) προφήτης οὐκ ἐγείρεται; and 1:46: Ἐκ Ναζαρὲθ δύναταί τι ἀγαθὸν εἶναι; (although this latter question may be due to local rivalry between Cana and Nazareth rather than to an especially bad reputation of Nazareth)—also Mt 26:73, concerning Galilean pronunciation, ridiculed by Judaeans. Cf. also Black's view, above, p. 100, n. 2.

[6] Note the thought of contempt in Is 14:19: "But thou art cast out of thy grave like an abominable branch."

[7] So also "eruditi Hebraei," according to Jerome on Is 11:1. P. Winter would derive נצרת from נצר, "to keep watch," on the basis of the town's position on a hill (*NTS*, 3 [1956/57], 138f.).

to the general tenor of the prophets, for elsewhere in the Matthaean fulfilment-quotations Isaianic passages are always identified as such (except in 1:23, where the quotation is reported as that of the angel; 'Ησαΐου is present in D *pc* it syr$^{sin, cur}$).[1] In the remaining, "prophet" is always in the singular.[2, 3]

It has long been recognized that Is 11:1 received a Messianic interpretation in the Targum and rabbinical literature. In the latter, "Branch"-passages are interpreted as meaning the Messiah will come out of obscurity and a low estate.[4] The matter stands in even clearer light since the discovery of the Qumran scrolls, in which there is a strong נצר-motif.[5] Of great significance is *The Nezer and the Submission in Suffering Hymn from the Dead Sea Scrolls* edited by M. Wallenstein.[6] Here we find the combination of נצר with the thoughts of lowliness, despisedness, and suffering—with a clear allusion in line 6 to Is 11:1. The theme epitomized in line 30, "I thus became the [des]pised," is developed throughout the hymn. Thus, Mt builds his citation upon the נצר = lowliness motif as well as upon phonetic similarity. In Jesus' growing up in Nazareth there is both an outer correspondence to Is 11:1 and related passages in the place-name, based on נצר, and an inner correspondence in the obscurity of such a place as the Messiah's home-town.[7]

---

[1] 3:3; 4:14; 8:17; 12:17; 13:14; 15:7.

[2] Zahn finds ὅπως (instead of ἵνα) and the absence of λεγόντων significant. He also interprets ὅτι as causal, on the assumption it cannot introduce an indirect quotation (*Introduction*, II, 539, 568; *Mt*, 112-117). But it is doubtful the ancients made a sharp distinction between direct and indirect quotations.

[3] Προφητῶν has also been taken as a reference to the part of the OT canon so designated. But then Mt would surely have written ἐν τοῖς προφηταῖς, as in Jn 6:45 and Acts 13:40. The one case in point is Acts 15:15: καὶ τούτῳ συμφωνοῦσιν οἱ λόγοι τῶν προφητῶν, καθὼς γέγραπται. But perhaps there the quotation is to be considered one example from among other pertinent OT passages. V. Burch (*Testimonies*, II, 63) and Hunt (*op. cit.*, 163) conjecture προφητῶν is a name for the Testimony Book. H. J. Holtzmann (*Die Synoptiker*[3] [Tübingen, 1901], 194) and Bacon (*Studies in Mt*, 164) say that Mt simply did not know the origin of the citation—a very unlikely assumption, in view of his other citations of Is by name.

[4] See Strack-Billerbeck, *op. cit.*, I, 93-96.

[5] See the Hodayoth (VI, 15; VII, 19; VIII, 6, 8, 10); Gärtner, *op. cit.*, 23f.; 4QpIsa^{a}—J. M. Allegro, *JBL*, 75 (1956), 180.

[6] (Istanbul, 1957).

[7] Stendahl stresses the apologetic motive behind Mt's defense of Jesus' coming from Nazareth (in *Judentum, Urchristentum, Kirche* [J. Jeremias *Festschrift*; Berlin, 1960], 94-100).

Mt 4:15, 16	Is 8:23; 9:1 MT	LXX
γῆ Ζαβουλὼν	ארצה זבלון	χώρα Ζαβουλών
καὶ γῆ Νεφθαλίμ	וארצה נפתלי	ἡ γῆ Νεφθαλίμ
	והאחרון הכביד	ὁδὸν θαλάσσης
ὁδὸν θαλάσσης	דרך הים	καὶ οἱ λοιποὶ οἱ τὴν παραλίαν κατοικοῦντες
πέραν τοῦ Ἰορδάνου	עבר הירדן	καὶ πέραν τοῦ Ἰορδάνου
Γαλιλαία τῶν ἐθνῶν	גליל הגוים	Γαλιλαία τῶν ἐθνῶν τὰ μέρη τῆς Ἰουδαίας
ὁ λαὸς ὁ καθήμενος	העם ההלכים	ὁ λαὸς ὁ πορευόμενος
ἐν σκοτίᾳ	בחשך	ἐν σκότει
φῶς εἶδεν μέγα	ראו אור גדול	ἴδετε φῶς μέγα
καὶ τοῖς καθημένοις ἐν	ישבי בארץ	οἱ κατοικοῦντες ἐν χώρᾳ
χώρᾳ κ. σκιᾷ θανάτου	צלמות	καὶ σκιᾷ θανάτου
φῶς ἀνέτειλεν αὐτοῖς	אור נגה עליהם	φῶς λάμψει ἐφ' ὑμᾶς

τοῖς καθημένοις] οἱ -οι D it syr sah
καί] *om* D (= assimilation to LXX^{B}א*)

Cf. Lk 1:78, 79: . . . ἐπισκέψεται ἡμᾶς ἀνατολὴ ἐξ ὕψους, ἐπιφᾶναι τοῖς ἐν σκότει καὶ σκιᾷ θανάτου καθημένοις

ὁδὸν θαλ. Aא^{ca}Q] *om* Bא*V LucC sah syh
κατοικ. 1° Aא^{ca}QThdt] *om* Bא*Vsyh LucC (*sub obelo* Q)
Γαλιλαία] *pr* τὰ μέρη τῆς Γαλιλαίας Luc
τὰ μέρη τῆς Ἰουδ. AQ] *om* BVsyhLucC
πορ.] καθήμενος A
ἴδετε] εἶδεν LucCא^{c}
καὶ σκιᾷ 965Aא^{c}QC] *om* καί Bא*; σκιᾶς Luc

Where the LXX prefers the synonyms χώρα and γῆ for the same Hebrew word (ארצה), Mt more literally renders twice with γῆ. Yet contact with the LXX is seen in the final *mu* of Νεφθαλίμ. The LXX has vaguely understood האחרון ("at the last") as from אחר ("to be after, stay behind") and so renders by οἱ λοιποί, perhaps reading אחרים. Thereby the LXX-translator is left in the embarrassing position of being unable to render הכביד, which he omits. Mt leaves out this whole phrase as irrelevant to his purpose. He wishes to string together all the geographical terms in unbroken succession to emphasize the specifically geographical fulfilment, as further shown by the complete lack of grammatical relationship between the list and the rest of the quotation. In the MT the geographical terms are in accusative relationship to the preceding part of the verse, unquoted by Mt. In the LXX they are vocatives; Mt makes out of them an absolute construction.

Though accepted by Rahlfs and Ziegler,[1] ὁδὸν θαλάσσης in LXX^{AQ}א^{ca} appears to be an awkward insertion from the NT—

[1] Ziegler, however, vacillates (*Is*, 67).

awkward because it should follow οἱ λοιποί, since דרך הים follows והאחרון. Furthermore, in LXX^AQℵca^ דרך הים is later translated in its proper position by οἱ τὴν παραλίαν κατοικοῦντες, the looseness of the rendering speaking for its genuineness (Lagarde's second canon).[1] Were ὁδὸν θαλάσσης original, then, the translator would have skipped over והאחרון הכביד, rendered דרך הים, gone back to והאחרון הכביד, and finally returned to render דרך הים a second time. This is hardly probable. It may also be significant that a note in the margin of LXX^Q^ says, τίνες οὐκ ἔχ[ουσιν] ὁδὸν θαλάσσης. Therefore, just as LXX^A^'s καθήμενος in the next verse represents assimilation to the NT [2] and as the gloss τὰ μέρη τῆς Ἰουδαίας betrays the hand of a Christian scribe,[3] so also does ὁδὸν θαλάσσης. The Matthaean use of ὁδόν for דרך as a preposition meaning "toward" is Hebraistic, but already established in the LXX.[4] Hence, there is no necessity to see contact between Mt and Aquila and Theodotion at this point.[5]

Mt omits the LXX's καί before πέραν, also missing in the MT and the OT Peshitta. However, he follows the contemporization Γαλιλαία in the LXX for גליל ("circuit, region," but always specifically of a district in northern Palestine).[6] Mt again omits the expressions in LXX^AQLuc^ which contain τὰ μέρη and for which the Hebrew has no equivalent.

In ὁ καθήμενος Mt either anticipates τοῖς καθημένοις or works from a different text, a conjecture suggested by Lk's τοῖς καθημένοις. One may perhaps see parallel influence in Mt (and Lk) or in his Greek or Hebrew *Vorlage* from Ps 107 (106):10, where the LXX has καθημένους ἐν σκότει καὶ σκιᾷ θανάτου and the MT ישבי חשך וצלמות.[7] The singular participle agrees with the LXX against the MT, but this is probably due to stylistic considerations in the Greek: οἱ καθήμενοι would have been awkward after ὁ λαός.

Mt and LXX^LucCℵc^ agree in εἶδεν against the second person

---

[1] The whole expression comes by parallel influence from Ezek 25:16 LXX. Seeligmann, *op. cit.*, 74, 80f.

[2] Ziegler (ed.), *Is*, 27.

[3] Toy, *op. cit.*, 26. Q^mg^ εν αλλ[οις] ου κειται τα μερη της ιουδαιας.

[4] A & G, s.v. ὁδός; Bl-D § 161:1. The parallelism with עבר-πέραν shows דרך-ὁδόν is a preposition, not a noun referring to the Damascus-Mediterranean caravan route. The meaning "toward the Mediterranean," i.e., the western side of the Galilean circuit, is to be preferred.

[5] Against Wellhausen, *Mt*, 11.

[6] Cf. Seeligmann, *loc. cit.*, Aq θινας (-νες Pr.); Sym οριον.

[7] So Anger, I, 29; II, 4, 25, 29.

plural imperative of the LXX^{rell} (= the pointing רְאוּ) and the third person plural perfect of the MT. It may be doubted, however, that Mt works from an Ur-Lucianic text, for he goes against Lucian by omitting Lucian's τὰ μέρη τῆς Γαλιλαίας and he disagrees with Lucian's genitive σκιᾶς. Lucian may be influenced by Mt in εἶδεν; or he may merely be improving the style of the LXX, in which the plural ἴδετε is somewhat harsh after ὁ λαός.

In φῶς εἶδεν μέγα the emphatic word order of Mt disagrees with both the MT and the LXX. The reading οἱ καθήμενοι in the Western text of Mt is assimilation to the LXX. Καθημένοις renders ישבי more literally than κατοικοῦντες (LXX). Mt agrees with the LXX in χώρᾳ; but inasmuch as Mt had rendered with γῆ twice before, he must have been searching for a synonym. Since, then, χώρα is frequent in the LXX for ארץ, he need not have been following the LXX here. Καί (for which the MT has no equivalent) σκιᾷ θανάτου (for צלמות, which is in construct relationship with בארץ) looks like certain dependence on the LXX$^{965AQ\aleph c}$. But closer examination casts doubt on the matter, for it is possible that the Hebrew *Vorlage* of Mt and the LXX read וצלם מות, from which a fusion of the two words was made and the *waw* dropped of necessity, or that the present text was read in this manner.[1] If so, Mt and the LXX may agree merely because they both render the Hebrew according to the common understanding.[2]

'Ανατολή in the Lucan allusion and דנח in the OT Peshitta may point to a common textual tradition behind Mt's ἀνέτειλεν,[3] which like דנח can mean "to shine brightly" [4] as well as "to rise, dawn". The LXX stands closer to the MT with λάμψει and also in ἐφ' (for

---

[1] The vowels of צַלְמָוֶת show it was considered to be compounded from צֵלֶם + מָוֶת. The original form was probably צַלְמוּת (see Koehler-Baumgartner, s.v.).

[2] Also possible is assimilation of these MSS of the LXX to the NT. A. L. Williams thinks σκιᾶς (LXX^{Luc}) is original, and that the final ς dropped out, necessitating the insertion of καί (*The Pulpit Commentary, Mt* [London, 1898], I, 108). On the other hand, the addition of καί and the change of σκιᾷ to the genitive are two different ways of overcoming the difficulty of the Greek asyndeton. See A. P. Wikgren, in *NT Manuscript Studies* (Chicago, 1950), 109. Torrey thinks καί was inserted because צלמות was regarded as an apposition to ארץ (*Documents*, 57).

[3] Cf. C. H. Dodd, *According to the Scriptures* (London, 1952), 80.

[4] A & G, s.v.; in *Barn.* 3:4 of the robes of the righteous. Against Lindars (p. 198), who does not recognize this meaning and therefore sees parallel influence from Num 24:17 and Mal 3:20, where the usual Hebrew word behind ἀνατέλλειν in the LXX occurs, viz., זרח.

על), where Mt has the dative. Mt, however, is closer to the Hebrew than is the LXX in the third person αὐτοῖς for הם– (LXX: ὑμᾶς) and in the aorist tense for the Hebrew perfect. This quotation, we conclude, shows some contact with the LXX, but is primarily an independent rendering of the Hebrew.

Mt 5:21; Ex 20:13; Dt 5:17 LXX: οὐ φονεύσεις
Ex 20:13; Dt 5:17 MT: לא תרצח
Mt = LXX = MT.

Mt 5:27; Ex 20:14; Dt 5:18 LXX: οὐ μοιχεύσεις
Ex 20:14; Dt 5:18 MT: לא תנאף
Mt = LXX = MT.

Mt 5:31: (ὃς ἂν ἀπολύσῃ τὴν γυναῖκα αὐτοῦ) δότω αὐτῇ ἀποστάσιον
Dt 24:1 (3) LXX: γράψει αὐτῇ βιβλίον ἀποστασίου καὶ δώσει εἰς τὰς χεῖρας αὐτῆς
MT: כתב לה ספר כריתת ונתן בידה

As in 19:7, Mt reaches into the next clause of the OT text for the verb "to give." But unlike the allusion in 19:7, Mt here gives an abbreviated ἀποστάσιον, against the MT and the LXX.

Mt 5:33	Lev 19:12 LXX	MT
οὐκ ἐπιορκήσεις	καὶ οὐκ ὀμεῖσθε	ולא תשבעו
	τῷ ὀνόματί μου	בשמי
	ἐπ' ἀδίκῳ	לשקר
	Ps 50 (49):14 LXX	MT
ἀποδώσεις δὲ	καὶ ἀπόδος	ושלם
τῷ κυρίῳ	τῷ ὑψίστῳ	לעליון
τοὺς ὅρκους σου	τὰς εὐχάς σου	נדריך

Cf. Num 30:3; Dt 23:22-24.

Ἐπιορκήσεις ("swear falsely") pithily renders the Hebrew תשבעו ... לשקר, for which the LXX has a not quite exact ὀμεῖσθε . . . ἐπ' ἀδίκῳ ("swear unjustly").

Ἀποδοῦναι τινι ὅρκον is rare for fulfilling an oath and means "to give an oath,"[1] whereas the sense required here is "to perform an oath." Therefore, dependence on Ps 50 (49):14 LXX is clear. Mt, however, substitutes the more usual τῷ κυρίῳ for τῷ ὑψίστῳ and τοὺς ὅρκους for τὰς εὐχάς (correctly by the LXX for נדר, "vow"). The former substitution may come from the parallel passage Num 30:3 (ליהוה—[τῷ A] κυρίῳ). The latter substitution may also be influenced by Num 30:3, where נדר-εὐχή, שבעה-ὅρκος, and אסר-ὁρισμός are parallel and synonymous; and it unifies the statement

[1] A & G, s.v. ὅρκος.

by making τοὺς ὅρκους correspond to ἐπιορκήσεις. Thus, the quotation is both Septuagintal and non-Septuagintal.

Mt 5:38; Ex 21:24; Lev 24:20; Dt 19:21 LXX: ὀφθαλμὸν ἀντὶ ὀφθαλμοῦ καὶ ὀδόντα ἀντ ὀδόντος
Mt καί] *om* D it
LXX *om* καί
Ex 21:24; Lev 24:20 MT: עין תחת עין שן תחת שן
Dt 19:21 MT: עין בעין שן בשן

Mt = LXX = MT. The καί may have been inserted by Mt as a connecting link; or we may omit it with the Western text (although the probability is that the Western text assimilates to the OT texts). The accusatives, where we would expect nominatives, stem from Ex 21:24, where the phrases are objects of the verb "give" in verse 23. Thereafter in the LXX and in Mt the accusatives are retained because the words have assumed proverbial form.[1]

Mt 5:43; Lev 19:18 LXX: ἀγαπήσεις τὸν πλησίον σου
Lev 19:18 MT: אהבת לרעך
Mt = LXX = MT.

Mt 8:17	Is 53:4 MT	LXX
αὐτὸς	אכן חלינו	οὗτος
τὰς ἀσθενείας ἡμῶν	הוא	τὰς ἁμαρτίας ἡμῶν
ἔλαβεν	נשא	φέρει
καὶ τὰς νόσους	ומכאבינו	καὶ περὶ ἡμῶν
ἐβάστασεν	סבלם	ὀδυνᾶται

Is 53:4 Aq (Cod. 86), Sym: ὄντως αὐτὸς (*om* Sym) τὰς νόσους (ἁμαρτίας Pr.) ἡμῶν (+ αὐτὸς Sym) ἀνέλαβε(ν) καὶ τοὺς πολέμους (πόνους Sym) ἡμῶν ὑπέμεινεν

Mt's one contact with the LXX is the omission of אכן. Αὐτός is closer to הוא than οὗτος (LXX). Τὰς ἀσθενείας ἡμῶν literally renders חלינו against the spiritualizing interpretations of the LXX and the Targum. Needless difficulty has been caused by the supposition that the Matthaean context requires ἔλαβεν and ἐβάστασεν to be taken in the sense of removal, which סבל, it is said, cannot bear.[2]

---

[1] See Anger, I, 14; H. Alford, *The Greek Testament*[6] (London, 1868), I, 52.

[2] Deissmann thinks Mt transposes the verbs, since βαστάζειν renders נשא in II Kings 18:14; Job 21:3 (A) LXX; and in the four extant passages where Aquila uses the word, Is 40:11; 53:11; 66:12; Jer 10:5 (*Bible Studies*, 102f.). But λαμβάνειν is frequent for נשא in the LXX, especially in Is; and in Is 53:11 Aq's βαστάζειν stands for סבל, not נשא! As Deissmann admits, he still has not gotten over the difficulty that סבל does not mean "to take away." In similar fashion E. Massebieau thinks Mt transposes חלינו and מכאבינו (*Examen des citations de l'Ancien Testament dans l'évangile selon saint Matthieu* [Paris, 1885], 19). This also is unnecessary, especially since the connotation of weakness in both ἀσθενεία and חלי suits the words to each other.

Mt 12:18-21	Is 42:1-4 LXX	MT	Targ	Hag 2:23	Theod
ἰδοὺ ὁ παῖς μου	Ἰακὼβ ὁ παῖς μου	הן עבדי	הא עבדי	σε ἡρέτισα	ἰδοὺ ὁ παῖς[1] μου
ὃν ἡρέτισα	ἀντιλήμψομαι αὐτοῦ	אתמך בו	אקרבניה	בך בחרתי	ἀντιλήψομαι αὐτοῦ
ὁ ἀγαπητός μου	Ἰσραὴλ ὁ ἐκλεκτός μου	בחירי	בחירי	Is 41:8	ὁ ἐκλεκτός μου
ὃν εὐδόκησεν	προσεδέξατο αὐτὸν	רצתה	דאתרעי	ὃν ἠγάπησα	ὃν εὐδόκησεν
ἡ ψυχή μου	ἡ ψυχή μου	נפשי	ביה מימרי	אהבי	ἡ ψυχή μου
θήσω	ἔδωκα	נתתי	אתין	Is 44:2	Aq
τὸ πνεῦμά μου	τὸ πνεῦμά μου	רוחי	רוח קודשי	ὁ ἠγαπημένος	ἰδοὺ ὁ δοῦλος μου
ἐπ' αὐτόν	ἐπ' αὐτόν	עליו	עלוהי	ישרון	ἀντιλήψομαι ἐν
καὶ κρίσιν	κρίσιν	משפט	דיני		αὐτῷ. . .εὐδόκησεν
τοῖς ἔθνεσιν	τοῖς ἔθνεσιν	לגוים	לעממין		Sym
ἀπαγγελεῖ	ἐξοίσει	יוציא	יגלי		ἰδοὺ ὁ δοῦλος μου
οὐκ ἐρίσει	οὐ κεκράξεται	לא יצעק	לא יצוח		ἀνθέξομαι αὐτοῦ
οὐδὲ κραυγάσει	οὐδὲ ἀνήσει	ולא ישא	ולא יכלי		ὁ ἐκλεκτός μου
οὐδὲ ἀκούσει τις	οὐδὲ ἀκουσθήσεται	ולא ישמיע	ולא ירים		ὃν εὐδόκησεν
ἐν ταῖς πλατείαις	ἔξω	בחוץ	בברא		ἡ ψυχή μου
τὴν φωνὴν αὐτοῦ	ἡ φωνὴ αὐτοῦ	קולו	קליה		Theod
κάλαμον συντετριμ-μένον	κάλαμον τεθλασ-μένον	קנה רצוץ	ענותניא דכקני רעיע		καὶ στιππύον ἀμαυ-ρόν οὐ σβέσει
οὐ κατεάξει	οὐ συντρίψει	לא ישבור	לא יתבר		Aq
καὶ λίνον τυφόμενον	καὶ λίνον καπνιζό-μενον	ופשתה כהה	וחשיכיא דכבוצין עמי		καὶ λίνον ἀμαυρὸν οὐ σβέσει
οὐ σβέσει	οὐ σβέσει . . .	לא יכבנה ...	לא יטפי ...	Hab 1:4	Sym
ἕως ἂν ἐκβάλῃ	ἕως ἂν θῇ	עד ישים	עד דיתקין	εἰς τέλος	οὐδὲ λίνον ἀμαυρὸν
εἰς νῖκος	ἐπὶ τῆς γῆς	בארץ	בארעא	κρίμα	σβέσει
τὴν κρίσιν	κρίσιν	משפט	דינא	יצא לנצח	Theod, Aq, Sym
καὶ τῷ ὀνόματι αὐτοῦ	καὶ ἐπὶ τῷ ὀνόματι αὐτοῦ	ולתורתו	ולאוריתיה	משפט	καὶ τῷ νόμῳ αὐτο
ἔθνη	ἔθνη	איים	נגוון		ἔθνη (νησοι *recte* Pr.
ἐλπιοῦσιν	ἐλπιοῦσιν	ייחלו	יכתרון		ἐλπιοῦσιν

ὅν 2° Bℵ**pc* eth Eus^{semel}]
εἰς ὅν ℵ^{b}C^{2}LW Θ 565 700 *pm*;
ἐν ᾧ C*D*al*Ir^{lat}
τῷ ὀνόματι] *pr* ἐν D it vg syr$^{pesh, hk}$ sah boh eth arm

ומשפט [משפט 1QIs^{a} boh
ולתורתו] לתורתיו 1QIs^{a}

[1] Text: Qsyh. Thdt says Theod ha[s] δοῦλος, as he ha[s] elsewhere for **עבד**.

Although it is true that סבל does not express the thought of taking *away*, nevertheless its connotation of burden-bearing is not opposed to the thought of removal. Even more to the point, the Matthaean context requires removal only from the sick to Jesus, but not a subsequent taking away. With this thought of transference the Hebrew words are perfectly in accord. Mt, then, presents a rendering of the Hebrew almost wholly independent from the LXX.[1]

Mt 9:13; 12:7; Hos 6:6 LXX^{AQOr} Ziegler Rahlfs: ἔλεος θέλω καὶ οὐ θυσίαν
Hos 6:6 LXX$^{BQ^{c}Luc}$ La^{w} boh eth arm Th Tert Cypr Ir^{lat} Or^{lat} Aug: ἔλεος θέλω ἤ θυσίαν
MT: חסד חפצתי ולא זבח
Targ: בעבדי חיסדא רעווא קדמי מדדבח

Ἤ should be preferred as the original reading of the LXX, because it disagrees with the MT and because it agrees with the Targum.[2] Although it is possible καὶ οὐ in LXX^{AQOr} is a pre-Christian assimilation to the MT, the probability is that the reading is hexaplaric (for if καὶ οὐ were original and better attested, it is difficult to see why Or^{lat} should support ἤ while Or supports καὶ οὐ) and is influenced by the NT. If so, Mt independently renders the Hebrew.

Mt 12:18-21, *etc.*

Mt follows the LXX in having παῖς rather than δοῦλος,[3] but he rejects Ἰακώβ and Ἰσραήλ, for which the Hebrew has no equivalent and which one may even conjecture were not in the original text of the LXX, but were inserted by advocates of the collective inter-

---

[1] K. F. Euler argues that Mt has utilized an older Septuagintal text which contained the interpretation that the Servant relieves mankind of physical sufferings, this interpretation ousted by the Christian view that Jesus' passion fulfils Is 53. Euler notes that ἁμαρτία no where else in the LXX renders חלי, and περὶ ἡμῶν ὀδυνᾶται for ומכאבינו סבלם is curious (*Die Verkündigung vom leidenden Gottesknecht aus Jes* 53 *in der griechischen Bibel* [Stuttgart, 1934], 59-63; Stendahl [pp. 106f.] cites H. S. Nyberg as following this view [*Svensk Exegetisk Årsbok*, 7 (1942), 13]). But the LXX Is-translator frequently indulges in exceptional renderings; and here he may have been influenced by verses 5 and 6, where sins are explicitly mentioned (Seeligmann, *op. cit.*, 29). As Stendahl points out, the spiritualizing interpretation in the Targum makes quite unnecessary the conjecture that the spiritualizing interpretation in the LXX is a product of later, Christian correction (*loc. cit.*).

[2] The following prefer ἤ: W. Staerk, *ZWT*, 40 (1897), 257; Zahn, *Einl.*, II, 316; Hänel, *op. cit.*, 117. T. W. Manson speaks favorably of it (*BJRL*, 34 [1951/52], 321). Whether original or not, ἤ is due to parallelism with the next clause (מן-ἤ).

[3] On the waning use of παῖς and the increasing employment of δοῦλος, see P. Katz, *TZ*, 5 (1949), 17.

pretation of the Servant from the parallel passages 41:8, 9; 44:2. Note that the OT Peshitta does not go with the present reading of the LXX. The similarity between Mt and Theodotion need not rest on an Ur-Theodotionic text. Both merely have an eye on the Hebrew text, rejecting the LXX's obvious interpolations. Furthermore, παῖς in Theodotion is uncertain, and Mt's deviation from Theodotion in the next two phrases militates against a connection with Theodotion here.

Ὅν ᾑρέτισα in Mt presents several possibilities. The evangelist may have understood תמך in the sense of "taking hold of to acquire, to bring or adopt to oneself."[1] Very similar is the Targum: אקרבניה, "I will bring him near." Or αἱρετίζειν may anticipate the thought of ἐκλεκτός in the next phrase of the LXX.[2] Or parallel influence from Hag 2:23, where σε ᾑρέτισα (LXX) renders בך בחרתי, may enter. Yet again, Mt's Hebrew text may have read or he himself may have brought in בחרתי בו from Is 44:2 (cf. 41:8, 9: בחרתיך; in both passages the LXX has ὃν ἐξελεξάμην).[3] Since this provides a reason for Mt's aorist, against the future of the LXX and the imperfects of the MT and the Targum in Is 42:1, and since αἱρετίζειν is usual in the LXX for בחר, the last view is preferable, with the added consideration that Mt brings in בחרתי בו not in place of אתמך בו so much as by omission of the latter in anticipation of בחירי—to make room for ὁ ἀγαπητός μου from the voice at Jesus' baptism [4] and transfiguration, where it stems from the Targum to Ps 2:7.[5] Thereby Mt has brought into focus the double signification of בחר, choice and love.[6] Again, the parallel passages Is 44:2; 41:8, 9 contain the ἀγαπητός-motif and may have suggested or encouraged the insertion from the baptismal and transfiguration narratives.

Mt rejects προσεδέξατο αὐτόν in the LXX [7] and renders independently by ὃν εὐδόκησεν. The agreement with Theodotion is not signifi-

---

[1] So Massebieau, *op. cit.*, 22. On αἱρετίζειν = "to adopt," see Allen, *Mt*, 130f.; A & G, s.v.

[2] So Stendahl, 110.

[3] So Torrey, *Documents*, 64.

[4] Made easier if for the evangelist v. 18 alludes to the baptismal voice, v. 19 to the Sermon on the Mount, v. 20 to the healing ministry, and v. 21 to the incident concerning the Gentile centurion (A. B. Bruce, *op. cit.*, 185).

[5] Cf. Plooij, in *Amicitiae Corolla*, 250; Chevallier, *op. cit.*, 73, n. 2.

[6] Torrey's supposed ידידי behind ἀγαπητός is unnecessary (*Documents*, 64).

[7] This is a possible rendering (cf. esp. Mal 1:8, where רצה is in synonymous parallelism with נשא in the sense "to accept"), but foreign to the progression of thought in Is.

cant, for εὐδοκεῖν with the accusative is frequent in Biblical and extra-Biblical Greek.[1] The naturalness of the rendering is shown by the fact that Symmachus, who has diverged from Theodotion in ἀνθέξομαι and perhaps in δοῦλος, and Aquila also have ὃν εὐδόκησεν. There is the further possibility that the reading ὅν in Mt is mechanical conformation to ὃν ᾑρέτισα, so that we should prefer εἰς ὅν (ἐν ᾧ being assimilation to the words at Jesus' baptism and transfiguration).[2]

Θήσω in Mt agrees with the Targum (אתין) both in word choice and in tense against the MT (נתתי) and the LXX (ἔδωκα).[3] Ἀπαγγελεῖ (less literal than the LXX's ἐξοίσει) agrees with the Targum in understanding יוציא in the sense of promulgation, as indeed the Hebrew word often means.[4] The idea of accomplishment does not seem to be present in the *hiphil* of יצא. Mt's καί before κρίσιν agrees with 1QIs[a] and the Bohairic against all other known texts.[5]

The parallelism with κραυγάσει shows that ἐρίσει takes, as often,[6] the sense of *verbal* wrangling, and thus correctly renders צעק (here probably in the forensic sense of disputation or complaining accusation[7]). It is quite unnecessary, therefore, to see ἐρίσει as reflecting נריב ("to cry out") in the OT Peshitta, נריב being read in the manner of West Aramaic, in which the word means "to contend."[8] Besides, we cannot be certain that in NT times East and

[1] See A & G, s.v. εὐδοκέω.

[2] So B. Weiss, *Textkritik der vier Evangelien* (= *Texte u. Untersuchungen*, N. F., Bd. 4, Heft 2; Leipzig, 1899), 97. The reading εἰς ὅν in II Pet 1:17 may reflect the original reading in Mt. On the other hand, εἰς ὅν in Mt may be scribal assimilation to II Pet 1:17 or to the tradition behind II Pet. And Mt may have intended a parallel with ὃν ᾑρέτισα, this being the reason he does not conform to ἐν ᾧ at the baptism and the transfiguration.

[3] Anger doubts contact with the Targ, saying Mt and the Targ both happen to put the prophetic perfect into the future tense (I, 31f.). But it is more than accident that they agree in vocabulary as well.

[4] See, e.g., Num 14:37; Dt 22:14, 19; Neh 6:19. The LXX renders יצא (*hiphil*) by ἀναγγέλλειν in Is 48:20. So also the word used in the OT Peshitta, נפק, often has an oral connotation. See Payne Smith, *Thesaurus Syriacus*, s.v. McNeile's emendation, יודיע, is thus unnecessary (*Mt*, 172). Here and concerning θήσω, G. Barth without reason doubts any contact with the Targum (G. Bornkamm, G. Barth, and H. J. Held, *Überlieferung u. Auslegung im Matthäusevangelium* [Neukirchen, 1960], 118, n. 5).

[5] See above, p. 95, n. 4, on insertion and deletion of the *waw*.

[6] See L & S, s.v.

[7] Cf. B. Gärtner, *Studia Theologica*, 8 (1954), 20. So also the Targum's צוח. The Isaianic context will not allow צעק to be taken in its usual connotation of a cry for help.

[8] So Stendahl, 111f., 198, who lays great stress on this, not as a misunder-

West Aramaic were sufficiently different for us to assume a cleavage in the meaning of נריב.[1]

In κραυγάσει Mt again follows the Targum (יכלי, "cry aloud"). Probably the Targumic rendering does not imply a different Hebrew text containing ישאג (Kittel-Kahle), for both Mt and the Targum want to avoid the clumsiness of an unexpressed or deferred קולו-τὴν φωνὴν αὐτοῦ (MT, LXX).[2] The *hiphil* יַשְׁמִיעַ of the MT Mt renders by an active ἀκούσει with τις against the passive ἀκουσθήσεται of the LXX, and thereby retains the properly accusative force of קולו (LXX: ἡ φωνὴ αὐτοῦ). The LXX may have read the verb as *niphal*, יִשָּׁמַע. The Targum belatedly renders ישא by ירים, consequently omitting ישמיע. Ἔξω (LXX) is a more exact translation of בחוץ than Mt's ἐν ταῖς πλατείαις. However, חוץ, בר (Targ), and שוק (OT Pesh) all have narrower connotations as well;[3] and a narrower connotation would seem to be required in Is, where the thought is hardly that of shouting in the open fields.[4]

Συντετριμμένον and τυφόμενον in Mt and τεθλασμένον and καπνιζόμενον in the LXX are equally close to the Hebrew. Mt's κατεάξει ("break off or in pieces") is closer to ישבור (same meaning) than συντρίψει ("rub together, crush"—LXX).

The striking ἐκβάλῃ in Mt is much more forceful than ישים or θῇ and is introduced in anticipation of the following εἰς νῖκος, which suggests a contest or struggle in which the opponents of the Servant are routed. Also, ἐκβάλλειν is frequent in Mt, especially in this chapter (verses 24, 26, 27[bis], 28, 35[bis]).[5] Εἰς νῖκος comes from

---

standing, but as his prime example of *pesher*-type manipulation by a Matthaean school. The recognition that ἐρίζειν and צעק both refer to verbal disputation likewise renders superfluous other discussions regarding contact with the OT Peshitta and an Aramaic Ur-Mt: E. Nestle, *ET*, 20 (1908/09), 92f., 189; W. C. Allen, *ET*, 20 (1908/09), 140f.

[1] The farther back we go, the closer East and West Aramaic become. See C. C. Torrey, *ZAW*, 65 (1953), 228-247, esp. 229; Black, *op. cit.*, 13-15, 30.

[2] The difficulty of expression leads to omission in Tert., *Adv. Marc.* iv. 23; *Adv. Jud.* ix; Cypr., *Test.* ii. 13—cited by Hatch, *op. cit.*, 201.

[3] See the lexicons of Levy, Jastrow, Brockelmann, and Payne Smith. The words are used of streets, market-places, squares, etc. E.g., נפקת ברא in Gen 34: 31 (Targum) means "prostitute," and is practically equivalent to our "woman of the street."

[4] Against Stendahl, who sees the Matthaean school tendentiously fitting the OT text to the NT circumstances (pp. 112f.).

[5] Stendahl's discussion of ἐκβάλλειν rests on the faulty assumption that the word translates יוציא (p. 114). But ἕως ἄν (= עד) shows that Mt has already skipped verses 3b and 4a in Is.

Hab 1:4, where the use of יצא and משפט, both words twice, made easy the connection with Is 42.[1] Since נצח in Aramaic means "victory," the rendering by νῖκος may be an Aramaism. However, נצח may mean "victory" already in the Hebrew text of Hab, since the context speaks of justice unaccomplished. Although in Hab 1:4 the LXX has εἰς τέλος, the common rendering of לנצח is εἰς νῖκος; and this occurs as the rendering elsewhere in the LXX[2] and regularly in Aquila.[3] Thus, Mt's translation is not unique. It should be noted, moreover, that Mt substitutes his rendering of לנצח as a kind of compensation for לאמת in the omitted portion of Is 42:3 and in place of בארץ in Is 42:4.[4]

Mt's ὀνόματι agrees with the LXX[5] against ולתורתו (MT). But the simple dative (with ἐλπίζειν = a classical Greek construction)[6] demonstrates independence from the LXX (ἐπί with the dative). This fact lends support to the possibility that since all the early recensions of the LXX and the early Latin versions agree in τῷ ὀνόματι αὐτοῦ ἔθνη ἐλπιοῦσιν, we are dealing with lost variants in the Hebrew text; for it is strange we do not meet assimilation to the MT earlier than Aq, Sym, and Theod.[7] Furthermore, it is almost inconceivable that a reference to the *Torah* would have been displaced; but it seems very possible that the dominant Jewish concept of Messiah's expounding the Torah in his kingdom[8] would provide impetus for the reading of the MT. The plural form לתורתיו in 1QIs[a] may also hint at the variant nature of the word. Similarly, ἔθνη in Mt and the LXX presupposes גואים (or גויים or גוים) instead of

[1] Note that the connection cannot rest on the LXX, which has in Hab διεξάγειν, ἐξέρχεσθαι, and κρίμα, and that it is even easier with the variant ותוצא in DST iv. 25 (= M.G. ii. 46), to which Rabin calls attention (*JTS*, 6 [1955], 178f.).

[2] II Sam 2:26; Amos 1:11; 8:7; Jer 3:5; Lam 5:20.

[3] See A. Rahlfs, *ZNW*, 20 (1921), 186-189.

[4] This fact renders improbable the hypothesis of homoioteulon in Mt's Hebrew text (משפט ··· משפט—so Bacon, *Studies in Mt*, 131) or Greek OT text (κρίμα . . . κρίσιν—so Hatch, *loc. cit.*, who conjectures another κρίσιν in place of κρίμα). Mt may have realized that the play on רצץ and כהה in the omitted portion would be difficult to reproduce in Greek.

[5] The scribal error ὀνόματι for νόμῳ assumed by Ziegler ([ed.], *Is, ad loc.*) and J. Jeremias (*TWNT*, V, 698) neither explains the total lack of evidence for the supposedly primitive reading nor takes into account the further divergence from the MT in ἔθνη.

[6] McNeile, *Mt*, 173.

[7] See Hatch, *loc. cit.*; Woods, *HDB*, IV, 187.

[8] Cf. Targum Onkelos to Gen 49:10; Teeple, *op. cit.*, 14ff.; W. D. Davies, *Torah in the Messianic Age and/or the Age to Come* (Philadelphia, 1952).

איים (also in Is 41:5 the LXX has ἔθνη for איים). A softly gutteral pronunciation of the initial א could easily lead to confusion of the two words.[1] In the Habakkuk Commentary from Qumran there is a deliberate play on איים (the Hab text) and גואים (the commentary) (col. 3:2). It is possible, therefore, that Mt and the LXX agree together not against, but with their Hebrew *Vorlagen*. Even otherwise, the mixed text-character of other quotations makes unjustifiable the view that the Septuagintal stamp of verse 21 shows it to be from a later hand.[2]

Mt 13:14, 15; Acts 28:26, 27; Is 6:9, 10 LXX: πορεύθητι καὶ εἰπὸν τῷ λαῷ τούτῳ ἀκοῇ ἀκούσετε καὶ οὐ μὴ συνῆτε καὶ βλέποντες βλέψετε καὶ οὐ μὴ ἴδητε· ἐπαχύνθη γὰρ ἡ καρδία τοῦ λαοῦ τούτου καὶ τοῖς ὠσὶν αὐτῶν βαρέως ἤκουσαν καὶ τοὺς ὀφθαλμοὺς αὐτῶν ἐκκάμμυσαν· μήποτε ἴδωσιν τοῖς ὀφθαλμοῖς καὶ τοῖς ὠσὶν ἀκούσωσιν καὶ τῇ καρδίᾳ συνῶσιν καὶ ἐπιστρέψωσιν καὶ ἰάσομαι αὐτούς

LXX αὐτῶν 1°] *om* א*. αὐτῶν 2°] *om* B 393

Acts πορ. κ. εἰπὸν τῷ λαῷ τούτῳ] πορ. πρὸς τὸν λαὸν τοῦτον καὶ εἰπόν
αὐτῶν 1°] *om*

Mt IF: καὶ ἀναπληροῦται αὐτοῖς ἡ προφητεία Ἠσαΐου ἡ λέγουσα

ἀναπληροῦται] τότε πληροῦται f1; τότε πληρωθήσεται ἐπ' D*pc*it

Mt omits πορεύθητι . . . τούτῳ, except in D it (εἰπέ).

αὐτῶν 1° אCΦ 33 *pc* it syr[sin, cur, pesh] sah boh eth arm] *om rell*

Is 6:9, 10 MT: לך ואמרת לעם הזה שמעו שמוע ואל תבינו וראו ראו ואל תדעו: השמן לב העם הזה ואזניו הכבד ועיניו השע פן יראה בעיניו ובאזניו ישמע ולבבו יבין ושב ורפא לו

ישמע] ישמעו 1QIs[a]
ולבבו] בלבבו 1QIs[a]

The main question in this quotation concerns its genuineness. Objectors to its genuineness put forward several arguments:[3]

1) The IF is un-Matthaean, containing two *hapax legomena* in Mt, ἀναπληροῦν and προφητεία. However, ἀναπληροῦν is common in the LXX (thirteen times) and elsewhere in Greek literature (Eur., Luc., Plat., Demos., Josephus, papyri). In I Esdras 1:54 the word occurs in exactly the sense required in Mt: εἰς ἀναπλήρωσιν τοῦ

---

[1] J. Kennedy, *op. cit.*, 12. Cf. Job 2:10, where εἰ in the LXX presupposes אם instead of the MT's גם (also Zech 3:7). An imperfectly formed א sometimes resembles ג (*ibid.*, 36). Chr. Wordsworth suggests ἔθνη is a Hellenizing reading, for νῆσοι would not give the intended meaning "Gentiles" to the Greek ear (*The Greek Testament* [London, 1874], I, 42).

[2] Against Schlatter, *op. cit.*, 401f.; Bacon, *Studies in Mt*, 474 f.; Kilpatrick, *Origins*, 94; Jeremias, *The Servant of God*, 80; T. W. Manson, *BJRL*, 34 (1951/52), 323. On the other hand, omission of the verse in min. 33 provides a legitimate, but not sufficient basis for this view.

[3] See Torrey, *Documents*, 66f.; Stendahl, 131f.; S. E. Johnson, *op. cit.*, 137f.

ῥήματος τοῦ κυρίου ἐν στόματι Ἰερεμίου. We cannot assume, therefore, that ἀναπληροῦν was foreign to Mt's vocabulary. Rather, the prefixing of ἀνά, the vivid present tense in Mt, and the first position show a deliberate emphasis on the word; i.e., the quotation, partially fulfilled in Isaiah's generation, now receives a full measure of fulfilment. Also, the immediately preceding allusive quotation of the same passage in Is [1] necessitated a more emphatic IF for the full, explicit quotation—to save from awkwardness and anticlimax. As for προφητείᾳ although it occurs in the sense of written OT prophecy elsewhere in the NT only in II Pet 1:20, yet it is often used throughout the OT and NT of the prophetic message, a distinction between written and oral not in view. Even in the sense of written OT prophecy Mt was by no means the first to use προφητεία: γέγραπται ἐν τῇ προφητείᾳ Ἠσαΐου (II Chron 32:32 LXX); τῆς προφητείας Αμώς (Tob. 2:6); αἱ προφητεῖαι = the second section of the OT canon in Sir. *prol.* 18.

2) The great difference between Cod. D and other MSS points to the ungenuineness of the quotation. Cf. Mt 27:35, where Δ Θ f1 f13 *al* it vg^{cl}ς = Jn 19:24 in the quotation of Ps 22:19 LXX. As is obvious, however, parallel influence is rife in Cod. D throughout these verses and verse 13. The phrase ἐπ' αὐτοῖς in D (against the simple dative) reveals a Semitic background.[2] Presumably, then, the harmonistic and Semitic elements betray Tatianic influence on Cod. D. The lack of manuscript evidence for omission of Mt 13:14, 15 destroys the parallel with the textual situation in Mt 27:35.

3) The lengthy quotation here is tautological after the allusive quotation in verse 13. But it is not likely Mt abridged Mk's allusion, omitting the entire last clause, without compensation; for elsewhere he is usually more expansive in quotation material. We must rather assume that verse 13 leads up to the formal quotation in verses 14, 15. This can be seen in verse 13 in the causal ὅτι (against ἵνα in Mk, Lk, and Jn), which harmonizes with the γάρ-clause of the Septuagintal quotation to follow. If verses 14, 15 were an interpolation, we should almost have to say that an original ἵνα in verse

---

[1] V. 13 in Mt (par Mk 4:12). See above, pp. 33-35.

[2] In statements concerning what the scripture says about certain people, על was regularly used. See W. Bacher, *Die exegetische Terminologie der jüdischen Traditionsliteratur* (Leipzig, 1899), I, 5; B. M. Metzger, *JBL*, 70 (1951), 300; C. Taylor, *op. cit.*, p. xiv. Cf. esp. I Kings 2:27, where מלא in the meaning of fulfilment is construed with the clause, "which he spoke על the house of Eli."

13 was changed to ὅτι to conform with the interpretation of the LXX. This requires too much cleverness on the part of the interpolator.

4) The pure Septuagintal form is out of character with Matthaean formula-citations. Not so, for 1:23 is almost and perhaps wholly Septuagintal. And if individual phrases and entire clauses agree with the LXX against the MT in other formula-citations, a whole citation in the Septuagintal style should occasion no surprise.

5) The exact agreement with Acts, even in the omission of the first αὐτῶν [but this is textually disputed in Mt], shows the quotation has been interpolated from Acts. However, because of an identical purpose to show the OT passage has already been fulfilled, for which the Hebrew is not suitable, Mt and Acts may independently follow the same Septuagintal text, represented by Cod. ℵ* in its omission of the first αὐτῶν in Is *against its own reading in Mt*. Moreover, in interpolation one would have expected the introductory πορεύθητι . . . τούτῳ to have been brought over from Acts.

We therefore accept the originality of verses 14, 15 in Mt and note the pure Septuagintal form in the rendering of the Hebrew idiom of a conjugated verb-form with an infinitive absolute first by a finite verb with a cognate noun and then by a finite verb with a participle, in the indicatives against the Hebrew imperatives, in the insertion of γάρ, the omission of possessives, ἰάσομαι ("I shall or should heal") for the impersonal רפא, and in the identical vocabulary throughout.

Mt 13:35	Ps 78 (77):2 LXX	MT
ἀνοίξω	ἀνοίξω	אפתחה
ἐν παραβολαῖς	ἐν παραβολαῖς	במשל
τὸ στόμα μου	τὸ στόμα μου	פי
ἐρεύξομαι	φθέγξομαι	אביעה
κεκρυμμένα	προβλήματα	חידות
ἀπὸ καταβολῆς	ἀπ' ἀρχῆς	מני קדם
καταβολῆς Bℵ^{b}1 *pc*ek (syr$^{sin, cur}$) Or] + κόσμου ℵ*DWΘ f13 28 *pl* lat ς	παραβολαῖς] παραβολῇ ℵ*Aq	

Mt follows the LXX in the first clause, even in the plural παραβολαῖς for the collective singular משל (as do also the OT Pesh and the Vg).[1] The plural rendering arose through the parallelism with חידות.

[1] Cf. Ps 49:5, where the MT, LXX, Vg, and Targ have the singular (משל), but the OT Pesh the plural.

Ἐρεύξομαι ("belch forth, utter") is an exact etymological rendering of אביעה ("bubble or belch forth, utter"), though the LXX would have been suitable.[1] Προβλήματα ("tasks, problems"—LXX) is not a very close rendering of חידות ("enigmas"), for which Mt has a loose, but closer κεκρυμμένα ("hidden or unknown things"). The phrase ἀπὸ καταβολῆς is usually completed with κόσμου (Mt 25:34 and throughout the NT, also with πρό), for which reason some MSS in Mt contain κόσμου. Either Mt leaves κόσμου to be implied, or he drops κόσμου and uses καταβολῆς of an indefinite beginning to conform with the indefinite מני קדם ("from of old"—in Prov 8:23 parallel to מראש, "from the beginning"). The stereotyped character of the Greek expression with κόσμου favors that the omission is intentional conformity to the Hebrew.[2]

---

[1] In Ps 19:3 the LXX has ἐρεύγεσθαι for נבע.

[2] In the IF, Ἡσαΐου is read by א* Θ f13 1 *al.* According to Jerome, "In Asaph propheta . . . invenitur in omnibus veteribus codicibus" (*Brev. in Ps* 77 [MPL XXVI, 1108]). Jerome thought a scribe, knowing nothing of a prophet "Asaph," inserted "Isaiah" as a better known name. The reading Ἡσαΐου was also known to Eusebius (*in Ps* 77 [MPG XXIII, 901ff.]), who says the "accurate" MSS omit. Porphyry used the reading Ἡσαΐου to ridicule Mt's ignorance. The offensiveness of the reading, more keenly felt because of Porphyry, is in its favor. It is also said that an "erroneous correction" is not probable. See Zahn, *Einl.*, II, 596; *idem, Mt,* 477ff. F. J. A. Hort defends the genuineness of Ἡσαΐου by arguing that out of five other places where the true text simply has τοῦ προφήτου, in two no name is inserted (Mt 2:15; Acts 7:48); in two a name is inserted on trivial evidence (Mt 2:5—"Mic" correctly, 4 cop$^{boh[1 MS]}$, "Is" wrongly, a; Mt 21:4—"Is" correctly for the first phrase only, r^2 vg [3 MSS], "Zech" correctly, M^{mg} 42 ach cop$^{boh[1 MS]}$ Hil); in Mt 1:22 "Is" is correctly inserted in D*pc* it syr $^{sin, cur}$; and "Is" erroneously replaces "Jer" in Mt 27:9 21 l. See Westcott & Hort, *The NT in the Original Greek* (Cambridge, 1881), II, 13. Since Hort wrote, we have discovered that syr^{sin} erroneously inserts "Is" in Mt 2:15. It should also be noted that Justin refers Num 24:17 to Is (1 *Apol.* xxxii. 12 [MPG VI, 380]—against his correct ascription in *Dial.* cvi. 4) and Jer 9:26 to Is (1 *Apol.* liii. 3, 10, 11 [MPG VI, 408]). Thus, scribal misascription seems as possible as misascription by Mt, and more probable in view of Mt's usually not naming the prophet except when quoting Is, a custom which renders it unlikely he would make a mistake concerning a book very familiar to him and likely that a scribe used to seeing Ἡσαΐου in (1:22); 3:3; 4:14; 8:17; 12:17; 13:14 would insert the name here. See Blass, *op. cit.*, 33f.; Lagrange, *Mt*, 271. A. L. Williams (*Adversus Judaeos* [Cambridge, 1935], 9) and Hunt (*op. cit.*, 162f.) accept the misascription and explain by the Testimony Book hypothesis. Strack-Billerbeck cite rabbinical passages in which the words of one prophet are given as through another prophet as well (*op. cit.*, I, 670f.). Mt may use προφήτου because of the prophetic nature of the word itself or because Asaph is called a prophet in II Chron 29:30 (τοῦ προφήτου LXX—החזה MT) and I Chron 25:2 (note the variant reading in some Hebrew MSS, on which see Stendahl, 119, n. 1).

Mt 21:5	Is 62:11 LXX	MT	Jn 12:15
εἴπατε τῇ	εἴπατε τῇ	אמרו	μὴ φοβοῦ
θυγατρὶ Σιών	θυγατρὶ Σιών	לבת ציון	θυγάτηρ Σιών
	Zech 9:9 LXX	MT	
ἰδού	ἰδού	הנה	ἰδού
ὁ βασιλεύς σου	ὁ βασιλεύς σου	מלכך	ὁ βασιλεύς σου
ἔρχεταί σοι	ἔρχεταί σοι	יבוא לך	ἔρχεται
	δίκαιος καὶ	צדיק	
	σῴζων αὐτὸς	ונושע הוא	
πραῢς	πραῢς	עני	
καὶ ἐπιβεβηκὼς	καὶ ἐπιβεβηκὼς	ורכב	καθήμενος
ἐπὶ ὄνον	ἐπὶ ὑποζύγιον	על חמור	
καὶ ἐπὶ πῶλον	καὶ πῶλον	ועל עיר	ἐπὶ πῶλον
υἱὸν ὑποζυγίου	νέον	בן אתנות	ὄνου

Curiously, where Mt begins with Is 62:11 (= LXX = MT), Jn begins with Is 40:9 (אל תיראי, MT, against μὴ φοβεῖσθε, LXX). The omission of δίκαιος . . . αὐτός in Mt and Jn emphasizes πραΰς.[1] Mt may also have reasoned that at this time Jesus was hardly the just and victorious king according to the prevalent Jewish expectation of divine vindication of Israel and deliverance from foreign domination. It remained for later events to reveal the Christian concept of Messiah as the Just One and Saviour, and yet remains for his full victory to be unveiled at his return.[2] Mt agrees with the LXX, Aquila, the OT Peshitta, and the Targum in understanding עני as ענו. Mt also follows the LXX in ἐπιβεβηκώς ("mounted") for רֹכֵב ("riding").

'Υποζύγιον (LXX) Mt replaces with ὄνον, which correctly renders חמור ("a working or riding ass," rendered usually by ὄνος in the LXX). Mt translates the second על, which the LXX omits. Both Mt and the LXX have πῶλον, correctly, for עיר ("a young ass," rendered usually by πῶλος in the LXX).[3] But the LXX rejects the Semitic בן אתנות in favor of νέον; [4] whereas Mt renders the Hebrew

[1] G. Barth, *op. cit.*, 121.

[2] Cf. H. Gough, *The NT Quotations* (London, 1855), 326.

[3] As L. Köhler rightly observes, the circumstance that the עיר is ridden upon and the parallel with חמור show that עיר means not a young colt, but a strong young jackass (*Kleine Lichter* [Zürich, 1945], 52ff.). But against Köhler, πῶλος can also mean a strong young jackass (e.g., Jdg 10:4; 12:14 LXX—of riding-asses; Is 30:6 LXX—for carrying loads). H.-W. Kuhn (*ZNW*, 50 [1959], 82ff.) and O. Michel (*NTS*, 6 [1959], 81f.) have decisively refuted W. Bauer's contention that outside a zoological context, as in Mk 11:1ff., πῶλος means a horse (*JBL*, 72 [1953], 220-229) by showing that in spite of Hellenistic usage πῶλος alone usually means an ass in the Egyptian and Palestinian milieu (so the LXX).

[4] See Deissmann, *Bible Studies*, 164.

phrase fully, in agreement with the singular אתן of the Targum and the OT Peshitta (presupposed also in Sym and Theod). Ὑποζυγίου ("pack-animal," a donkey only by context) [1] is not exact for אתנות, but is as good as any unused synonym at hand.

Mt 21:16; Ps 8:3 LXX: ἐκ στόματος νηπίων καὶ θηλαζόντων κατηρτίσω αἶνον
Ps 8:3 MT: מפי עוללים וינקים יסדת עז

Dependence upon the LXX is especially close in κατηρτίσω ("prepare [for oneself]") for יסדת ("found, establish") and in αἶνον for עז.[2] The meaning of עז in the OT text is much disputed. Since the word ordinarily means "bulwark, strength," emendations of the Hebrew text have been suggested.[3] However, the meaning "praise" need not be doubted in the light of such passages as Ps 29:1 and 96:7: "Give to Yahweh כבוד and עז"; 68:35: "Give עז to God"; Ex 15:2: "Yah (is) my עז and my song. . . I will praise him. . . I will exalt him."[4] As in Rev 4:11; 5:12, 13, the divine attribute praised becomes so identified with the act of praise that it comes to mean the praise itself. In Ps 8:3 the Lord silences the hostile speech of his enemies by the praise of children, עז being chosen because the other side of its double meaning, "strength," emphasizes Yahweh's might working through the weakness of children. No other meaning than "praise" will stand with מפי.[5] The Midrash thus interprets, and the rabbinical tradition concerning the children who sang at the crossing of the Red Sea rests on Ps 8:3.[6] It is probable that the

---

[1] On ὑποζύγιον in the narrow meaning "ass" in the LXX, Theod, Sym, and the papyri, *ibid.*, 161.

[2] Zahn supposes the Greek translator of the Aramaic Ur-Mt used the LXX's αἶνον to preserve an assonant relationship between עושנא ("strength") in the Targum to the psalm and "Hosanna" (an expression of praise) in the Matthaean context (*Einl.*, II, 318).

[3] H. Gunkel reads יִסַּרְתָּ עָז and translates, "Out of the mouth of children you have rebuked the insolent" (*Die Psalmen* [Göttingen, 1926], 29). G. E. Paulus thinks מפי should be מפני, "Because of . . ., you have ordained a bulwark" (*Commentar* [1812], cited by Bertram, *TWNT*, IV, 916). With Duhm, P. A. H. de Boer doubts any sense can be made from "establishing strength out of the crying of babes and sucklings" and therefore translates, "Thy impressiveness upon the heavens, louder than the crying of children and sucklings! Thou hast established a bulwark, because of Thy adversaries, to still Enemy and Avenger . . ." (*Oudtestamentische Studien* [Leiden, 1943], II, 175, 190).

[4] And perhaps II Chron 30:21: ". . . praised Yahweh with כלי עז ('instruments of praise,' but possibly 'loud instruments')."

[5] Thus the LXX, Vg, the Latin version of Jerome, the OT Pesh, Sym, Bar Hebraeus. See further Briggs, *op. cit.*, I, 63; Kraus, *op. cit.*, 69.

[6] See Strack-Billerbeck, *op. cit.*, I, 854.

psalmist himself had in mind this tradition and Ex 15:2, where עז is in synonymous parallelism with "song (זמרת)."

Mt 27:5, 6, 9	Zech 11:13 LXX		MT
καὶ ῥίψας τὰ ἀργύρια	καὶ ἐνέβαλον αὐτοὺς		ואשליך אתו
εἰς τὸν ναὸν	εἰς τὸν οἶκον κυρίου	V	בית יהוה
(ἀνεχώρησεν . . .)	εἰς τὸ χωνευτήριον		אל היוצר
οἱ δὲ ἀρχιερεῖς			
λαβόντες τὰ ἀργύρια			
εἶπαν			
οὐκ ἔξεστιν βαλεῖν	κάθες αὐτοὺς	II	השליכהו
αὐτὰ εἰς τὸν κορβανᾶν	εἰς τὸ χωνευτήριον		אל היוצר
. . .			
τότε ἐπληρώθη			
τὸ ῥηθὲν διὰ Ἰερεμίου			
τοῦ προφήτου			
λέγοντος·			
καὶ ἔλαβον	καὶ ἔλαβον	IV	ואקחה
τὰ τριάκοντα ἀργύρια	τοὺς τριάκοντα ἀργυροῦς		שלשים הכסף
τὴν τιμὴν	καὶ σκέψαι	III	אדר
τοῦ τετιμημένου	εἰ δόκιμόν ἐστιν		היקר
ὃν ἐτιμήσαντο	ὃν τρόπον ἐδοκιμάσθην		אשר יקרתי
ἀπὸ υἱῶν Ἰσραήλ,	ὑπὲρ αὐτῶν		מעליהם
καὶ ἔδωκαν αὐτὰ			
εἰς τὸν ἀγρὸν			
τοῦ κεραμέως			
καθὰ συνέταξέν	καὶ εἶπεν	I	ויאמר
μοι κύριος	κύριος πρός με		יהוה אלי
	Ex 40:25; Num 8:3, 22; 9:5; 27:11; 31:31, etc.		
	καθὰ συνέταξεν		כאשר צוה
	κύριος τῷ Μωυσεῖ		יהוה את משה

ἔδωκαν] ἔδωκα ℵW*pl*syr

Zech בית] *pr* אל 4 MSS Ken היוצר] אוצר 1 MS Ken OT Pesh; בית יוצר 4 MSS Ken, 1 MS De-R מעליהם] מעליכם 8 MSS Ken, 8 MSS De-R, 1 MS Ginsb

Since Wellhausen, it has been customary to see in Mt a "double fulfilment" of two readings in Zech, εἰς τὸν κορβανᾶν, presupposing אל האוצר, and εἰς τὸν ἀγρὸν τοῦ κεραμέως, pointing to אל היוצר.[1] Perhaps the chief priests made a play on the words, "We cannot put

[1] Wellhausen, *Mt*, 145, followed by almost everyone. But see J. Jeremias, *Jerusalem zur Zeit Jesu* (Leipzig, 1923), II, A, 55ff.

the money into the אוצר, so let us give it to the יוצר." But whether or not Mt himself knew of another reading, he cannot have intended εἰς τὸν κορβανᾶν to have fulfilled a reading אוצר in Zech; for his narrative expressly states that it was not permissible to put the money εἰς τὸν κορβανᾶν, and Judas had merely thrown the money εἰς τὸν ναόν.[1] Similarly, the attempt by Torrey and Eissfeldt to establish יוצר both in Zech and in II Kings 12:5-17; 22:3-6 as an official "founder" to melt down and cast metals offered in the Temple falls short.[2] In II Kings there is no thought of melting and casting offerings. The offerings in coins are merely counted and paid to the repairmen. In Zech the LXX's χωνευτήριον ("furnace") does not, as Torrey thinks, rest on an understanding of יוצר as "founder," but upon an interpretation in which the money is tested to determine whether it is genuine. Aquila's πλάστης is a literal rendering which may mean "potter" (cf. Ro 9:20, 21) [3] as well as "founder." אמרכלא in the Targum is a general term for "official," and thus supports neither "founder" nor "treasury." For "treasury" the Hebrew and the Targum regularly have אוצר, and for "treasurer" גזבר.

אוצר in the Peshitta of Zech 11:13 and 1 MS Ken may be a mere mistake due to the similarity of the words in sight and sound, or an interpretative attempt, as in the LXX and the Targum. If אוצר be original, the change to יוצר is difficult to explain.[4] Neither "founder" nor "treasury" fits the symbolic action required by the context in Zech. The paltry sum must be repudiated, not brought as an offering. And since the prophet impersonates Yahweh, bringing the money as an offering is tantamount to Yahweh's giving it to himself— but he does not want it! [5]

---

[1] The argument stands whether the latter phrase means Judas entered the sanctuary in reckless abandon, or threw the money into the sanctuary from just outside, or threw it down ἐν τῷ ἱερῷ. Whatever the precise signification of ναός, the implication is that Judas had not put the money εἰς τὸν κορβανᾶν. There is a faint possibility, but too faint for serious consideration in view of prevalent usage, that ναός means "treasury," as at Delphi. See L. Dyer, *Journal of Hellenic Studies*, 25 (1905), 311f.; E. Power, *Biblica*, 9 (1928), 263.

[2] C. C. Torrey, *JBL*, 55 (1936), 247-260; O. Eissfeldt, *Ras Schamra u. Sanchunjaton* (Halle, 1939), 42-46; F. F. Bruce, *BJRL*, 43 (1961), 341.

[3] So sometimes in classical Greek. See L & S, s.v.

[4] Allen suggests יוצר was substituted because the paltry sum was considered not good enough for the sacred treasury (*Mt*, 288). One wonders whether the irony of the passage would have been missed so entirely.

[5] Cf. J. Chr. K. Hofmann, *Weissagung u. Erfüllung* (Nördlingen, 1841-44), I, 325f.; Lange, *op. cit.*, 506.

It is impossible to be certain what is the exact reference in Zech, but to cast the coins "to the potter" must have had something to do with an answering contempt to the contempt with which Yahweh was valued.[1] J. Chr. K. Hofmann suggests a connotation of impurity and contemptibility was attached to the potter, since the field where potters obtained their clay was in the Valley of Hinnom (cf. Jer 18:2).[2] Perhaps it is best to think that the prophet was to throw the money to the potter who sold vessels for offerings of grain, wine, and oil in the Temple precincts (much as the sellers of sacrificial animals and fowl) merely to get rid of it as quickly as possible and in a public way. Because Judas' money is given to a potter (that it is for the purchase of his field is wholly incidental so far as Zech 11 is concerned) Mt sees a coincidence so singular that when combined with the other parallels—the rejection, the contemptible price, the return of the money in the Temple—it must be fulfilled prophecy.

It is very unlikely that Mt brings in Jer 18:1, 2; 32:6 ff. There is no evidence that the potter of Jer 18 is Hanamel of Jer 32. Rather, the identification is improbable, since the potter is working in the environs of Jerusalem, perhaps in the Valley of Hinnom, to which Jer "goes down" (cf. Jer 18:1, 2); whereas Hanamel, a cousin of Jer and therefore from a priestly family (Jer 1:1) and not likely a potter, presumably lives in Anathoth, where his field is located. In Jer 18 a potter is mentioned, but no field, in Jer 32 a field, but no potter. In Jer 32:14 the deeds are deposited in an earthen vessel (כלי חרש), but this is quite irrelevant to a "potter's field."[3] The juxtaposition of כסף and שקל in both Jer 32:9 and Zech 11:12 proves nothing, for it is very common (Ex 22:16; I Kings 20:39; Is 46:6; 55:2).[4] In Jer 32 the price is seventeen shekels of silver, in Zech 11 thirty pieces of silver. We cannot assume that Mt connected two such unrelated passages in Jer with each other and then with Zech 11.

There is, however, one point of connection with Jer; that is with Jer 19:1-13. Here Jer takes a potter's earthen bottle, goes down into the Valley of Hinnom, or Topheth, breaks the bottle, and

---

[1] Reinke compares the phrases "zum Henker" and "zum Schinder" (*op. cit.*, IV, ii, p. 144).

[2] *Op. cit.*, 327.

[3] Against Torrey, *Documents*, 87; *idem*, *JBL*, 55 (1936), 252.

[4] Against Doeve, *op. cit.*, 185f.

prophesies that because Judah and Jerusalem have shed "the blood of innocents (דם נקים—αἱμάτων ἀθῴων)" Topheth will become a burial place for their inhabitants from thenceforth called "The Valley of Slaughter." Mt sees parallels between the guilt of Judah and Jerusalem in shedding innocent blood and that of Judas (ἥμαρτον παραδοὺς αἷμα ἀθῷον, Mt 27:4), between the two occurrences of יוצר in Jer 19:1, 11 (probably the symbolism of a potter's vessel was chosen because the Valley of Hinnom, "which is by the entry of the Gate of Potsherds" [v. 2], was a source of clay for potters) and the circumstance that the chief priests bought the field *of a potter*, between the prominence of "the elders" and "the (chief) priests" in both passages, between the burial of the Judaeans in the Valley of Hinnom and the burial of Judas in the potter's field (which Mt may have known was located in the Valley of Hinnom, if the field was an exhausted source of clay for the former owner—the traditional site is in Hinnom), and between the names "The Valley of Slaughter" and "The Field of Blood" (note the similarity of expression: "wherefore this place shall be called. . ." [Jer 19:6]; "wherefore that field was called. . ." [Mt 27:8]). Thereby the end of Judas becomes repetitive of the judgment on Judah and prophetically typifies the end of the Jewish nation in their rejection of Jesus Christ.

Mt, then, sees two separate prophecies, one typical and one explicit, fulfilled in one event, and makes the ascription to Jer because the manifestness of the quotation from Zech and the lack of verbal resemblance to Jer would cause the Jer-side of the prophecies to be lost. The naming of one author in a composite allusion is not unknown elsewhere. For example, the allusive quotation in II Chron 36:21 is verbally drawn from Lev 26:34 f., yet ascribed to "Jer" (25:12; 29:10), from which the number of years, "seventy," is drawn.[1] Also, it was a rabbinical practice to quote various persons under one name if a similarity existed between the characters or actions of the persons.[2, 3]

---

[1] C. C. Torrey, *Ezra Studies* (Chicago, 1910), 120.

[2] See Z. H. Chajes, *The Student's Guide through the Talmud* (London, 1952), 172ff.

[3] Other views on the ascription to Jer are as follows: (1) It is a mistake by Mt (Stendahl, 123). (2) The textual evidence for omission is to be accepted (A. S. Lewis, *Light on the Four Gospels from the Sinai Palimpsest* [London, 1913], 61ff.). (3) "Jer" is a general reference to the prophetic section of the OT canon, in which in ancient times Jer stood first (thus in *Baba Bathra* 14b,

In the LXX ἔλαβον is first person singular (= אקחה). In Mt it is impossible to determine whether the parallelism with ἔδωκαν (third person plural) or the parallelism with the OT text is the stronger factor. The latter is possible since the quotation breaks off at Ἰσραήλ. It may even be that ἔδωκαν is an assimilation to the Matthaean context, rather than ἔδωκα (אW*pl*syr—cf. μοι) an assimilation to ἔλαβον taken as the first person. In any case, Mt felt no difficulty in the fact that in Zech the prophet gives the money to the potter and in his own narrative the chief priests give the money, for the essential point is that the money is paid *to the potter*.

Τὰ τριάκοντα ἀργύρια (Mt) shows independence from the LXX (τοὺς τρ. ἀργυροῦς). Τὴν τιμήν retains both its meanings, "price" and "honor," in rendering the ironic אדר ("magnificence, excellence"). הַיְקָר ("the price") becomes read as הַיָּקָר or הַיָּקָר ("the honored one"—so also the OT Pesh) and translated by τοῦ τετιμημένου. יקרתי is then adapted from first person to third in order to fit Mt's partitive understanding of מעליהם as "(those) from among them" (-αντο ἀπὸ υἱῶν Ἰσραήλ) instead of the instrumental sense, "by them."[1] Υἱῶν

five MSS of Ginsburg, and the Aramaic book-list in Byrennios) (Carpzov, *A Defence of the Hebrew Bible* [London, 1729], 107; Strack-Billerbeck, *op. cit.*, I, 1030; C. D. Ginsburg, *Introduction to the Massoretico-Critical Edition of the Hebrew Bible* [London, 1897], 6; J.-P. Audet, *JTS*, 1 [1950], 136, 138, 150; H. F. D. Sparks, *JTS*, 1 [1950], 155; E. F. Sutcliffe, *JTS*, 3 [1952], 227f.; Torrey-Eissfeldt, *TLZ*, 77 [1952], 249-254; C. C. Torrey, *ZNW*, 44 [1952/53], 217-223). (4) In a vulgar Hebrew text the passage from Zech had been inserted into Jer (E. Böhl, *Die alttestamentliche Citate im NT* [Wien, 1878], 75f.—Böhl's *Volksbibel*). (5) Zech 9-11 was written by Jer and inserted into Zech, a theory originated by Joseph Mede to account for the misascription, but eventuating in the Deutero-Zech hypothesis (see P. J. Gloag, *Introduction to the Synoptic Gospels* [Edinburgh, 1895], 161; E. J. Young, *An Introduction to the OT* [London, 1953], 270). (6) Ζρι̅ου̅ was confounded with Ιρι̅ου̅ (Toy, *op. cit.*, 71). (7) Διὰ τοῦ προφήτου reflects ביד נביא, which was misread as ביר and taken for an abbreviation of the name "Jeremiah" (Baumstark, *op. cit.*, 301, following J. Kremer, *Die Hirtenallegorie im Buche Zacharias auf ihre Messianität hin untersucht* [Münster, 1930], 99). On ביד in introductory formulae, see Num 10:13; Jer 26:13 (LXX); 37 (44):2; Zech 7:7; CDC 3:21; 4:13 (Rabin's second edition, pp. 12, 16). (8) The quotation was taken from a Testimony Book, in which it stood close to or in connection with a quotation (or quotations) from Jer (Harris, *Testimonies*, I, 56-60; Findlay, *Jesus in the First Gospel*, 21f.). (9) The quotation comes from an apocryphal text of Jer (Jerome, *Comm. in Mt*, ad 27:9 [MPL XXVI, 205]; Lohmeyer-Schmauch, *op. cit.*, 378f.; cf. Origen, *Comm. in Mt*, ad 27:9 [ed. Klostermann (Leipzig, 1933), II, 249f.]). (10) The Jews deleted the passage from Jer (Eus., *Dem. Ev.* x. 4 [MPG XXII, 745]).

[1] Stendahl thinks Mt distinguished the authorities from the people and blamed the former (p. 126, n. 1).

Ἰσραήλ merely identifies הם- and does not presuppose a different Hebrew text.[1] The inserted clause about the purchase of the field points to Jer 19. Καθὰ συνέταξέν μοι κύριος imitates the statement concerning Moses repeated in the Pentateuch,[2] but maintains contact with Zech through μοι (= אלי).[3]

Allusive Quotations Peculiar to Matthew

The allusive quotations peculiar to Mt will display the same mixed text-form that is prominent in all the other groups of quotations except the formal citations in common with Mk.

Mt 1:21	Tit 2:14	Ps 130 (129):8 LXX	MT
αὐτὸς γὰρ	ἵνα	καὶ αὐτὸς	והוא
σώσει	λυτρώσηται	λυτρώσεται	יפדה
τὸν λαὸν αὐτοῦ	ἡμᾶς	τὸν Ἰσραὴλ	את ישראל
ἀπὸ τῶν	ἀπὸ πάσης	ἐκ πασῶν τῶν	מכל
ἁμαρτιῶν αὐτῶν	ἀνομίας	ἀνομιῶν αὐτοῦ	עונתיו

Cf. Philo, *De Mut. Nom.* cxxi (Cohn-Wendland, III, 177).

The most remarkable thing about this quotation is that although it is given as the reason for the name Ἰησοῦς, פדה instead of ישע appears in the Hebrew. Lest the allusion be doubted on that account, notice should be taken of the striking verbal resemblance to the OT text and of the circumstance that in Tit there are similarities both with Mt against the MT and LXX and with the LXX against Mt. Unless word-substitution occurred in the MT, we must say that פדה and ישע were treated as synonyms.[4]

Mt's γάρ ties the quotation to the context, as ἵνα does in Tit. Αὐτός agrees with the LXX, but is a self-evident translation of הוא (unrendered in Tit). Mt puts σώσει in place of λυτρώσηται, because in the LXX σῴζειν usually stands for ישע, the root from which

---

[1] The Targums very often expand with the phrase, "children of Israel." See Baumstark, *op. cit.*, 300.

[2] I owe this observation to Anger, I, 41; II, 4f., 29.

[3] Baumstark thinks this clause in Mt goes back to a reading ביד יהוה for בית יהוה (*op. cit.*, 302f.). However, when used of the word of the Lord, יד denotes instrumentality and is construed with a word of speaking (see references above, p. 125f., n. 3 [7]). Alone, it denotes supervision (Ex 38:21; Num 7:8). The Matthaean μοι clearly points to אלי in the introductory clause of Zech.

[4] Another possibility exists, viz., parallel influence from Jdg 13:5: והוא יחל להושיע את ישראל מיד פלשתים (F. W. Danker, *Multipurpose Tools for Bible Study* [St. Louis, 1960], 92). If a reference to Jdg 13:5 in Mt 2:23 be rejected (see above, pp. 98-100), this explanation is less probable.

Ἰησοῦς is derived. For "Israel" Mt substitutes "his people," perhaps in view of the catholicity of the Church. In Tit ἡμᾶς is due to the context. Mt and Tit agree in ἀπό against ἐκ (LXX); but Mt drops כל and renders עונתיו ("his iniquities") by ἁμαρτιῶν αὐτῶν ("their sins"). One wonders if a Hebrew text in which כל was missing is reflected. Ἁμαρτία and ἀνομία stand side by side in the LXX as translations of עון. Αὐτῶν might reflect the suffix ־ימו, a poetic form of the third person plural, which because of its rarity may have been changed to ־יו. Tit agrees with the LXX in rendering כל and in the choice of ἀνομία, but goes its own way in the singular (maybe because of the Pauline emphasis on the sin-principle) and in the dropping of the possessive pronoun. Ἡμῶν might have been added, but would have overloaded the sentence since ἡμῶν and ἡμᾶς had just been used.

Thus, the Matthaean quotation is wholly independent from the LXX and shows signs of targumic adaptation.[1]

Mt 2:1, 2: μάγοι ἀπὸ ἀνατολῶν . . . εἴδομεν γὰρ αὐτοῦ τὸν ἀστέρα ἐν τῇ ἀνατολῇ
Num 23:7 LXX: ἐξ ὀρέων ἀπ' ἀνατολῶν
MT: מהררי קדם
24:17 LXX: ἀνατελεῖ ἄστρον ἐξ Ἰακώβ, καὶ ἀναστήσεται ἄνθρωπος ἐξ Ἰσραήλ
MT: דרך כוכב מיעקב וקם שבט מישראל

The Magi, like Balaam, come ἀπὸ ἀνατολῶν.[2] The peculiar expression ἐν τῇ ἀνατολῇ (also v. 9) must mean "at its rising," because it is unlikely Mt would change to the singular after using the plural for "east" in verse 1.[3] This is the only place the LXX translates דרך by ἀνατέλλειν.[4] "Star" in the singular occurs elsewhere in the OT only in Amos 5:26.[5] Num 24:17 is Messianically interpreted in

---

[1] Kilpatrick supposes the IF to 1:23 originally belonged to 1:21, since the latter is non-Septuagintal and the former Septuagintal (*Origins*, 57, 93). This is unjustifiable because of the heterogeneous textual character of the formula-citations as a group, because of the non-Septuagintal character of many allusive quotations, because γάρ in 1:21 makes superfluous an IF, and because 1:23 is then left hanging in the air. See also Lindars, 214.

[2] The reading "from the east" in v. 2 syr^{sin} may derive from Num 23:7.

[3] See A & G, s.v. ἀνατολή, and the literature cited. The objection that "at its rising" would require an αὐτοῦ (Alford, *op. cit.*, I, 12) does not reckon with the possibility the definite article weakly fulfils the same function. Αὐτοῦ may have fallen out through frequent use of the expression. A. S. Lewis would construe the phrase with "we" (-ομεν), but this is unnatural (*ET*, 19 [1907/08], 138).

[4] A fact noted by Stendahl, 136. On the Messianic coloring ἀνατέλλειν gained, see H. Schlier, *TWNT*, I, 354f.

[5] See E. A. Abbott, *The Expositor*, 22, 8th Series (1916), 404f.

the LXX (ἄνθρωπος for שבט, "sceptre"!), the Targums (Jon and Onk), the *Testament of Judah* 24, Qumran literature,[1] and patristic literature.[2] The OT and NT passages both deal with the king of Israel (cf. Num 24:7). We must therefore say that Mt's play on ἀνατολή is a conscious allusion to Num 23 and 24, based on the LXX.[3]

Mt 2:11	Ps 72 (71):10, 11 LXX	MT
	βασιλεῖς . . . δῶρα	מלכי ··· מנחה
	προσοίσουσιν, βασιλεῖς	ישיבו מלכי ···
	. . . δῶρα προσάξουσιν	אשכר יקריבו
καὶ πεσόντες	καὶ	
προσεκύνησαν αὐτῷ	προσκυνήσουσιν αὐτῷ	וישתחוו לו
	πάντες οἱ βασιλεῖς	כל מלכים
	Is 60:6 LXX	MT
. . . προσήνεγκαν	φέροντες	
αὐτῷ δῶρα		
χρυσὸν	χρυσίον	זהב
καὶ λίβανον	καὶ λίβανον	ולבונה
	οἴσουσιν	ישאו
καὶ σμύρναν		

This OT allusion buttresses Mt's purpose of showing that the Messiah, rejected by his own nation, has been received by the Gentiles. Sheba, mentioned in both OT passages, was a region of Arabia and noted for its gold and spices.[4] The earliest tradition traces the

[1] See F. F. Bruce, *op. cit.*, 46ff.; J. Daniélou, *Vigiliae Christianae*, 11 (1957), 121-138.

[2] Justin, 1 *Apol.* xxxii (MPG VI, 380); *Dial.* cvi. 4 (MPG VI, 724); Iren., *Epideixis* 58 (J. A. Robinson, *St. Irenaeus*: *The Demonstration of the Apostolic Preaching* [London, 1920], 121).

[3] The objection that in Num the star *is* the Messiah, whereas in Mt it is only the sign of his coming (Klostermann, *Mt*, 12; Weiss-Bousset, *op. cit.*, I, 234f.; M. M. Bourke, *CBQ*, 22 [1960], 166), misses the metaphorical nature of the OT expression and the representative function of the star in Mt. The further objection that Mt would surely have explicitly quoted Num does not take into account that many OT quotations in the NT are not formal (see K. J. Woollcombe, *Essays in Typology* [London, 1957], 46). Stendahl argues that in Mt 2 only the geographically oriented quotations are quoted explicitly because the main point of the chapter is to show why the Messiah came from Nazareth (in *Judentum, Urchristentum, Kirche*, 99f.). Other interesting parallels between Num and Mt are that in both passages the ones from the East come to an anti-Jewish king, with whom their relationship is finally broken off by divine interjunction in the form of visions; יהוה אלהיו עמו in Num 23:21 is close to "Immanuel" in Mt 1:23; and although Balaam's coming to get treasure contrasts with the bringing of treasures by the Magi, in both cases the treasures play a central role.

[4] See also Ps 72:15; I Kings 10:1ff.; Ezek 27:22; Herodotus iii. 107; Strabo XVI. iv. 25; I. Löw, *Die Flora der Juden* (Wien, 1928), I, 312.

Magi to Arabia.[1] Except for πεσόντες, which Mt likes to add to προσκυνεῖν (see 4:9), and σμύρναν, all of Mt's words are paralleled in the LXX.

Mt 2:13	Ex 2:15 LXX	MT
μέλλει γὰρ Ἡρῴδης	Φαραὼ . . .	פרעה ···
ζητεῖν	καὶ ἐζήτει	ויבקש
τὸ παιδίον		
τοῦ ἀπολέσαι αὐτό	ἀνελεῖν Μωυσῆν.	להרג את משה
. . . καὶ ἀνεχώρησεν	Ἀνεχώρησε δὲ . . .	ויברח

The *Midrash Rabba* on the birth of Moses in Ex tells of Pharaoh's astrologers perceiving that the mother of Israel's redeemer was pregnant. Not knowing if the redeemer was to be Israelite or Egyptian, Pharaoh ordered all children from henceforth to be drowned. But when the Egyptians remonstrated, the edict was restricted to Israelitish infants. Since this story was known to Josephus,[2] it was current in apostolic times and may well have suggested the Moses-Jesus parallel here and in verses 20, 21.

In the choice of ἀπ λλυμι and in the use of the articular infinitive Mt renders the Hebrew independently from the LXX.[3]

Mt 2:20, 21	Ex 4:19, 20 MT	LXX
καὶ πορεύου	לך	βάδιζε
	שב	ἄπελθε
εἰς γῆν Ἰσραήλ	מצרים	εἰς Αἴγυπτον
τεθνήκασιν γὰρ	כי מתו	τεθνήκασιν γὰρ
	כל האנשים	πάντες
οἱ ζητοῦντες	המבקשים	οἱ ζητοῦντές
τὴν ψυχὴν τοῦ παιδίου	את נפשך	σου τὴν ψυχήν
δὲ . . . παρέλαβεν	ויקח משה	ἀναλάβων δὲ Μωυσῆς
τὸ παιδίον καὶ	את אשתו	τὴν γυναῖκα καὶ
τὴν μητέρα αὐτοῦ	ואת בניו ···	τὰ παιδία . . .
καὶ εἰσῆλθεν	וישב	καὶ ἐπέστρεψεν
εἰς γῆν Ἰσραήλ	ארצה מצרים	εἰς Αἴγυπτον

In Mt the Hebraistic ζητεῖν τὴν ψυχήν and the *plural* τεθνήκασιν γὰρ οἱ ζητοῦντες immediately after the genitive absolute in the singular (τελευτήσαντος δὲ τοῦ Ἡρῴδου) and in construction with τὴν

---

[1] See Tert., *Adv. Marc.*, iii. 13. 8; *Adv. Jud.*, ix. 12; Lagrange, *Mt*, 20, 31; Edersheim, *Life and Times*, I, 203.

[2] *Ant.* II. ix. 2. On the *Midrash*, see G. H. Box, *ZNW*, 6 (1905), 89.

[3] See M. S. Enslin, *JBL*, 59 (1940), 332; Lohmeyer-Schmauch, *op. cit.*, 31, n. 1, for this allusion. An allusive quotation here might have been doubted but for the clear allusion to Ex 4:19, 20 in Mt 2:20, 21.

ψυχήν must reflect Ex.[1] So also does the fact that "land of Israel" occurs only here in the NT, answering to ארצה מצרים. The LXX is reflected in the omission of האנשים. But in the choice of πορεύεσθαι, παραλαμβάνειν, and εἰσέρχεσθαι Mt translates independently from the LXX, which would have been suitable. Ἄπελθε and ἐπέστρεψεν would have provided even better shades of meaning than the words Mt chooses. However, Mt is closer to the Hebrew in rendering ויקח by a finite verb rather than by a participle and in retaining ארצה, omitted by the LXX.

Mt 3:4	Mk 1:6	II Kings 1:8 LXX	MT
αὐτὸς δὲ	καὶ ἦν		
ὁ Ἰωάννης εἶχεν	ὁ Ἰωάννης	ἀνὴρ	איש
τὸ ἔνδυμα αὐτοῦ	ἐνδεδυμένος		בעל
ἀπὸ τριχῶν	τρίχας	δασὺς	שער
καμήλου	καμήλου		
καὶ ζώνην	καὶ ζώνην	καὶ ζώνην	ואזור
δερματίνην	δερματίνην	δερματίνην	עור
περὶ τὴν	περὶ τὴν	περιεζωσμένος	אזור
ὀσφὺν αὐτοῦ	ὀσφὺν αὐτοῦ	τὴν ὀσφὺν αὐτοῦ	במתניו

τρίχας] δέρριν Da
καὶ ζώνην . . . αὐτοῦ] *om* D it

Δέρριν is usually explained as a corruption from Zech 13:4, where deceivers are said to pose as prophets by donning δέρριν τριχίνην.[2] However, the obscurity of the passage in Zech and the impropriety and the unlikelihood of a comparison between the practice of lying prophets and the dress of John the Baptist render this explanation doubtful. Nor is the omission in the Western text then accounted for. The inter-synoptic harmonistic element rife elsewhere in Cod. D [3] and the usually greater fulness of the Western text [4] make more valuable the shorter reading here, which disagrees with Mt. Therefore, prefer as a Western non-interpolation [5]

[1] The plural has otherwise been explained as a plural of category, a plural of majesty, a generalizing plural to conceal the identity of Herod [!] or to show respect for the dead [!] or to include Herod's accomplices. Besides the commentaries, see Bl-D § 141; Robertson, *Grammar*, 392. There are notable differences between the stories, particularly in geographical direction, as Nepper-Christensen has pointed out (*op. cit.*, 165f.); but this in no way destroys the obvious borrowing of phraseology from Ex.

[2] So Swete, *Mk*, 5; Moulton & Milligan, *The Vocabulary of the Greek Testament* (London, 1928), 142; Cranfield, *Mk*, 47.

[3] See above, p. 29, n. 4.

[4] Westcott & Hort, *op. cit.*, II, 122; A. Souter, *Text and Canon*, 112.

[5] On preferring Western omissions, see Westcott & Hort, *op. cit.*, II,

the reading καὶ ἦν ὁ Ἰωάννης ἐνδεδυμένος δέρριν καμήλου and regard the longer reading as assimilation to Mt,[1] perhaps occasioned by the rarity and vulgarity of δέρριν. In this case, Mt characteristically casts the Marcan narrative in OT phraseology to bring out the parallel between John and Elijah.

The expression καὶ ζώνην δερματίνην περὶ (LXX: -εζωσμένος) τὴν ὀσφὺν αὐτοῦ is Septuagintal. But τὸ ἔνδυμα αὐτοῦ ἀπὸ τριχῶν καμήλου alludes to the Hebrew expression בעל שער ("lord of hair"). The LXX interprets the Hebrew to mean that Elijah was a hairy man (ἀνὴρ δασύς); [2] whereas Mt interprets it to mean that Elijah (and John) wore a garment of hair-cloth or a shaggy coat of untanned skin with the hair outward.[3]

Mt 5:4: οἱ πενθοῦντες . . . παρακληθήσονται
Is 61:2 LXX: παρακαλέσαι πάντας τοὺς πενθοῦντας
MT: לנחם כל אבלים

The Lucan form of this beatitude is far from OT phraseology: μακάριοι οἱ κλαίοντες νῦν, ὅτι γελάσετε (Lk 6:21).[4] Mt, the LXX, and the MT agree with one another.

Mt 5:5: οἱ πραεῖς, . . . κληρονομήσουσιν τὴν γῆν
Ps 37 (36):11 LXX: οἱ δὲ πραεῖς κληρονομήσουσιν γῆν
MT: וענוים יירשו ארץ

The genuineness of this verse in Mt has been doubted because it is obviously drawn from Ps 37:11 and because verses 4 and 5 are transposed in Tatian 33 Δ D Θ 700 565 28 544 b q f r² syr^cur Clem-Al

175f.; A. T. Robertson, *An Introduction to the Textual Criticism of the NT*, 225ff.; Kenyon, *Handbook to the Textual Criticism of the NT*, 327, 362f.

[1] So J. Weiss, *Das älteste Evangelium* (Göttingen, 1903), 124f.; E. Nestle and E. von Dobschütz, *Einführung in das griechische NT*⁴ (Göttingen, 1923), 7; C. H. Turner, *JTS*, 28 (1927), 151. Scribal assimilation tended to be toward Mt. See F. F. Bruce, *The Books and the Parchments* (London, 1950), 170.

[2] J. A. T. Robinson thinks the LXX is "almost certainly right," since "this is the sort of man a prophet was expected to be, . . ." (*NTS*, 4 [1958], 263f.). One may question, however, that prophets were expected to have hairy bodies. Robinson claims the support of C. H. Kraeling in arguing there is no reference to Elijah in the description of John, but Kraeling merely doubts that John intentionally imitated Elijah. Kraeling does see an allusion to II King 1:8 in the NT (*John the Baptist* [New York, 1951], 14f.).

[3] Cf. R. Kittel, *Die Bücher der Könige* (Göttingen, 1900), 183; Alexander, *op. cit.*, 52.

[4] On this account J. H. Moulton regards Lk as preserving the form of Greek Q and Mt as assimilating to the OT (*The Expositor*, 2, 7th Series [1906], 102). It may be, however, that Jesus himself modelled the beatitudes after OT passages. See Flusser, *op. cit.*, 11 f.

Or Bas Greg of Nyss Aphraates.[1] But verse 5 also contains an OT allusion, as well as most of the Matthaean beatitudes. Ps 37:11 is not a beatitude, so that it is doubtful an invention would have been based thereupon.[2] We might as well suspect verse 4 as verse 5 on account of the transposition in some MSS.[3]

With one exception, Mt, the LXX, and the MT agree. The exception is that in Mt the article with γῆν reflects the Targum (ארעא)—a further indication of genuineness.[4]

Mt 5:7: μακάριοι οἱ ἐλεήμονες, ὅτι αὐτοὶ ἐλεηθήσονται
Ps 18 (17):26 MT: עם חסיד תתחסד
LXX: μετὰ ὁσίου ὁσιωθήσῃ

This beatitude is obviously patterned upon a correct rendering of the Hebrew text against the LXX.[5]

Mt 5:8: μακάριοι οἱ καθαροὶ τῇ καρδίᾳ, ὅτι αὐτοὶ τὸν θεὸν ὄψονται
Ps 24 (23):3, 4 LXX: τίς ἀναβήσεται εἰς τὸ ὄρος τοῦ κυρίου, καὶ τίς στήσεται ἐν τόπῳ ἁγίῳ αὐτοῦ; . . . καθαρὸς τῇ καρδίᾳ
MT: מי יעלה בהר יהוה ומי יקום במקום קדשו ··· בר לבב

Except for the definite article with καθαροί and the plural, both through conformity with the other beatitudes, Mt agrees with the LXX and the MT in the expression "the pure of heart." "They shall see God" adapts the thought in the psalm of going up to the hill of Yahweh and standing in His holy place.

---

[1] Wellhausen, *Mt*, 14f.; A. Harnack, *The Sayings of Jesus* (London, 1908), 48; M. Goguel, *Introduction au NT* (Paris, 1923), I, 415; Streeter, *op. cit.*, 252; Bultmann, *Geschichte der synoptischen Tradition*² (Göttingen, 1931), 115; Benoit, *Mt*, 52.

[2] See Michaelis, *Mt*, I, 202f.

[3] This is exactly what R. H. Charles does (*ET*, 28 [1916/17], 537f.). Others adopt the order of Tat 33 etc. (e.g., Lagrange, *Mt*, 83). But Schniewind argues that because of their similarity, verses 4 and 5 would probably not have been separated had they been together originally; verses 3 and 4 do belong together because both are reminiscent of Is 61:1, 2 (*op. cit.*, 41). M. Black, on the other hand, argues that verses 3 and 5 together make a four-line stanza, which stems from a play on עניים (πτωχοί) and ענוים (πραεῖς) (*ET*, 64 [1952/53], 125). Cf. the Qumran *pesher* to Ps 37:11, in which ענוים in the text of the psalm is interpreted by אביונים (edited by J. M. Allegro, *PEQ* [1954], 69ff.). Yet others regard verse 5 as a redactional addition by the evangelist (Pfleiderer, *op. cit.*, II, 319; J. Dupont, *Les béatitudes* [Louvain, 1954], 89f.).

[4] Against most others, I must agree with Holtzmann that τὴν γῆν retains the limited meaning, the Promised Land, original to the psalm (*op. cit.*, 203).

[5] I owe the notice of this allusion to Toy, *op. cit.*, 26f.

Mt 5:34: μήτε ἐν τῷ οὐρανῷ, ὅτι θρόνος ἐστὶν τοῦ θεοῦ
Is 66:1 LXX: οὕτως λέγει κύριος, ὁ οὐρανός μοι θρόνος
μοι Rahlfs] μου BQ
MT: כה אמר יהוה השמים כסאי
Acts 7:49: ὁ οὐρανός μοι θρόνος

Mt puts θέος with the article for יהוה-κύριος and uses the genitive. If the genitive in LXX^BQ is hexaplaric, as would seem to be so in view of μοι in Acts 7:49, the two divergences in Mt probably display independence from the LXX.

Mt 5:35	Is 66:1 LXX; Acts 7:49	MT
μήτε ἐν τῇ γῇ	ἡ δὲ γῆ	והארץ
ὅτι ὑποπόδιόν ἐστιν	ὑποπόδιον	הדם
τῶν ποδῶν αὐτοῦ	τῶν ποδῶν μου	רגלי
	Ps 48 (47):3 LXX	MT
μήτε εἰς Ἰεροσόλυμα		
ὅτι πόλις ἐστὶν	ἡ πόλις	קרית
τοῦ μεγάλου βασιλέως	τοῦ βασιλέως τοῦ μεγάλου	מלך רב

There is no variation and little chance for such in the first half of the quotation. In the second half Mt omits the definite article with πόλις in the LXX and smooths out the style by transposing βασιλέως and μεγάλου and by dropping the article with the adjective.

Mt 6:6	Is 26:20 LXX	MT	II Kings 4:33 LXX	MT
εἴσελθε εἰς	εἴσελθε εἰς	בא	εἰσῆλθεν . . . εἰς	ויבא
τὸ ταμεῖόν σου	τὰ ταμίειά σου	בחדריך	τὸν οἶκον	
καὶ κλείσας	ἀπόκλεισον	וסגר	κ. ἀπέκλεισεν	ויסגר
τὴν θύραν σου	τὴν θύραν σου	דלתיך	τὴν θύραν . . .	הדלת ...
πρόσευξαι			κ. προσηύξατο	ויתפלל
τῷ πατρί σου			πρὸς κύριον	אל יהוה

The first part of the quotation stands closer to Is 26:20 in the imperative and in ταμεῖον.[1] In view of the *Qere* reading דלתך (singular— also the LXX and many MSS of Kennicott and De-Rossi), Mt's singular τὸ ταμεῖον may reflect a parallel singular reading בחדרך.[2] Mt prefers the simplex κλείειν to ἀποκλείειν in the LXX of both passages. Προσεύχεσθαι stems from II Kings and is a self-evident rendering of פלל. The following dative in Mt differs from πρός with the accusative in the LXX. The use of πατήρ is an assimilation to the Matthaean context. Thus, Mt departs from the LXX in minor, but definite points.

[1] Ταμίειον (LXX) was later contracted to ταμεῖον. Delitzsch interprets Is 26:20 with reference to protection of those hidden in the place of prayer (*Is*, I, 452f.).

[2] Omission and addition of the *yodh* were common mistakes. See J. Kennedy, *op. cit.*, 9f.

Mt 7:22: οὐ τῷ σῷ ὀνόματι ἐπροφητεύσαμεν;
Jer 14:14; 27 (34):15 (12) LXX: προφητεύουσιν τῷ ὀνόματί μου
τῷ] *pr* ἐπί 14:14 and Cod. A in 34:12
MT: נבאים בשמי

Both passages in Jer concern false prophets, as does Mt 7:22. Throughout Mt and the rest of the NT the expression "(in) the name of. . ." regularly takes a preposition.[1] Here the Hebrew has בְּ. Therefore, Mt's simple dative shows slavish dependence on the LXX of Jer 34:12.

Mt 10:6; 15:24: πρὸς [15:24: εἰς] τὰ πρόβατα τὰ ἀπολωλότα οἴκου Ἰσραήλ
15:24 τά 2°] *pr* ταῦτα D syr$^{\text{sin, cur}}$ [2]
Jer 50 (27):6 LXX: πρόβατα ἀπολωλότα ἐγενήθη ὁ λαός μου
MT: צאן אבדות היה עמי

The texts agree with one another. The Targum to Jer 50:6 provides the link with the closely related allusion in Mt 9:36 through its reference to scattering: עאן מבדרא הוו עמי. It would therefore seem that both allusions took shape in a Semitic milieu.

Mt 10:29: καὶ ἓν ἐξ αὐτῶν [στρουθία] οὐ πεσεῖται ἐπὶ τὴν γῆν ἄνευ τοῦ πατρὸς ὑμῶν
ἐπὶ τὴν γῆν] εἰς παγίδα Or
Am 3:5 LXX: εἰ πεσεῖται ὄρνεον ἐπὶ τὴν γῆν ἄνευ ἰξευτοῦ
τὴν γῆν] τῆς γῆς A
MT: התפל צפור על פח הארץ ומוקש אין לה

This verse was early recognized as an allusion to Am 3:5, as is shown by the reading εἰς παγίδα, answering to על פח, in Origen, the Pseudo-Clementine Homilies, and Chrysostom.[3] The allusion is based wholly upon the LXX in the omission of פח, the use of ἄνευ, and the contrast between the caring heavenly πατρός and the hunting ἰξευτοῦ ("fowler," for מוקש, "noose, snare").

Mt 11:28	Jer 31 (38):25 LXX	MT
δεῦτε πρός με	ὅτι ἐμέθυσα	כי הרויתי
πάντες	πᾶσαν	
οἱ κοπιῶντες	ψυχὴν διψῶσαν	נפש עיפה
καὶ	καὶ πᾶσαν ψυχὴν	וכל נפש
πεφορτισμένοι	πεινῶσαν	דאבה
	ἐνέπλησα	מלאתי
	Ex 33:14 LXX	MT
κἀγὼ ἀναπαύσω	καὶ καταπαύσω	והנחתי
ὑμᾶς	σε	לך

[1] See the concordance, s.v. ὄνομα, for a host of references.
[2] See M. Black, *JTS*, 49 (1948), 164, on Aramaic influence.
[3] E. Hautsch, *Die Evangelienzitate des Origenes* (= *Texte u. Untersuchungen*, 3. Reihe, Bd. 4, Heft 2a; Leipzig, 1909), 29f.

The Hebrew words in Jer denote one who is languishing and weary, especially through toil. Hence, Mt's οἱ κοπιῶντες (= "wearied through toil") and πεφορτισμένοι (= "languishing under heavy burdens") come much closer to the Hebrew than the LXX's διψῶσαν ("thirsting") and πεινῶσαν ("hungering"). In view of the poor state of the Hebrew text in Jer, the agreement between Mt and the LXX in πᾶς may attest another כל before the first נפש. Alternatively, since Mt has no article and no πάντες before πεφορτισμένοι, he may have worked from a Hebrew text in which כל was present before the first נפש only.

In the allusion to Ex the prefix ἀνα- differs from the prefix κατα- in the LXX. The plurals in Mt are due to the context.

Mt 11:29: καὶ εὑρήσετε ἀνάπαυσιν ταῖς ψυχαῖς ὑμῶν
Jer 6:16 LXX: καὶ εὑρήσετε ἁγνισμὸν ταῖς ψυχαῖς ὑμῶν
ἁγνισμόν B] ἁγιασμόν A
MT: ומצאו מרגוע לנפשכם

Mt's ἀνάπαυσιν ("rest") correctly renders מרגוע against both readings in the LXX (ἁγνισμόν, "purification"; ἁγιασμόν, "sanctification"). But Mt agrees with the LXX in the future indicative verb against the imperative of the Hebrew and in the plural ταῖς ψυχαῖς for the collective singular of the Hebrew.[1]

Although this pericope may reflect a stereotyped form of speech used by Oriental teachers,[2] the saturation in OT language and thought [3] and the paronomasia in the Aramaic [4] speak for authenticity.

Mt 12:40; Jon 2:1 LXX: ἦν Ἰωνᾶς ἐν τῇ κοιλίᾳ τοῦ κήτους τρεῖς ἡμέρας καὶ τρεῖς νύκτας
MT: ויהי יונה במעי הדג שלשה ימים ושלשה לילות

Mt, the LXX, and the MT agree, if we regard κῆτος ("sea-monster") as a legitimate rendering in this context of דג ("fish"). This verse has been widely regarded as an interpolation, because

---

[1] The Gospel of Thomas, logion 90, rejects the Semitic use of ψυχή as a reflexive in this saying.

[2] See A. Fridrichsen, in *Synoptische Studien*, 83-85. The parallels most frequently drawn are Sir. 51:23ff.; 24:19ff. and the Hermetic tractate *Poimandres*. Fridrichsen adds Epictetus, *Diss.* iv. 8. 28. It may be that Jesus impersonates the Divine Wisdom. See further E. Norden, *op. cit.*, 277-308; D. Völter, *Die Grundfrage des Lebens Jesu* (Stuttgart, 1936), 167ff.; T. Arvedson, *Das Mysterium Christi* (Uppsala, 1937).

[3] Schniewind, *op. cit.*, 144f.; L. Cerfaux, *Ephemerides Theologicae Lovanienses*, 31 (1955), 331-342; Percy, *op. cit.*, 109.

[4] A. Meyer, *op. cit.*, 83f.: אֲנִיחַ (ἀναπαύειν)—נִיחַ (πρᾶυς)—נִיחָא (ἀνάπαυσις).

the parallel, Lk 11:30, mentions nothing of Jonah's adventure in the belly of the sea-monster and because Justin, in quoting the passage and drawing the parallel to Jesus' rising the third day, omits verse 40.[1] But in Lk as well as in Mt the sign is placed in the future and a specific Messianic proof is in question, so that Jesus' mere preaching of repentance does not meet the requirements. The difficulty that Jesus was in the grave but two nights militates both against interpolation and against a *vaticinium ex eventu* [2] and provides a reason for Justin's omission.[3] The view which would connect "the sign of Jonah" with "the sign of the Son of man" at the second advent (Mt 24:30) [4] misses the distinction between the meaning "ensign" in 24:30 [5] and the meaning "proof" in 12:40.

Mt 13:41: τὰ σκάνδαλα καὶ τοὺς ποιοῦντας τὴν ἀνομίαν
Zeph 1:3 MT: אסף ··· והמכשלות את הרשעים

The Septuagintal text adopted by Ziegler and Rahlfs omits after אסף: + καὶ τὰ (*om* W*) σκάνδαλα σὺν τοῖς ἀσέβεσι(ν) W* 36 48mg Thdt (= MT); + κ. τὰ σκάνδ. σὺν (*om* 22) τ. ἀσ./ καὶ ἀσθενήσουσιν οἱ ἀσεβεῖς 22 763 (tr.); + (·※· Hi.) καὶ ἀσθενήσουσιν οἱ ἀσεβεῖς *rell* (48 txt). These additions are late assimilations to the Hebrew text.

Inasmuch as the LXX omits, Mt goes directly to the Hebrew. Τὰ σκάνδαλα in the parabolic context and by parallelism with ποιοῦντας should refer to persons. But since it renders המכשלות, a feminine noun probably meaning the idols [6] which will be swept away with their worshippers, τὰ σκάνδαλα may not refer to persons. If the reference is to persons, Mt has adapted the word; or he has read המכשלים (*hiphil* participle) and taken את as the sign of the accusa-

[1] *Dial.* cvii. 2 (MPG VI, 724f.). See J. A. Findlay, in *Amicitiae Corolla*, 58.

[2] See Cullmann, *Christology*, 62f.

[3] So Lagrange, *Mt*, 249. The fathers were uneasy about the "three nights" (see B. M. Metzger, *JTS*, 8 [1957], 119, who cites the Syriac *Didascalia Apostolorum*, ed. Lagarde, lxxxviii, pp. 18f.; Cyril, *Cat.* xiii. 24 [MPG XXXIII, 801]; and Stendahl, 133, n. 1, on the marginal note in min. 899). On the Jewish method of reckoning time by a part for the whole, see Strack-Billerbeck, *op. cit.*, I, 649; I Sam 30:12, 13; II Chron 10:5, 12; Esther 4:16; 5:1. Alternatively, "three days and three nights" is an indefinitely short period of time (J. Bauer, *Biblica*, 39 [1958], 354-358).

[4] See A. Vögtle, in *Synoptische Studien*, 230-277—also for a full discussion of other views.

[5] See Is 5:26; 11:12; 13:2; 18:3; 49:22; 62:10 and E. C. S. Gibson, *op. cit.*, 86ff.; *idem*, *The Expositor*, 1, 2nd Series (1881), 298.

[6] In the only other OT occurrence in Is 3:6, the word means "ruin." J. M. P. Smith states "ruins" is the only possible translation in Zeph 1:3 (*op. cit.*, 186); but it is precarious to rule out the meaning "offence," when the word occurs only twice and the meaning in question fits the etymology of the word. The Targum uses תקלת, "stumbling-block."

tive, inserting a *waw* conjunctive. The Hebrew text is suspected of corruption, so that the Matthaean version may reflect a different Hebrew text.

Τοὺς ποιοῦντας τὴν ἀνομίαν looks like a targumic expansion for הרשעים, because the verb עבד is frequently inserted into the renderings of the Targum. Another possibility exists, viz., that the expression derives from Ps 37 (36):1: τοὺς ποιοῦντας τὴν ἀνομίαν (LXX); (ב)עשי עולה.[1]

Mt 13:43: τότε οἱ δίκαιοι ἐκλάμψουσιν ὡς ὁ ἥλιος
ἐκλάμψουσιν] λάμψουσιν D *pc*
Dan 12:3 LXX: καὶ οἱ συνιέντες φανοῦσιν ὡς φωστῆρες τοῦ οὐρανοῦ καὶ οἱ κατίσχοντες τοὺς λόγους μου ὡσεὶ τὰ ἄστρα τοῦ οὐρανοῦ
Theod: καὶ οἱ συνιέντες ἐκλάμψουσιν ὡς ἡ λαμπρότης τοῦ στερεώματος καὶ ἀπὸ τῶν δικαίων τῶν πολλῶν ὡς οἱ ἀστέρες . . .
ἐκλάμψουσιν] λάμψουσιν B
MT: ··· והמשכלים יזהרו כזהר הרקיע ומצדיקי הרבים ככוכבים

The allusion compresses the two clauses of Dan 12:3 into one by drawing οἱ δίκαιοι from the second clause, either as a free adaptation of מצדיקי or in agreement with Theodotion ("those from the many righteous," against "they who make many righteous"[2]), by utilizing the verb of the first clause in Theodotion, and by gathering up the thought of the comparative phrases into ὡς ὁ ἥλιος.

Mt 16:27: καὶ τότε ἀποδώσει ἑκάστῳ κατὰ τὴν πρᾶξιν αὐτοῦ
τὴν πρᾶξιν] τὰ ἔργα א*F 1 28 *al* lat syr cop arm Cyril Chrys Ambr
Ps 62 (61):13 LXX: ὅτι σὺ ἀποδώσεις ἑκάστῳ κατὰ τὰ ἔργα αὐτοῦ
MT: כי אתה תשלם לאיש כמעשהו
Prov 24:12 LXX: ὃς ἀποδίδωσιν ἑκάστῳ κατὰ τὰ ἔργα αὐτοῦ
MT: והשיב לאדם כפעלו

This allusion is extremely common, occurring also in *Tanch.* וישלח 30.130 [3] and, in accordance with the LXX (τὰ ἔργα), in Ro 2:6; II Tim 4:14; Rev 2:23; 20:12; II Clem 11:6 (τῶν ἔργων). The reading τὰ ἔργα in Mt is thus influenced by the prevailing text elsewhere. This makes the original reading, τὴν πρᾶξιν, stand out all the more in its non-Septuagintal character. Τὴν πρᾶξιν is a successful attempt to render the collective singular in the Hebrew by a corresponding singular in the Greek.

---

[1] A. L. Williams, *Mt*, II, 11.
[2] In מצדיקי in the MT, the *mem* is the sign of the participle. Theod and perhaps Mt take it as the preposition מן.
[3] Cited by Schlatter, *op. cit.*, 524.

Mt 18:16: ἵνα ἐπὶ στόματος δύο μαρτύρων ἢ τριῶν σταθῇ πᾶν ῥῆμα
μαρτύρων] *om* Dd; *trps* with δύο L124*pc*; *post* τριῶν ℵΘ 1 700 *pc*
Dt 19:15 LXX[B]: ἐπὶ στόματος δύο μαρτύρων καὶ ἐπὶ στόματος τριῶν μαρτύρων στήσεται πᾶν ῥῆμα
μαρτύρων 1°] *om* Luc (75) arm Cyr$\frac{10}{11}$
καὶ ἐπὶ στόματος] ἢ Luc (75bw)
μαρτύρων 2°] *om* bw
στήσεται] σταθήσεται AFMNΘ Luc
MT: על פי שני עדים או על פי שלשה עדים יקום דבר
על פי 2°] *om* 3 MSS Ken, 3 MSS De-R, vg, both arabic texts of Saadia, Targ Jon
II Cor 13:1: ἐπὶ στόματος δύο μαρτύρων καὶ τριῶν σταθήσεται πᾶν ῥῆμα
καί] ἢ ℵ (it)
I Tim 5:19: ἐκτὸς εἰ μὴ ἐπὶ δύο ἢ τριῶν μαρτύρων

When allowance is made for ἵνα with the subjunctive, Mt's text[1] agrees wholly with Lagarde's discredited Lucianic text (bw). It is doubtful that Mt utilized the Lucianic text represented by 75 in ἢ and the omission of ἐπὶ στόματος (2°), because in 75 these are necessitated by the omission of the first μαρτύρων, an omission Mt does not share.[2] The passive form of the verb is well-attested in the LXX. Πᾶν may represent a lost כל in the Hebrew.[3] Or insertion of πᾶν may be a natural way of overcoming the awkwardness in Greek of the Semitic idiom.[4]

Mt has either utilized an Ur-Lucianic text of the type represented by b w, or translated directly from a Semitic text which omitted the second על פי. Mt's omission of the second "witnesses" against all Semitic texts and the over-all agreement with II Cor 13:1 (except, possibly, for καί) favor the former possibility. The passive יתקיים in the Targums corresponds to Mt's σταθῇ; but this must not be pressed, because σταθήσεται in the Septuagintal tradition is also passive.

Mt 18:22: ἕως ἑβδομηκοντάκις ἑπτά
ἑπτά] ἑπτάκις D*
Gen 4:24 LXX: ἑβδομηκοντάκις ἑπτά
MT: שבעים ושבעה

---

[1] The total omission of μαρτύρων in Dd, although the most difficult reading, must be regarded as a slip; for it is not likely to have been original. Both other variants in Mt are stylistic, seeking to draw together δύο and τριῶν.

[2] I Tim 5:19 agrees with 75, but perhaps only because both are stylistically motivated. Cf. ℵΘ 1 700 *pc* in Mt.

[3] See above, p. 76, n. 3, on addition and omission of כל.

[4] Torrey, *Documents*, 73. Cf. πᾶν before ῥῆμα for the indefinite דבר in Gen 18:14 LXX[Luc (75)].

Out of Lamech's formula of revenge Jesus makes a formula of forgiveness.[1] E. J. Goodspeed has strongly defended the meaning 70+7 in agreement with Gen 4:24, as opposed to 70x7.[2] He argues that 70x7 would be ἑβδομηκοντάκις ἑπτάκις (so Cod. D* in Mt). The single occurrence of the suffix -κις shows the meaning is 70+7, as confirmed by this same translation in the LXX for the Hebrew 70+7 (Gen 4:24). Generally in the NT καί is not added after numbers from twenty to ninety (e.g., Jn 6:19). Ἑβδομήκοντα with an accompanying numeral in the sense of addition occurs in Lk 10:1, 17; Acts 7:14; 27:37—and καί is always absent. The understanding 70+7 by Origen, Augustine, and the Gospel of Hebrews (fragment quoted by Jerome) more than compensates for the understanding 70x7 in the *Testament of Benjamin* 7:4.

Mt 21:14: καὶ προσῆλθον αὐτῷ τυφλοὶ καὶ χωλοὶ ἐν τῷ ἱερῷ
II Sam 5:8 LXX: τυφλοὶ καὶ χωλοὶ οὐκ εἰσελεύσονται εἰς οἶκον κυρίου
MT: עור ופסח לא יבוא אל הבית

The OT text is probably a gloss inserted to explain the exclusion of mendicants from the Temple.[3] Mt follows the LXX in taking הבית as a reference to the Temple.[4] The allusion displays a kind of antithetic typology. David hated the blind and the lame,[5] who came to be excluded from the Temple. The greater Son of David receives the blind and the lame within the Temple and heals them, thus making them fit to be there.

Mt 21:41: οἵτινες ἀποδώσουσιν αὐτῷ τοὺς καρποὺς ἐν τοῖς καιροῖς αὐτῶν
Ps 1:3 LXX: ὃ τὸν καρπὸν αὐτοῦ δώσει ἐν καιρῷ αὐτοῦ
MT: אשר פריו יתן בעתו

---

[1] See W. Vischer, *Die evangelische Gemeindeordnung Mt* 16, 13-20, 28 (Zollikon-Zürich, 1946), 74.

[2] *Problems of NT Translation* (Chicago, 1945), 29-31. See also Moulton-Howard, *Grammar*, I, 98, II, 175; Moulton & Milligan, *op. cit.*, s.v. ἑβδομηκοντάκις; Bl-D § 248:2.

[3] See S. R. Driver, *Notes on the Hebrew Text and the Topography of the Books of Samuel*[2] (Oxford, 1913), 260f.; B. D. Eerdmans, *The Hebrew Book of Ps* (*Oudtestamentische Studien*, IV; Leiden, 1947), 504. Dalman denies the blind and the lame were thus excluded (*Sacred Sites and Ways* [London, 1935], 288ff.), but see Acts 3:2, 8.

[4] For בית alone as a temple, see I Kings 6:5; Is 44:13; 66:1. In the proverbial context הבית (note the article) was naturally understood as the house of Yahweh. The Targum retains the unexpanded expression, but spiritualizes the preceding with reference to sinners (חטאייא וחייבייא).

[5] In II Sam, the Jebusites are so sure of their position that they contemptuously tell David that even their blind and lame can keep David and his men outside the walls. The point of David's answer is that even the Je-

Mt smooths the word order and in the plurals assimilates to his context (vv. 34, 43). Minor divergences from the LXX are the compound verb and the article with καιροῖς.[1]

Mt 22:34: συνήχθησαν ἐπὶ τὸ αὐτό
ἐπὶ τὸ αὐτό] ἐπ' αὐτόν D it syr$^{sin, cur}$
Acts 4:26; Ps 2:2 LXX: καὶ οἱ ἄρχοντες συνήχθησαν ἐπὶ τὸ αὐτό
MT: ורוזנים נוסדו יחד

The above-adopted reading in Mt has been suspected of assimilation to the OT text, especially in view of Acts 4:26.[2] But comparison of Mt and the Marcan parallel (12:28 ff.) shows Mt has rearranged the wording to gain an allusion to Ps 2:2. In Mk one of the scribes comes, hears the discussion with the Sadducees, and asks his question. In Mt, the Pharisees, having heard of Jesus' discussion with the Sadducees, *gather together first*, and only then does one of them ask his question. Therefore, we must regard the Western reading as a characteristic harmonization to συνήγαγον ἐπ' αὐτόν in Mt 27:27, or an error due to the similarity of the phrases and the naturalness with which ἐπ' αὐτόν blends into the flow of thought.

Mt is in strict agreement with the LXX in the use of συνάγειν for יסד (*niphal*: "to hold council") and ἐπὶ τὸ αὐτό ("to the same place") for יחד ("together").[3]

Mt 23:19: τὸ θυσιαστήριον τὸ ἁγιάζον τὸ δῶρον
Ex 29:37 LXX: πᾶς ὁ ἁπτόμενος τοῦ θυσιαστηρίου ἁγιασθήσεται
MT: כל הנגע במזבח יקדש

Mt takes the indeterminate Hebrew as a thing, the offering; the LXX, the OT Peshitta, and the Targums (except the Old Palestinian) understand a person, the priest. Mt and the LXX agree with the MT,[4] the Old Palestinian Targum,[5] and rabbinical tradition[6] in understanding that whatever or whoever touches the altar shall become holy on contact; the OT Peshitta and Targums Jonathan and Onkelos understand that consecration is prerequisite for the priest

busites' strongest warriors (hated by David) will be as helpless as the blind and the lame before his attack.

[1] I owe the notice of this allusion to Lagrange, *Mt*, 417.

[2] Merx, *op. cit.*, I, i, p. 312; Lagrange, *Mt*, 430; Torrey, *The Four Gospels*, 295.

[3] In Ps 31 (30):14 the LXX has ἐν τῷ συναχθῆναι αὐτοὺς ἅμα for בהוסדם יחד.

[4] *Kal*. For the same understanding the verb may be pointed as a *niphal*, יִקָּדֵשׁ. Cf. Ex 29:43.

[5] יתווי קדש. The marginal reading conforms to the other Targums.

[6] H. Danby, *The Mishnah* (Oxford, 1933), 481 (*Zeb*. 9.1); Strack-Billerbeck, *op. cit.*, I, 932.

who touches the altar.[1] Mt, then, is dependent upon the Hebrew and may show contact with the Old Palestinian Targum.

Mt 24:10: καὶ τότε σκανδαλισθήσονται πολλοί
Dan 11:41 LXX *om*] + ·※· καὶ πολλαὶ σκανδαλισθήσονται 88-syh
Theod: καὶ πολλοὶ ἀσθενήσουσιν
MT: ורבות יכשלו

The hexaplaric addition in the LXX may be disregarded. Mt agrees with Theodotion in the masculine πολλοί against the feminine of the MT; but his σκανδαλισθήσονται agrees with the MT against Theodotion's poor rendering, ἀσθενήσουσιν.

Mt 25:31: καὶ πάντες οἱ ἄγγελοι μετ' αὐτοῦ
ἄγγελοι] *pr* ἅγιοι AW f13 700 *al* boh^{pc} ς
Zech 14:5 LXX: καὶ πάντες οἱ ἅγιοι μετ' αὐτοῦ
MT: כל קדשים עמך
Targ: וכל קדישוהי עימיה
I Thess 3:13: μετὰ πάντων τῶν ἁγίων αὐτοῦ

Mt works from a Hebrew text (also attested by the LXX, the OT Peshitta, the Vulgate, and the Targum) which reads the *waw* conjunctive before כל and the third personal pronoun with the preposition. The MT must be corrupt, for "Jehovah my God shall come, and all the holy ones with thee" does not make good sense. Unlike Paul, who adopts τῶν ἁγίων from the LXX, Mt interpretatively (and correctly) renders קדשים by οἱ ἄγγελοι.

Mt 25:35, 36	Is 58:7 LXX	MT
ἐπείνασα γὰρ καὶ	διάθρυπτε πεινῶντι	הלוא פרס
ἐδώκατέ μοι φαγεῖν	τὸν ἄρτον σου	לרעב לחמך
ἐδίψησα καὶ		
ἐποτίσατέ με		
ξένος ἤμην καὶ	καὶ πτωχοὺς ἀστέγους	ועניים מרודים
συνηγάγετέ με	εἴσαγε εἰς τὸν οἶκόν σου	תביא בית
γυμνὸς καὶ	ἐὰν ἴδῃς γυμνὸν	כי תראה ערם
περιεβάλετέ με	περίβαλε	וכסיתו
ἠσθένησα καὶ	καὶ ἀπὸ τῶν οἰκείων	ומבשרך
ἐπεσκέψασθέ με	τοῦ σπέρματός σου	
ἐν φυλακῇ ἤμην		
καὶ ἤλθατε πρός με	οὐχ ὑπερόψῃ	לא תתעלם

The Matthaean passage is a targumic adaptation of Is 58:7. To the thought of feeding the hungry is added that of giving drink to

[1] This is the significance of the passive stems in the OT Pesh (נתקדש) and Targums Jon and Onk (יתקדש). Cf. Ex 19:22; II Sam 11:4; II Chron 5:11; 29:15. Perhaps a *pual* pointing is presupposed, יְקֻדַּשׁ. Cf. II Chron 26:18; 31:6; Is 13:3; Ezek 48:11.

the thirsty. Unsheltered poor who are taken in become unsheltered strangers. The thought of clothing the naked remains unchanged. Taking notice of one's own is expanded into visiting the sick and the imprisoned.[1]

Mt 25:46	Dan 12:2 LXX	Theod	MT	
καὶ ἀπελεύσονται		καὶ		
οὗτοι	οἱ δὲ	οὗτοι		ואלה
εἰς κόλασιν	εἰς ὀνειδισμόν	εἰς ὀνειδισμὸν		לחרפות
	οἱ δὲ	καὶ	II	
	εἰς διασπορὰν	εἰς		
	καὶ αἰσχύνην	αἰσχύνην		לדראון
αἰώνιον	αἰώνιον	αἰώνιον		עולם
οἱ δὲ δίκαιοι	οἱ μὲν	οὗτοι		אלה
εἰς ζωὴν	εἰς ζωὴν	εἰς ζωὴν	I	לחיי
αἰώνιον	αἰώνιον	αἰώνιον		עולם

Mt reverses the order of the phrases. חרפות, "reproach," comes from חרף, "to pluck off (fruit)." Κόλασιν comes from κολάζειν, "to prune off." The similar horticultural connotation in the root meanings of both words may provide the basis for the Greek translation.[2] Οἱ δίκαιοι stems from the following verse in Dan.[3] The final phrase agrees with the LXX, Theodotion, and the MT. That we should have another allusion to Dan 12 at the very end of the Olivet Discourse in Mt points to the unity of the Matthaean version. That is, it shows the inner connection of the latter part, peculiar to Mt, with that which Mt has in common with Mk, where allusions to Dan 11 and 12 abound.

Mt 26:15: οἱ δὲ ἔστησαν αὐτῷ τριάκοντα ἀργύρια
ἀργύρια] στατῆρας Dabqr[1], [2]; στατ. ἀργυρίου f1 h
Zech 11:12 LXX: καὶ ἔστησαν τὸν μισθόν μου τριάκοντα ἀργυροῦς
MT: וישקלו את שכרי שלשים כסף

The use of ἱστάναι for שקל in the meaning "to weigh out (money)"

---

[1] The oft-noted parallel to Mt 25:35, 36, *Test. Joseph* i. 5-7, is due to influence from the NT, since the present form of the *Testaments* probably post-dates the NT (J. T. Milik, *Ten Years of Discovery in the Wilderness of Judaea* [London, 1959], 34f.; *idem RB*, 62 [1955], 398-406; M. de Jonge, in *Studia Evangelica*, 546-556; M. Burrows, *More Light on the Dead Sea Scrolls*, 179f.; Kahle, *The Cairo Genizah*[2], 27; P. W. Skehan, *CBQ*, 21 [1959], 73). OT influence in Mt is more likely than influence from the *Testaments*.

[2] Κόλασις αἰώνιος occurs in *Test. Reub.* v. 5; *Asher* vii. 5. But see the preceding note.

[3] See above, p. 138.

is very common in the LXX. 'Αργύρια is poor Greek as compared with ἀργυροῦς [1] and shows independence from the LXX.

Mt 26:52: πάντες γὰρ οἱ λαβόντες μάχαιραν ἐν μαχαίρῃ ἀπολοῦνται
Is 50:11 LXX: ἰδοὺ πάντες ὑμεῖς . . . κατισχύετε φλόγα· πορεύεσθε . . . τῇ φλογί, ᾗ ἐξεκαύσατε· . . . ἐν λύπῃ κοιμηθήσεσθε
MT: הן כלכם ··· מאזרי זיקות לכו ··· (ו)בזיקות בערתם ··· למעצבה תשכבון
Targ: הא כולכון ··· מתקפי חרב איזילו פילו ··· (ו)בחרב דתקיפתון ··· לתקלתכון תתובון

H. Kosmala has noted that Mt 26:52, usually referred to Gen 9:6 and the *ius talionis*, really quotes the italicized phrases in the targumic version of Is 50:11: "*All you. . .who take a sword*, go, fall . . .*on* (or, *by*) *the sword* which you have taken. . . you will return *to your destruction.*"[2] Neither the MT nor the LXX mentions a sword or destruction.

Mt 27:24: λαβὼν ὕδωρ ἀπενίψατο τὰς χεῖρας . . . λέγων· ἀθῷός εἰμι ἀπὸ τοῦ αἵματος τούτου
τούτου BDΘ it syr^{sin}] *pr* (= A*pc*) τοῦ δικαίου אW f1 f13 565 700 *pl* lat ς
Dt 21:6, 9 LXX: νίψονται τὰς χεῖρας . . . σὺ δὲ ἐξαρεῖς τὸ αἷμα τὸ ἀναίτιον
νίψονται] ἀπονίψονται b w
MT: ירחצו את ידיהם ··· ואתה תבער הדם הנקי
Susanna 46 (Theod): ἀθῷος ἐγὼ ἀπὸ τοῦ αἵματος ταύτης
Cf. Ps 73 (72):13.

The interesting agreement with Lagarde's Lucianic text in the compound verb, ἀπονίπτειν, and the lack of a possessive pronoun in Mt and the LXX (against the MT and where we would expect one) confirm the influence on Mt's language from the LXX of Dt.[3] The use of ἀθῷος instead of ἀναίτιος, the unusual and Hebraistic ἀθῷος ἀπό instead of the simple genitive,[4] and the almost exact verbal parallelism may well display influence from Susanna 46 (Theod).

Mt 27:34: ἔδωκαν αὐτῷ πιεῖν οἶνον μετὰ χολῆς μεμιγμένον
οἶνον אBDΘ f1 69 *al* lat syr^{sin}] ὄξος AW 565 700 *pm* it boh (3) ς
Ps 69 (68):22 LXX: καὶ ἔδωκαν εἰς τὸ βρῶμά μου χολὴν καὶ εἰς τὴν δίψαν μου ἐπότισάν με ὄξος
MT: ויתנו בברותי ראש ולצמאי ישקוני חמץ

Ἔδωκαν conforms to the LXX (Mk 15:23 has ἐδίδουν). The

---

[1] Cf. X. Léon-Dufour, *Biblica*, 40 (1959), 688. The variant readings in Mt stumble against the un-Greek ἀργύρια.
[2] *NovTest*, 4 (1960), 3-5.
[3] For examples of symbolic hand-washing in classical Greek and Latin authors, see J. Elsner, *Observationes Sacrae in Novi Foederis Libros* (1770), I, 122f. But according to Origen, it was a Jewish, not a Roman custom (*Comm. Mt* [ed., Klostermann, II, 259]).
[4] See Bl-D § 182:3.

variant ὄξος in Mt is a further assimilation to the LXX. Χολῆς depends closely on the LXX, since the meaning of ראש is somewhat uncertain.[1]

Mt 27:43	Ps 22(21):9 LXX	MT
πέποιθεν	ἤλπισεν	גֹּל
ἐπὶ τὸν θεόν	ἐπὶ κύριον	אל יהוה
ῥυσάσθω νῦν	ῥυσάσθω αὐτόν	יפלטהו
	σωσάτω αὐτόν	יצילהו
εἰ θέλει αὐτόν	ὅτι θέλει αὐτόν	כי חפץ בו
πέποιθεν] *pr* εἰ DΘf1 *pc* it cop τὸν θεόν] τῷ θεῷ B 213 abhlq(r[1])vg(*pler*) νῦν] *om* A565*al*boh; + αὐτόν DΘ *pl* ς αὐτόν] *om* אBL 33 *pc*	ὅτι θέλει] ἐθέλει U; εἰ θέλει 1221 boh sah Luc*pau*	

With the LXX, the OT Peshitta, and Jerome, Mt reads the perfect indicative גַּל instead of the imperative of the MT. Πέποιθεν with ἐπί and the accusative is similar to the OT Peshitta (אתתכל על, "he put confidence upon") and somewhat more exact for גלל than ἤλπισεν (LXX). Πεποιθέναι never occurs in the LXX for גלל. Θεόν for יהוה also diverges from the LXX. Ῥυσάσθω agrees with the LXX. Νῦν is a natural insertion in view of the context and may have been intended to compensate partially for the omission of the next clause. The variant omission of νῦν and the addition of αὐτόν represent attempts at assimilation to the LXX.

It has been suggested that LXX^{U} really reads εἰ θέλει, since in that MS ε stands for ει in verses 1, 7, 9, 16 of Ps 22, and that Mt's εἰ depends on this form of the Septuagintal text. But Mt's divergence from the LXX elsewhere in the quotation favors NT influence on LXX$^{U1221\ Luc}$ boh sah [2] or another explanation, viz., that ἐθέλει was meant to be the classical form of that verb, but was misunderstood for εἰ θέλει because of ε for ει elsewhere in Cod. U or because of the reading in Mt. Mt's εἰ is not based on a Greek OT text or upon a distantly possible conditional sense of כי.[3] In the psalm the state-

[1] The word properly means a poisonous plant (cf. Hos 10:4), hence, poison itself. But since bitterness and poison are correlative notions, ראש comes to mean gall as the most bitter of the bitter (in Dt 29:17; Lam 3:19 alongside wormwood and in Ps 69:22 alongside vinegar).

[2] So A. Rahlfs, *Septuaginta-Studien* (Göttingen, 1904-11), II, 149, 154, n. 6, against P. L. Hedley, *HTR*, 26 (1933), 70.

[3] Gesenius-Kautzsch-Cowley, *Hebrew Grammar* (Oxford, 1910), § 159aa,bb.

ment is ironic. But in a passing allusion the larger context of the psalm could not be brought into view. Therefore, Mt has εἰ for ὅτι to avoid the possibility his reader might miss the irony and so not catch the point of the statement. Θέλειν is common in the LXX for חפץ. Thus, the quotation shows no necessary relationship with the LXX.

MT 27:57: ἄνθρωπος πλούσιος
Is 53:9 LXX: καὶ δώσω . . . τοὺς πλουσίους ἀντὶ τοῦ θανάτου αὐτοῦ
MT: [1] ויתן ··· קברו ואת עשיר במתיו

The Marcan parallel (15:43) has εὐσχήμων βουλευτής. Mt draws the description of Joseph of Arimathaea, in whose grave Jesus was buried, into line with OT prophecy. Clearly Mt works from the MT, which means, "They made his grave. . . with the rich in his death"; for neither the interpretation of the LXX ("I will give. . .the rich [plural] for his death") nor that of the Targum ("He will deliver. . . the rich [plural]. . .unto the death of destruction") is suitable to Mt's application.

MT 28:3	Dan 10:6 Theod	LXX	MT
ἦν δὲ	καὶ τὸ	καὶ τὸ	
ἡ εἰδέα αὐτοῦ	πρόσωπον αὐτοῦ	πρόσωπον αὐτοῦ	ופניו
ὡς	ὡσεὶ ὅρασις	ὡσεὶ ὅρασις	כמראה
ἀστραπή	ἀστραπῆς	ἀστραπῆς	ברק
	Dan 7:9 Theod	LXX	MT
κ. τὸ ἔνδυμα	κ. τὸ ἔνδυμα	ἔχων περιβολὴν	לבושה
αὐτοῦ	αὐτοῦ		
λευκὸν	ὡσεὶ	ὡσεὶ	כתלג
ὡς χιών	χιὼν λευκόν	χιόνα λευκήν	חור

A comparison of Mt with the parallel passages in Mk and Lk [2] shows that Mt has assimilated his description of the angel at the empty tomb to the phrases in Dan. He renders פניו independently from Theodotion and the LXX by ἡ εἰδέα αὐτοῦ ("his countenance"), and he jumps directly to the simile of lightning, dropping מראה. The part drawn from Dan 7:9 agrees with Theodotion and the MT, except for the smoothing of "as white snow" into "white as snow" (cf. Is 1:18).

Mt 28:10: ἀπαγγείλατε τοῖς ἀδελφοῖς μου
Heb 2:12: ἀπαγγελῶ τὸ ὄνομά σου τοῖς ἀδελφοῖς μου
Ps 22 (21):23 LXX: διηγήσομαι τὸ ὄνομά σου τοῖς ἀδελφοῖς μου
MT: אספרה שמך לאחי
Cf. Jn 20:17.

---

[1] 1QIs[a]: בומתו (see W. F. Albright, *VT Supplement IV*, 242-258).

[2] Mk 16:5: περιβεβλημένον στολὴν λευκήν; Lk 24:4: ἐν ἐσθῆτι ἀστραπτούσῃ.

In view of the Septuagintal character of the OT quotations in Heb, the agreement of Mt and Heb against the LXX in ἀπαγγέλλειν is remarkable and surely implies some kind of connection.[1]

Mt 28:18	Dan 7:14 LXX	Theod	MT
ἐδόθη μοι	ἐδόθη αὐτῷ	αὐτῷ ἐδόθη	לה יהיב
	ἐξουσία	ἡ ἀρχή	שלטן
	Dan 4:14 LXX	Theod	MT
	ἕως ἂν γνῷ	ἵνα γνῶσιν	די ינדעון
	τὸν κύριον	οἱ ζῶντες	חייא
	τοῦ οὐρανοῦ	ὅτι κύριός	די שליט
πᾶσα ἐξουσία	ἐξουσίαν ἔχειν	ἐστιν ὁ ὕψιστος	עליא
	πάντων τῶν	τῆς βασιλείας	במלכות
ἐν οὐρανῷ	ἐν τῷ οὐρανῷ	τῶν ἀνθρώπων	אנושא
καὶ	καὶ τῶν		
ἐπὶ τῆς γῆς	ἐπὶ τῆς γῆς		

The background of Dan 7 is generally recognized. Schlatter also compares the LXX of Dan 4:14, from which the use of πᾶς and the phrases ἐν οὐρανῷ and ἐπὶ τῆς γῆς seem to stem.[2] The double allusion produces a very fine contrast between Nebuchadnezzar, divested of his authority, and the Son of man, to whom all authority in heaven and upon earth is given. Mt is dependent on the LXX—against Theodotion in the reference to 7:14, and in the reference to 4:14 wholly against Theodotion and the MT, which have nothing even remotely equivalent.

Mt 28:20: πάσας τὰς ἡμέρας ἕως τῆς συντελείας τοῦ αἰῶνος
Dan 12:13 LXX Theod: εἰς συντέλειαν ἡμερῶν
MT: לקץ הימין

Mt retains his set formula, συντέλεια τοῦ αἰῶνος (also in 13:39, 40, 49; 24:3), but prefixes πάσας τὰς ἡμέρας to gain the allusion to Dan 12:13.

The Text-Form of the Matthaean Quotations: A Summary of the Foregoing Treatment[3]

Of the sixteen formal quotations common to Mt and Mk, in one a Hebrew verb is pointed and rendered differently from the LXX (Mt

---

[1] Cf. S. Kistemaker, *The Psalm Citations in the Epistle to the Hebrews* (Amsterdam, 1961), 31f., against Atkinson, who sees a mere lapse of memory in Heb (*op. cit.*, 41f.), and K. J. Thomas, who sees assimilation in Heb toward εὐαγγελίζεσθαι (*op. cit.*, 39ff.).

[2] *Op. cit.*, 798.

[3] I refrain from the word-counting method for several reasons: (1) it would be hazardous in the extreme when one is dealing with allusive quotations;

11:10 = Mk 1:2). One in Mk (10:19) shows significant divergence from the LXX; but it is a catechetical text, the decalogue, and there are wide variations in the texts of both the OT and the NT. Another catechetical text in Mk (12:29, 30), the *shema'*, shows some divergence, but is essentially Septuagintal. Very slight stylistic changes of the LXX occur in Mt 3:3 (= Mk 1:3); 11:10 (= Mk 1:2); 15:8, 9 (= Mk 7:6, 7). Mt strays somewhat from both Mk and the LXX in 15:4a; 19:5, 18, 19; 22:32, 37; 26:31. The remaining quotations in Mt and Mk agree wholly with the LXX.[1] Thus, the Marcan formal quotations are almost purely Septuagintal and the Matthaean parallels a little less so.

Mt and Mk share forty allusive quotations. Eleven are Septuagintal.[2] Twelve are non-Septuagintal.[3, 4] Eight display a mixed Septuagintal and non-Septuagintal form.[5] In three Mk differs from and Mt agrees with the LXX.[6] In two allusions to Dan there is disagreement with both the LXX and Theodotion,[7] in two a mixture of agreement with the LXX against Theodotion and agreement with Theodotion against the LXX,[8] in one a mixture of agreement with the LXX against Theodotion and disagreement with both,[9] and in one a mixture of agreement with Theodotion against the LXX and disagreement with both.[10] Six show possible contact with

(2) it gives a misimpression when there is little room for disagreement in the translation of the Hebrew; (3) the word-counting method distorts the picture where a few long quotations because of their high number of words outweigh many more short quotations; (4) the oft-times important significance of textual points of contact involving a single word or a very few words is lost in mere word-counting and percentage figures; (5) sometimes there is complete agreement between texts in wording, but the words *in context* show mutually exclusive interpretations of the Hebrew text.

1 Mt 15:4b; 19:4; 21:13a, 13b, 42; 22:39, 44 and parallels.

2 Mt 8:4; 10:21; 12:4; 21:33; 22:24; 24:6b; 26:3f., 38, 67; 27:35, 48 and parallels.

3 Mt 3:17; 9:36; 14:16; 17:5; 19:7; 20:28; 24:24; 26:11, 28, 41; 27:39, 46 and parallels.

4 It should be noted that disagreements with the LXX do not always imply greater proximity to the MT. Sometimes the translation is poorer. Sometimes there is targumic-style freedom, paraphrase, or expansion.

5 Mt 19:26; 21:9; 24:6a, 7, 21, 29, 31; 26:64 and parallels.

6 Mt 3:16; 13:13; 17:11 and parallels. In 3:16 Mt alludes to a different OT passage, which could hardly be rendered otherwise. In the Marcan parallel to 17:11, Mk is dependent on the LXX, but does not agree exactly.

7 Mt 24:15b, 34.

8 Mt 13:32; 24:30 and parallels.

9 Mt 24:15a and parallel.

10 Mt 24:13 and parallel.

one or more of the Targums.[1] Five display possible contact with the OT Peshitta.[2] One may reflect an apocryphal passage [3] and one rabbinical tradition.[4]

Of the four formal quotations common to Mt and Lk, all in the Temptation narrative, two are Septuagintal.[5] The textual situation in the remaining two is uncertain; but probably they show divergence from the LXX.[6]

Of the twenty-six allusive quotations common to Mt and Lk, six are Septuagintal.[7] Thirteen are non-Septuagintal.[8] Four display a mixture of agreement and disagreement with the LXX.[9] In one Mt differs from and Lk agrees with the LXX.[10] In one allusion to Dan there is agreement with Theodotion against the LXX and disagreement with both.[11] Six show possible contact with one or more of the Targums,[12] two with the OT Peshitta,[13] one with the Qumran War Scroll,[14] two with rabbinical tradition,[15] and one with Josephus.[16]

Of the twenty formal quotations peculiar to Mt, seven are Septuagintal.[17] Seven are non-Septuagintal.[18] In six there is a mixture of Septuagintal and non-Septuagintal.[19] Possible contacts with the Targum are seen in two,[20] with the OT Peshitta in two,[21] and with Qumran literature in one.[22]

Of the forty-two allusive quotations peculiar to Mt, fifteen are

---

[1] Mt 3:17; 17:5; 24:24, 31; 26:28 and parallels, and Mk 4:12.
[2] Mt 19:26; 24:31; 26:28; 27:39 and parallels, and Mk 4:12.
[3] Mt 24:21.
[4] Mt 14:16 and parallel.
[5] Mt 4:6, 7 and parallels.
[6] Mt 4:4, 10.
[7] Mt 5:3, 39; 11:5; 18:15; 23:38 (?); 24:38 and parallels.
[8] Mt 5:11, 12, 48; 6:11; 8:11, 12; 10:32f.; 11:19; 12:42; 17:2, 17; 23:12; 24:28 and parallels.
[9] Mt 7:23; 11:23; 23:35f.; 24:45 and parallels.
[10] Mt 10:35f. and parallel.
[11] Mt 21:44 and parallel.
[12] Mt 5:12, 48; 6:11; 8:11; 10:32f.; 11:19 and parallels.
[13] Mt 10:35f. and 24:28 and parallel.
[14] Mt 5:3.
[15] Mt 17:2; 23:35f. and parallels.
[16] Mt 12:42 and parallel.
[17] 1:23; 5:21, 27, 38, 43; 13:14f.; 21:16.
[18] 2:6, 15, 18, 23; 5:31; 9:13 = 12:7; 27:9f.
[19] 4:15f.; 5:33; 8:17 (possibly should be put in the preceding group); 12:18-21; 13:35; 21:5.
[20] 2:6; 12:18-21.
[21] 2:6; 4:15f.
[22] 2:23—in the נצר-concept.

Septuagintal.[1] Seventeen are non-Septuagintal.[2] Three display mixture of the Septuagintal and the non-Septuagintal.[3] In allusions to Dan, two show agreement with Theodotion against the LXX,[4] one with the LXX against Theodotion,[5] one a mixture of agreement with Theodotion and disagreement with both Theodotion and the LXX,[6] and one disagreement with both Theodotion and the LXX.[7] One depends wholly on the Targum.[8] Two show possible contact with the Targums,[9] one with the OT Peshitta,[10] and one with apocryphal literature.[11] Two display targumic-style paraphrase.[12]

Although there is room for disagreement with the writer on individual points in appraisal of the text-form and on inclusion and exclusion of some allusive quotations,[13] two facts are so outstanding and indisputable that they are not affected by such differences of opinion here and there. First, the formal quotations in the Marcan tradition are almost purely Septuagintal. Second, a mixed textual tradition is displayed elsewhere—in all strata of the synoptic material and in all forms (narrative, didactic, apocalyptic, etc.).

---

[1] 2:1f., 11; 5:4, 5, 8; 7:22; 10:6, 29; 12:40; 18:22; 21:14; 22:34; 27:34; and 18:16; 27:24 agree with Lagarde's Lucianic text.

[2] 1:21; 2:13; 5:7, 34, 35; 6:6; 11:28; 13:41; 16:27; 21:41; 23:19; 25:31; 26:15, 52; 27:43, 57; 28:10.

[3] 2:20f.; 3:4; 11:29.

[4] 13:43; 24:10.

[5] 28:18.

[6] 28:3.

[7] 25:46.

[8] 26:52.

[9] 5:5; 23:19.

[10] 27:43.

[11] 27:24.

[12] 25:35f.; 28:10.

[13] E.g., I myself have some doubt about the allusions in Mt 10:32f.; 14:16.

CHAPTER TWO

EXPLANATION OF THE TEXT-FORM

Documentary-Redactional Views

Various hypotheses about the origin of Mt and the quotations in Mt have been advanced.[1] Purely documentary-redactional views are not so much in vogue now as they used to be,[2] but they continue to be proposed.

According to Resch, Mt 1 and 2 derives from a pre-canonical source, a Greek document translated from Hebrew.[3] Canonical Mk was taken over and a Hebrew *Urevangelium* for the discourse material, to which were added bits of Petrine-Jerusalem tradition. The twelve formula-quotations were added by the final redactor.[4]

Soltau sees Mt as a combination of Mk and an Ur-Matthaean gospel based on Q, with the formula-citations mechanically inserted.[5]

Bacon sees the same combination of Mk and "S" by a compiler who had Greek as his mother-tongue and relied on the LXX. The formula-citations are part and parcel of "N," an Aramaic Targum of Mk to which scripture fulfilments and the nativity narratives had been added. Quotations in "S" display various stages of assimilation to the LXX.[6]

According to P. Parker, Mt and Mk utilized an early Jewish-Christian gospel (K). Mk excised seemingly anti-Gentile portions

---

[1] Some do not deserve consideration, e.g., Deissmann's view that Mt diverges from the LXX only when he failed to find the passage in the LXX or could not identify the quotation (*Bible Studies*, 162f.).

[2] For reactions against purely documentary-redactional hypotheses, see E. Hirsch, *Frühgeschichte des Evangeliums* (Tübingen, 1941), II, 290-301; Kilpatrick, *Origins*, 1.

[3] That these chapters belong to the hand of the evangelist because of expressions characteristic of Mt, see Burkitt, *Evangelion da-Mepharreshe*, II, 259; Hawkins, *op. cit.*, 4-10; J. G. Machen, *The Virgin Birth of Christ* (London, 1930), 170ff.

[4] Resch, *op. cit.*, II, 20-28.

[5] *ZNW*, 1 (1900), 219-248. *Mechanical* insertion is ruled out by the drastic revision of Mk to introduce citations, e.g., in 4:12f.; 8:16f.; 12:15ff.; 13:13-15, 34f.; 21:4f. (see T. Stephenson, *JTS*, 20 [1919], 227-229).

[6] *Studies in Mt*, 13-17, 20, 21, 156-164, 475, 476.

and revised the remainder in the interests of Gentile Christianity. Mt combined K and the pro-Gentile Q. Material peculiar to Mt (M) is simply what Mk omitted in K. (Lk combined Mk and Q.) The compiler of Mt or the author or translator of K in his own comment has depended on his own recollection of the Jewish OT, but in quotations on the lips of Jesus has conformed to the standard of the LXX.[1]

As far as the quotation material is concerned, these redactional theories have two basic faults. First, they treat the formula-citations in Mt as a special group homogeneous in text-form. The assumption is erroneous. It cannot be emphasized too much that the only thing which binds the formula-citations together is the fulfilment-formulae with which they are introduced. In text-form they are no more non-Septuagintal than the rest of the synoptic quotation material, outside Marcan formal quotations, and they range from the purely Septuagintal to the wholly non-Septuagintal. Second, the redactional theories fail to recognize the large non-Septuagintal element in the allusive quotations throughout the synoptic tradition.[2] Thus, from the textual standpoint no need exists to posit a separate redactional stage for the formula-citations or for the citations in Mt 1 and 2. It is not the non-Septuagintal element in the synoptics, but the pure Septuagintal form of the Marcan formal quotations which stands out and calls for explanation.

Torrey's Metrical Hebrew [3]

C. C. Torrey holds that in Aramaic Mt and Mk the quotations stood in metrical Hebrew and that the Greek translator of Mt took over Greek-Mk in the quotations common to both gospels, but elsewhere rendered the Hebrew independently and accurately.[4]

---

[1] *Op. cit.*, 5, 90ff.

[2] The exception is Bacon, who recognized the non-Septuagintal element in "S." But then he has no reason to draw the line between S-quotations and N-quotations. Nor can we agree with Bacon that the final redactor of Mt was restricted to the LXX, in view of assimilation of Mk to the Hebrew OT, such as occurs in Mt 27:57. Parker's view that quotations on the lips of Jesus are conformed to the LXX is simply not true, for the majority of the allusive quotations which diverge from the LXX represent words of Jesus.

[3] Inasmuch as Torrey's theory has not received general acceptance and was refuted in detail by S. E. Johnson (*op. cit.*, 135-153), I confine myself to several general criticisms.

[4] *Documents*, 41-90.

Where Mt-Greek differs from the LXX, Torrey reconstructs Mt-Hebrew according to Mt-Greek and exultingly proclaims that the Greek translator of Mt translated exactly. Of course, when Torrey has made Greek-Mt the basis of his reconstructed Hebrew! When the reconstructed Hebrew differs from the MT, Torrey says Mt-Aramaic quoted the MT freely. Can we take such *circulum in probando* seriously? Torrey has neither proved his case nor explained anything which could not be otherwise explained by less arbitrary procedure. Positively against Torrey's hypothesis is the sizeable number of non-Marcan formal and allusive quotations and parts of quotations which agree with the LXX against the MT.[1] Many of these are not even considered by Torrey, but from his discussion of a few such instances one may guess his answer: the LXX has been assimilated to the NT. Needless to say, wholesale revision of the LXX toward the NT is very improbable, especially in allusive quotations, which would hardly come to the mind of LXX-copyists.

The Liturgical-Homiletical Hypothesis

G. D. Kilpatrick advocates the view that the documentary source-material for Mt, Mk, Q, and M (*discourse* tradition peculiar to Mt) had been read liturgically and expounded homiletically until it gained a certain stereotyped form, which was written down as our first gospel for further liturgical use. It is axiomatic with Kilpatrick that the compilation took place in a Greek-speaking milieu, so that variation from the LXX means the quotation was not first provided by the evangelist. A Septuagintal quotation may or may not have been first introduced by the evangelist. Because of their independence from the LXX, the formula-citations with their IF belong to the oral homiletical tradition.[2]

It is a little difficult to criticize Kilpatrick's view, because he can refer Septuagintal as well as non-Septuagintal quotations to homiletical tradition.[3] But having provided this way of escape, Kilpatrick really fails to explain the text-form of the Matthaean quotations, for he has no criterion by which to judge whether a

[1] See above, pp. 149f.

[2] Kilpatrick, *Origins*, esp. 52-57, 93-95.

[3] Therefore, Kilpatrick's supposition that the IF to 1:23, a Septuagintal quotation, originally belonged to 1:21, a non-Septuagintal quotation, is quite needless from his own standpoint (pp. 57, 93). Against transference of the IF, see above, p. 128, n. 1.

Septuagintal quotation comes from the evangelist or from oral liturgical-homiletical tradition. And if the Septuagintal and the non-Septuagintal can exist side by side in the liturgical-homiletical tradition, there is no need to posit such tradition, for the evangelist himself might exhibit these characteristics. In the final analysis, then, the text-form of the quotations neither supports the hypothesis nor is explained by it.

The liturgical-homiletical hypothesis will have to be judged on other grounds. Though the OT scriptures were certainly read in Christian worship-services,[1] no evidence exists that the books of the NT were read liturgically at an early date.[2] And there is certainly no evidence the books of the NT were expounded homiletically at an early date.[3] Unless this practice can be demonstrated, Kilpatrick's hypothesis falls to the ground.

Our supposition must be against such a practice, for in Judaism reading and expounding was based on the authority of the OT. We cannot take for granted that Christian pericopes introducing new subject-matter and lacking authority up to that moment immediately replaced the OT lections.[4] The expositional material admitted to liturgical use in the synagogue was not so admitted until after a span of centuries, at least not until the first century A.D.; [5] yet the hypothesis under consideration requires the same process to have taken place in less than half a century. The picture we get from the NT of early church services indicates they were less liturgical than the synagogue service, giving free play for the exercise of the various

---

[1] I Tim 4:13; II Tim 3:15. Clement of Rome, Ignatius, Polycarp, and Barnabas take for granted in their epistles that their readers are familiar with the OT. Justin expressly mentions the practice (1 *Apol.* lxvii [MPG VI, 429]), which was carried over from the synagogue (see A. Harnack, *Bible Reading in the Early Church* [London, 1912], 33; Oesterley, *The Jewish Background of the Christian Liturgy*, 113; Dugmore, *op. cit.*, 8, 71, 72).

[2] I Thess 5:27; Col 4:16; *ad Polycarp* v. 1 imply no more than informal, public reading of epistles for encouragement and edification. After all, epistles addressed to a church were expected to be read to the church.

[3] Kilpatrick admits this: "About the sermon we are less well informed" (p. 65). He cites Melito's *Homily* as the first piece of evidence for such a practice; but G. Zuntz has shown that Melito refers to a reading of the Hebrew OT followed by a Greek translation (*HTR*, 36 [1943], 299-315).

[4] See W. D. Davies, in *The Background of the NT and Its Eschatology* (Cambridge, 1956), 124-152; O. Piper, *JBL*, 78 (1959), 119.

[5] So J. Mann, who is considered to have pushed back the date of the connection between the lections of the Palestinian Triennial Cycle and the homiletic Midrashim as far as one dares (*op. cit.*).

charismata.[1] Kilpatrick is able to give astonishingly few and inconclusive indications of liturgical-homiletical usage in Mt.[2] The evangelistic, apologetic, and historical elements far outweigh any liturgical-homiletical element in Mt.

THE SCHOOL OF ST. MATTHEW

In his book, *The School of St. Matthew*, K. Stendahl advances the hypothesis that the first gospel emanates from a "school" which practiced a *pesher*-type exegesis in choosing from among and adapting known variant readings of the OT text. To support his thesis Stendahl emphasizes the mixed text displayed in the formula-citations, which belong to the final stage in the development of Mt, and draws a parallel with the Habakkuk Commentary, which emanates from the Qumran "school" and displays a similar use of variant readings.

We must first consider introductory arguments which Stendahl uses to support his thesis. He argues that since Jesus was a rabbi, there is every reason to suppose that the social pattern of the rabbi and his disciples made a deep impression on the early life of the church.[3] It may be doubted, however, that the rabbinical school became a pattern in the primitive church. For the early Christians there was but one rabbi, Jesus Christ. The relationship between Jesus and his disciples while he was on earth was unique. In Jesus' absence the great Teacher became the Holy Spirit, who spoke through the apostles and through those who possessed the various *charismata*—and certainly the spiritual gifts were not exercised in the formal atmosphere of a semi-rabbinical school.

Mt itself provides us with the clearest possible evidence against

---

[1] See esp. I Cor 14. Cf. O. Cullmann, *Early Christian Worship* (London, 1953), 32f.

[2] P. 72. E.g., stylistic changes of Mk to increase lucidity, omission of unnecessary details, grouping of like subject-matter, editorial additions, introduction of antithesis and parallelism, repetition of formulae, and carefully balanced and rounded phraseology may all be set down to literary style rather than to liturgical-homiletical usage. The same may be said about the catechetical hypothesis, to which these literary characteristics are said to point. For the catechetical view of Mt, see E. von Dobschütz, *ZNW*, 27 (1928), 338-348; and for a critique, see Kilpatrick, *Origins*, 78f. (summarized and evaluated by Stendahl, 22ff.). H. Riesenfeld cogently argues that the catechetical theory cannot explain the absence of direct citation of Jesus' words in the epistles (*Studia Evangelica*, 50ff.).

[3] P. 34.

the continuation of the rabbinical pattern. "Be not ye called Rabbi: for one is your teacher, and all ye are brethren" (Mt 23:8). Stendahl indeed thinks that this prohibition has significance only if something similar to rabbinical schools existed.[1] But we would hardly expect to find the one clear injunction against rabbinical practice preserved in (and only in) the gospel which supposedly emanates from a semi-rabbinical milieu. Jesus' words are to be understood against the background of the scribes and Pharisees, not against a background of schools within the church, in which teachers were setting up themselves as rabbis.

The synagogue, not the rabbinical school, became in large measure the pattern for the early church. Stendahl seizes also on this fact, and suggests that the Christian ὑπηρέται τοῦ λόγου (Lk 1:2), who correspond to the חזן in the synagogue,[2] were instructors in the "schools." However, the חזן, who had charge of the scrolls (Lk 4:20), exercised a teaching function only as a side-activity and primarily in small congregations. When he did teach, the teaching method was not to comment and explain, but to catechize the pupils by rote.[3] This is hardly the kind of *Sitz im Leben* required for a Matthaean school in which advanced textual research and hermeneutical adaptation were carried out.[4] The prevailing connotation of ὑπηρέτης is that of an official having to do with documents.[5] There is no connotation of research or instruction. The word is chosen in Lk 1:2 because it emphasizes the safe-keeping and accuracy of the gospel tradition.

The closest analogy to the kind of school Stendahl has in mind is the Qumran community. But even here there is a difficulty. The Qumran community was reclusive and monastic, whereas the gospel of Mt is outgoing and evangelistic (cf. 9:37, 38; 10:5-11:1; 24:14; 28:18-20) and must have come from such a source. Stendahl maintains that since the free manner of quotation in the formula-citations did not lessen their authority, the authority of a school

---

[1] P. 30.

[2] I. Elbogen, *Der jüdische Gottesdienst*[3] (Frankfurt, 1931), 485; Zuntz, *op. cit.*, 310.

[3] R. O. P. Taylor, *The Groundwork of the Gospels* (Oxford, 1946), 21-26.

[4] Stendahl admits as much when he notes that the חזן was confined to the בית הספר, in which basic teaching was given, whereas higher education, to which Matthaean interpretation is analogous, was given in the בית המדרש (p. 35).

[5] See B. T. Holmes, *JBL*, 54 (1935), 63-72.

must have stood behind them.[1] However, both in Qumran literature and in Mt it is the eschatological fulfilment, exposing the true and full meaning of the text, which gives authority to the free quotation. There is no question of imprimatur from a school.

As a starting-point for his primary argument from the aberrant text-form of the formula-citations, Stendahl utilizes Hawkins' statistical analysis of the quotations in Mt.[2] The severe limitations of the word-counting method have been pointed out above.[3] But accepting for the moment Hawkins' statistics, we should note several phenomena for which Stendahl's hypothesis does not account. First, the quotations peculiar to Mt in the Sermon on the Mount, which are not preceded by fulfilment-formulae, show as much divergence from the LXX as the formula-citations. Second, quotations only in Mt but in the course of the double or triple narrative are Septuagintal. If these are due to the Matthaean school, one would have expected a non-Septuagintal form. If they stem from another tradition, one wonders why the quotations peculiar to Mt in the Sermon on the Mount are not likewise Septuagintal. Third, Hawkins' statistics demonstrate that the twelve formula-citations are not a homogeneous group in their text-form.[4] Half of them, 2:6; 4:15 f.; 8:17; 12:18-21; 21:5; 27:9 f., account for ninety-five out of the one hundred and twelve non-Septuagintal words. In the remaining half, the proportion of non-Septuagintal to Septuagintal words is seventeen to forty-eight, or eighteen to ninety-five if 13:14, 15 is included, as it should be.[5] The formula-citations range from the Septuagintal (1:23; 3:3; 13:14 f.) to the half and half (2:18; 4:15 f.; 13:35; 21:5) to the non-Septuagintal (8:17; 27:9 f.).

The really big fault in Stendahl's treatment of the Matthaean quotations is that he does not take seriously non-Septuagintal quotations outside the formula-quotations. Some he brushes aside

---

[1] P. 201.

[2] Stendahl, 43-45; Hawkins, *op. cit.*, 154-156.

[3] See above, p. 147, n. 3, continued on p. 148.

[4] The formula-citations are 1:23; 2:15, 18, 23; 3:3; 4:15f.; 8:17; 12:18-21; 13:35; 21:5; 27:9f.—and 2:6, which Stendahl includes because of its non-Septuagintal form, even though it is not introduced by a fulfilment-formula.

[5] See above, pp. 116-118, against Torrey's and Stendahl's attempts to eliminate, without evidence from the MSS, this quotation from the original text of Mt. It is preceded by a fulfilment-formula, and comparison with Mk makes obvious that it is an editorial insertion.

as allusive,[1] some as apocalyptic[2] (though it is not clear why apocalyptic quotations diverging from the LXX should not imply a "school," if the formula-citations do), and some he does not mention. The overwhelmingly mixed text-form in all groups of synoptic quotations, except Marcan formal quotations, demolishes the very foundation of the school-hypothesis, viz., the distinctiveness of the formula-citations. The statement that "there is scarcely any tradition of translation or interpretation which does not emerge in Matthew's manner of understanding his [formula-] quotations"[3] might also have been written concerning the mass of allusive quotations throughout the synoptics.

Stendahl does admit a few Semitic features in quotations other than the formula-citations, but regards them as "a survival of that Aramaic form in which the words and deeds of Jesus were originally recounted."[4] That is, these few quotations happened to escape assimilation to the LXX. But if a non-Septuagintal form stands at the beginning of the process, it cannot be proved that the non-Septuagintal form of the formula-citations makes them stand at the end of the process. The implication might rather be that they also belong to the most primitive milieu of the evangelic tradition.

The parallel between the formula-citations and the Habakkuk Commentary[5] is no more convincing. H. F. D. Sparks notes that the *lemmata* in the Habakkuk Commentary are not nearly so aberrant in text-form as the formula-citations in Mt.[6] In the very nature of the case, all that is proved and all that can be proved from the mixed texts at Qumran and in the synoptics is that in NT times there existed a vulgar text of the OT containing readings some of which appear later in separate streams of textual tradition.

The Dead Sea Scrolls have demonstrated that the streams of textual tradition had not entirely divided by NT times,[7] so that

---

[1] E.g., pp. 146f. See above, pp. 2-5, for the relevance of allusive quotations.

[2] E.g., pp. 79f., 146f., 158f.

[3] Stendahl, 127.

[4] P. 146.

[5] Stendahl, 183-202.

[6] *JTS*, 7 (1956), 104.

[7] See W. F. Albright, *BASOR*, 140 (1955), 27-33; M. Burrows, *More Light on the Dead Sea Scrolls*, 158ff.; F. M. Cross, Jr., *The Ancient Library of Qumrân* (London, 1958), 126-140, 163f.; *idem, BASOR*, 132 (1953), 15-26; *idem, RB*, 63 (1956), 56-58; R. Gordis, *VT*, 7 (1957), 193; H. M. Orlinsky, *JBL*, 78 (1959), 32f.; Rabin, *JTS*, 6 (1955), 180ff.; B. J. Roberts, *BJRL*, 42 (1959), 134; J. A. Sanders, *Journal of Religion*, 39 (1959), 238; P. W.

there is little force in Stendahl's argument that the Habakkuk commentator and the Matthaean school picked from among variant readings known to them. This is probably true in a few cases in the Habakkuk Commentary,[1] but cannot at all be demonstrated in Mt [2] and cannot be the main basis for the mixed text in either. We can draw a line from the Habakkuk Commentary and from Mt (and the other synoptics) to the state of the OT text, but we cannot infer a Matthaean school similar to the Qumran community. An individual exegete of the OT may have shown likenesses to the Habakkuk commentator simply because he, like the Habakkuk commentator, used a mixed text, the only kind of text then existent.[3]

The *midrash pesher* style is not at the base of the mixed text at Qumran, for the same freedom and the same textual contacts with the LXX, the Targum, the Peshitta, and the Vulgate appear also in minor, untendentious items in the Habakkuk Commentary and in allusive quotations throughout Qumran literature, where the hermeneutical motive does not enter.[4] Thus, although Stendahl's discussion of the text-form in the Matthaean quotations is often admirable, we must write *non sequitur* over his thesis as a whole.

Lindars' *NT Apologetic*

Rejecting Stendahl's theory of a local "school," Lindars proposes that the text-form of Mt's formula-citations is due to successive reworkings of the OT texts in the church at large. Anti-Judaic apologetic motivated these reworkings. Thus, different stages of

---

Skehan, *BASOR*, 136 (1954), 12-15; *idem*, in *VT Supplement IV* (1957), 149ff.; *idem*, *JBL*, 78 (1959), 21-25. Thus, Kahle's advocacy of a vulgar Hebrew text has been vindicated (*The Cairo Geniza*[1] [London, 1947], 148). Greenberg suggests that because Qumran was isolated from the mainstream of Judaism, it used forms of the OT text already rejected by the more orthodox leaders of Judaism (*op. cit.*, 157-167). Perhaps we see reflections of cast-off MSS in the NT.

[1] K. Elliger (*Studien zum Habakuk-Kommentar vom Toten Meer* [Tübingen, 1953], 132f.) and B. Gärtner (*Studia Theologica*, 8 [1954], 2f.) challenge the use of dual readings in 1QpHab (against A. Dupont-Sommer, *RHR*, 137 [1950], 143; W. H. Brownlee, *BA*, 14 [1951], 54-76; *idem*, *The Text of Habakkuk in the Ancient Commentary from Qumran*, 122). The debate is not directly relevant to us, since there are no instances of dual readings in Mt.

[2] See above, pp. 122f., that Mt 27:6, 10 is not such an example.

[3] Cf. E. E. Ellis, *NTS*, 2 (1955/56), 133.

[4] See literature cited above, p. 4.

apologetic development can be detected in the various textual deviations of OT quotations (outside Mt as well as within Mt). The final editor of Mt was largely unaware of the apologetic-textual developments and applied the formula-citations independently of their text-form and on the basis of a "pictorial" correspondence to Jesus' life. Text-form becomes divorced from the Matthaean context and tied to an allegedly traceable pattern of prior apologetic evolution.[1]

But Lindars does embrace Stendahl's emphasis on *pesher* style exegesis, and adds his own special emphasis that the desire to answer Jewish objections against Jesus' Messiahship by showing how Jesus fit OT Messianism dominated the use of the OT in the early church. The hypothesis is that apologetic use of the OT began with applications to Jesus' resurrection. After it had been established that the resurrection revealed Jesus' Messiahship in accordance with the OT, the church began by means of the OT and under pressure from Jewish objections to read back the revelation of Jesus' Messiahship into successively earlier phases and aspects of Jesus' career: from the resurrection to the crucifixion, to the ministry, to the baptism, to the birth, to pre-existence. On the basis of this reconstruction, Lindars constantly conjectures a more primitive use of an OT quotation than the use which actually stands in the NT passage.

Although Lindars must be credited with many penetrating observations, undemonstrated presuppositions reduce the probability of his reconstruction as a whole. The first is that despite the recognition that not all OT quotation material is apologetic in character,[2] Lindars forces too much of the material into the apologetic mold. Strengthening of faith and instruction *within* the church were also motives. Luke indicates that in the post-resurrection ministry Jesus used the OT for teaching and confirmation. His earlier ministry to the disciples exhibits the same kinds of usage. Christians may also have applied OT texts to Jesus' career simply

---

[1] E.g., the textual phenomena in 12:18-21 lead Stendahl to posit a Matthaean school which adapted the OT text to the Matthaean context. But they lead Lindars to posit four chronologically successive stages of applying Is 42 to Jesus' resurrection, baptism, and gentle ministry, and to the Gentile mission (pp. 150f.). At the most, only the final reworking of the OT text by the editor of the gospel could bear direct relationship to the gospel context (according to Lindars). See pp. 16, 148, 259ff.

[2] P. 251.

because a correspondence was patent, as well as because they felt an apologetic need.

A second, recurring presupposition is that a Septuagintal element in a quotation indicates a late stage of development.[1] But the Septuagintal element in allusive quotations in all strata of the synoptic tradition, alongside Semitic elements, and apart from interpretive motives shows that Septuagintisms do not at all necessitate later dating.[2]

A third presupposition is that literal interpretation of the OT preceded typological interpretation, so that where a typological interpretation appears, Lindars automatically assigns it to a later stage of apologetic development. This rule of thumb is unwarranted, because Jews (including Jesus himself) may be expected to have dealt in typology from the very beginning of Christian interpretation (cf. the picturing of the restoration as a second exodus as far back as the OT prophets).

Yet another unfounded assumption is that the OT began to be used apologetically in connection with Jesus' resurrection and only later began to be read further and further back into the life of Jesus. Thus, the possibility that during his ministry Jesus indicated applications of the OT to himself in messianic self-disclosure is gratuitously ruled out from the very first. For example, Lindars maintains that OT texts explaining why Jesus was rejected were not used until after the resurrection when unbelieving Jews objected that surely the Messiah would not have been rejected as Jesus had been. But against Lindars, the rejection of Jesus began during his ministry, so that there is no reason to deny that Jesus himself utilized such texts.[3] Although the resurrection certainly was

[1] *Passim.*

[2] Cf. R. H. Gundry, "The Language Milieu of First-Century Palestine: Its Bearing on the Authenticity of the Gospel Tradition," in *JBL*, 83 (1964), 404ff.

[3] Another example is Lindars' contention that the baptismal voice originally referred only to Is 42:1 and was deliberately conflated with Ps 2:7 at a later stage, later because Acts 13:33 shows that at first Ps 2:7 was applied to Jesus' resurrection, not to his baptism (pp. 139f.). Quite apart from the faulty premise that a non-resurrection usage must be later, this interpretation of Acts 13:33 is questionable. "Raised up" probably means "raised up on the scene" (at the baptism) in contradistinction to being raised up "from the dead" in verse 34. See F. F. Bruce, *Acts* (New International Commentary on the NT; Grand Rapids, 1960), 275. Verses 32-37 reinforce with OT prooftexts what has already been reviewed in verses 23-31 about Jesus' ministry from John the Baptist to the resurrection. Paul simply steps

decisive for early Christian thought, not everything began with it.

Frequently Lindars assumes a somewhat radical scepticism toward the reliability of the gospel records and a high estimation of the distortive and creative powers of the Christian community. Unless one grants this negative approach, the further part of his discussions will not seem cogent.[1] At this point, however, Lindars' method suffers from erraticism. He maintains, for example, that Ps 110:1 was read back into the mouth of Jesus, but refuses to say that Jesus' predictions about his death and resurrection were similarly put into his mouth.[2] The sceptical viewpoint seems to be regarded as valid where it works to the advantage of the proposed apologetic development, but not elsewhere. Lindars' work may illustrate that devaluation of historicity and source-criticism tends toward fanciful overinterpretation of the theological motives of the evangelists.

Since much of the highly developed apologetic in Lindars' scheme appears already in early books of the NT,[3] it may be doubted that apologetic development could have been so neatly progressive as Lindars leaves the impression it was. It might also be easier to account for the early date of such variegated development by holding that Jesus himself instituted apologetic uses of OT texts as Jewish rejection of him became plainer and more imminent—instead of postponing apologetic use of the OT till after the resurrection and leaving the disciples without guidelines. Alongside advanced apologetic in early NT books Lindars frequently detects primitive apologetic in late NT books. Such a topsy-turvy situation is not impossible, but it does cast doubt on the chronological validity of Lindars' reconstruction.

As in the case of Stendahl, however, the really big fault in Lindars' work is a disregard of the mixed text-forms in the untendentious material of many allusive quotations throughout the synoptics.

---

back to show divine authentication at the inauguration of the ministry (so the quotation in verse 33 of Ps 2:7, reminiscent of the baptismal pronouncement) and at the climax (so the quotation in verses 34f. of Is 55:3 and Ps 16:10, referring to the resurrection). The occurrences of Ps 2:7 in Heb 1:5; 5:5; 7:28 leave the question open by mentioning neither the baptism nor the resurrection. The juxtaposition with Ps 110:1 in Heb may again point to initial and final authentications of Jesus' ministry, as in Acts 13. Cf. Acts 4:24-30; 10:38, which Lindars must consider as results of later application of Ps 2:7 to Jesus' baptism, in order not to spoil his reconstruction.

[1] Against sceptical form-criticism see below, pp. 189ff.

[2] Pp. 46f., 60ff., 251f.

[3] E.g., Davidic sonship in Ro 1:3—see Lindars, 189.

In some instances, of course, the developing exegesis of an OT text is obvious. But the labyrinthian textual developments which Lindars imagines against an apologetic backdrop are at best *non liquets* because of identical textual phenomena in allusive quotations where fulfilment and apologetic motives are absent.

The Testimony Book

A very popular hypothesis has been that the NT writers utilized a "Testimony Book," i.e., a catena of OT proof-texts.[1] General arguments for the hypothesis are the recurrence in the NT and in patristic writings of quotations which agree in text-form against all known OT texts, the combination of OT passages (sometimes leading to misascription), the recurrence of such combinations, and the actual Testimony Book edited by Cyprian, traces of which appear in earlier church fathers.

These arguments are not wholly convincing. Influence from the NT itself rules out the argument from agreement in text-form with patristic writings.[2] Also, the fathers used one another.[3] Often NT texts disagree with each other and with the patristic texts. There are other explanations for misascriptions. Composite quotations are not unknown outside testimony tradition.[4] The recurrence of the combination of "stone"-passages is unique. The formation of a Testimony Book by Cyprian gives us no right to suppose he worked on a model antedating the canonical books of the NT. Some NT quotations supposedly derived from the Testimony Book are too woven into or dependent upon their contexts to have been thus derived.[5] The testimony hypothesis tends to underrate the ability

---

[1] This hypothesis is connected primarily with the name of J. R. Harris (*Testimonies* [1916-20]). But as early as 1889, E. Hatch was proposing essentially the same thing in Judaism (*op. cit.*, 203-214). On the German side, Harris was anticipated by Ungern-Sternberg, *Der traditionelle alttestamentliche Schriftbeweis* . . . (Halle, 1913).

[2] This is especially so in Mt, which exercised a dominant influence in patristic literature. See É. Massaux, *Influence de l'évangile de saint Mt sur la littérature chrétienne avant saint Irénée* (Louvain, 1950).

[3] A. Kraemer, *Philologische Wochenschrift*, 58 (1938), 73-83; J. A. Robinson, *St. Irenaeus*: *Demonstration*, 6-23.

[4] E.g. CDC 8:14f. Cf. the חרז-method of quoting from the three sections of the OT canon, on which see G. Surenhusius, ספר המשוה *sive* ΒΙΒΛΟΣ ΚΑΤΑΛΛΑΓΗΣ (Amsterdam, 1713), 339-345; Ellis, *Paul's Use of the OT*, 46, 49, 50.

[5] E.g., Mt 2:15, 18; 27:9, 10.

of the NT authors to work from the OT text. It is also somewhat strange that such a basic work was omitted from the NT canon and did not emerge again till Cyprian.[1]

The Testimony Book was supposedly written in Aramaic.[2] Yet, it was utilized in Greek translation.[3] T. W. Manson prefers to think of an oral tradition.[4] To some, Mt inserted quotations in his gospel from the Testimony Book. To others, the Testimony Book is Q, in large measure forms the substratum of the first gospel, and is to be equated with τὰ λόγια of Mt in Papias.[5]

But just when the Testimony Book seemed almost toppled, the discovery of a catena of Messianic texts at Qumran Cave Four gave new life to the hypothesis. J. M. Allegro well writes that "it must now be regarded as more than a possibility that the first Christians were able to take over and use collections of Hebrew *testimonia* already current."[6]

As one surveys the situation, the following conclusions seem to emerge. First, it is probable that the early Christians availed themselves of already existing Jewish catenae of Messianic texts and, following the Jewish example, compiled their own. No reason invites us to think, however, that but one Christian Testimony Book *par excellence* existed[7] or that it had special connection with

---

[1] For these general criticisms, see Dodd, *According to the Scriptures*, 26f.

[2] See esp. D. Plooij, *Studies in the Testimony Book* (Amsterdam, 1932).

[3] Thus it is argued that the formula-citations must not come from the hand of the first evangelist, because elsewhere he utilizes only the LXX and conforms Mk to the LXX (W. C. Allen, *ET*, 12 [1900/01], 284f.; Stanton, *op. cit.*, II, 342ff.; Burkitt, *The Gospel History and Its Transmission*, 124ff.; McNeile, *Mt*, p. xi). We have seen that the first evangelist most certainly is not limited to the LXX and that the conforming of Mk to the LXX occurs in places where the Marcan style is rough.

[4] *JTS*, 46 (1945), 132. W. L. Knox combines the documentary and the oral (*op. cit.*, II, 127).

[5] So especially J. B. Gregory, *op. cit.*; E. C. Selwyn, *op. cit.*; T. H. Bindley, *op. cit.*; Hunt, *op. cit.*; cf. Harris, who identifies a reference to a five-part work of Matthew the Monk against the Jews in a late MS from Mt. Athos with the Testimony Book, which was attributed to Mt the apostle and became the basis for Papias' commentary (*Testimonies*, I, 100ff.; against which see B. W. Bacon, *The Expositor*, 15, 8th Series [1918], 60ff., and an answer to Bacon by T. H. Bindley in the same journal, 318-320). J. A. Findlay at first thought the fivefold division of the first gospel derived from the Testimony Book (*The Expositor*, 20, 8th Series [1920], 388-400).

[6] *JBL*, 75 (1956), 186. Cf. *idem*, *JBL*, 77 (1958), 350; R. M. Grant, *op. cit.*, 46.

[7] P. Carrington speaks of testimony collections in the plural (*The Primitive Christian Calendar* [Cambridge, 1952], I, 107-109). So also A. L. Williams, *Adversus Judaeos*, 6f. C. H. Roberts found Rylands Papyrus Greek 460 and

Mt. J. A. Findlay, at first a strong advocate of such a view, abandoned it because his further research showed "subsequent collections of testimonies do not follow his [Mt's] model either in order or language."[1]

Second, it is impossible to determine which quotations might have belonged to testimony traditions. Misascription, compositeness, recurrence, etc., are not reliable clues.

Third, the heavy Semitic element throughout synoptic quotations, outside Marcan formal quotations, means that a Semitic text-form does not imply testimony origin. Many of these Semitic quotations are not of the testimony kind. And the Septuagintal imprint on some of the formula-citations forbids our saying this group as a whole comes from a Testimony Book because of the group's Semitic imprint.[2] The hypothesis simply does not help explain the text-form of Mt's quotations.

Fourth, the Testimony Book is not to be equated with τὰ λόγια [3] which Papias said Mt wrote in the Hebrew dialect.[4] In the LXX λόγια does not explicitly indicate the "writtenness" of the divine revelation; but that the words of God were in fact written down as scripture lent that connotation to the term.[5] Papias must have meant the Gospel of Mt, for in his reference to the Gospel of Mk, τὰ ὑπὸ τοῦ κυρίου ἢ λεχθέντα ἢ πραχθέντα are immediately described as τὰ κυριακὰ λόγια,[6] and the Matthaean λόγια are contrasted with Mk's gospel. So Irenaeus understood Papias' statement.[7] As for Papias' commentary, it is hardly credible that he wrote five books of commentary on a half dozen formula-citations

---

Papyrus Osloensis 11 to be parts of one leaf, took them as a fragment of a Testimony Book, and argued from the appearance of passages not occurring in other *testimonia* that more than one such anthology existed (*BJRL*, 20 [1936], 237-244).

[1] In *Amicitiae Corolla*, 69.

[2] J. Moffatt finds two types of testimonies, Semitic and Septuagintal (*An Introduction to the Literature of the NT*[3] [Edinburgh, 1918], 23-25, 258). The text-form cannot then be used as a criterion.

[3] Against Burkitt, *The Gospel History and Its Transmission*, 126; Harris, *Testimonies*, I, 124ff.; F. C. Grant, *op. cit.*, 65.

[4] Eusebius, *H.E.* iii. 39.

[5] See J. Donovan, *The Logia in Ancient and Recent Literature* (Cambridge, 1924), 10ff. So also in Philo, Josephus, and the NT. T. W. Manson neglects this acquired connotation (*BJRL*, 29 [1946], 7ff.).

[6] See Wikenhauser, *op. cit.*, 180.

[7] *Haer.* III.i.1.

collected by Mt and later made the basis of the first gospel.[1]

Thus, the Testimony Book is a partially confirmed hypothesis which disappointingly explains little or nothing.

Written Greek Targums

P. Kahle [2] has strongly advocated the view that non-Septuagintal quotations and readings within quotations in the NT display the text-forms of written Greek Targums which were widely used before Christianity adopted the LXX as its standard version of the OT.[3]

[1] See A. Wright, *The Critical Review*, 5 (1895), 16f. Bacon thinks Papias' commentary was based on the pentateuchal format of the first gospel (*The Expositor*, 15 [1918], 60ff.). E. Nestle thinks Mt and Papias independently derived the five-fold division from the OT (*ZNW*, 1 [1900], 252-254).

[2] Besides the full treatment in his chapter on the LXX in *The Cairo Geniza*, see *Theol. Stud. u. Krit.*, 88 (1915), 410ff.; *Festschrift Otto Eissfeldt* (Halle, 1947), 161-180; *Studia Patristica* (= *Texte u. Untersuchungen*, 5. Reihe, Bd. 8; Berlin, 1957), I, iv, pp. 328-338. Kahle's view is not entirely new. L. Cappellus concluded the apostles cited from the Greek, not from the Hebrew, seemingly implying something akin to Kahle's view (*Critica Sacra* [Paris, 1650], 444-557). G. Roepe thought some of Paul's divergences from the LXX might stem from other Greek versions (*De Veteris Testamenti locorum in apostolorum libris allegatione* [1827], cited by O. Michel, *Paulus u. seine Bibel* [Gütersloh, 1929], 1f.). P. Katz cites J. Ussher (17th century), Z. Frankel (1841), and L. Diestel (1869) as forerunners of Kahle (in *Actes du Premier Congrès de la Fédération Internationale des Associations d'Études Classiques* [Paris, 1951], 166; the German version of this article is in *TZ*, 5 [1949], 1-24).

[3] A. Sperber holds a special view that the Hexapla was based on two independent Greek translations of the Hebrew Bible, Origen marking with an *obelus* variant readings representing the translation based on a Hebrew text akin to the Samaritan Pentateuch and reflected in LXX^B and with an *asterisk* the translation based on a Hebrew text akin to the MT and reflected in LXX^A and in NT quotations (*op. cit.*, 193-293; *Tarbiz*, 6 [1934], 1-29). Because Sperber must reject the ancient tradition preserved in Jerome concerning the Hexapla and because he rather arbitrarily sets up LXX^B and LXX^A as norms, the hypothesis has generally been rejected. See Seeligmann, *op. cit.*, 14; I. Soisalon-Soininen, *Die Textformen der Septuaginta-Übersetzung des Richterbuches* (Helsinki, 1951), 12f. Sperber admits LXX^B and LXX^A contain somewhat mixed texts, but the mixture is more than his thesis will allow, and neither codex is uniform throughout the OT books in textual relationships, so that it is invalid to set them up as norms (cf. P. Katz, *ZNW*, 49 [1958], 221f.). Ever since A. F. Kautzsch noted Paul's quotations often agreed with A against B (*De Veteris Testamenti locis a Paulo Apostolo allegatis* [Lipsiae, 1867], 108ff.), the same phenomenon has often been noted elsewhere in the NT. W. Staerk strongly opposed wholesale influence from the NT on Cod. A (*ZWT*, 40 [1897], 249ff.). But against using the agreements of LXX^A and the NT as a basis for a theory such as Sperber's, agreement of LXX^B and the NT against LXX^A occurs not a few times. I have noted the following instances in Mt: 2:18; 5:34; 7:22; 8:11; 10:35; 24:29; 24:45; 26:3f. Cf. Thomas, *op. cit.*, 180ff.

This view is tied to Kahle's contention that there was no original LXX, but only various Greek Targums which were gradually assimilated to one another and finally standardized into the present "Septuagint." The Letter of Aristeas does not contain even a kernel of truth about the origin of the LXX. Rather, that letter is but a propaganda-piece to promote one Greek translation of the Pentateuch among other earlier ones. To substantiate his view Kahle draws a parallel with the development of the Aramaic Targums, points to several intimations that the LXX was not the only and not the first Greek translation of the OT,[1] and regards much of the variation within the LXX itself[2] and within quotation material in Philo, Josephus,[3] Justin, Clement of Alexandria, and others as evidence of diverse origins instead of recensional branching off from a prototype.

One may grant that other Greek translations of the OT, or parts of the OT, existed in early times. For example, an Ur-Theodotionic

---

[1] In a book by Aristobulus of Alexandria dedicated to Ptolemy Philometor (184-141 B.C.), fragments of which are preserved by Clement of Alexandria (*Stromata* i.150.1-4) and Eusebius (*Praeparatio Evangelica* ix.6; xiii.12) (texts in Swete, *An Introduction to the OT in Greek*, 1f.); and in the *Letter of Aristeas* §§ 30, 314-316.

[2] Outstanding examples are the Greek texts of Jdg, the Lucianic text of Esther, the Ur-Theodotionic text of Dan, the texts of Tobit in B and א, the three additional translations in the Hexapla to the Psalms.

[3] It is difficult to understand why Kahle regards the agreement between Josephus' quotations from the historical books and the Lucianic text as due to alteration by Christian copyists (*Geniza*², 233f.), when the opposite view would fit his thesis. As it is, Kahle leaves himself no basis from which to argue for the genuineness of the aberrant text in some Philonic quotations, which Katz says were omitted as *lemmata* and subsequently reinserted from later recensions and translations (*Philo's Bible* [Cambridge, 1950]). The same is true about Kahle's agreement with W. Bousset that Justin's quotations were later revised according to the Lucianic text (*Geniza*², 229; Bousset, *Die Evangeliencitate Justins des Märtyrers* [Göttingen, 1891], 18-32). (P. Katz cautions that the only evidence for Justin's text is a carelessly copied fourteenth century MS [*Studia Patristica*, I, 343]; see W. Schmid, *ZNW*, 40 [1941], 87-138). Kahle would have to show that the revisions of Josephus and Justin were not only pre-Lucianic (based on an Ur-Lucianic text), but also that the Ur-Lucianic text was based on a pre-Christian Greek translation alongside other translations. This he cannot do from Josephus and Justin if he admits the possibility of later tampering with their texts, a possibility increased by the known assimilation of the NT text to the LXX in many passages and in many MSS (against Kahle, *Geniza*², 249) (e.g., in Mt 1:23 (D *pc* d^{c}); 3:3 (b sy^{cur} Ir); 4:4 (D a b d g^{1} Cl Tert Aug), 15f. (D); 27:34 (AW 565 700 *pm* it boh [3]); Lk 3:22 (D it Ju [Cl] Or).

translation of Dan seems beyond doubt.[1] But it is another thing to reject the tradition regarding the origin of the LXX, to show that the LXX grew by amalgamation, and to demonstrate that other translations besides the "Alexandrian version" exercised significant influence on what has been regarded as the Septuagintal tradition proper and on the NT.

One's view of the Letter of Aristeas is crucial. We may accept with Kahle the date 130-100 B.C. But the reasoning that "nobody makes propaganda for something a hundred or more years old" and that therefore "we can be sure that the translation had just been made" and the letter "attempts to show it was the first translation ever made" is unacceptable.[2] It cannot be supposed the letter is a wholly fictitious propaganda-piece for a contemporary translation, because the very contemporaneousness would leave the letter open to the most obvious exposé, as the author would know full well.[3] The author would have been incredibly stupid to think he could convince those who were in the habit of using previous Greek translations that the Alexandrian version was the first.[4]

Kahle's concern to discover Septuagintal origins has misled him into thinking the Letter of Aristeas was written with the same subject in view. The story of the translation actually occupies but a small fraction of the letter's length. G. Zuntz has shown that the letter was designed to present the most glorious of Hellenistic kings as a devout admirer of Jewish wisdom and to invite Greeks to study the Torah, which was available for them in a perfect translation.[5] Thus, the most space is occupied by the wise answers of the Jewish scholars to the king's questions. The purpose of the letter is propagandist for the Jewish faith in general, not for a particular version of the Greek OT against others.

The subordination of the actual account of translation heightens the possibility of an historical residuum in the account. For what

---

[1] It may be doubted, however, that A and B in Jdg represent different translations. See O. Pretzl, *Biblica*, 7 (1926), 233ff., 353ff.; Soisalon-Soininen, *op. cit.*

[2] *Geniza*², 211f.

[3] When Kahle says that "Ben Sira's grandson [c. 110 B.C.] regards himself as the immediate successor of the Bible translators and we can take it for granted that he was in Egypt when some of the biblical translation work was still being done" (*Geniza*², 217), he outruns the text of the *Prologue to Ecclesiasticus*, in which there is no implication of immediacy whatsoever.

[4] Cf. G. Zuntz, *JSS*, 4 (1959), 123.

[5] *Ibid.*, 126.

could be the purpose of inserting a wholly fictitious story into a work which, as we have noted, was not written with Septuagintal origins primarily in view? Rather, the legendary elements must be regarded as accretions upon a core of historical facts,[1] which give us the right to see the LXX as originating in Alexandria some time before the Letter of Aristeas. This tradition is corroborated by Philo, who describes an annual festival on Pharos in celebration of the translation.[2]

The parallel with the growth of the Aramaic Targum is not close. In the first place, at least for the Pentateuch we have a variety of Targums; unity was never attained. In the second place, the evolution of the Aramaic Targum(s) continued much later into the Christian era. Why did the amalgamation of the Greek Targums take so much less time? Christian standardization cannot be the answer, for the Septuagintal element is heavily predominant in the NT (except for the bulk of the synoptic quotation material) at the very dawn of the Christian era. Furthermore, there is no historical data indicating the LXX as we know it was formed and canonized by the Christians. Were the analogy perfect, it still would not necessitate the same development for the LXX as for the Aramaic Targum(s).

Kahle's is essentially a superficial view of the state of the Septuagintal text. P. Katz has shown that the bewildering mass of variant readings on closer inspection does indeed present a discernible pattern of development from an archetype.[3] The outstanding example of what can be done along Lagardian lines to disentangle the variants is M. L. Margolis' work on the text of Joshua.[4] Had independent translations gone to make up the LXX, we would have had very much more variation between LXX MSS, such as exists between the LXX, Theodotion, Aquila, and Symmachus.[5]

We may grant that Lucian utilized an older Antiochean textual tradition of the LXX; [6] but that does not imply an Ur-Lucianic in-

---

[1] Contra Zuntz, *ibid.*, who sees no historical worth at all.

[2] *De Vita Mosis* ii. 41-43.

[3] In the above-mentioned article in *Actes du Premier Congrès . . .*, 165-182; *TZ*, 5 (1949), 1-24.

[4] In *Jewish Studies in Memory of Israel Abrahams* (New York, 1927), 307-323.

[5] Cf. B. J. Roberts, *The OT Text and Versions*, 114.

[6] Cf. T. W. Manson, *Dominican Studies*, 2 (1949), 187f. The great age of the tradition utilized by Lucian is shown by Lucianic readings in the Old Latin (Driver, *Sam*, pp. lxxviff.), in the Chester Beatty Papyri (A. Allgeier, *DLZ*, 61 [1940], 602), in Rylands Papyrus Greek 458 (2nd century B.C.) (A.

dependent translation, for we can discern reasons for divergences, such as simple errors of sight and sound, principles of stylistic and grammatical change, etc. In the Qumran papyrus fragments of Lev 2-5, the leather fragments of parts of Num 3 and 4 and Lev 26:2-16, and the Minor Prophets leather scroll,[1] Kahle points to some striking readings.[2] But more than isolated word-substitutions, striking though they may be, are required to demonstrate independent translation. The fact that in the fragments of Lev 26:2-16 nine of the ten unique readings are farther from the MT confirms what is most damaging to Kahle's thesis, viz., that from earliest times the LXX was subject to assimilation toward the Hebrew text,[3] which itself was in a fluid state.[4] Kahle himself recognizes this, but seems blind to the fact it undermines his view of the LXX; [5] for if constant revision according to the Hebrew occurred, no need exists to posit independent translations in order to account for striking variants.[6] And the early dates of the papyri and of the leather fragments and scroll, in which Kahle exults, combined with the *general* agreement with later MSS of the LXX strikes the death-blow to Kahle's theory; because it is inconceivable that independent translations immediately interacted with one another to bring about this general uniformity overnight. In fact, Kahle has the Rylands Papyrus in general agreement with the LXX—but antedating it.

For several reasons Kahle's view does not receive support from or help explain the text-form of NT quotations.[7] The major premise

---

Vaccari, *Biblica*, 17 [1936], 501-504), and elsewhere (Hedley, *op. cit.*, 69-71). See further Wevers, *op. cit.*, 98ff.

[1] On which see Barthélemy, *RB*, 60 (1953), 18-29, who thinks it represents the Quinta and was used by Aq, Theod, and Sym. The scroll shows agreements with Justin.

[2] *Geniza*², 223ff.

[3] Perhaps, then, the Lev fragments represent the LXX *before* assimilation to the Hebrew, rather than vice versa. Against P. W. Skehan, in *VT Supplement IV* (1957), 158.

[4] See F. M. Cross, Jr., *BA*, 17 (1954), 12f.; *idem*, *The Ancient Library at Qumrân*, 129; D. W. Gooding, *Recensions of the Septuagint Pentateuch* (London, 1955), 4; P. Katz, *ZNW*, 49 (1958), 220; P. W. Skehan, in *VT Supplement IV* (1957), 156-158; *idem*, *JBL*, 78 (1959), 21f.; and references above, p. 13, n. 4.

[5] *TLZ*, 79 (1954), 88; *Opera Minora* (Leiden, 1956), 123; *Geniza*², 228, 245, 255.

[6] Cf. F. M. Cross, Jr., *The Ancient Library at Qumrân*, 126f.

[7] It is perhaps instructive that Torrey, Stendahl, and Kahle all put forward Mt 12:18-21 as their prize exhibit in favor of their mutually exclusive hypotheses.

that "the [Greek] texts were used exactly as they stood by Christians" [1] cannot be taken for granted. In favor of that premise A. Baumstark argues that one who undertakes, like Mt, to prove from OT prophecies that Jesus is the Messiah could not have treated his OT citations carelessly or over-boldly without losing the point of his argument.[2] However, it is common knowledge that the ancients did not scruple against quoting interpretatively. Neither the historian in the Graeco-Latin classical tradition [3] nor the Jewish targumist [4] had the modern concept of the sacrosanctity of direct quotation. Rather, a certain freedom of interpretation and adaptation was expected in order to show one's grasp of the material, to bring out its inner meaning and significance, and to apply it to the subject at hand. The Targums themselves are concrete evidence against the premise of Kahle and Baumstark.

Nor can it be taken for granted that the NT authors responsible for non-Septuagintal quotations were limited to Greek. The numerous contacts with Semitic textual tradition argue otherwise. In reality, the higher the number of Greek OT texts differing more or less from later MSS of the LXX and the greater the vicissitudes of the LXX through repeated assimilation to the Hebrew text, the less need there is to assume the NT authors used written Greek targums. For if direct recourse to the Semitic texts was widely practiced by Greek targumists and Greek copyists, how much more likely it was practiced in compositional work, where hermeneutical, evangelistic, didactic, and hortatory motives came into play. Until pre-Christian Greek OT MSS are found which exhibit the same aberrant texts as NT quotations, the supposition must be that the NT authors made their own *ad hoc* renderings.[5]

---

[1] *Geniza*[2], 238; cf. 250f.

[2] *ZDMG*, 89 (1935), 114.

[3] See M. Dibelius, *Studies in the Acts of the Apostles* (London, 1956), 138-144; F. Johnson, *op. cit.*, 32ff.

[4] The Talmud says, "Whoever targums a verse in its closely literal form is a liar" (*Kidd.* 49a; cited by Edersheim, *Life and Times*, I, 206). See also, Stenning, *op. cit.*, p. x.

[5] The finding of pre-Christian Greek OT texts differing somewhat from the LXX but agreeing with quotations in the church fathers (as the Leather Scroll of the Minor Prophets and Justin) is not significant for NT quotations because most of the church fathers had no knowledge of the Semitic OT and because we have not found LXX MSS agreeing with aberrant NT quotations of the OT.

Matthew the Targumist

The recourse to the Hebrew displayed in the working over of the Septuagintal text gives us the cue to restate and re-establish the traditional view that Mt was his own targumist and drew on a knowledge of the Hebrew, Aramaic, and Greek [1] textual traditions of the OT.[2] This must be the supposition, unless pre-Christian MSS are discovered which agree with the aberrant text of the quotations. It is also favored by positive considerations.

The original milieu of Christianity was Jewish. Hence, "the Christian Church must have passed through a state of Targumism, if it emerges from the synagogue in which Targumism prevails."[3] B. Gärtner gleans evidence from Acts 3:18; 9:20-22; 13:27; 17:2 f.; 28:23 that the primitive Christian mission to the Jews took advantage of the synagogical practice of scripture-reading to prove Jesus the Messiah.[4] This practice received its sanction from Jesus himself (Lk 4:16 ff.; 24:27). We must therefore think that not only the practice, but also the style of reading and interpreting the OT conformed to synagogical targumizing, both because the audience was used to that style and because the first Christian preachers were themselves Palestinian Jews [5] and knew only that style.

Among Christian preachers the prophetic consciousness reinforced their right of targumic adaptation.[6] For this also there is concrete

---

[1] Edersheim (*Life and Times*, I, 445) and Elbogen (*op. cit.*, 188) both suggest use was made of the LXX by the methurgeman of the synagogue.

[2] So Jerome: "eos [apostolos evangelistas] ubi Septuaginta ab Hebraico discrepant, Hebraeum sensum suis expressisse sermonibus" (*Epistula ad Aglasiam* lvii [MPL XXII, 574f.]); Carpzov, *op. cit.*, 104-183; *idem, Critica Sacra Veteris Testamenti* (Lipsiae, 1728), 120ff.; S. Davidson, in T. H. Horne's *Introduction*[10] (London, 1856), II, 182; H. J. Holtzmann, *Die synoptischen Evangelien* (Leipzig, 1863), 258ff.; B. F. Westcott, *An Introduction to the Study of the Gospels*[4] (London, 1872), 229; Edersheim, *Life and Times*, I, 445; Swete, *Introduction to the OT in Greek*, 398; S. E. Johnson, *op. cit.*, 141; *idem, The Interpreter's Bible* (New York, 1951), VII, 238 (Johnson also sees reminiscences of other Greek translations); M. Black, *Journal of the Manchester University Egyptian and Oriental Society*, 23 (1942), 4; Karnetzki, 255ff. E. E. Ellis concludes the same for Pauline quotations which diverge from the LXX (*Paul's Use of the OT*; *NTS*, 2 [1955/56], 131).

[3] J. R. Harris, *ET*, 32 (1920/21), 373-376.

[4] *Studia Theologica*, 8 (1954), 22ff.

[5] So also in Hellenistic Jewry. On Philo's frequently targumic method of quotation, see C. Siegfried, *ZWT*, 16 (1873), 217-238; H. E. Ryle, *Philo and Holy Scripture* (London, 1895), pp. xxxvff.; Swete, *Introduction to the OT in Greek*, 374-376.

[6] Cf. Ellis, *Paul's Use of the OT*, 107-112.

evidence. In Acts 4:8-11 Peter, "filled with the Spirit," targumically quotes Ps 118 (117):22 as fulfilled prophecy, adapting the text so that the chief priests and scribes, often called the "building men" in rabbinical literature, become "the builders" who reject Jesus, just as in the Targum to Ps 118 "the learned" or "the scribes" reject "the young man (טליא)."[1] We can do no better than to quote the words of T. W. Manson:

> We are long accustomed to distinguish carefully between the text, which—in more senses than one—is sacred, and the commentary upon it or the expositions of it. We tend to think of the text as objective fact and interpretation as subjective opinion. It may be doubted whether the early Jewish and Christian translators and expositors of Scripture made any such sharp distinction . . . accurate reproduction of the traditional wording of the Divine oracles took second place to publication of what was held to be their essential meaning and immediate application. Odd as it may seem to us, the freedom with which they handled the Biblical text is a direct result of the supreme importance which they attached to it.[2]

The argument is confirmed by the fact that not only in oral targumizing, but also in the copying of the sacred text itself, a certain freedom in harmonization, expansion, etc., was exercised. This we have learned from the Biblical texts of the Dead Sea Scrolls.[3] Further confirmation comes from the Christian practice, alluded to by Melito, of reading the scripture-lesson in Hebrew and then targumizing it into Greek (probably with the aid of the LXX) [4] and by the Christian targumizing of the canonical Greek gospels into Aramaic as late as the fourth century.[5] These practices stemmed from the adoption of targumism by the early church.

In an article confined to Mt's non-Septuagintal citations from the Minor Prophets, A. Baumstark has shown that every phenomenon of textual variation and adaptation finds a parallel in the Targums.[6] This and the fact Mt's deviations from the LXX and

---

[1] Gärtner, *Studia Theologica*, 8 (1954), 22ff.

[2] *JTS*, 46 (1945), 135f.

[3] See esp. Skehan, *JBL*, 78 (1959), 24f., who draws the parallel with NT quotations.

[4] G. Zuntz, *HTR*, 36 (1943), 299-315.

[5] For full discussions, see T. Zahn, *Geschichte des neutestamentlichen Kanons* (Erlangen, 1888-90), II, 2, App. ix, 3, pp. 665ff.; Bacon, *Studies in Mt*, 13-17, 20f., who draws heavily on Zahn.

[6] *Biblica*, 37 (1956), 305ff. Baumstark's own view is that the texts in Mt are based on a lost Aramaic Targum, which in turn was based on a vulgar Hebrew text similar to the Samaritan Pentateuch.

even from the MT do not in the majority of instances betray hermeneutical motivation combine to reduce the significance of the parallel, often drawn nowadays, to Qumran *midrash-pesher*. What is *midrash-pesher* but the targumic method applied to prophecy believed to be fulfilled or on the verge of fulfilment in an eschatological situation? It is the fulfilment-motif which gives NT interpretation of the OT affinity to Qumran *pesher*. But in the mechanics of text-handling, both rest on the targumic method.[1]

The Language Situation Presupposed By the Matthaean Quotations

The Matthaean and indeed all the synoptic quotations, except Marcan formal quotations, present a combination of Septuagintal, Aramaic, and Hebrew textual elements. Inasmuch as the combination meets us at all levels of the synoptic tradition and in all literary forms, we cannot parcel out the Septuagintal to a Hellenistic milieu, the Aramaic to a Syrian or a Palestinian, the Hebrew to a Palestinian, and say that the final redactor threw together the component parts. The way the various elements are intertwined, even within single quotations, defies unravelling and forbids the supposition of redactional stages, whether conceived of in terms of documentary editing or in terms of evolution under oral influences. Rather, the combination appears to be orignal to the tradition itself.

We must now ask out of what language milieu this phenomenon could have arisen. Where were Greek, Aramaic, and Hebrew all used in NT times? The answer is, Palestine.

The language situation in Palestine during NT times has long been a subject for debate. Thus far in the present century the Aramaists, led by A. Meyer, G. Dalman, A. J. Wensinck, J. Jeremias, C. C. Torrey, and M. Black, have been in the ascendancy. Protests in favor of Hebrew have been made by M. H. Segal[2] and now by

[1] I relegate to a footnote two weak objections against Mt's being a targumist with knowledge of the Semitic as well as the Greek OT text. (1) The first evangelist was limited to Greek, because he rejects Mk's Aramaisms (P. Wernle, *Die synoptische Frage* [Leipzig, 1897], 146). This shows only that Mt had a better feeling for Greek style than Mk. He translates κορβᾶν and ἀββᾶ, thereby seeming to indicate a knowledge of the Semitic tongue. (2) No one would have dared substitute his own rendering for the venerated LXX (Hunt, *op. cit.*, 151). But in any case, someone did!

[2] *A Grammar of Mishnaic Hebrew* (Oxford, 1927), 16f. Cf. T. W. Manson, *The Teaching of Jesus*, 46ff.

J. M. Grintz, H. Birkeland, and I. Rabinowitz.[1] Proponents of Greek have not been so vocal as A. Roberts [2] and T. K. Abbott [3] in the last century, but have not been lacking.[4] Special mention should be made of S. Lieberman's notable contribution, *Greek in Jewish Palestine*.[5] Here he has shown, largely from rabbinical sources, that Hellenism (including the use of Greek) had deeply penetrated all classes of Jews in Palestine.

The purpose here is not to enumerate or evaluate the arguments pro and con.[6] The present writer would observe, however, that usually the strongest arguments in favor of conflicting views are left largely unrefuted, the weight of discussion being put on evidence favorable to the particular author's viewpoint.[7] This has happened for a very good reason: proof now exists that *all three languages* in question—Hebrew, Aramaic, and Greek—were commonly used by Jews in first-century Palestine. We are not dealing with an either/or, but with a both/and.

A difficulty has been that scholars were forced to infer their views from scattered literary intimations. But now we have archaeological data at hand to settle the question. J. T. Milik notes the presence of Greek, Aramaic, and Hebrew on ossuaries dating from NT times.[8] Excavations by the Franciscans on Mt. Olivet have un-

---

[1] Grintz, *JBL*, 79 (1960), 32-47; Birkeland, *The Language of Jesus* (Oslo, 1954); Rabinowitz, *ZNW*, 53 (1962), 229-238. The debate about the kind of Hebrew that was possibly spoken is irrelevant here.

[2] *Greek the Language of Christ and His Apostles* (London, 1888).

[3] *Essays on the Original Texts of the Old and New Testaments* (London, 1891), 129-182.

[4] J. P. Mahaffy, *The Progress of Hellenism in Alexander's Empire* (London, 1905), 128ff.; A. T. Robertson, *Grammar*, 26ff.; G. A. Smith, in R. O. P. Taylor, *op. cit.*, 91-95; R. O. P. Taylor, *ibid.*, 5ff., 96-105; *idem*, *ET*, 56 (1944/45), 95-97; T. Nicklin, *Gospel Gleanings* (London, 1950), 290ff.; and a well-balanced treatment from the last century in Hug, *Introduction to the NT* (Andover, 1836), 326ff.

[5] (New York, 1942). Lieberman was not the first to gather evidence for the use of Greek from rabbinical literature. See Edersheim, *Life and Times*, I, 29f.; and also W. L. Knox in the Schweich Lectures delivered the same year that Lieberman's study was published (*Some Hellenistic Elements in Primitive Christianity* [London, 1944], 30ff.).

[6] For surveys up to their respective times, see A. Schweitzer, *The Quest of the Historical Jesus* (London, 1910), 269ff.; and W. C. Allen, in *Studies in the Synoptic Problem* (Oxford, 1911), 288ff.

[7] A classic example is Dalman's well-known chapter on the three languages in *Jesus-Jeshua*, 1-37. His own discussion of Greek contains evidence that it was used much more than he is willing to admit or attempts to refute.

[8] *Ten Years of Discovery*, 130f.

earthed ossuaries predating the Jewish War (A.D. 66-73). On seven of these ossuaries the language is Hebrew, on eleven it is Aramaic, and on eleven it is Greek.[1] Whatever the correct interpretation of the Talpioth ossuaries,[2] of significance are the use of the Greek alphabet, the Greek form of the name "Jesus," and the mixture of Hebrew, Aramaic, and Greek inscriptions on the ossuaries.

N. Avigad notes that on ossuaries in a first-century tomb discovered in 1941 by E. L. Sukenik and himself, eight out of twelve personal names were Greek, most of them never before found in Palestine. Eight of the ossuaries have Greek inscriptions, one inscription is bilingual (Greek and Hebrew), and one is in Hebrew. Even though Avigad's conjecture that the tomb belonged to a family of the diaspora from Cyrenaica seems probable, we still have evidence of a mixed language milieu—if for no other reason than the influx of the diaspora into Palestine.[3] Sukenik mentions the presence of Greek as well as Hebrew and Aramaic on many ossuaries in other finds.[4] Similarly, the ossuaries discovered long ago by Charles Clermont-Ganneau on the Mount of Olives near Bethany bore both Hebrew and Greek inscriptions.[5] One would think that in the presence of death a language of the heart would be used, a language in which people habitually thought and spoke. Yet all three languages in question appear on the ossuary finds in roughly equal proportions.

Y. Yadin's recent Dead Sea expedition brought to light fifteen letters dating from the Bar-Kokhba revolt. These letters again employ Hebrew, Aramaic, and Greek. They show that Bar-Kokhba's officers understood these languages and suggest the use of these languages among the people of Palestine at large. In a re-excavation later in Yadin's expedition, a large number of additional documents

---

[1] B. Bagatti and J. T. Milik, *Gli scavi del "Dominus Flevit," La necropoli del periodo romano* (Jerusalem, 1958)—summarized and evaluated by R. de Vaux, *RB*, 66 (1959), 299-301.

[2] See E. L. Sukenik, *American Journal of Archaeology*, 51 (1947), 351-365; B. Gustafsson, *NTS*, 3 (1956/57), 65-69; D. Fishwick, *NTS*, 10 (1963), 49-61, and other literature cited by Fishwick, p. 51, n. 3.

[3] *Israel Exploration Journal*, 12 (1962), 1-12.

[4] *Op cit.*, 363f. See also S. Klein, *Jüdisch-palaestin. Corpus Inscriptionum* (1920), 8ff.; Lieberman, *op. cit.*, 30, 37-39; H. J. Leon, *The Jews of Ancient Rome*, 75—cited by Fishwick, *op. cit.*, p. 53, n. 1; and M. Hadas, *Hellenistic Culture: Fusion and Diffusion* (New York, 1959), 35f., 48f.

[5] C. Clermont-Ganneau, *Palestine Exploration Fund: Quarterly Statement* (London, 1874), 7-10. Fishwick, *op. cit.*, 50, cites in addition *Archaeological Researches in Palestine*, 1 (1899), 381ff., but I have been unable to check that reference.

of other kinds (contracts, receipts, etc.) were found—written yet again in Hebrew, Aramaic, and Greek.[1]

It is striking that such finds have been made in southern Palestine. Scholars have always recognized that Galilean Jews, farther removed from the center of Judaism, closer to Gentile areas like the Decapolis, and located on the Via Maris trade route, were more hellenized than Judean Jews. Yet the archaeological discoveries show that even in the South Greek was commonly used. How much more likely it is, then, that Jesus the Galilean and the apostles, who were predominantly if not exclusively Galilean, commonly used Greek in addition to the Semitic tongues.[2] If so, much of the gospel tradition may have been originally cast into Greek as well as Aramaic and Hebrew molds.

The hardcore archaeological evidence therefore gives confirmation to our examination of the synoptic texts themselves. Apparently the explicit quotations in the Marcan tradition became hellenized exactly because they were explicit. They stood out, were recognized, and were assimilated to the LXX. The mass of allusive quotations escaped assimilation precisely because they were allusive. Beneath the surface, overlooked, and hard-to-be-changed because they were grammatically tied to nonquotation material, the allusive quotations did not become hellenized.

We are not dealing with partial hellenization of an originally pure Semitic quotation tradition, because the very point of the quotation sometimes rests on the LXX against the Hebrew, Aramaic, and Syriac readings. And since the allusive quotations compose part of the very fabric of the synoptic tradition, they belong to its earliest stage so far as that can be ascertained by us. It is surely significant, then, that this early quotation material exhibits the same threefold language milieu which archaeological data should have taught us to expect. That the trilingual mixture in the synoptic quotations (except formal quotations in the Marcan tradition)

---

[1] Y. Yadin, *BA*, 24 (1961), 34-50, 86-95. See also a preliminary report by M. Wallenstein, *The Guardian* (Manchester, Saturday, February 4, 1961), p. 6.

[2] Cf. the Greek names "Andrew" and "Philip" within the circle of the twelve, and Dalman's admission, "Anyone brought up in Bethsaida would not only have understood Greek, but would also have been polished by intercourse with foreigners and have had some Greek culture" (*Sacred Sites and Ways*, 165). Philip, Andrew, and Peter came from Bethsaida. Jn 12:21 takes for granted Philip understood Greek when he was approached by the Greeks who asked to see Jesus.

agrees with the physical evidence for a trilingual situation in first-century Palestine suggests first-century Palestine as the origin of the gospel tradition. For where else were these three languages used alongside one another? [1]

Here then is the milieu of the bulk of synoptic quotation material. Our analysis of the quotation material confirms the archaeological data; the archaeological data confirms our analysis, and also the contention that the strands of textual tradition cannot and need not be disentangled. It is perfectly possible that the first evangelist was his own targumist, ranging with easy familiarity from one textual tradition to another.[2]

Implications for the Synoptic Problem And the Origin of Matthew

The triple textual tradition in Matthaean quotations calls for Palestinian origin, as we have noted above. More particularly, the contacts with the Hebrew OT call for this geographical origin. "In no other part of the Empire can we assume a knowledge of the Old Testament in the original language."[3] Also, scrolls of the Hebrew OT must have been confined largely to Palestine.[4] A Palestinian origin accords with external tradition [5] and with numerous other internal indications.[6]

The working upon the Hebrew text of the OT also suggests an

---

[1] For further consideration of the implications of the threefold language milieu for the authenticity of the gospel tradition, see my article in *JBL*, 83 (1964), 404ff., entitled, "The Language Milieu of First-Century Palestine: Its Bearing on the Authenticity of the Gospel Tradition." See also G. H. Thompson, "To What Extent Did Jesus Use Greek?", *Religion in Life*, 32 (1962/63), 103-115; and (unavailable to me) M. Bobichon, "Grec, araméen et hébreu: les langues de Palestine au premier siècle chrétien," *Bible et Terre Sainte*, 58 (1963), 4f.

[2] The heavy Semitic element in the Matthaean quotations and the correspondence between the trilingual language situation in first century Palestine and the quotations present a formidable obstacle in the way of S. G. F. Brandon's thesis that Mt emanates from Alexandria, where the Septuagintal would surely have been predominant (*op. cit.*).

[3] Burkitt, *The Gospel History and Its Transmission*, 127f.

[4] Gloag, *op. cit.*, 150.

[5] E.g., the Anti-Marcionite prologue to Lk. See Wikenhauser, *op. cit.*, 181.

[6] See Allen, *Mt*, 310f.; Schniewind, *op. cit.*, 203; X. Léon-Dufour, in *Introduction a la Bible* (Tournai, 1959), II, 192f. Bacon's arguments for geographical remoteness from Palestine are quite indecisive (*Studies in Mt*, 17f.). E.g., the addition of demonstrative pronouns to several Marcan expressions may be purely a matter of emphasis.

early date for the first gospel, for access to Hebrew scrolls must have been difficult after complete break with the synagogue.[1] Material which includes allusive quotations—and this comprehends practically the whole of the synoptic tradition—must be dated very early, because the mixed text shows the material emerged from the Palestinian language milieu and escaped wholesale Hellenization (in contrast with Marcan formal quotations). Had the material arisen or undergone revision in a later, extra-Palestinian milieu, the Septuagintal element almost surely would have been dominant. Not only so, it becomes unnecessary and even disadvantageous to regard the Matthaean formula-citations with their strong Semitic coloring as belonging to a late stage. They are obviously inserted in the final stage of composition, but the final stage is not late.[2]

That the Matthaean parallels to Marcan formal quotations are almost as purely Septuagintal as Mk confirms that Greek-Mt utilized Mk.[3] But how is it that Marcan formal quotations stand out from all

[1] A. G. Hebert, *The Authority of the OT* (London, n.d.), 204.

[2] Not even Mt 22:7 necessarily points to a date after A.D. 70, since recent studies conclude Jesus did predict the calamities to befall Jerusalem. See C. J. Cadoux, *The Historic Mission of Jesus* (London, 1941), 266ff.; C. H. Dodd, *Journal of Roman Studies*, 37 (1947), 47-54; V. Taylor, *The Life and Ministry of Jesus* (London, 1955), 172; and earlier, T. H. Robinson, *Mt* (London, 1928), 198. Wikenhauser's argument for a post-70 date from a comparison between Mt 22:2-14 and Lk 14:16-24 rests on the doubtful assumption that these two passages are parallel (*op. cit.*, 197f.). Qumran parallels have dramatically crushed the arguments from Mt 16:18 ("I will build my church") and 18:15-17 (disciplinary regulations) that Mt is the late ecclesiastical gospel (see W. H. Brownlee, *NTS*, 3 [1956/57], 16f.). On the other hand, with Marcan priority over Mt we are forced to a date near 70 for Mt *if* ἔξοδος in Iren., *Haer.* III.i.1 means "decease" and not "departure" and *if* Irenaeus' testimony is to be taken at face-value. The latter is not certain, since Irenaeus may be limited to information from Papias and interpreting it (cf. R. Heard, *NTS*, 1 [1954/55], 122ff.). Irenaeus' testimony does not harmonize with Lk-Acts if our Lk depends on Mk and antedates Acts and if Acts records events about as far as they had progressed. It is further suspect because the statement that Peter and Paul founded the church in Rome conflicts with the Epistle to the Romans.

[3] I write "Greek-Mt," because Lagrange's suggestion that the Greek translator of Aramaic-Mt conformed to Mk's Septuagintal form in parallel passages remains possible (*Mt*, pp. cxxiiff.). Note that in the two Matthaean quotations from Mic 7:6, the one peculiar to Mt is non-Septuagintal (10:35f.) and the one paralleled in Mk is Septuagintal (10:21; Mk 13:12). We cannot argue for Marcan priority from assimilation of Mk by Mt toward the LXX (like Allen, *ET*, 12 [1900/01], 281ff.; Bacon, *Studies in Mt*, 470; Stendahl, 147f.), because the assimilation is usually stylistic and because the opposite, Mt straying from Mk and the LXX, is seen in 15:4a; 19:5, 18, 19; 22:32, 37; 26:31.

other quotation material in the synoptics as almost purely Septuagintal? The general answer is that these formal quotations were easily recognizable and so were conformed to the LXX in a Hellenistic milieu. Allusive quotations escaped the process because they were, so to speak, incognito. The specific answer may be that the Hellenization took place in Rome, where Mk wrote for Gentiles, just as the tradition says.[1]

Passing from the formal quotations in the Marcan tradition, we can appreciate the significance of the mixed text in the other synoptic quotations only against the background of the predominantly Septuagintal form of quotations throughout the rest of the NT.[2] That this mixed text character pervades all three gospels—not just Q material or Matthaean material Lk might have copied from Mt, for Marcan allusive quotations are included—suggests a common body of tradition behind *all three* synoptic gospels.

The Q hypothesis as usually held has been plagued by certain unresolved difficulties. General agreement on the extent of Q has never existed.[3] B. H. Streeter's attempts at explaining the "minor" agreements of Mt and Lk against Mk seem strained at numerous points.[4] Therefore, we have the old Ur-Markus theory, Bacon's "S" (a complete gospel inclusive of Q and containing a passion narrative), Schniewind's "G" (for *Geschichtenüberlieferung*, a source similar to Mk on which Mt and Lk draw when agreeing against

---

[1] For a survey and discussion of this tradition, see Streeter, *op. cit.*, 488-491. Cf. Atkinson, *op. cit.*, 56, who, however, sees Matthaean priority and Mk (or Peter) drawing from Mt only those quotations he could reconcile with the LXX.

[2] We may adopt in general the figures of Atkinson, *ibid.*, 39, concerning agreement with the LXX: Acts—19/20; Pauline epistles—9/10; pastorals—100%; Hebrews—11/12; catholic epistles—4/5; Rev—6/7.

[3] See S. Petrie, *NovTest*, 3 (1959), 28-33.

[4] *Op. cit.*, 295-331. Streeter escapes many instances of Mt and Lk agreeing against Mk by including in Q John the Baptist's preaching, Jesus' baptism and temptation, the Beelzebub controversy, the mission charge, and the parable of the mustard seed. What kind of document would contain only these bits of narrative? And if this much narrative material is allowable in Q, what prevents an even greater extension to account for the mixed text in *all three* synoptics, so that Q becomes an Ur-Matthaean gospel, or a body of note-material as suggested below. In other words, if one does not include a sizeable amount of narrative material in Q, the agreements of Mt and Lk against Mk become an insuperable problem. But if one does include a sizeable amount of narrative material in Q, the very nature of the document becomes a problem—and the door is opened for further hypotheses concerning its nature.

Mk),[1] an overlapping of Mk and Q in the triple narrative where Mt and Lk agree against Mk (in which case another synoptic problem arises: Whence the general agreement of Mk and Q at these points?), and the view that Mk sometimes utilized Q.[2] The matter is clearly stated by V. A. Dearing: "From the textual point of view, the agreements explained as arising from common dependence upon Q are simply clearer and larger manifestations of the state of affairs indicated by the 'minor agreements.' "[3] Neither does the view that Lk used Mt seem destined to succeed. From our perspective, neither a Q limited to Mt and Lk nor Lucan dependence on Mt is favored by the same mixed text in Marcan allusive quotations as in Matthaean quotations.

The suggestion of a common source for all three synoptics because of their common mixed text-form in quotations invites us to think of an Aramaic or Hebrew Ur-Mt. Undeniably, an Ur-Mt best accords with the tradition of the early church, as usually interpreted.[4] Ur-Mt also provides a basis for the agreements of Greek-Mt and Lk against Mk and for the Semitic element in the substratum of quotation material throughout the synoptics. But there is one insurmountable difficulty. A formal gospel written in a Semitic language cannot account for the Septuagintal element which, along with the Semitic, is woven into the warp and woof of the synoptic tradition. It is not conceivable that this comes from partial assimilation to the LXX.[5] The allusions are too subtle. The combinations of text-forms within single quotations are too intricate. Sometimes the quotation depends on the LXX. All three gospels, therefore, must have originally been written in Greek.[6]

There is but one hypothesis known to the present writer which can

---

[1] J. Schniewind, *Mk* (Göttingen, 1937), 36f.

[2] So Rawlinson, *op. cit.*, pp. xxxviiiff.; C. A. Briggs, *JBL*, 23 (1904), 191ff., who sees an influx of Q into Mk, where originally Q was absent; Streeter, in Oxford *Studies in the Synoptic Problem*, 165-183 (Streeter's original position, with W. Sanday's concurrence, pp. xvif.); T. E. F. Honey, *JBL*, 62 (1943), 319-331; F. C. Grant, *op. cit.*, 60.

[3] *A Manual of Textual Analysis* (Berkeley, 1959), 95.

[4] The various hypotheses of Roman Catholic scholars who accept dependence of Greek-Mt on Mk—Lagrange, Cerfaux, Benoit, Vaganay, Wikenhauser, J. Levie, Léon-Dufour— all include a Semitic Ur-Mt of some form.

[5] Against Karnetzki, 255-264, 269ff.

[6] The original Greek unity of Mt is the main burden of Anger's study. See Anger for detailed discussion of this debate, which loomed large in the last century.

meet the requirements of the data which has been discovered in this study. It is the hypothesis that the Apostle Matthew was a note-taker during the earthly ministry of Jesus and that his notes provided the basis for the bulk of the apostolic gospel tradition.[1] The use of notebooks which were carried on one's person was very common in the Graeco-Roman world.[2] In ancient schools outline notes (γράμματα ὑπομνηματικά) were often taken by pupils as the teacher lectured. The notes became the common possession of the schools and circulated without the name of the lecturer. Sometimes an author would take this material as the basis for a book to be published (γράμματα συνταγματικά).[3] Shorthand was used possibly as early as the fourth century B.C. and certainly by Jesus' time.[4] The Oxyrhynchus papyri show that scribes and clerks were often trained in shorthand.[5] Rabbinic tradition was transmitted by the employment of catchwords and phrases which were written down in shorthand notes.[6] Thus, from both the Hellenistic side and the

[1] This hypothesis has been revived by E. J. Goodspeed, *Mt, Apostle and Evangelist* (Philadelphia, 1959). See also B. F. C. Atkinson, in *The New Bible Commentary* (Grand Rapids, 1954), 771; A. T. Robertson, *Studies in Mark's Gospel* (New York, 1919), 28; *idem, The Expositor*, 23, 8th Series (1922), 108f.

[2] F. G. Kenyon, *Books and Readers in Greece and Rome*[2] (Oxford, 1951), 91f.

[3] On the above-outlined practice, see W. Bousset, *Jüdisch-Christlicher Schultrieb* (Göttingen, 1915), 2-5; and for further references and discussion, B. Gerhardsson, *Memory and Manuscript* (Uppsala, 1961), 157-163, cf. 200-202.

[4] See G. Milligan, *The NT Documents* (London, 1913), 241-247; further references in Gerhardsson, *op. cit.*, p. 156, n. 3.

[5] Goodspeed is at his best when drawing on his knowledge of the papyri to show the practice of note-taking, the use of shorthand, and the qualifications of a tax-collector such as Mt. His attempted parallel between Jesus and Isaiah is less than convincing (in the above-mentioned book on *Mt*).

[6] See L. Finkelstein, *HUCA*, 16 (1941), 115ff. The above remarks, written before the appearance of Gerhardsson's book, do not imply whole-hearted acceptance of the Riesenfeld-Gerhardsson thesis. In particular, the notorious paucity of rabbinic sayings from before A.D. 70, the informality and freshness of Jesus' teaching style, and the synoptic agreement in *narrative* material (whereas rabbinic tradition is primarily expository) reduce the value of the thesis. The Scandinavian scholars have, however, correctly re-emphasized the general importance of memory and note-taking in the NT milieu. Granted that the early Christian methodology of preserving tradition must have been less formally structured than rabbinic methodology at a somewhat later date, preservation of Jesus' teaching must nevertheless have been effected by some such methods; for otherwise we would not have the broad agreement which has led to the Q-hypothesis. For reactions to Gerhardsson's book, see A. N. Wilder and W. D. Davies, in *Neotestamentica et Patristica* (*Freundesgabe* O. Cullmann; Leiden, 1962), 3-34; M. Smith, *JBL*, 82 (1963), 169-176; H. K.

Judaistic side it is wholly plausible to suppose that one from the apostolic band was a note-taker—especially since the relationship of Jesus to his disciples was that of a teacher, or rabbi, to his pupils.

As an ex-publican, whose employment and post near Capernaum on the Great West Road would have required and given a good command of Greek and instilled the habit of jotting down information, and perhaps as a Levite,[1] whose background would have given him acquaintance with the OT in its Semitic as well as Greek forms, Mt the Apostle was admirably fitted for such a function among the unlettered disciples.[2] We can then understand how all strands of textual tradition made their way into the whole of the synoptic material, for the looseness and informality of such notes made it possible for Hebrew, Aramaic, and Greek all to appear in them.

Thus also we can account for the wide variation in the degree of agreement between Mt and Lk in Q-material, a variation which led to Bussmann's division of Q into ד (Greek) and R (Aramaic, Mt and Lk using different translations). The difficulty in fixing the exact boundaries of Q is accounted for, because such notes would have circulated in varying forms. Their brevity on occasion may have called for expansion; and some sections may have circulated independently.

We can also understand why the first three evangelists were content to present by and large the same outline of Jesus' life and ministry. Since the Jesus-tradition embraces only a fraction of what took place and was spoken, why is there broad agreement among the synoptics? Surely not for lack of tradition. A single authoritative, apostolic source behind the bulk of synoptic tradition best answers the question. Otherwise, the tradition would have been hopelessly fragmented, and no synoptic problem would exist. Finally, the persistent feeling that Mk is sometimes parallel to Q or used Q or another parallel source is satisfied by the hypothesis that Mt was a note-taker from whose material the synoptists drew.

Here we might stop, but the question of the authorship of the first gospel forces itself upon us. Has the text-form of the Matthaean quotations anything to say on this question? Perhaps—and to appreciate the argument we must again call to mind the predomi-

---

McArthur, *Interpretation*, 18 (1964), 44. My own hypothesis stresses note-taking, whereas Gerhardsson stresses memorization.

[1] The alternate name "Levi" may indicate a Levitical background.

[2] Acts 4:13: ἄνθρωποι ἀγράμματοί εἰσιν καὶ ἰδιῶται.

nantly Septuagintal form of NT quotations outside the synoptics and also the Hellenistic strain within Mk and the occasional assimilation to the LXX in Lk. The quotations peculiar to Mt, and notably the formula-citations, which appear most certainly to come from the author of the gospel, display the same mixed text that appears elsewhere throughout the synoptics. If then we accept as a working hypothesis that the Apostle Mt stands behind the mixed text elsewhere, it is natural to think the same concerning the formula-citations and the first gospel itself. There is thus no advantage in thinking that the name "Mt" was erroneously attached to the first gospel because that apostle stood behind an earlier tradition incorporated into the gospel. The distinctive mixed text may betray his presence behind both.

Immediate objections to Matthaean authorship will spring up, prime among which is that an eyewitness such as Mt the Apostle would never have depended on Mk. However, if Mk represents Petrine tradition, Mt is using apostolic tradition. And if Peter perchance used Matthaean "notes," [1] Mt would be using a form of his own tradition. Is it too difficult to think that Mt wished to preserve the unity of the apostolic gospel tradition and therefore utilized Mk? Perhaps we should not speak so much of "dependence" as of "agreement." Attention should also be paid to the fact that Mt maintains a certain independence from Mk at numerous points where stylistic and theological reasons seem not to enter.[2] The parallel to practice in ancient schools is again instructive, for note-material was considered common property and freely drawn upon, there being no feeling of slavish dependence or of plagiarism.[3, 4]

---

[1] Could this be the reason for signs of abridgement in Mk? See the list in Parker, *op. cit.*, 52ff.

[2] For this phenomenon in the passion narrative, see Léon-Dufour, *Biblica*, 40 (1959), 684-696.

[3] Bousset, *Jüdisch-Christlicher Schultrieb*, 2-5.

[4] Another objection to Matthaean authorship often heard is that Mt's frequent disinterest in the vivid details of Mk shows him not to have been an eyewitness. But this may be purely a matter of individual interest and style. For further answers to the common objections against Matthaean authorship, see Gloag, *op. cit.*, 98-104. I need not expand the various arguments for Matthaean authorship: the early tradition, the popularity of the gospel, the question why the gospel should have been falsely ascribed to an apostle of Mt's obscurity, the special mention of Capernaum, the home-town of Mt the publican, in 4:13, the dropping of αὐτοῦ (Mk 2:15) in the phrase ἐν τῇ οἰκίᾳ αὐτοῦ regarding the supper in the house of Mt the publican (9:10), the special

Whether or not the Apostle be regarded as the author of Greek-Mt, under the note-taking hypothesis two possibilities are open concerning the tradition of a Semitic Ur-Mt. The first is that this tradition is simply irrelevant. Greek-Mt may bear no special relationship to the Semitic book, although both may work largely upon the same traditions. The second possibility is that Papias' notice [1] does not mean Mt wrote a Hebrew (or Aramaic) gospel. J. Kürzinger has put forward the interpretation that since Papias' main concern is to apologize for the lack of literary σύνταξις in Mk, in contrast with Mt, Ἑβραΐδι διαλέκτῳ (note the anarthrous form) is to be understood in the connotation of literary style, and ἡρμήνευσεν (not μεθηρμήνευσεν) refers to exposition, not to translation.[2] Despite its novelty, this view merits serious consideration; Kürzinger's presentation should be studied in full.

---

interest shown in money (10:9f.; 18:23ff.; 20:1ff.; 28:12ff.), the juggling of figures in the genealogy.

[1] Preserved in Eusebius, *H.E.* iii. 39.

[2] *BZ*, 4 (1960), 19-38.

PART TWO

THE MATTHAEAN ARGUMENT FROM THE FULFILMENT OF MESSIANIC PROPHECY

". . . With Special Reference to the Messianic Hope"

CHAPTER THREE

THE QUESTION OF HISTORICITY

Historical Pessimism and the Form-Critical Method

The foregoing suggestions have obviously presupposed a negative attitude toward radical form-criticism. For this reason and as an introduction to the problem of historicity as it relates to OT quotations, it is necessary to give a brief critique of the form-critical method.[1]

As manifest in historical scepticism regarding our ability to know very much about the historical Jesus, form-criticism minimizes the personality and the ministry of Jesus and can hardly explain the origin of the Church. Whence came the Church if the tradition upon which it purports to be based is its own creation? The problem is aggravated when we remember that it is a man who died as a criminal who became the object of faith. The very existence of the Church and of its Christology demands that Jesus was a person of tremendous impact, and this in turn demands a vivid recollection of his words and deeds as the basis for the new faith and the new community. If, as radical form-criticism supposes, the gospels really describe the history of the early church, and yet the central concern of the early church was to proclaim the redemptive history of Jesus Christ, it is quite needless to say that the historical Jesus was largely forgotten—the strongest motive existed for remembering him. The evangelistic motive for remembrance was complemented by the ideal for Christian life, living in accordance with the words

---

[1] Rather than burden the following treatment with numerous footnotes, I acknowledge general indebtedness to W. F. Albright, *From the Stone Age to Christianity*[2] (Baltimore, 1946), 38f., 297f.; A. Barr, *ET*, 49 (1937/38), 401-408; P. E. Davies, *JBL*, 73 (1954), 197-202; B. S. Easton, *The Gospel before the Gospels* (London, 1928); I. Henderson, *Myth in the NT* (London, 1952); J. Jeremias, *ET*, 69 (1957/58), 333-339; W. Manson, *op. cit.*; V. T. O'Keefe, *CBQ*, 21 (1959), 171-189; E. F. Scott, *The Validity of the Gospel Record* (London, 1938); V. Taylor, *The Formation of the Gospel Tradition* (London, 1935); H. G. Wood, *NTS*, 4 (1958), 169-182. I must emphasize that the following critique is directed against that side of form-criticism which denies historicity where it discovers motives. Considerations of space forbid a more detailed discussion.

of Christ. Even Paul, who had not known Jesus, could quote no higher authority.[1]

Radical form-criticism does not sufficiently take into account the restraint which the mere presence of the apostles and other eyewitnesses, hostile as well as friendly, must have exercised against free invention of tradition to meet the needs of the community. Numerous references throughout the NT indicate the Church was very interested in eyewitness testimony.[2] Not only would eyewitnesses have provided a restraining influence, but also their recollection of the deeds, the example, and the teaching of Jesus would have been called upon for solutions to ecclesiastical problems, for answers to inquiring questions from prospective converts, and for apology in the face of false and malicious charges. The shortness of the time between the events and the gospel records combines with the eyewitness factor to rule out serious modification of the historical tradition and the analogy of folk-literature.

Radical form-criticism does not judge fairly the written records. The chief interest of the gospels is historical, as expressly stated in Lk 1:1-4. Matter-of-fact restraint is shown in description of the spectacular.[3] Even the artificial literary forms may be a mark of veracity, since more flexible modes of narration would give more room for alteration. The original poetic form discernible in many of Jesus' reported sayings [4] points to authenticity. So also do the lack of romantic and psychological interest in the workings of Jesus' inner consciousness, the preservation of enigmatic sayings and incidents discreditable to the apostles and Jesus' brethren, and the vivid geographical and biographical details—in contrast with the tendency toward simplification, not elaboration, seen in Mt and Lk (over against Mk) and in modern studies of human memory.[5]

---

[1] See J. Weiss, *The History of Primitive Christianity* (London, 1937), I, 77ff.

[2] Lk 1:1-4; Jn 19:35; 21:24; Acts 1:8, 21f.; 10:39, 41; I Cor 15:1ff.; I Pet 5:1; II Pet 1:16; I Jn 1:1-3; Papias in Eusebius, *H.E.* iii. 39.

[3] W. Manson singles out Mk 9:26, where "like one dead" would surely have turned the story into a tale of raising the dead, in an uncontrolled tradition (*op. cit.*, 46).

[4] C. F. Burney, *The Poetry of Our Lord* (Oxford, 1925).

[5] See W. S. Taylor, *Theology Today*, 15 (1959), 470-479, with dependence on F. C. Bartlett, *Remembering* (Cambridge, 1932), and Taylor's own article in *The British Journal of Psychology*, Vol. 38, Part 1 (1947), 7-19. When lack of detail is taken as evidence of stereotyping and generalizing for community needs and presence of detail is taken as attempt at verisimilitude, a predisposition against the gospels is evident.

Radical form-criticism does not appreciate the improbability that eyewitnesses of Jesus' life gladly endured suffering and martyrdom for a confession of faith known by them not to have originated with Jesus himself. Knowledge that the kerygmatic Jesus was the historical Jesus provides a credible psychological basis for the eagerness of the early disciples to proclaim Christ at the risk and cost of their lives, but free invention of Christological tradition provides no such basis.

Radical form-criticism mistakes the role of the Christian community. That she was the guardian, not the inventor of the evangelic tradition is evident from the absence of Pauline terminology in the gospels, from the meticulous way Paul distinguishes his teaching from that of Jesus, and from the unregulated tradition in the *agrapha* and the apocryphal literature. With free invention under differing local conditions, we certainly would not have had the *syn*optics.[1] Nor is the primarily evangelistic thrust of the gospels [2] consonant with evolvement from and for community needs, to say nothing of the fact we do not really know what the needs of the community were. In Acts and the epistles, the comparative infrequency of formal citations of *verba Christi* does not imply the absence of a firm tradition about Jesus' teaching. It is rather due to the fact that the Jewish-Palestinian background of Jesus' teaching made much of it not directly applicable to Gentile-Jewish problems outside Palestine in the church at large. Thus, the details of Jesus' life and teaching do not crop up very often in Acts and the epistles, as would have been the case had these details been fabricated to meet the needs of the early church.[3] The expectation that Jesus might soon return must have tended to suppress the feeling of need for further information than was already available concerning him and his teaching.

It is therefore a fair judgment to say that sceptical form-criticism rests on three doubtful presuppositions. The historical presupposition is that we cannot trust the authenticity of anything in the gospel tradition which might have derived from Judaism or from the beliefs and needs of the early church.[4] But no historian, Biblical

---

[1] Cf. Piper, *op. cit.*, 124.

[2] See C. F. D. Moule, in *NT Essays*, 165-179.

[3] See R. P. Casey, in *Quantalacumque* (K. Lake *Festschrift*; London, 1937), 115f.

[4] This rule of thumb is explicitly advocated, e.g., by H. Conzelmann, *RGG*[3],

or "secular," can reasonably adopt the negative attitude that any data for which a motive can be found is invalid. Motives may be used to explain the *preservation* of data and they may be used to call in question data *which conflict with other data,* but they cannot be used to shift the burden of proof to the side of pro-historicity when the data is otherwise acceptable. The result of a consistent application of this rule of thumb is that we can know absolutely nothing about the historical Jesus, for we should have to possess omniscience concerning Judaism and the life-situation of the early church, and any continuity whatsoever with the life and message of the historical Jesus (be it ethical or explicitly or implicitly eschatological) would immediately be exposed to the charge of derivation from the *Sitz im Leben der alten Kirche.*[1]

The philosophical presupposition is anti-supernaturalism. Since the evangelic tradition is steeped in the supernatural, it must be rejected. One can only say that anti-supernaturalism prejudices historical enquiry and is theologically and scientifically out-of-date, for it rests on the rationalistic concept of a closed universe and a rigid concept of natural law.

The theological presupposition is that objectively verifiable proof is not necessary and is even a stumbling-block to true faith.[2] The proof-text, II Cor 5:16, is quite unconvincing. In context Paul's statement that we do not know Christ any more after the flesh contrasts our attitude toward Christ before and after conversion and has nothing to do with a denial of historical basis for faith, which Paul elsewhere affirms (e.g., in I Cor 15).[3] It is true that the

---

III, 623; J. M. Robinson, *A New Quest of the Historical Jesus* (London, 1959), 37ff.

[1] For this reason the post-Bultmannian new quest for the historical Jesus by Käsemann, Fuchs, Ebeling, Bornkamm, Conzelmann, and J. M. Robinson is doomed to failure before it starts. Even the slightest historical continuity between Jesus and the Church cannot coexist with the sceptical axiom. Since the school of Bultmann uses Jesus' eschatological message as an existential handle (illegitimately, since according to Jesus his own person created the eschatological crisis—yet Bultmannians reject such a Christology and regard Jesus' eschatological expectations as having been crushed), it must be emphasized that the eschatological can be derived from Judaism and the early church as easily as any other part of the gospel tradition.

[2] So R. Bultmann, *Theology of the NT* (London, 1952), I, 238f.; *idem, Glauben u. Verstehen* (Tübingen, 1954), I, 207; J. M. Robinson, *op. cit.*, 44, 56, 76.

[3] See J. G. Machen, *The Origin of Paul's Religion* (London, 1921), 54ff.; P. Althaus, *The So-Called Kerygma and the Historical Jesus* (Edinburgh, 1959), 35f.

theological meaning of historical facts cannot be apprehended from the bare facts themselves. But several questions arise here. Does not the NT present the resurrection of Christ as objective verification for the theological message on which faith is to seize? Must faith cling to historical nothingness in order to be faith? Is a purely existential faith the only alternative to a purely rationalistic faith? Can it seriously be contended that the NT presents absence of historical foundation for faith as the offence of Christianity? Does the NT equate unbelief with the desire to know the Jesus of history, or with rejection of the Jesus whose work it portrays on a historical canvas? Purely existential faith receives no help from modern historiography, for although existentialism has invaded that field, historians continue to work with the very practical recognition that historical data range in reliability from the highest level of certainty humanly attainable to the lowest level of conjecture.[1]

Thus, we have been justified in by-passing the results of left-wing form-critical study in our suggestions concerning the origin of the gospel tradition and can now examine the effect of the fulfilment-motif on the tradition without an initial prejudice against it.

The Effect of the Fulfilment-Motif On the Evangelic Tradition

The question is to what extent the fulfilment-motif exercised a formative, or even creative influence on the evangelic tradition. Generalizations will not suffice, so that it is necessary to examine individual passages about which there is the greatest suspicion. Nevertheless, some miscellaneous remarks of a general nature may serve to introduce this aspect of the study.

First, the presence of a Septuagintal element in quotation material does not constitute grounds for questioning its authenticity.[2] The Septuagintal element is embedded along with the Semitic in the earliest layers of the synoptic tradition; and its presence there is

[1] See W. F. Albright, *JBL*, 77 (1958), 244-248. Existential historiography does not hold the field. See C. G. Singer, *Christianity Today*, 4 (1960), 534ff. Cf. D. M. Mackinnon's criticism of R. G. Collingwood (*The Idea of History*) for demanding "an autonomy for the historian which comes very near allowing him to 'make history' by his re-living of the past" (*JTS*, 48 [1947], 251).

[2] Against, e.g., Burkitt, *The Earliest Sources for the Life of Jesus*, 24ff.; Loisy, *op. cit.*, I, 953; Glasson, *ET* 69 (1957/58), 213ff. See the author's article in *JBL*, 83 (1964), 404ff.

justified by the now known language situation in Palestine at the beginning of the Christian era.

Second, the bulk of the gospel tradition cannot be traced to a reading of prophecy into the life of Jesus, for several reasons. The NT does not exploit the whole corpus of Messianic prediction.[1] Indeed, OT passages easily susceptible to fulfilment-interpretation were neglected.[2] Many of the passages the NT does exploit were not, so far as we can tell, Messianically interpreted in contemporary Judaism. Also, the prevalent Jewish concept of a conquering king is absent. The obvious inference is that "a true historical memory determined the use of prophecy by the Church." [3]

Because of the intended readers Mt's conforming Marcan material to the OT does not necessarily represent later accretion of unhistorical tradition. If, as is generally agreed, Mt is addressed to Jews and Mk to a wider audience, it is only natural that the former should pay more attention to the OT than the latter. In material usually assigned to Q, Lk more than once suppresses or loses the allusion to the OT. We must therefore not too readily assume allusions in Mt are due to the first evangelist.[4] The looseness with which many Matthaean citations from the OT are appended shows that the direction is from tradition to prophecy, not vice versa.[5] Assimilation to OT language in allusive quotation likewise depends on an already existing correspondence. Even in Qumran literature, where the desire to find fulfilment is so strong that the OT text is tortuously treated, invention of "history" to fit prophecy is not seen.

There is a concentration of quotations in Mt 1 and 2, the nativity narrative. It is therefore maintained that OT prophecy was the source of much of the nativity tradition.[6] But N. B. Stonehouse suggests that when Jesus began his public ministry, his deeds and words served to indicate the divine nature of his person and mission, so that a special need for authentication was felt in the

---

[1] C. H. Dodd, *History and the Gospel* (London, 1938), 61f.

[2] E.g., Mic 4:14. We would also have expected a developed Joseph-Jesus typology. See further J. J. O'Rourke, *CBQ*, 24 (1962), 402f.

[3] *Ibid.*

[4] See E. A. Edghill, *An Enquiry into the Evidential Value of Prophecy* (London, 1906), 416f.

[5] H. E. W. Turner, *ET*, 68 (1956/57), 15.

[6] F. Kattenbusch, *Theol. Stud. u. Krit.*, 102 (1930), 461.

nativity tradition, and was provided by fulfilled prophecy.[1] The unbridged interval between Jesus' birth and his baptism certainly favors the historicity of Mt 1 and 2; for apocryphal tradition about the childhood (as in the later NT apocrypha) would surely have been spun out at the same time to meet the conditions of supposed prophecies, were this being done to produce the nativity narrative. As it is, the apologetic, not the apocryphal, dominates Mt 1 and 2. Zahn shows that the apologetic motive stands behind the mention of the women in the genealogy.[2] Is 7:14 is introduced to combat Jewish slander regarding the manner of Jesus' birth.[3] The birth in Bethlehem, in accord with the prophecy, counteracts insinuations against Jesus' sojourn in Egypt and his growing up in Nazareth. The sojourn in Egypt and the slaughter of the infants are pictured as divinely intended to reduplicate the history of Israel. The return to live in the obscure and despised town of Nazareth plays a part in Christ's being despised and rejected by men.[4] Why the invention of tradition for which a need is felt to apologize by appeal to OT prophecy?

This line of thought finds confirmation in the citations. Is 7:14 was not interpreted Messianically in Judaism,[5] so that the nativity tradition must have molded the interpretation of Is 7:14, rather than vice versa. The most obvious testimonies, Num 24:17 and Is 60:6; Ps 72:10, are not formally cited, as they surely would have been had they been the source of the magi-story. The birth in Bethlehem receives independent support from Lk, where the verse from Mic does not figure at all.[6] The citations from Hos 11:1 and

[1] *The Witness of Mt and Mk to Christ* (Grand Rapids, 1958), 190.

[2] As shown, e.g., by Bathsheba's being called (ἐκ) τῆς τοῦ Οὐρίου (v. 6). Other explanations for mention of the women have been proposed, but none can evade the obvious intention behind this expression, which reminds Jewish readers of their ancestor David's sin lest they read the nativity story with haughty prejudice based on slanderous presuppositions. It is a humbling reminder that God works in irregular ways. See R. Bloch, in *Mélanges bibliques rédigés en l'honneur de A. Robert* (Paris, 1957), 381-389; Stendahl, in *Judentum, Urchristentum, Kirche*, 101-104. M. Krämer underrates the apologetic element in Mt 1 and 2, but rightly cautions that other themes are also evident (*Biblica*, 45 [1964], 2ff.).

[3] On which see R. T. Herford, *Christianity in Talmud and Midrash* (London, 1903), 43-45.

[4] Zahn, *Introduction to the NT*, II, 536-539, 560, 561.

[5] That παρθένος in the LXX does not imply a Messianic interpretation, see G. B. Gray, *The Expositor*, 1, 8th Series (1911), 301f.

[6] Cf. E. Stauffer, *Jesus and His Story* (London, 1960), 26f., who also emphasizes the absence of Jewish dispute against Jesus' birth in Bethlehem.

Jer 31:15 are so obscure that no one would have thought of them as bases for invention of the stories to which Mt relates them. The account of Moses' flight from Egypt has influenced the form of statement in Mt, but the differences between the narratives—Moses' fleeing as an adult from Egypt at his own will and returning to Egypt, Jesus' taken as an infant to Egypt at divine behest and returning to Palestine—rule out the story's having been built upon the OT passage or upon Jewish folklore concerning Moses' experiences.[1] Is 11:1, the primary reference in Mt 2:23, is a prominent

[1] Against P. Winter, *The Hibbert Journal*, 53 (1954/55), 34-42. For the parallels with rabbinic sources and Josephus, see R. Bloch, in *Moïse, l'homme de l'alliance* (Paris, 1955), 164-166. S. M. Iglesias sees the same parallel between Mt 1 and 2 and midrashic stories concerning Moses, but does not regard the haggadic genre of Mt 1 and 2 as a legitimate criterion for judging historicity (*Estudios Bíblicos*, 17 [1958], 272f.). D. Daube believes this section in Mt builds upon the haggadic story connected with the Passover recitation, in which Laban attempts to destroy all Jacob's children, male and female, in order to prevent the Star coming out of Jacob; but Jacob and his family escape to Egypt, having been warned in a dream (Midrash on Dt 26:5-8) (*The NT and Rabbinic Judaism*, 190f.; *NTS*, 5 [1959], 184f.; followed by C. H. Cave, *NTS*, 9 [1963], 382-390). Although one must admit Daube draws attention to some striking parallels with the story of Laban and Jacob, they are incidental in comparison with the larger Moses-Jesus typology throughout Mt (see above, pp. 82, 83) and with the clear verbal reminiscences of Ex 2:15; 4:19, 20 in Mt 2:13, 20, 21. It is therefore preferable to regard the parallel between Jesus' and Jacob's flights to Egypt as due to the relationship of both stories to the account of Moses. Daube's strongest argument, that Mt's παῖδας in v. 16 and τέκνα in place of υἱοῖς for על בניה in the quotation of Jer 31:15 reflect Laban's attempt to kill *all* Jacob's children (whereas Pharaoh killed only male infants), is not entirely convincing. Both of Mt's words may refer to male children only (cf. Mt 21:28; 22:24; the LXX of Hos 11:1 [MT: לבני], just quoted in Mt 2:15) (see M. M. Bourke, *CBQ*, 22 [1960], 170); and if Herod did have infants of both sexes slaughtered, it would accord with what we know from extra-Biblical sources of his cruelty—and therefore need not derive from the story of Laban and Jacob. In the Midrash, only the first short paragraph deals with Laban. Immediately after the reference to Laban, Jacob's going down to Egypt is attributed to the famine, as in Gen 47:4. L. Finkelstein regards the reference to Laban as an effort to placate the Egyptian government, when Palestine was under Egyptian suzerainty (3rd century B.C.), by denouncing Egypt's rival, Syria (*HTR*, 31 [1938], 299ff.). Since, then, the reference to Laban appears to be an extraneous insertion, the political reason for which had dropped out by NT times, it may be questioned whether this part of the Passover recitation was used. That striking parallels can also be drawn to heathen stories suggests the comparative method does not here help us determine historical origins. For heathen parallels, see E. Norden, *Die Geburt des Kindes* (Leipzig, 1924); C. Clemen, *Religionsgeschichtliche Erklärung des NT*[2] (Giessen, 1924), 192ff.; E. Brunner-Traut, *Zeitschr. für Religions- u. Geistesgeschichte*, 12 (1960), 97-111.

Messianic passage; but the way in which Mt uses it, drawing a phonetic parallel between נצר and Nazareth based on a thought-correspondence between prophecies of Messiah's lowliness and the fact of Jesus' lowliness, must rest on a precedence of the tradition over the prophecy.

In 4:12, 13, Mt adds references to Capernaum "by the sea," Zebulon, and Naphtali, after following Mk's statement that Jesus withdrew into Galilee (also Lk 4:14). Thus he gains a clearer parallel with Is 8:23-9:1, where these geographical references occur. The substance of the tradition has not been falsified; but the form of statement has been modified by expansion.

In 13:13-15, the fulfilment-citation in verses 14, 15 is obviously an editorial expansion of the allusive quotation in verse 13 and parallels. Again it is expansion rather than falsification. One also wonders whether the first evangelist did not intend the reader to recognize by the fulfilment-formula an editorial insertion here.

Of all Mt's fulfilment-citations, that of Zech 9:9 in Mt 21:5 is most universally considered an instance of prophecy creating tradition. There is no question but that the OT passage refers by synonymous parallelism to one animal. Both חמור and עיר are masculine, the former emphasizing the function of carrying people or loads, the latter emphasizing youth. In contrast with the other gospels, Mt introduces into his narrative a mother animal alongside the πῶλος which carried Jesus, and he immediately quotes Zech 9:9. The charge is that Mt misunderstood the synonymous parallelism for synthetic parallelism and introduced a second animal in the narrative to correspond to what he mistakenly supposed was a second animal in the prophecy. This charge is carried farthest by O. Michel, who sees Mt thinking of an Oriental throne-seat over two animals,[1] and reaches its peak of sarcasm in D. F. Strauss, who ridicules Mt for making Jesus ride on two animals at once.[2]

According to Mk, the donkey on which Jesus rode had never been sat upon (Mk 11:2). This has been regarded as legendary accretion based upon the sacredness of an unused animal; but it is just as likely that Jesus deliberately chose an unused donkey for the sacred occasion.[3] Mk betrays no reminiscence of Zech 9:9, neither

[1] *TWNT*, VI, 961. [2] *The Life of Jesus*[6] (London, 1913), 553f.

[3] So Cranfield, *Mk*, 349; against Michel, *TWNT*, V, 286. On the importance of an unused animal or thing for sacred purposes, see Num 19:2; Dt 21:3; I Sam 6:7; II Sam 6:3; Lk 23:53.

quoting the passage nor using the Septuagintal expression, πῶλον νέον, by which he could have avoided the periphrastic ἐφ' ὃν οὐδεὶς οὔπω ἀνθρώπων ἐκάθισεν.[1]

We now ask whether Mt really intended his quotation to refer to both animals in his narrative.[2] An affirmative answer is usually assumed because the phrases in the quotation, ἐπὶ ὄνον and ἐπὶ πῶλον υἱὸν ὑποζυγίου, easily correspond to ὄνον and πῶλον in the narrative (v. 2). But we must not jump too hastily to the equation of ὄνος in the narrative with ὄνος in the quotation, for ὄνος can be masculine as well as feminine. A number of factors argue against the equation.

First, it would require us to suppose that Mt misunderstood the common Hebrew word for a working he-ass, חמור, as a mother-ass. But if anything is clear from the Matthaean quotations of the OT, it is that the first evangelist was very familiar with the Hebrew language, specifically with the Hebrew text of the OT. Second, it is just as doubtful that Mt would have deliberately perpetrated such an obvious error in writing to evangelize Jews, who could have easily detected the error—and this in the face of rabbinic tradition, which knew only one animal in Zech 9:9,[3] and seemingly against the rest of the gospel tradition. Third, it is very clear from Mt's disagreements with the LXX in this quotation that he had the Hebrew text before him and was endeavoring to give a closer rendering of the Hebrew than the LXX had done. Fourth, if Mt had been intent on identifying the ὄνος in the quotation with the mother ὄνος in the narrative, he might have translated the second phrase in Zech quite simply, "and upon a colt, the foal of an ὄνος (instead of ὑποζύγιον)," i.e., repeated the word ὄνος in the second line of the parallel structure to make clear he was referring to a mother ὄνος in the first line. He had all the more reason to do this because ὄνος is the usual equivalent for אתון in the LXX. As it is, Mt gives the much less natural rendering ὑποζυγίου, as if he wished *not* to identify the mother animal in his narrative with the ὄνος in the first part of the quotation.

---

[1] This refutes Bacon (*Studies in Mt*, 470f.) and H.-W. Kuhn (*ZNW*, 50 [1959], 89), who see Mk deriving the idea of a donkey not previously ridden from πῶλον νέον.

[2] The condensed form of the quotation in Jn 12:15, ἐπὶ πῶλον ὄνου, may be considered a correction of Mt (cf. C. K. Barrett, *Jn* [London, 1955], 349) or a correction of a misunderstanding of Mt.

[3] See J. Klausner, *The Messianic Idea in Israel* (London, 1956), 439.

One may therefore doubt that Mt intended to break up the parallelism in Zech and that the prophecy led to the introduction of a second animal. The ὄνος in the narrative is feminine and refers to the mother animal. The ὄνος in the first line of the quotation is masculine and refers to the same young male animal as is referred to in the second line. Mk emphasizes the young donkey had never been ridden. But it is not likely an unbroken young donkey would have submitted to being ridden through milling, shouting crowds —unless its mother were led closely alongside to quiet the younger animal.[1] It is therefore not unreasonable to suppose Mt was working with a genuinely historical tradition.[2]

Mt emphasizes the presence of the mother animal, not to equate her with the masculine חמור in the quotation, but to underscore that the young donkey really was, as Mk said, unused.[3] The true equation brings together the mother animal and the אתנות-ὑποζυγίου, the express mention of which in Zech Mt may have considered to have implied the unusedness of the young donkey. The quotation is then introduced *before* the account of the entry in order to emphasize that the donkey was unused—with stress on υἱὸν ὑποζυγίου— and as a kind of introduction to the following scene to avoid the awkwardness of this quotation's standing side by side with the "Hosanna" quotation, which dominates the last part of the pericope.[4]

---

[1] Cf. the comment of Cyril of Alexandria: ὅτι δὲ ὁ μὲν Ματθαῖος ὄνον καὶ πῶλον ἀγηοχέναι τῷ κυρίῳ λέγει, Λουκᾶς δὲ καὶ Μᾶρκος ἑνὸς μόνου ὑποζυγίου ἀπεμνημόνευσαν, οὐ μάχης τὸ εἰρημένον· τοῦ γὰρ πώλου ἀγομένου κατὰ τὸ κελευσθὲν ὑπὸ τῶν μαθητῶν ἐφήλατο καὶ ἡ ὄνος τῷ αὐτῆς τέκνῳ ἀκολουθοῦσα ὡς φιλόστοργος μήτηρ (J. Reuss [ed.], *Matthäus-Kommentar aus der griechischen Kirche* [= *Texte u. Untersuchungen*, 5. Reihe, Bd. 6], 230).

[2] Lindars thinks Mt deduced the mother donkey from the unusedness of the young male donkey in Mk's text, and then made the text of Zech fit the deduction (p. 114). But Mt's evident working from the Hebrew text of Zech makes such a deduction from Mk just as unlikely as the same deduction from Zech.

[3] See J. H. A. Ebrard, *Wissenschaftliche Kritik der evangelischen Geschichte* (Frankfurt, 1842), 591.

[4] That the disciples place ἐπ' αὐτῶν τὰ ἱμάτια and that Jesus ἐπεκάθισεν ἐπάνω αὐτῶν (Mt 21:7) are, of course, inconclusive for the view Mt broke up the OT parallelism, as many of the proponents of that view admit. The garments may have been placed upon both animals merely because both were to form part of the procession or because the disciples were unsure upon which animal Jesus would sit. Ἐπάνω αὐτῶν may refer to the garments (cf. II [IV] Kings 9:13 and U. Holzmeister, *Biblica*, 14 [1933], 75), the change of reference betrayed by the change from ἐπ' to the awkward ἐπάνω,

The allusiveness of the reference to II Sam 5:8 in Mt 21:14 and the obscurity of the OT verse speak against derivation of Jesus' healing in the Temple from II Sam. Since Jesus' teaching, mentioned in the Marcan and Lucan parallels, was regularly accompanied by healing and since both Mk and Lk speak of the astonishment of the crowds at Jesus' Temple ministry on this occasion, nothing prevents our thinking the Matthaean account rests on authentic tradition.

Although Ps 8, quoted in Mt 21:16, is quoted prominently elsewhere in the NT,[1] the interrogative use of ἀναγινώσκειν in the IF is peculiarly typical of Jesus [2] and is not used in the NT except by him. It is therefore unlikely the story of the children singing in the Temple was spun out of Ps 8:3 and the quotation put in Jesus' mouth.[3]

The same is true of Mt 21:42, where ἀναγινώσκειν again appears in the IF. In this quotation Mt receives the support of Mk (12:10 f.) and Lk (20:17). Although the appending of the quotation may seem somewhat awkward and out of place at the end of the parable,[4] yet scriptural quotations sometimes appear at the close of rabbinic parables.[5]

The susceptibility of Jesus' use of Ps 110:1 (Mt 22:44 and parallels) to a doctrine which denies that the Messiah must be of Davidic lineage [6] argues strongly against Christians' having put the words in Jesus' mouth, for the Davidic sonship of Jesus is taught throughout the NT.[7]

---

unusual in the sense "upon" (Plummer, *op. cit.*, 286). Or it is a general expression in which the animals are considered as a pair. Or the true reading is ἐπάνω αὐτοῦ (DΘ it) or ἐπάνω αὐτόν (ℵ^{c}lat), the corruption coming from the preceding αὐτῶν.

[1] I Cor 15:27; Eph 1:22; Heb 2:6-9. Parallel influence from Ps 8 is seen in quotations of Ps 110:1 in Mt 22:44; Mk 12:36.

[2] Mt 12:3, 5; 19:4; 21:16, 42; 22:31; Mk 2:25; 12:10, 26; Lk 6:3; 10:26.

[3] Cf. Edghill, *op. cit.*, 470.

[4] So Easton, *op. cit.*, 96, who on this account rejects the quotation as intrusion of Christian apologetic.

[5] P. Fiebig, *Die Gleichnisreden Jesu im Lichte der rabbinischen Gleichnisse des neutestamentlichen Zeitalters* (Tübingen, 1912), 78.

[6] So many modern commentators interpret Jesus' meaning.

[7] See Mt 1:1ff.; 9:27; 12:23; 15:22; 20:30f.; 21:9, 15; Mk 10:47f.; 11:10; Lk 1:32; 18:38f.; Ro 1:3; II Tim 2:8; Rev 3:7; 5:5; 22:16. Bultmann's view that the pericope comes from a Hellenistic community which wished to depreciate Davidic sonship in favor of divine sonship rests on the mistaken notion that the two were considered in opposition to each other (*Gesch. synopt. Trad.*, 145f.). Jesus does not deny the necessity

In the passion narrative we meet another concentration of quotation material. H. Conzelmann writes, "Ganze Motive, ja Szenen . . sind aus dem AT herausgesponnen." [1] Bundy declares that the crucifixion story could very well be a dramatization of Psalms 22 and 69.[2] Against this extreme position, we may quote Alan Richardson:

> If anyone feels inclined to believe that practically the whole of the Passion story (in the form in which it has reached us in our Gospels) is unhistorical, on the ground that it is built up from *a priori* attempts to fulfil Old Testament prophecy, let him reread Is liii., Ps xii. [sic], and lxix., and see for himself how many details are to be found in these passages which there have been no attempts to fulfil. [3]

The mistreatment of Jesus by the Sanhedrin (Mt 26:67 and parallels), in the description of which an allusion to Is 50:6 occurs, is wholly probable. The taunting challenge to prophesy, which cannot derive from Is, lends a touch of authenticity to the whole scene.

---

of Davidic descent for the Messiah, because it is unthinkable he contradicted the clear testimony of the OT (see references in V. Taylor, *Mk*, 491), a contradiction which surely would have been brought up as a charge against him (see A. Schweitzer, *The Quest of the Historical Jesus*, 393). The question is πῶς . . . ἐστιν, not as if Jesus had implied a negative with μὴ υἱὸς αὐτοῦ ἐστιν; (H. A. W. Meyer, *op. cit.*, II, 96). Jesus means that Messiah is the Son of God as well as the Son of David (Schniewind, *Mt*, 218). Zahn points out that Jesus had already hinted at this in his claim to be a greater than Solomon (Mt 12:42) (*Lk*, 647; *Mt* 640). Lindars objects that the question of Jesus' Davidic sonship could have arisen only at a later date (pp. 46f.). But why could not Jesus himself have formed the paradox between Davidic descent and divine lordship? By the time of Passion Week, the Jews had long since broached the question of Jesus' Messiahship, to which the question of Davidic descent was a corollary. And Jesus' self-application of the transcendent term "Son of man" makes plausible his originating the paradox. On "Son of man" see below, pp. 213f., 231ff. Lindars also thinks that Is 8:23-9:1 (quoted in Mt 4:15f.) was originally used to prove a Galilean birth for the Messiah and was limited to the Messiah's sphere of preaching only after the Bethlehem birth of Jesus became an established belief (p. 198). But it is extremely doubtful that the OT text was ever used to defend a Galilean birth for the Messiah, because in spite of the Messianic blessing upon Galilee, the reference in Is 9:6 to "the throne of David" clearly implies the Judean origin of the Messianic child.

[1] *RGG*³, III, 646f.

[2] *Op. cit.*, 536. See more fully F. K. Feigel, *Der Einfluss des Weissagungsbeweises u. anderer Motive auf die Leidensgeschichte* (Tübingen, 1910); K. Weidel, *Theol. Stud. u. Krit.*, 83 (1910), 83-109, 163-195, 267-286; M. Dibelius, *Beihefte zur ZAW*, 33 (Giessen, 1918), 125-150; and pertinent sections in Bultmann, *Gesch. synopt. Trad.*

[3] *The Gospels in the Making* (London, 1938), 73.

The quotation of Zech 11:13 in Mt 26:15; 27:9, 10 presents more serious problems. That the story of the thirty silver pieces does not as a whole rest on Zech is evident from the independent tradition in Acts 1:18, 19, from the absence of correspondence in character between the prophet (who casts down the money in Zech) and Judas, from the unmention of a field in Zech, from the circumstance that the prophet gives the money to the potter in Zech and in Mt the chief priests give the money, from the attempts to avoid the word "potter" in the LXX and the OT Peshitta, and from Mt's omission of εἰς τὸν οἶκον κυρίου, an extremely suitable phrase in view of εἰς τὸν ναόν in the narrative (v. 5).[1] The connection with and the typological interpretation of Jer 19 would never have suggested itself apart from a prior tradition of the potter's field. In Mt's mention of the exact sum of money it is possible, but not necessary to see intrusion of the prophecy upon the tradition. The publican may have taken special note of the pecuniary aspect of the transaction.

In 27:34, Mt conforms to Ps 69:22 by changing Mk's "wine flavored with myrrh" (15:23) to "wine mixed with gall." Had this incident been based on the OT text, we should have had ὄξος, as in the Ps, rather than οἶνον. The word ראש, used in the Ps, refers to a poisonous plant, to the poison itself, to anything bitter (since bitterness and poison are correlative notions), and to gall as the most bitter of the bitter.[2] Χολή likewise refers to anything bitter or poisonous.[3] If Mt is thinking of the bitter property of myrrh, he is justified in conforming to ראש-χολή in the sense of a bitter substance. Χολώδης δὲ καὶ κατάπικρος ἡ σμύρνα (Cyril, *Cat.* xiii. 29 [MPG XXXIII, 808]).[4] It does not seem that myrrh stupefies or deadens pain,[5] so that in all three passages—Mt, Mk, and Ps 69—the offer of the bitter drink is not an act of mercy, but an act of mockery.[6]

---

[1] See further J. H. Bernard, *The Expositor*, 9, 6th Series (1904), 422ff.

[2] See above, p. 145, n. 1.

[3] In Prov 5:4; Lam 3:15 LXX for לענה, "wormwood"; in Job 20:14 LXX and in classical Greek (see L & S) of venom.

[4] It is thus not necessary to see in the background a confusion between מורה ("myrrh") and מררה ("gall") (as do Plummer, *op. cit.*, 394f.; J. Döller, *Biblica*, 4 [1923], 165).

[5] See J. J. S. Perowne, *Ps*[7] (London, 1890), I, 568f. Elsewhere I have been unable to find mention of any pain-killing properties in myrrh.

[6] Edersheim cites the custom practiced by certain women in Jerusalem of giving drugged wine to those about to be executed, and thinks the NT speaks of a merciful gesture (*Life and Times*, II, 589f.). But if Jesus had been

It is doubtful that the parting of Jesus' garments in Mt 27:35 and parallels was made up from Ps 22:19; for we surely would also have had in the synoptics a description of Jesus' piercing, in conformity to the nearby verse, Ps 22:17.[1] Both the parting of the garments by the soldiers and the reviling by the bystanders, described in phraseology borrowed from Lam 2:15 and Ps 22:8 (Mt 27:39 and parallels), are inherently possible. Considering the circumstances of Jesus' death and the way in which the reviling is connected with the accusation concerning Jesus' destroying the Temple and rebuilding it, they appear probable.

Edersheim maintains that the loose way in which the Jews quoted scripture makes possible that the Sanhedrinists actually quoted Ps 22:9 (Mt 27:43).[2] If not, to quote from another writing in order to convey the standpoint of other persons was a recognized literary usage.[3] The quotation is in perfect accord with the mocking at Jesus' helplessness and the challenge to come down from the cross (in both Mt and Mk).

Concerning the cry of dereliction, it is hardly possible that legend would have put the language of despair into the mouth of Jesus.[4] The apparent reflection of the ancient form *eliya* [5] and the whole misunderstanding concerning Elijah exclude derivation of this scene from Ps 22:2, where nothing could have suggested such an incident. On the other hand, a genuine reference to Ps 22:2 by Jesus explains the confusion with Elijah and is wholly fitting for Jesus to have made in his last moments on the cross.

In Mt 27:48 and Mk 15:36 a further reference to Ps 69:22 occurs. Legend, building upon the OT text, would have produced but one incident. The details of the sponge and the reed and the connection with the misunderstanding concerning Elijah also speak for authenticity. Again we must reject a merciful motive behind the ac-

---

intent on refusing succour, he would hardly have tasted the wine before refusing it. We must therefore think that what customarily was an act of mercy was in Jesus' case perverted into cruelest mockery and that Jesus tasted the wine, discerned it had been made bitter to mock him, and refused any more.

[1] Lindars argues that the evangelists do not refer to the piercing in Ps 22:17 because the Hebrew text of the verse was corrupt (p. 92). But they could have used the LXX, as they often do elsewhere.

[2] *Op. cit.*, II, 597, n. 2.

[3] See R. Gordis, *HUCA*, 22 (1949), 166ff.

[4] H. A. W. Meyer, *op. cit.*, II, 274.

[5] See above, p. 63.

tion. In Mk, the man offering the vinegar says to the others, "Let us see [1] if Elijah comes to take him down." In Mt, the others echo in agreement, "Let us see if Elijah comes to save him." Both gospels picture the action as designed to sustain Jesus a little while longer—so that they might watch in mocking unexpectancy whether Elijah would come to deliver him.

In 27:57, Mt's description of Joseph of Arimathaea as "a rich man," in conformity to Is 53:9, changes the phraseology of the Marcan tradition, but not the essential meaning.

Something always prevents our seeing evolvement of the gospel tradition from OT prophecy. Some of the OT texts were not Messianically interpreted in Judaism. Others are only fleetingly alluded to. Mt sometimes receives independent support from one or both of the other synoptics, where no fulfilment-motif is present. Some of the OT passages are so obscure that no one could have thought of them as Messianic prophecies unless given the gospel tradition first. Fairly wide differences between OT and NT cannot be accounted for on the theory that the former was the source for the latter. The gospel tradition has an inner fitness and inherent likelihood. Sometimes the quotation is introduced by a formula peculiarly characteristic of Jesus. Verisimilar details which cannot come from the prophecy are often present, as are also essential relationships to the NT context which cannot derive from the prophecy. Repugnance to Christian piety and susceptibility to interpretation contrary to primitive Christian doctrine make Christian invention from OT prophecy improbable. Had the tradition been erected upon the OT text, we would not have had the absence of elements in the OT text which were extremely suitable. In two or three instances, it cannot be shown one way or the other whether or not an incidental detail derived from the prophecy. What is certain is a conforming of descriptive phraseology to OT language to make patent the latent correspondence between prophecy and event.[2]

---

[1] Thus ἀφίημι with another verb should be translated. Cf. Mt 7:4. Ἀφίημι is not to be understood in the sense of restraint or of leaving Jesus alone. See Cranfield, *Mk*, 459.

[2] See O'Rourke, *loc. cit.*

CHAPTER FOUR

THE PROBLEM OF LEGITIMACY

MATTHAEAN HERMENEUTICS AND THE MESSIANIC HOPE

In Qumran and rabbinical literature and in Mt, the mechanics of treating the OT text are targumically oriented.[1] A certain similarity exists between Qumran and NT interpretation of the OT in the common themes of eschatological fulfilment and of illumination of the full meaning of the OT text through that fulfilment.[2] This similarity lends a fervency to the NT and Qumran which stands in contrast to the arid academicism of the rabbis.[3] Qumran, however, stands in the midst of the fulfilment-process, whereas the dominant NT perspective is that prophecies have already reached fulfilment.[4] Also, in the NT the person of Jesus Christ looms much larger than the Teacher of Righteousness.[5] Jesus' role is pre-eminently redemptive, but that of the Teacher of Righteousness is not.[6]

Both Qumran hermeneutics and rabbinical hermeneutics are supremely oblivious to contextual exegesis whenever they wish.[7] The major question which now confronts us is whether the hermeneutical principles upon which Mt worked display the same atomization of the OT text.

C. H. Dodd's study, *According to the Scriptures*, constitutes an initial consideration against an affirmative answer to the question.

---

[1] See above, pp. 172ff.

[2] F. F. Bruce, *Biblical Exegesis in the Qumran Texts*, 7-10, 66f.

[3] Elliger, *op. cit.*, 156-164; J. C. G. Greig, in *Studia Evangelica*, 595.

[4] I. Rabinowitz, *JBL*, 73 (1954), 11-35; B. Gärtner, *Studia Theologica*, 8 (1954), 6f.; *et al.*

[5] F. F. Bruce, *Biblical Exegesis*, 67f.

[6] Greig, *op. cit.*, 597.

[7] On atomizing exegesis in Qumran literature, see Elliger, *op. cit.*, 139ff.; F. F. Bruce, *Biblical Exegesis*, 11ff.; Milik, *Ten Years of Discovery*, 40; and in rabbinical literature, see F. Weber, *Jüdische Theologie*[2] (Leipzig, 1897), 86f.; F. Johnson, *op. cit.*, 376f.; B. J. Roberts, *BJRL*, 36 (1953/54), 78f. This similarity led W. H. Brownlee to see no essential difference between rabbinical exegesis and Qumran exegesis (*BA*, 14 [1951], 71-75). On reflections of atomization in the LXX, see Seeligmann, *op. cit.*, 41; and in the Targum, see P. Seidelin, *ZNW*, 35 (1936), 195.

Dodd shows that the mainstream of quotation material which relates to Jesus and the Church [1] tends to concentrate in certain areas of the OT.[2] From this discovery Dodd concludes that the NT authors were not engaged in searching through the OT for isolated proof-texts, but that they exploited "whole contexts selected as the varying expression of certain fundamental and permanent elements in the biblical revelation."[3]

All OT quotations in Mt which show the fulfilment-motif fall into Dodd's text-plots, except these which will now be considered. The quotations from Mic 5:1 (Mt 2:6) and 7:6 (Mt 10:21, 35 f. and synoptic parallels) do not fall in a text-plot. However, Mic 5 is a prominent Messianic passage, also alluded to in Jn 7:42. Lk 1:32, 33 quotes Mic 4:7, and Rev 12:3 quotes Mic 4:10. Mic 7:6 is quoted in an unparallel passage, Mk 13:12. Lk 1:55 quotes Mic 7:20. This number of references from such varying NT sources warrants the establishment of another supplementary text-plot, Mic 4-5, 7.

Num 23-24, alluded to in Mt 2:1, 2, is another prominent Messianic section, so interpreted in Judaism. Interestingly, Heb 8:2 quotes Num 24:6 LXX in an entirely different connection.

Mt 2:11 alludes to Is 60:6. But allusions to the last chapters of Is (outside the boundaries of Dodd's text-plots) are very numerous throughout the NT. The other half of the allusion in Mt 2:11 refers to Ps 72:10. In the Lucan nativity narrative Ps 72:18 is quoted (Lk 1:68).

Mt 2:13, 20 f. plays on the experiences of Moses in Ex 2 and 4. The Moses-Jesus typology rests (in part, at least) on Dt 18:15, which does fall in one of Dodd's text-plots. However, Ex 1-4 seems itself to be another text-plot, for Stephen alludes to these chapters about fourteen times in Acts 7, and further quotations occur in Mt 22:32;

---

[1] Failure to recognize this qualification underlies the adverse criticisms of Sundberg, *op. cit.*, 271ff.

[2] Dodd's listing and classification of text-plots is as follows: I. Apocalyptic-Eschatological Scriptures—Joel 2-3; Zech 9-14; Dan 7 (primary): Mal 3:1-6; Dan 12 (supplementary). II. Scriptures of the New Israel—Hosea; Is 6:1-9:7; 11:1-10; 28:16; 40:1-11; Jer 31:10-34 (primary): Is 29:9-14; Jer 7:1-15; Hab 1-2 (supplementary). III. Scriptures of the Servant of the Lord and the Righteous Sufferer—Is 42:1-44:5; 49:1-13; 50:4-11; 52:13-53:12; 61; Ps 69; 22; 31; 38; 88; 34; 118; 41; 42-43; 80 (primary): Is 58; 6-10 (supplementary). IV. Unclassified Scriptures—Ps 8; 110; 2; Gen 12:3; 22:18; Dt 18:15, 19 (primary): Ps 132; 16; II Sam 7:13, 14; Is 55:3; Am 9:11, 12 (supplementary). See *According to the Scriptures*, 107f.

[3] *Ibid.*, 132f.

Mk 12:26; Lk 20:37; Acts 3:13; 18:10; Ro 9:18; Heb 11:23, 24; Rev 1:4, 8; 4:8; 11:17; 16:5.

Similarly, the allusion to II Kings 1:8 in Mt 3:4 regarding the likeness of John the Baptist to Elijah stems from the Elijah-John typology, which is based on Mal 3, another of Dodd's text-plots. Again, references to II Kings 1 (verses 10, 12) occur in such widely different sources and contexts as Lk 9:54 and Rev 11:5 (Elijah redivivus?); 20:9.

Mt 11:5 (= Lk 7:22) alludes to Is 35:5, 6. Another allusion to these same verses occurs in Acts 26:18. Heb 12:12 quotes verse 3 of Is 35, and Rev 21:4 quotes verse 10.

The quotation of Jon 2:1 in Mt 12:40 stands alone.

Dodd does not include Ps 78, quoted in Mt 13:35, among the text-plots. But different verses throughout the psalm are quoted in Jn 6:31; Acts 8:21; Rev 2:17; 16:4.

Mt 17:2 alludes to Ex 34:29. Paul makes very extensive use of Ex 34:29-35 in his comparison between the old covenant and the new, and, just as Mt, between the shining face of Moses and the glory of Christ (II Cor 3:7-16). Rev 15:3 alludes to Ex 34:10, again with a juxtaposition of Moses and Jesus ("the Lamb").

The quotation of Mal 3:23 in Mt 17:11 (= Mk 9:12) stands very near to and has close thought-connection with the text-plot Mal 3:1-6 and should therefore be attached to it. Confirmation of this comes from the quotation of the next verse in Mal in Lk 1:17, again concerning John's fulfilling the ministry of Elijah.

The allusion to II Sam 5:8 in Mt 21:14 rests on the David-Jesus typology, which appears in several text-plots. More interesting is the fact that Mt's quotation of Mic 5:1 (Mt 2:6) concludes with a clause from II Sam 5:2, a verse regarding the throne-right of David.

The apocalyptic text-plot, Dan 12, should reach back to include the last part of Dan 11 so that allusions to Dan 11:44, 41 in Mt 24:6, 10 (and to Dan 11:36 in II Thess 2:4; Rev 13:5) may be accommodated. Similarly Dan 2 should be accorded a place, since quotations from that chapter occur in Mt 21:44; 24:6 (and parallels) and in no fewer than eleven allusions in the Rev.

Mt 24:7 and I Cor 1:20 allude to different verses in Is 19. Mt 24:24 and 24:31 allude to verses close to each other in Dt 13. The latter allusion in Mt (24:31) comes in a composite quotation of Is 27:13; Zech 2:6; Dt 13:7; 30:4. We may surmise the background of a catena of parallel passages, *testimonia*, concerning Israel's regathering. Ro 11:27 quotes Is 27:9 of Israel's final forgiveness. Zech 1-6 is quoted ten times in Rev, and in Jude 9, 23 and Heb 10:21.

Mt 24:29 quotes Is 13:10, also quoted in Rev 6:12. Ro 9:22 quotes Is 13:5, and Rev 18:2 quotes verse 21. The other part of Mt 24:29 refers to Is 34:4, quoted also in Rev 6:13, 14. Rev 14:11; 19:3 allude to Is 34:9, 10, and Rev 18:2 to Is 34:11, 14.

The allusion to Ex 24:8 in Mt 26:28 and parallels is perfectly understandable in the context of the Last Supper. But it is remarkable that Ex 24 is quoted also in II Cor 3:3, 18; Heb 9:20; 10:29.

Thus, upon close examination of the Matthaean quotations, Dodd's main thesis that NT quotations tend to be drawn from OT contexts which are exploited as a whole by various NT authors is remarkably confirmed and is found to hold true even in the allusive quotations. The text-plots are somewhat more extensive than Dodd has indicated.

It is established, then, that in common with the other NT writers Mt does not deal atomistically with the OT in the sense that he does not search either haphazardly or systematically for isolated proof-texts, but in the main confines himself to areas of the OT which the church recognized as having special bearing upon the ministry of Jesus Christ, upon the new dispensation inaugurated by him, and upon his expected return and the events connected with it. We now ask if within the OT text-plots Mt displays an atomizing treatment of the individual verses quoted. Rather than draw out the discussion to undue lengths by examining the hermeneutics behind each quotation, there follows a classification of the quotations which Jesus applies to himself and which the evangelist applies to Jesus, according to the hermeneutical principles underlying them. *The very fact that all the quotations can thus be classified under specific lines of interpretation constitutes the best demonstration that Mt's hermeneutical method is not atomistic.*

I. Quotations assuming direct applicability to Jesus

A. Jesus fills the role of the royal Messiah supernaturally born (1:23) in Bethlehem (2:6), growing up in obscurity like a branch out of the cut-off stump of David (2:23), pronounced the royal son of God (3:17), shedding Messianic light upon the Galilean region (4:15 f.), riding into Jerusalem on a donkey (21:5), plotted against

(22:34), designated as "Lord" (22:44), and seated at God's right hand (26:64).

B. Jesus fills the role of the Isaianic Servant receiving God's commendation (3:17), bearing the sicknesses of others (8:17), bringing good news to the poor (11:5),[1] despising popularity (12:18-21), giving his life for us (20:28), enduring shame and suffering (26:67), and lying buried in a rich man's tomb (27:57).

C. Jesus fills the role of the Danielic Son of man, for he will come with the clouds of heaven (24:30; 26:64) and has already received all authority (28:18).

D. Jesus fills the role of the Shepherd of Israel, smitten in his passion (26:31), but yet to smite his enemies (21:44) and to become the object of Israel's repentant mourning at his return (24:30).[2]

E. Jesus fills the role of Yahweh, who saves from sin (1:21), whose coming demands repentance (3:3 f.), who requires public allegiance (10:32 f.), who heals, cleanses, and makes alive (11:5), whose way is prepared by a forerunner (11:10; 17:11), who satisfies the weary soul (11:28), gives rest to the heavy laden (11:29), will purge the stumbling-blocks out of his kingdom (13:41), render to every man according to his deeds (16:27), gather his elect (24:31), and bring with him his holy angels (25:31), and who is valued at the despicable price of thirty pieces of silver (26:15; 27:9 f.).

II. Quotations resting on typological [3] application to Jesus

A. Jesus is the greater Moses fleeing the wrath of a wicked king (2:13) and returning (2:20 f.), shining with glory on a mountain (17:2), and instituting a covenant in blood (26:28).

---

[1] I put Is 61:1, alluded to in Mt 11:5, with Servant passages. See Delitzsch, *Is*, II, 424f., and for a list of commentators advocating this view, F. F. Bruce, *Acts* (New London Commentary; London, 1954), 227, n. 47, 231, n. 62.

[2] See F. F. Bruce, *BJRL*, 43 (1961), 336-353. I put the "stone" quotation in 21:44 under this classification because both figures indicate rulership. Note Gen 49:24: "From thence is the shepherd, the stone of Israel" (I owe this reference to Professor Bruce).

[3] "Typological" involves reiterative recapitulation; i.e., what happens to the type happens to the antitype. See K. J. Woollcombe, *Essays on Typology*, 42ff. As distinct from Hellenistic allegorizing, which is a philosophic quest for a rationale underlying the OT, and Eastern allegorizing, which is suited to homiletical purposes, typology rests on a telic, eschatological view of history. See Edersheim, *Life and Times*, I, 35; J. Daniélou, in *Studia Evangelica*, 28f.; *idem*, *Sacramentum futuri*, 257f.; *idem*, *Theology*, 57 (1945), 85.

B. Jesus is the greater Son of David receiving worship "from the east" (2:1 f.) and tribute from the Gentiles (2:11), exhibiting greater wisdom than Solomon (12:42), and (in a piece of *antithetic* typology, contrasting with David) receiving and healing the blind and the lame in the Temple (21:14).

C. Jesus is the representative prophet, like Jonah buried three days and three nights (12:40), like Isaiah teaching the spiritually dull and unreceptive (13:13-15), like Asaph expressing in narrative form the profound dealings of God with men (13:35), like Elisha commanding that people be fed with miraculously multiplied bread (14:16), and like all the prophetic successors of Moses deserving to be heard (17:5).[1]

D. Jesus is the representative Israelite in whose individual history the history of the whole nation, apart from its sin and apostasy, is recapitulated and anticipated. Like Israel in the Messianic times he receives the homage of Gentiles (2:11). He is preserved in and comes out of Egypt (2:15). Just as the mourning of the Israelite mothers for the Babylonian exiles preluded a brighter future through divine preservation in a foreign land and restoration to Palestine, so the mourning by the mothers of the Bethlehem innocents is a prelude to the Messianic future through divine preservation of the infant Messiah in a foreign land and his later restoration to Palestine (2:18). In the temptation narrative, the quotation of three Deuteronomic verses having to do with Israel's probation in the wilderness draws a parallel between Jesus' temptation in the wilderness and Israel's temptation in the wilderness (4:4, 7, 10).

E. Jesus is the representative righteous sufferer rejected by men but made the corner- or capstone by God (21:9, 42; 23:39), overcome with sorrow (26:38), given vinegar and gall (27:34, 48), robbed of his clothes through their distribution by lot (27:35), mocked by passers-by who wag their heads (27:39), taunted to call upon God for rescue (27:43), asking why God has forsaken him

---

[1] Cullmann thinks Jesus and the disciples regarded John the Baptist as "the Prophet" (*Christology*, 28, 36f.). He does not mention the voice at the transfiguration. Cullmann's whole discussion needs to be re-thought along the line that John was regarded as the forerunner-prophet and Jesus himself as the prophet *par excellence*, "like unto Moses."

(27:46), but at last triumphantly proclaiming to his brethren God's vindication of him (28:10).[1]

Several remarks on the above classification are necessary. The quotations in 3:4 and 17:11 deal directly with Elijah-John the Baptist typology; but they are included under Jesus' filling the role of Yahweh, because as Elijah is the precursor of Yahweh in the OT, so John is the precursor of Jesus. Similarly, in Zech 11:13 (Mt 26:15; 27:9 f.) it is Yahweh whom the prophet impersonates. The quotations in 3:17; 22:34 might be put under Jesus as the greater Son of David rather than under direct Messianic prophecies of the royal Messiah. Contrary to the usual understanding, the quotation in 13:35 is not based solely on the occurrence of the word "parable" in Ps 78:2, but on Jesus' coming forward as a teaching prophet to express the riddle of God's dealings with his people, just as does Asaph the prophet (I Chron 25:2; II Chron 29:30) in the psalm. Note that this quotation closely follows those in 12:40 and 13:13, 14 f., which are based on comparisons of Jesus with the prophets Jonah and Isaiah. Both passages emphasize both the difficulty of fully comprehending spiritual truth and the possibility of doing so through spiritual attentiveness (cf. vv. 10-17 in Mt). The parabolic psalm and Jesus' parabolic stories are also similar in their common narrative style. As the greater Son of David and as the representative Israelite, Jesus receives gifts from the Gentiles, just as gifts are brought by the Gentiles to Solomon (Ps 72:10) and to the nation of Israel in the Messianic time (Is 60:6) (Mt 2:11). The quotation in 2:15 is based on the idea that the preservation in and the return from Egypt of the representative Israelite were divinely designed to recapitulate the same experience of the whole nation. Similarly, 2:18 rests on the correspondence between Judah's captivity and Herod's massacre, in both of which the future of the nation is threatened[2] and Jewish mothers mourn, but the very disaster heralds a joyful future. See the context in Jer 31.[3] Finally, special

[1] Cf. on a wider scale S. Amsler's categorizing of Christological hermeneutics in OT quotations throughout the NT (*L'Ancien Testament dans l'église* [Neuchatel, 1960], 135-152).

[2] In the NT, the nation's hopes would have been hopelessly crushed had the Messianic infant been killed.

[3] Cf. H. Milton, *JBL*, 81 (1962), 179. A comment by C. Taylor is worth quoting: "To Him [Jesus] one side of the nation's history was applicable; not the nation's shortcomings, but whatever was expressive of Jehovah's unchanging purpose toward them" (*op. cit.*, 59). Since Mt rejects "Ephra-

attention should be paid to the absence of fulfilment citations with a merely rhetorical or illustrative function.[1]

It may be objected that a classification of hermeneutical principles like the above is an imposition upon the NT and that Mt himself did not consciously think in such categories.[2] The objection might have force, except for the self-evidence of the various principles. It does not require great cleverness to extract them or to recognize on what principle a quotation is based. Had the author been unconscious of the hermeneutical principles along which he was working and approached the OT in a random manner, neither the principles nor their applications would have been so easily discernible. Indeed, we should have had so great a number of "hermeneutical principles" that it would become doubtful they were principles at all. Only one would really exist—the one that by any means a fulfilment must be wrenched from the OT text, as in Qumran literature.

The rabbis were conscious that in application of OT passages to later events, prophecy (in the narrow sense) was not always to be as-

---

thah" in his quotation of Mic 5:1 (Mt 2:6), his comparison between the mourning in Bethlehem and the mourning in Ramah (Jer 31:15) probably does not rest on a mistaken locating of Rachel's sepulchre in Bethlehem Ephrathah, instead of at or near Ramah. Gen 35:16, 19; 48:7 explicitly state Jacob had just left Bethel and was some distance from Bethlehem Ephrath, his destination, when Rachel died and was buried (cf. I Sam 10:2); she was buried *on the way toward* Bethlehem Ephrath. This latter fact may have facilitated Mt's comparison, but does not form its basis. Note also that the parenthetical gloss in Gen 35:19; 48:7 equates *Ephrath*, not Rachel's burial-place, with Bethlehem. Jer, knowing Rachel was buried at or near Ramah, pictures her weeping for the captives of the northern kingdom, the leading tribe of which was descended from her grandson, Ephraim (see vv. 1-22 and F. Johnson, *op. cit.*, 293ff.; thus, no connection exists between the mention of Ramah here and the gathering of the captives from *Judah* at Ramah [cf. 40:1]). Since then Rachel weeps for those not properly her own already in the OT text, Mt felt no difficulty in his making her weep for descendants of Judah. She was Jacob's favorite wife and Israel's representative mother. Neither geography nor genealogy is in the forefront of Mt's comparison (against McNeile, *Mt*, 18; S. L. Edgar, *NTS*, 5 [1958], 52).

[1] Such usage is often assumed and was most pressed by J. G. Palfrey, *Lowell Lectures on the Evidences of Christianity* (Boston, 1843), II, 224ff.; *idem*, *The Relation between Judaism and Christianity* (Boston, 1854), 17-33; to a somewhat lesser extent by L. Woods, *The Works of . . .* (Boston, 1851), I, 116-133.

[2] See, e.g., Friedrich, *TWNT*, VI, 835: "Die Unterscheidung von Zustandsschilderung und Prophetie liegt nicht im Sinne der neutestamentlichen Schriftsteller."

sumed.[1] That a NT author could recognize the difference between the original sense and a divine ὑπόνοια is evident from Jn 11:51, where the intended meaning of Caiaphas is distinguished from the higher intention of God.[2] We must not think that the ancients were so devoid of intelligence as not to appreciate that a passage like Hos 11:1, for example, has a historical reference to the Exodus.[3] Mt gives us one clear indication that he did distinguish between levels of prophecy. The IF which introduces Is 6:9, 10 in Mt 13:14 uses ἀναπληροῦν, "to fulfil completely," or perhaps even, "to fulfil again." Thereby is displayed a consciousness that the OT text had a meaning for Is's day and a further meaning for NT times.[4]

Having established in the Matthaean quotations an interpretation of the OT consciously based on certain hermeneutical principles, we now ask the origin of this kind of OT interpretation. Certainly it does not come from "the casuistic pilpulism" [5] of the rabbinical school.[6] Nor does it come from or stand parallel to Qumran, where each phrase of the OT text is made to fit a new historical situation regardless of context and where we meet far-fetched allegorical interpretations and ingenious word-play.[7] We seem to be dealing with a new and coherent hermeneutical approach to the OT.

The answer to the question of origin is the teaching of Jesus. According to the Matthaean tradition and the other synoptic tradition where parallel, every one of the hermeneutical principles outlined above found expression in OT quotations by Jesus himself.

---

[1] See Tholuck, *op. cit.*, 581ff.

[2] Cf. also Jn 17:12; 18:9, and see *ibid.*, 602f.

[3] Cf. Reinke, *op. cit.*, III, 111.

[4] Some commentators would add other examples, Mt 2:18 and 27:9, where the IF τότε ἐπληρώθη (instead of ἵνα or ὅπως πληρωθῇ) supposedly suggests analogy rather than fulfilment in a narrower sense (Zahn, *Mt*, 106f.; A. B. Bruce, *op. cit.*, 75f.; G. Friedrich, *TWNT*, VI, 833, n. 343). But it is doubtful that τότε was intended to weaken the meaning.

[5] B. J. Roberts, *BJRL*, 36 (1953/54), 79.

[6] Against J. W. Doeve's attempted revival of the view of J. C. C. Döpke (*Hermeneutik der neutestamentlichen Schriftsteller* [Leipzig, 1829]) that "there is no essential difference between rabbinic and New Testament use of Scripture" (Doeve, *op. cit.*, 29). Against the equation, see F. Johnson, *op. cit.*, 376-387.

[7] See F. F. Bruce, *Biblical Exegesis*, 11ff., 68f.; cf. Brownlee, *BA*, 14 (1951), 60-62, 73, n. 48, who rightly sees, as Stendahl amazingly does not (190ff.), the wide gulf between the thirteen hermeneutical devices he finds in the Habakkuk Commentary and NT interpretation of the OT. (I say "devices," because they are mainly means of textual manipulation rather than lines of interpretation as in Mt.) Against Greig, *op. cit.*, 598f.

He assumed the role of Yahweh: 10:32 f.; 11:5, 10, 28, 29; 13:41; 16:27; 17:11; 24:31; 25:31. He claimed to be the royal Messiah: 22:44; 26:64. He considered himself the Isaianic Servant: 11:5; 20:28. He applied to himself Daniel's description of the Son of man: 24:30; 26:64; 28:18.[1] He took upon himself the role of the Shepherd of Israel: 21:44; 24:30; 26:31. He acted as the greater Moses: 26:28 (cf. 5:21 f., 27 f., 31 f., 33 f., 38 f., 43 f.). As the royal son of David he said he was even greater than Solomon: 12:42. He spoke and acted as the representative prophet: 12:40; 13:13; 14:16. He regarded himself as the representative righteous sufferer: 21:42; 26:38; 27:46; 28:10. He assumed the role of the representative Israelite: 4:4, 7, 10.[2] It is significant that *the Matthaean quotations not attributed to Jesus do not transgress the hermeneutical boundaries indicated by him.*[3] One thinks especially of Luke's statement that Jesus "interpreted to the disciples in all the scriptures the things concerning himself" (24:27).

It may be said that the presence of all lines of interpretation in both the words of Jesus and the words of the evangelist shows that the evangelist and the early church consistently read their own

---

[1] I am not unaware of the view which would divide Son of man sayings into three groups and regard the apocalyptic as unauthentic or as not identifying Jesus and the Son of man, the predictions of suffering as *vaticinia ex eventu*, and the sayings concerning Jesus' ministry as meaning merely "man" or "I." However, in the authors I have checked, little or no attempt is made to answer the decisive objection that the title would not have appeared almost exclusively in Jesus' mouth if not original to him as a self-designation. I have checked Jackson and Lake, *The Beginnings of Christianity*, I, 368-384; J. Héring, *Le royaume de Dieu et sa venue* (Paris, 1937), 88ff.; Bultmann, *Theology of the NT*, I, 30f.; G. Bornkamm, *Jesus von Nazareth* (Stuttgart, 1956), 206ff.; R. P. Casey, *JTS*, 9 (1958), 263ff.; J. Knox, *Jesus, Lord and Christ* (New York, 1958), 92ff.; J. M. Robinson, *op. cit.*, 101ff.; H. Conzelmann, *RGG*³, III, 630f. For the objection, see G. Kittel, *RGG*², III, 2119; W. Manson, *op. cit.*, 114f., 160; Cullmann, *Christology*, 155; Stauffer, *op. cit.*, 133. In view of the frequency of the self-designation and the absence of a tendency to work in the title outside Jesus' own words, "Son of man" may preserve the more original form of the sayings in Mt 16:13, 28; Lk 12:8, in the parallel passages to which the title is missing (Mk 8:27; 9:1; Mt 10:32) (contra W. Manson, *loc. cit.*). P.S.: this footnote is now out of date.

[2] To counter Satan's temptations, Jesus in the wilderness chooses appropriate quotations from Deuteronomic contexts which deal with Israel in the wilderness. Cf. the belief of the Qumran sect that they would stay forty years in the Judaean desert (Milik, *op. cit.*, 115f.).

[3] S. L. Edgar's claim that Jesus shows far greater respect for OT context does not stand critical examination (*NTS*, 9 [1962], 55-62). Against Edgar from a different angle with inclusion of non-Messianic quotations, see R. T. Mead, *NTS*, 10 (1964), 279-289.

lines of interpretation back into the mouth of Jesus. But it is mathematically improbable that mere chance reading back would have resulted in representation of *all* the lines of Messianic interpretation in the reported words of Jesus. Deliberate reading back for Christological justification of the lines of interpretation is equally improbable, for that would attribute too much subtlety to the evangelist and early church. Besides, application of the OT passages concerning the Son of man and the Shepherd of Israel do not occur *outside* the words of Jesus. Most of all, the theological depth and coherence of the hermeneutical principles (in sharp contrast with Qumran and rabbinic exegesis) demand the unique genius of the kind of man Jesus must have been—they cannot reasonably be set down to *Gemeindetheologie*.

Modern Hermeneutics and The Messianic Hope

Having established a unity of OT interpretation between Mt and Jesus, we now probe further into the question of legitimacy. Are the hermeneutical principles displayed in Matthaean quotations valid, and are their applications consistent with a proper historical understanding of the OT? This question is pressed upon us from the side of OT scholarship: "He [the Christian scholar] must study the Old Testament in its own right. . . For this [typology] reads so much into the Old Testament, or treats things in the Old Testament not in their own right as valid revelation of God, ..."[1] It is also pressed from the side of NT scholarship by the reticence of the *heilsgeschichtliche* school to extend typology to matters of detail as does the NT[2] and by the current discussion of the *sensus plenior* in Roman Catholic circles.

The problem in its most nettling form is implied in the statement by A. Bentzen, "We must not forget that the historical understanding of the Old Testament in our own age must be respected, as in the Early Church their historical understanding, *which we*

---

[1] H. H. Rowley, *The Changing Pattern of OT Studies* (London, 1959), 27. See also J. A. Sanders, *op. cit.*, 234ff.

[2] This generalizing tendency originated with J. C. K. Hofmann, who extended typology to all world history (*op. cit.*, I, 15). Cf. O. Cullmann, *Christ and Time* (London, 1951), 94ff.; F. Baumgärtel, *Verheissung* (Gütersloh, 1952), 76; B. S. Childs, *Interpretation*, 12 (1958), 264ff.

cannot accept, was the starting point." [1] On the one hand, a generalizing view of *Heilsgeschichte* lacks the solid foundation of detailed fulfilments which would justify in addition the broader typological approach. On the other hand, the detailed fulfilments claimed in the NT are thought to rest on OT interpretation which offends modern OT scholarship. Although a really adequate treatment of this aspect of the study would call for a full discussion of OT prophecy and the Messianic hope, the attempt here will be to indicate avenues of thought which lead to the conclusion that Jesus' and Mt's use of the OT should not offend the best in modern OT scholarship.

Much of the difficulty lies in the question, when did the Messianic hope arise in Israel and under what impulses? Any discussion of the origins of the Messianic hope [2] must proceed with the realization that historical and theological questions are intertwined. If—regardless of what the OT writers had in mind—a remarkable correspondence exists between the OT and the ministry of Jesus and if this correspondence implies divine design,[3] we must reckon with the possibilities of direct revelation and of divine intention beyond that of the OT authors.[4] It is not enough to ask for the *Sitz im Leben* along

---

[1] *King and Messiah* (London, 1955), 110f. See further H. Braun, *ZTK*, 59 (1962), 16-31.

[2] For the progressively more technical and personal use of "Messiah," see the standard Bible dictionaries. Mowinckel would restrict the application of "Messianic" to the eschatological figure (*He That Cometh* [Oxford, 1956], 3f.); but it is legitimate to apply the term to the eschatological time-period, which may be described without specific reference to the Messiah himself (e.g., Is 2;25-27; 30:18-26; 35; Mic 4; Jer 31:27-40).

[3] H. H. Rowley: "If the anticipations rested on the activity of the Spirit of God in men, and the fulfilment represented the activity of God in history and experience, we have a sufficient explanation of all. But if we wish to reject this explanation, we are hard put to it to find another which is more scientific and more satisfying. If the anticipations had no basis but the false claim that men were the mouthpiece of God, their fulfilment becomes a problem. There could have been no power in such self-deception to influence future events. On the other hand, . . . the anticipations were quite certainly written down before the fulfilment took place" (*The Unity of the Bible* [London, 1953], 12). Cf. *idem, The Servant of the Lord* (London, 1952), 52; *idem, The Re-Discovery of the OT* (London, 1946), 292ff. The Scandinavian school likewise sees fulfilment in Christ. For a representative statement, see Mowinckel, *op. cit.*, 247. On true prescience in OT prophecy, see E. König, in Hastings' *Encyclopaedia of Religion and Ethics* (Edinburgh, 1918), X, 390ff.

[4] Cf. A. B. Davidson, *The Expositor*, 8, First Series (1878), 241ff.; *idem, OT Prophecy* (Edinburgh, 1912), 326ff.

purely naturalistic and evolutionary lines, or to set up *a priori* postulates concerning when and how the Messianic hope could not have arisen. Historical development on the horizontal plane and divine revelation on the vertical plane conditioned each other.[1]

One may see Messianic foregleams in the Protevangelium,[2] the promises of salvation through Abraham and his descendants,[3] the Shiloh prophecy,[4] and Balaam's oracle.[5] But E. Sellin [6] and J. Klausner have argued that the Messianic hope broke into view shortly after Moses.[7] Especially would Moses have become a Messianic prototype at the time of the judges, during which Israel longed for saviours from oppression. Klausner presses the argument that the Talmudic and Midrashic parallel between Moses and the Messiah preserves the original setting.[8] Support comes from the early Samaritan doctrine of the Messianic *Taheb* or "Restorer" like Moses and from the fact that the passages in 4Q Testimonia are those used by the Samaritans as Messianic *testimonia*.[9] Further support may come from the even earlier OT picture of the Messianic deliverance as a second exodus.[10]

The Messianic idea came into much clearer relief, however, with

---

[1] Mowinckel calls it "an unassailable theological thesis" that the Messianic concept came into existence by direct revelation (*op. cit.*, 129). He fails to understand we are not dealing with either/or alternatives.

[2] Gen 3:15. That victory is promised to the seed of the *woman* may have occasioned stress on the mother of the Messianic figure in Is 7:14; 49:1; Mic 5:3; and perhaps Jer 31:22. So J. A. Moyter, in *New Bible Dictionary* (Grand Rapids, 1962), 817.

[3] Gen 9:24-27; 12:1-3; 22:18; 26:4; 27:27-29; 28:14.

[4] Gen 49:10-12. The paradisaic fruitfulness mentioned in the passage goes beyond conditions attained under David. For convenient summaries of the possible meanings of "Shiloh," see N. K. Gottwald, in *IDB*, IV, p. 330; P. Heinisch, *Christ in Prophecy* (St. Paul, Minn., 1956), 36f.

[5] Num 24:15-19 probably refers to David, but is Messianically interpreted in the LXX, Targums Jonathan, Jerusalem, and Onkelos, *Test. Judah* 24, the DSS (see discussions by F. F. Bruce, *Biblical Exegesis in the Qumran Texts* [Den Haag, 1959], 46ff.; J. Daniélou, *Vigiliae Christianae*, 11 [1957], 121-138), rabbinical writings (references in Edersheim, *Life and Times*, I, 211f.), and patristic literature (Justin, *I Apol.* xxxii; *Dial.* cvi.4; Irenaeus, *Epideixis* 58 [J. A. Robinson, *St. Irenaeus' The Demonstration of the Apostolic Preaching* (London, 1920), 121]).

[6] *Der alttestamentliche Prophetismus* (Leipzig, 1912), 105-193.

[7] Cf. Dt 18:15-19, which refers to the line of prophets, but readily yields to a Messianic interpretation as well because of Moses' uniqueness (cf. Dt 34:10, and see Moyter, *op. cit.*, 812-814).

[8] *The Messianic Idea in Israel* (New York, 1955), 16ff.

[9] T. Gaster, *The Scriptures of the Dead Sea Sect* (London, 1957), 327f.

[10] Most clearly in Jer 23:5-8, but cf. Is 51:9-11; 52:12.

the institution of kingship in Israel, particularly as a result of the tension between human kingship and the ideal of Yahweh's sole sovereignty and as a result of failure by David's descendants to meet the conditions of the Davidic covenant.[1] OT scholars of the past generation denied Messianism during this early period by late-dating the pertinent OT passages and minimizing the import of their language. According to their view the crushing of Israel's nationalistic hopes by the Exile produced the Messianic hope. But it became increasingly evident that archaeological evidence prohibits late-dating and that minimizing exegesis must make up for the Messianic-like language in passages which are not late-dated.

Out of the bankruptcy of the old view arose the myth-ritual and Scandinavian schools. Any pre-exilic Messianic-sounding passage is supposed to reflect the pagan idealogy of divine kingship. True Messianism did not arise until the mythological wish-dreams connected with the cultic ritual of the New Year's Festival had been disappointed so often they were finally obliterated by the Exile.[2] The new view is already crumbling under several lines of attack.[3]

First, there are obstacles to assuming a cultic ritual pattern throughout the Fertile Crescent. Practical difficulties exist as to language, insight into alien modes of thought, and transmission of an esoteric "culture-pattern" to an alien people.[4] It is doubtful that the Ugaritic texts contain a myth-ritual pattern,[5] and it has been acknowledged for some time that kingship idealogies differed radically from one another.[6] OT literature does not picture Israel's kings as divine, but rather as sharing inviolability with the priests,[7]

---

[1] II Sam 7:1-17.

[2] In the reconstructed New Year's Festival, celebrated in the autumn, the "divine" king endured humiliation and suffering in an acted-out ritual, but finally triumphed in his annual enthronement.

[3] K.-H. Bernhardt argues with much more detail and documentation along many of the lines which appear below, written before his book appeared (*Das Problem der altorientalischen Königsidealogie im A. T.* [*VT* Supplement, VIII; Leiden, 1961]).

[4] S. G. F. Brandon, in *Myth, Ritual, and Kingship*, ed. S. H. Hooke (Oxford, 1958), 266ff.

[5] De Langhe, *ibid.*, 122-148.

[6] H. Frankfort, *The Problem of Similarity in Ancient Near Eastern Religions* (Oxford, 1951); *idem*, *Kingship and the Gods* (Chicago, 1948); E. A. Speiser, *Israel Exploration Journal*, 7 (1957), pp. 201-216; K. F. Euler, *ZAW*, 56 (1938), 296; S. Szikszai, in *IDB*, III, pp. 14f.; freely admitted by Mowinckel, *op. cit.*, 27-51.

[7] I Sam 22:17f.; I Kings 2:26.

denying divinity,[1] being prayed for instead of worshipped,[2] and often censured by the prophets—but never for divine claims.[3] Were the cultic view correct, we should have had in pre-exilic portions of the OT many more than the few theophorous proper names compounded with *melek* ("king").[4] Heavy influence from Canaanite religion on kingship in Israel is unlikely, because kingship in Canaan was already a spent force at the time of the Hebrew occupation.[5] Why did not eschatology develop in other nations which had cultic festivals? [6]

Second, the method of drawing conclusions from parallel phraseology in "enthronement" psalms and supposedly "cultic" texts is open to suspicion. O. Kaiser has shown that the sea, or water, in Egypt, Ugarit, and Israel was differently regarded as to religious significance.[7] The lesson is clear: peoples may live in close contact and borrow words, but not deeply influence one another's religious concepts. Similar terminology does not mean identical thought-content. Through long use much of the pagan terminology may have lost its mythological content. It is also dubious that many of the texts cultically interpreted should be so understood. Metasemasiological interpretations have been denied by scholars closely associated with research in the texts.[8] Supposing the Hebrew poets and prophets did envision a royal and priestly Messiah possessing divinity—apart from sacral kingship idealogy—how else can we expect them to have spoken than in terms which can be paralleled in pagan texts which speak of the king as a royal and priestly divinity? Even if it be granted that OT terminology is borrowed from oriental *Hofstil*, we cannot assume identity of reference, for what would be more natural than to apply these exalted phrases

---

[1] II Kings 5:7; cf. 6:26f.

[2] Ps 20:1-5; 72:15.

[3] See Szikszai, *IDB*, III, p. 15. That the Israelitish kings appear sometimes to have performed priestly functions is far from proving divine kingship.

[4] C. R. North, *The OT Interpretation of History* (London, 1946), 123f.

[5] A. Alt, *Die Staatenbildung der Israeliten in Palästina* (Leipzig, 1930), 31f.

[6] G. Pidoux, *Le Dieu qui vient* (Paris, 1947), 50. Mowinckel's answer, Israel's concept of Yahweh, the God of history, only strengthens the third objection below (*op. cit.*, 151).

[7] *Die mythologische Bedeutung des Meeres in Ägypten, Ugarit, und Israel* (Berlin, 1959).

[8] C. H. Gordon, *Ugaritic Literature* (Rome, 1949), 3ff.; H. L. Ginsberg, *JAOS*, 70 (1950), 157.

to the Messiah, in opposition to heathen idealogy? [1] Furthermore, the Psalms sometimes go beyond the *Hofstil*. For example, the *world*-dominion expressed in Psalm 2 speaks not of "einem urzeitlichen Kampf des Gotteskönigs mit Chaosmächten, sondern von einem solchem des Zionskönigs mit den Erdenkönigen," looking forward to the *Endzeit*.[2]

Third, Israel's worship of Yahweh was historically, not mythologically oriented, with Yahweh's redemption of Israel from Egypt the keystone.[3] "The precise content of any given conception can be discerned only when it is considered in the context of the particular system of thought to which it belongs." [4] Therefore, we must conclude Hebrew kingship never achieved the sanctity which prevailed elsewhere—this would contradict Yahwehism. Therefore, we must also conclude that cultic re-enactment of myth based on elements of sympathetic magic, essentially foreign to Israel's religion, is not to be inferred from parallel phraseology in OT texts and supposedly cultic texts—this would contradict the historical framework of Yahwehism.[5] From the psychological standpoint we must doubt a cultic origin for Messianism, for the directness of cultic experience generally gives way to a more rational life-philosophy.[6]

Fourth, the hypothesis of a New Year's Festival of the myth-ritual, divine kingship kind is open to doubt. It is passing strange that "the Old Testament offers little direct evidence as to the

---

[1] See G. von Rad, *Theologie des A. T.*, I (München, 1957), 317ff., who sees the taking over of the *Hofstil* in the royal psalms as designed to project the fulness of the Nathanic oracle. Thus, the royal psalms are a prophetic *Urbild* of the Messiah and his kingdom. Cf. the remarks of H. G. Mays on the utilization of pagan mythology in the OT and Qumran history and eschatology (*JBL*, 82 [1963], 1-14). Mays follows the Scandinavian approach, however.

[2] R. Press, *Theologische Zeitschrift* (Basel), 13 (1957), 324. See also H.-J. Kraus, *Die Psalmen* (Neukirchen, 1958), 14ff.

[3] See W. F. Albright, *From the Stone Age to Christianity*[2] (New York, 1957), 257ff.; *idem, Archaeology and the Religion of Israel*[3] (Baltimore, 1953), 142ff.

[4] Mowinckel, *op. cit.*, 27.

[5] This is the most decisive objection to the Scandinavian and myth-ritual schools. See C. R. North, *ZAW*, 50 (1932), 35-37; N. W. Porteous, *The Kingship of God in Pre-Exilic Hebrew Religion* (London, 1938), 6ff.; G. E. Wright, *BA*, 6 (1943), 7f.; *idem, The OT against Its Environment* (London, 1950), 65; A. Robert, in *Miscellanea Biblica B. Ubach* (1953), 216ff.; H.-J. Kraus, *Die Königsherrschaft Gottes im A. T.* (Tübingen, 1951), 30ff.; *idem, Gottesdienst in Israel* (München, 1954), 73.

[6] W. Eichrodt, *Theologie des A. T.*[3], (Berlin, 1948), I, p. 254.

ritual and mythology of this great autumnal festival in any of its forms; and even the little that is available is post-exilic in date." [1] Why the lack of evidence in historical-narrative portions of the OT if elements in poetic portions, primarily the Psalms, imply the existence of such a festival and cultic ritual? Why did not the "anti-Canaanite reaction," conjured up to meet this incongruity,[2] expurgate the poetic as well as the historical portions of the OT? The psalms Mowinckel associates with the New Year's Festival are nowhere in Jewish liturgies specially associated with the New Year. On the contrary, they are Sabbath psalms.[3] Data from rabbinical sources is too late to be valid for the pre-exilic period.[4]

Fifth, to work on the *a priori* assumption that a clear Messianic hope cannot have emerged until the Exile is unjustifiable. Unless the concept of an individual Messiah as set forth in passages such as Is 9 and 11 and Mic 5 was born in a day,[5] we must see a fairly clear Messianism before the Exile.[6] Then it becomes not at all difficult to see an early stage of Messianic doctrine and Messianic overtones in psalms which are said to reflect divine kingship idealogy. That the Exile was not the decisive factor in the *origin* of Messianism is shown by the fact that the Messianic king in Ezek, Hag, and Zech is less prominent than in passages like Is 9 and Mic 5, which link far better with such psalms as 2 and 110.[7] *Prima facie*, it is improbable the Messianic hope would arise in an epoch without a state or kingdom, in a community where the priesthood prevailed and an anti-dynastic tendency was evident.[8] Even if disappointment be

---

[1] A. R. Johnson, *Sacral Kingship* (Cardiff, 1955), 51, who proceeds to infer such a festival from Zech 14:16f. Cf. H. Ringgren, *The Messiah in the OT* (London, 1956), 8ff.; A. Bentzen, *King and Messiah* (London, 1955), 21.

[2] E.g., by Mowinckel, *op. cit.*, p. 88.

[3] N. H. Snaith, in *Record and Revelation*, ed. H.W. Robinson (Oxford, 1938), 260.

[4] L. J. Pap, *Das israelitische Neujahrefest* (Kampen, 1933), 47. Further against such a festival, see Kraus, *Die Königsherrschaft Gottes im A. T.*, 21ff.; *idem*, *Gottesdienst in Israel*, 97ff.

[5] S. B. Frost's post-exilic revision of the Ps with influx of futurist Messianism and his carving out Messianic passages in the prophets and late-dating them serve only to underscore the real presence of pre-exilic Messianism and the lengths requiied to do away with it (*OT Apocalyptic* [London, 1952], 61, 67-70).

[6] Cf. Klausner, *op. cit.*, 34f.

[7] Cf. H. L. Ellison, *The Centrality of the Messianic Idea for the OT* (London, 1953), 10.

[8] H. Schmidt, in *RGG*², III, cols. 2143f.

made the mainspring of Messianism, we must remember that the decline of Israel and Judah had become obvious long before the Exile, and the carrying into captivity was itself progressive over a period of many years.

Sixth, although the Gunkel-Gressmann view that Israel borrowed eschatology from other religions has rightly been rejected,[1] their recognition of eschatology in the Psalms has not been refuted and has been reaffirmed by A. R. Johnson, with the added touch of a Messianic hope connected with the house of David.[2] The prophets are not to be set apart from the cultus,[3] so that no barrier prevents the influx of eschatology into the Psalms. Mowinckel's remarkably brief dismissal of eschatology from the Psalms is not satisfactory. His arguments are that there is no prophetic style, that the present tense excludes the future, that prophetic formulae of introduction are missing, and that eschatology would be poetic fiction.[4] It may be countered that if by style is meant literary framework, the argument proves nothing. If content is included, that is the very matter in question, and the language easily lends itself to an eschatological understanding.[5] Why should not expressions of world-wide dominion, a great ruler, etc.—criteria by which we recognize later OT texts as Messianic—be considered indicative of Messianism in the Psalms and other pre-exilic passages? The present tense is not to be pressed in Hebrew, where even the past tense is used prophetically. Perfects and imperfects are mingled in Is 9:6, an admittedly Messianic prophecy.[6] Allowance must also be made for the fact we are dealing with different literary forms in the Psalms and in the prophets. Even so, in Ps 110, one of the psalms most in question, נאם יהוה ("The Lord says"), a regular prophetic formula, does introduce the psalm. For "poetic fiction" Mowinckel would substitute cultic-ritual fiction. It is true that Gunkel and Gressmann

---

[1] See Mowinckel, *op. cit.*, 123.

[2] *Op cit.*; *idem*, in *Myth, Ritual, and Kingship*, 234f. Johnson still works within the framework of the autumnal festival, however. Catholic scholars have all along maintained eschatology and Messianism in the Ps. See, e.g., A. Feuillet, *Nouvelle Revue Théologique*, 73 (1951), 244-260, 352, 363; A. Miller, in *Miscellanea Biblica B. Ubach*, 201-209; J. Coppens, in *L'attente du Messie* (Paris, 1954), 31ff.

[3] See H. H. Rowley, in *Myth, Ritual, and Kingship*, 240ff.

[4] *Psalmenstudien* (Kristiania, 1921), II, pp. 15f.

[5] See H. Gunkel, *Einleitung in die Psalmen* (Göttingen, 1933), 79ff., 94ff., 114-116, 329ff.

[6] Mowinckel, *He That Cometh*, 16.

deny the concept of an individual Messiah in the Psalms.[1] But this is wholly needless, for if eschatology, why not the central eschatological figure? The language fits the concept of an individual Messiah as easily as it fits eschatology in general.

The inadequacies of the old late-dating and the newer cultic-ritual views free us to see pre-exilic Messianism in both the Psalms and the prophets. A strong factor in the flowering of the Messianic hope during the period of monarchy was the attitude of suspicion to the institution of kingship by those who retained the old concept of Yahweh's sole sovereignty over Israel.[2] The narrative passage to which the Scandinavian school most appeals as proving the YHWH MLK concept grew out of the cult of divine or sacral kingship derived from surrounding religions, I Sam 8:4-22, rather teaches that the concept antedates the adoption of the monarchal system by Israel; for Samuel says that hitherto Yahweh has been their king. At the very least, the passage must indicate the concept arose in opposition to, not out of a cultus of divine kingship.[3] Thus, YHWH MLK did not derive from transference of divine kingship idealogy to Yahweh, but was itself the starting-point for the idea that the Israelite king was endued with a special portion of divine power and authority as Yahweh's vicegerent. This is not to deny outside influence on Israel's religion at the popular level. It is to say, however, that a cherishing of the old ideal, Yahweh is King, by the spiritual nucleus of the nation kindled Messianic hopes for a perfect representative and embodiment of Yahweh, this in the face of the manifest failure of human kingship as it actually was in Israel.

Such hopes would have been confirmed and enlarged by the grandeur promised to the seed of David in the Nathanic oracle (II Sam 7:5-16). The way in which the promise is concentrated on David's immediate successor ("him," singular), the attached condition of obedience for blessing, the subsequent failure to meet that condition, the consequent judgment, and yet the divine assurance that the Davidic throne "shall be established forever"

---

[1] Gunkel, *op. cit.*, 330; Gressmann, *Der Messias* (Göttingen, 1929), 212ff.

[2] Cf. G. S. Gunn, *God in the Ps* (Edinburgh, 1956), 71ff., 106ff. On the feeling in early Israel that Yahweh alone was king, see Jdg 8:22f. and M. Buber, *Königtum Gottes*[3] (Heidelberg, 1956), 11ff.

[3] That the passage in I Sam is not late, see I. Mendelsohn, *BASOR*, 143 (1956), 17-22.

even though the condition for blessing is not met—all these factors would further the expectation of an Anointed One in whom the old ideal, Yahweh alone is King, and the seemingly contradictory promise to David find a meeting-point. David himself in his last words and in prophetic ecstasy seizes on the hope for a perfect ruler (II Sam 23:2-4; cf. 7:18). If 4QFlor. can interpret the Nathanic oracle of the Davidic Messiah, there is no reason why the same interpretation could not have arisen soon after the oracle was given.[1] "The pre-exilic tension round the king consisted of the vision of one who should perfectly represent Yahweh, even as the heathen around Israel declared their 'divine kings' represented their gods, and the stark reality of one who, however great his office, fell far short of the vision." [2]

With the above view, which combines the old YHWH MLK ideal with disappointment in the Davidic line, what Mowinckel writes of the prophet-poet who authored the Servant-songs can be applied to pre-exilic prophets and poets who elsewhere paint pictures far brighter than were actually realized in Israel: "The poet has, of course, idealized the portrait. Every prophetic interpretation and transformation of historical reality is an idealization." [3] We are therefore not denying the *Sitz im Leben*, but merely affirming that factors *within* Israel's religion provide a better life-setting than does the Oriental *Umwelt*. Furthermore, the *Sitz im Leben* is not a kind of ceiling above which the thought of the pertinent OT passages cannot rise, but is a springboard from which the thought leaps beyond the immediate occasion.

All this is directly relevant to the question whether Jesus' and Mt's use of the OT is legitimate. For if the Messianic hope is to be seen in pre-exilic OT passages, there is no *a priori* objection to NT interpretation of pre-exilic passages as directly Messianic. And if the concept of Yahweh's sole sovereignty played the part suggested in the rise of the Messianic hope, the quotations in which Jesus fills the eschatological role of Yahweh stem from a correct understanding of OT Messianism. For the tension between Yahweh as the sole king

---

[1] On the importance of the Nathanic oracle and on the development of the hope for an eschatological *Heilskönig* answering Yahweh's requirements from the manifest unworthiness of the Davidic line, see Kraus, *Die Königsherrschaft Gottes im A. T.*, 90ff., 95f.; *idem, Gottesdienst in Israel*, 78; Y. Kaufmann, *The Religion of Israel* (Chicago, 1960), 272f.

[2] Ellison, *op. cit.*, 11.

[3] *He That Cometh*, pp. 250f.

and the promise of a perfect ruler from David's line is resolved in Jesus Christ, who as Son of God fills the eschatological role of Yahweh and as Son of David fulfils the role of the Davidic king.[1] All that remains is to see whether the particular OT passages interpreted as eschatological and directly Messianic sustain that interpretation.

In Is 40 (Mt 3:3) the themes of Israel's final restoration and complete forgiveness and Yahweh's coming and revealing his glory display Messianic[2] strains, as was recognized in rabbinical literature, where, as in the NT, the passage was associated with Elijah (in the NT, John in the role of Elijah).[3] Similarly, Is 35 (Mt 11:5) speaks of Yahweh's coming, the revelation of his glory, and the banishing of the results of sin.[4] In Zech 11:13 (Mt 26:15; 27:9) the prophet represents Yahweh, and on this basis Mt applies Israel's rejection of Yahweh to the nation's rejection of Jesus in the betrayal bargain. The last chapters in Zech are prevailingly eschatological.[5] The coming of Yahweh to cleanse and reinstate Israel in Mal 3:1, 23 (Mt 11:10; 17:11) is eschatological in tone and applied to Messianic times in rabbinical literature.[6] John the Baptist becomes the forerunner of Jesus just as "my messenger" "Elijah" prepares the way for the "Lord . . . even the messenger (or angel) of the covenant."[7] Thus, all the OT passages applied to Jesus in the role of Yahweh are Messianic or eschatological in tone, and the NT application is consistent with the intended meaning in those passages.

It has been indicated above why Ps 2 (Mt 3:17; 22:34) may be

---

[1] Cf. the fusion of Messiah and Yahweh beginning already in the OT: Is 9:5; 2:4 with 11:1-4; 24:23b with 9:5f.; 11:1-4; and 32:1; Jer 23:5f.; 33:15-17; Mic 2:12 with 5:3; Zeph 3:15-17; Zech 2:14-17 with 9:9f.; 14:9 with 9:9; 14:16-21.

[2] Here I use "Messianic" for characteristics of the *time* when Messiah reigns.

[3] Strack-Billerbeck, *op. cit.*, I, 66, 97.

[4] For recognition of the Messianic character of Is 35 in rabbinic literature, see Edersheim, *Life and Times*, II, 725; Strack-Billerbeck, *op. cit.*, I, 593ff.

[5] The rabbis regarded Zech 11:13 as Messianic, but interpreted the thirty pieces of silver as thirty precepts given by Messiah to the Gentiles (*Genesis*, R. 98.9).

[6] Strack-Billerbeck, *op. cit.*, I, 597; Edersheim, *Life and Times*, II, 736f.

[7] The NT identification of "my messenger" (Mal 3:1) with Elijah (Mal 3:23) is correct, because "my messenger" is a forerunner to "prepare the way," whereas the coming of "the messenger of the covenant" is placed in juxtaposition with and second in order to the coming of the Lord. See J. M. P. Smith, *op. cit.*, 63.

considered Messianic, the view which was earliest and most widespread in Judaism.[1] Not only the world-wide dominion of the Anointed (against the historical reality of the kings of Israel), but also the expectation that the faith of Israel will become the faith of the kings and the nations of the world is typically Messianic (cf. Is 11:9, 10).[2] Is 8:23-9:1 (Mt 4:15 f.) occurs in a prominent individually Messianic passage (see Is 9:5 f.).[3] The prophet proclaims the Lord's favor upon the northern Israelitish provinces, which had suffered the greatest affliction and degradation.[4] Mt applies the prophecy to Jesus' Galilean ministry. The Messianic character of Is 11:1 (Mt 2:23) is generally recognized. Mt's use of Is 11:1 to describe the lowliness and obscurity out of which Jesus came exactly corresponds to the Isaianic thought. Mic 5:1 (Mt 2:6) and Zech 9:9 (Mt 21:5) are generally accepted as Messianic.

Considerations of space forbid a full discussion of Is 7:14 (Mt 1:23). But it may briefly be pointed out that all views which do not see the prediction of a miraculous birth of the Messiah in Is 7:14 neglect to establish one of two things which must be established for those views to stand. First, if the *'almah* is virgin, she will lose her virginity, conceive, and bear. But we should have expected *'ishah* if marriage were contemplated before conceiving and giving birth.[5] The adjective emphasizes the state of the *'almah*'s pregnancy, as if it had already begun;[6] so that we must understand she conceives

---

[1] See Strack-Billerbeck, *op. cit.*, III, 675ff. On Rashi's statement that Ps 2 was indeed Messianic, but should be applied to David "to refute the heretics [Christians]" and the expunging of the quoted phrase in some later editions, see C. Taylor, *op. cit.*, p. xvii.

[2] W. E. Barnes, in *Cambridge Biblical Essays* (ed. H. B. Swete; London, 1909), 147ff.

[3] See Reinke, *op. cit.*, I, 118ff., that this passage cannot refer to Hezekiah. Mowinckel recognizes Is 9:1-6 as Messianic (*He That Cometh*, 16).

[4] With O. Procksch (*Jesaia I* [Leipzig, 1930], 143), therefore, I reject the interpretation which sees mention of the three Assyrian provinces, Dor (דרך הים—from Mt. Carmel to Aphek in the south), Gilead (עבר הירדן), and Megiddo (גליל הגוים) (E. Forrer, *Die Provinzeinteilung des assyrischen Reiches* [Leipzig, 1920], 59ff., 69; A. Alt, in *Festschrift für Alfred Bertholet* [Tübingen, 1950], 32ff. [= A. Alt, *Kleine Schriften zur Geschichte des Volkes Israel* (München, 1953), 209ff.]; Simons, *op. cit.*, 34, 433). Unless the Isaianic expressions refer to the Galilean area, the stated contrast between "the former time" and "the latter time" is lost.

[5] Procksch, *op. cit.*, 121.

[6] So also if הרה is pointed as a participle. Cf. S. R. Driver, *A Treatise on the Use of the Tenses in Hebrew*^{3} (Oxford, 1892), 165, 168.

and bears in her status as *'almah*.[1] The construction could not be more awkward for the supposition that the *'almah* becomes *'ishah* before pregnancy.

Second, if marriage is not contemplated, *'almah* is used in the sense of a young married woman. To this writer's knowledge, such a meaning for *'almah* has never been demonstrated.[2] *'Almah* refers to a mature young woman of marriageable age, but unmarried and presumably virgin unless otherwise stated (cf. Dt 22:20, 21).[3] In the similar[4] birth-annunciation formula twice occurring in the Ras Shamra text, Nikkal is designated once by the exact etymological counterpart of *'almah* (*glmt*) and once by the counterpart of *b^ethulah* (*btlt*).[5] Thus, it appears from a pre-Isaianic, even pre-Mosaic text that the use of *'almah* instead of *b^ethulah* in Is 7:14 is not significant and that *'almah* refers to an unmarried, but mature young virgin. In view, then, of *'almah,* the connection of the preiction with the house of David (v. 13), the frequency of individually Messianic prophecies throughout Is,[6] and the beautiful progression the Messianic interpretation yields—Messiah about to be born (7:14), Messiah born (9:5), Messiah reigning (11:1-5, 10) [7]—the Messianic interpretation is much to be preferred.[8]

---

[1] Zahn, *Mt,* 83; E. J. Young, *Studies in Is* (Grand Rapids, 1954), 161ff.

[2] L. Koehler's suggestion that a young lady is *'almah* until her firstborn appears not to be well-established (*ZAW,* 67 [1955], 50).

[3] The most detailed and extensive examination of the evidence is that by R. D. Wilson, *Princeton Theological Review,* 24 (1926), 308-316. In Cant 6:8 the word stands in contrast with queens and concubines. In Prov 30:18-20, the way of a man with an *'almah* refers to the infatuation of youthful love and contrasts with the infatuation of an adulterous woman (v. 20).

[4] Not identical, for the Ugaritic text has no counterpart for הרה.

[5] C. H. Gordon, *Journal of Bible and Religion,* 21 (1953), 106. That the *glmt-btlt* of the Ras Shamra text is non-virgin shows the moral indifference in Canaanite thought, but does not affect the point that the words were used as synonyms. In Biblical thought the words retain their high moral connotation unless otherwise indicated.

[6] 4:2; 8:8b, 10b; 9:1-6; 11:1-5, 10; 16:5; 32:1; and the Servant passages.

[7] Delitzsch, *Is,* I, 218.

[8] Note a partial return to this view by Mowinckel, *He That Cometh,* 111ff. Under the Messianic interpretation, in vv. 15ff. the far-future period of Immanuel's infancy becomes the measure of time for near-future events. Alternatively, vv. 15ff. represent a veiled shift (probably unrealized by the prophet, but divinely intended—if divine inspiration be allowed) from Immanuel to Shearjashub, whose presence in the pericope (v. 3) is otherwise purposeless apart from the meaning of his name. In the immediately following passage (8:1-4) Is's other son plays a central role, so that reference to Shearjashub would be natural in chapter 7.

Jesus' use of Ps 110 (Mt 22:44) presupposes the psalm was written by David and is directly Messianic. The Dead Sea Scrolls rule out a late date.[1] Authorship by David the royal poet is therefore as possible as authorship by someone else. Unless one holds to the theory of divine kingship in Israel, an early date almost necessitates a Messianic interpretation. David approaches, and perhaps enters a clear Messianism in II Sam 23:2 ff. World-wide dominion and victory over foes are typically Messianic themes. The eternity and the Melchizedek order of the priesthood lend themselves more easily to a person of Messianic stature than to a lesser figure. Finally, and perhaps decisively, the introduction to the psalm, נאם יהוה, is a well-known prophetic formula, occurring only here in the Psalter.

Possibly David wrote Ps 110 to legitimize Solomon on the throne. There was a power struggle among his sons during his old age, a struggle in which David supported Solomon (I Kings 1). At a date long after David's conquest of Jerusalem the reference to Melchizedek priesthood is not so likely to have been made as at an early date.[2] But the association with the old Jebusite priest-king is easily conceivable in the thought of David, who conquered the former city-kingdom of Melchizedek. E. König notes that David was the only king to live into the reign of his successor and that David's calling Solomon "Lord" because Solomon was the ruling king would agree with his earlier respect for Saul as the ruling king, even though Saul was his mortal enemy and David already knew that God had chosen him to be Saul's successor. König also suggests that Ps 110 is the poetic counterpart to David's dying charge to Solomon, in which he voices his hope that Solomon will fulfil the terms of the Nathanic oracle (I Kings 2:1-4).[3]

David's hope that his son would be the kind of ruler delineated in the Davidic covenant and anticipated in the psalm did not materialize. Nevertheless his description of the super-Davidic king remained

---

[1] The Dead Sea Scrolls exclude the old Maccabaean interpretation by showing the Psalter was a pre-Maccabaean compilation. See W. F. Albright, in *The OT and Modern Study* (ed. H. H. Rowley; Oxford, 1951), 25; M. Burrows, *More Light on the Dead Sea Scrolls*, 169ff. H. G. Jefferson dates the psalm early because of the unusually high percentage of words paralleled in Ugaritic (71%) (*JBL*, 73 [1954], 152ff.—also for a devastating attack on the Maccabaean view, now rendered unnecessary by the DSS).

[2] Cf. Kraus, *Ps*, 756.

[3] König, *Die messianischen Weissagungen des A.T.*, 150.

a classic expression to be fulfilled by someone greater than Solomon in David's line of successors. In Ps 110 (and Ps 2), then, we see the beginnings of eschatological Messianism. It is the stage at which there has arisen expectation of a great king who in a final sense measures up to the terms of the Davidic covenant. It is also the stage at which there exists optimism that the new or current ruler may turn out to be that king. Later comes dismay at the failure of the Davidic dynasty, a dismay which led to the enriching of the Messianic concept on the one hand by the doctrine of a suffering Servant (to bear the penalty of his predecessors' failures) and on the other hand by the doctrine of a transcendant Son of man (for a merely human Messiah could turn out to be no better than his predecessors).

To the Jews of Jesus' time the failure of Solomon and the other Davidic kings had made it obvious that the ultimate meaning of the psalm could be realized only in the Messiah. Jesus' point is that a Messianic interpretation heightens the meaning of any passage of scripture.[1] Therefore, the word "Lord" carries a full implication of deity beyond the weaker, representative sense intended by David, just as the phrases "at my right hand," "priest forever," and "after the order of Melchizedek" are pressed to their ultimate possible meanings elsewhere in the NT.[2]

Concerning the original meaning of the Isaianic Servant passages (quoted in Mt 3:17; 8:17; 12:18-21; 20:28; 26:67; 27:57), non-Messianic explanations have devoured one another. British scholarship, at least, seems to have come around to essentially the same view as Delitzsch's pyramid, Israel—the remnant—the Messiah.[3] The

---

[1] Cf. Peter's use of Ps 16:10, which originally referred to deliverance *before* death, but in its grander Messianic meaning refers to deliverance *after* death by resurrection. In the same way what the OT righteous sufferers intended to be figurative descriptions of their woes find exactly literal fulfilment in Jesus' passion according to NT authors. E.g., Mt (27:34, 48) takes the parallelism in Ps 69:22 separately and literally instead of synonymously and figuratively—not because of misunderstanding the OT text, but by way of intensification through Messianic application.

[2] Cf. the application of אלהים to rulers and judges as God's representatives in Ex 22:8, 28; Ps 82:6. Underlying Jesus' interpretation is the idea that scripture may contain a divinely intended significance higher (or deeper) than the human author intended.

[3] C. R. North, *The Suffering Servant in Deutero-Is* (Oxford, 1948); *idem*, in *Interpretationes ad Vetus Testamentum Pertinentes*, 141ff.; H. H. Rowley, *The Servant of the Lord*. Cf. E. J. Young, *Studies in Is*, 114ff. Morna D. Hooker's attempted revival of the collective view must be rejected (*op. cit.*,

prophecies in Is 40-66 are prevailingly eschatological.[1] The Servant's enduement with the Spirit, work of judgment upon the nations, restoration of Israel, exaltation in Israel and among the Gentiles, and ministry of salvation to the Gentiles are as typically Messianic as possible. These themes tie in perfectly with such acknowledged Messianic passages as Is (7), 9, and 11.[2] In the OT outside Is, the Messiah is called "my Servant" five times (Ezek 34:23 f.; 37:24 f.; Zech 3:8), and numerous times in *II Esdras* (*IV Ezra*)[3] and the Targum.[4] The reading in 1QIs[a] 52:14 ("I have anointed") betrays Messianic interpretation of the Servant at Qumran.[5] The Messianic view also finds support in rabbinic literature.[6] The evidence points to a Messianic intention behind the Servant passages and to a recognition of that intention from the beginning.

The application of Is 53:4 to Jesus' physical healings (Mt 8:17) calls for special comment. The prophet has in mind the Servant's taking the diseases of others upon himself through his suffering and death for their sin, the root cause of sickness and disease.[7] Insofar as Mt represents Jesus' healings as illustrations of his redemptive work, visible pledges of his taking away sin, and the compassion exercised and the healing virtue expended as beginnings of his passion, the evangelist has caught the thought of Is.[8] Mt's use of Is 53:4 may be partially based on the observation that the verse forms a transition from the Servant's growing up, being despised, and knowing sorrow and sickness on the one hand to his suffering and death on the other. Although part of the rabbinic tradition interpreted the verse of physical sickness,[9] the application

---

41ff.). For crushing blows against the collective view, see Mowinckel, *He That Cometh*, 213ff.; E. J. Young, *Studies in Is*, 105ff.

[1] "Eschatological" does not imply cessation, but consummation. That the prophets may have mistakenly expected the consummation in the near-future restoration from the exile says nothing against the note of finality in their message.

[2] See J. Bourke, *CBQ*, 22 (1960), 137ff.

[3] 7:28; 13:32, 37, 52; 14:9; 7:28 v.l., 29; also Syr. *Bar.* 70:9.

[4] Is 42:1; 43:10; 52:13; Ezek 34:23f.; 37:24f.; Zech 3:8. See J. Jeremias, *The Servant of God*, 49.

[5] W. H. Brownlee, *BASOR*, 132 (1953), 8ff.; 135 (1954), 33ff.

[6] Edersheim, *Life and Times*, II, 726f.; Strack-Billerbeck, *op. cit.*, I, 481ff.

[7] On the close relationship between sin, sickness, and suffering in Jewish thought, see Weber, *op. cit.*, 322ff.

[8] See Cullmann, *Christology*, 69; Wolff, *op. cit.*, 73f.; Oepke, *TWNT*, IV, 1090; Lange, *op. cit.*, 158; Apollinaris of Laodicea, in *Matthäus-Kommentare aus der griechischen Kirche* (ed., J. Reuss), 11.

[9] Strack-Billerbeck, *op. cit.*, I, 481f.

in Mt stands in contrast with the spiritualizing interpretation of the Targum. The allusion to Is 53:9 in the account of Jesus' burial (Mt 27:57) shows Mt also recognized the larger reference in Is 53 to the Servant's vicarious suffering and death.

Jesus' use of Dan 7:13 (Mt 24:30; 26:64; 28:18) presupposes that the passage speaks of a Messianic or eschatological figure of superhuman proportions. That the Danielic Son of man is indeed such an individual figure, who represents the saints and shares his rule with them (therefore the substitution of "saints" in the interpretation [v. 18]), and not a mere collective symbol for or personification of the saints is evident from a number of considerations. The Son of man stands in opposition to the "little horn," a king, not a people (vv. 8, 20-26). The four beasts are said to be four kings, i.e., representatives of their kingsdoms (cf. vv. 16 f. and 23).[1] A similar linking of king and people in apocalyptic is seen in Dan 2:37 f.; 8:20 f.; Rev 13.[2] Verse 14 makes a distinction between the Son of man and the kingdom he receives; and he is to be served and worshipped.[3] The clouds with which the Son of man comes are a theophanic symbol.[4] In Ezek 1:26 the divine being sitting above the cloud is described as one with "a likeness as the appearance of a man."[5] The saints are present in the vision before the destruction

[1] Cf. Gressmann, *op. cit.*, 140; Ellison, *op. cit.*, 13.

[2] *Ibid.*

[3] E. J. Young, *The Messianic Prophecies of Dan* (Grand Rapids, 1954), 46f.

[4] Ex 13:21f.; 19:9, 16; 34:5; Num 11:25; Ps 18:12f.; 97:2; 104:3; Is 19:1; Ezek 1:4ff. Cf. Baal in the Ugaritic texts, the god who "rides upon the clouds." R. B. Y. Scott's objection that it is strange the clouds are associated with a man-like figure instead of with the Ancient of days has force only if one does not recognize the superhuman stature of the Son of man (*NTS*, 5 [1959], 130). Scott's own view that "with the clouds of heaven" is not to be connected specifically with the coming of the Son of man, but forms the general introduction to a celestial scene, leaves the phrase hanging in the air without grammatical connection and regards vv. 11, 12 as parenthetically breaking the connection between vv. 9, 10 and 13, 14, whereas the phrase "at that time" shows that vv. 11, 12 epexegetically lay the scene on earth and prepare for the transference of dominion from the little horn and the fourth beast to the Son of man and the saints. The parallel Scott draws with Ezek 1 works to his own damage, for there the scene is located in the terrestial atmosphere. The bringing forward of the adverbial phrase to a position after "Behold"—usually, as Scott notes, the subject immediately follows the interjection and any adverbial phrase comes after (Dan 2:31; 4:7, 10; 7:2, 3, 8 [*bis*]; 8:3, 5; 12:5)—really emphasizes the theophanic significance of the clouds.

[5] "If Dan. vii.13 does not refer to a divine being, then it is the only exception out of about seventy passages in the O.T." (J. A. Emerton, *JTS*,

of the little horn (v. 21), consequently before the Son of man, and therefore are not to be equated with the Son of man.[1] There seems to be no intention to contrast the human and the bestial, for the lion of verse 4 stands upright as a man and is given human intelligence, and the little horn has the eyes of a man and a speaking mouth (v. 8).[2] If the Eastern concept of an *urmenschlicher* saviour of mankind does not provide the primary source for the Danielic Son of man, it does provide the best commentary on the kind of figure Dan must have wished to portray and the impression his first readers must have received.[3] This is confirmed by the heavenly eschatological man in apocalyptic literature (*I Enoch, II Esdras*) and by the purely Messianic interpretation of Dan 7:13 in the old synagogue.[4] The strikingly identical pattern of thought which Dan 7:13, 14 shares with Isaianic Servant passages and prophecies of the royal Messiah—universal and everlasting dominion, authority deriving from God, homage of the nations, close association with the restored and exalted nation of Israel [5]—gives final confirmation to the individually Messianic implication of Dan 7:13.

Jesus alludes to Dan 7:13 in Mt 24:30, where he describes his return as a descent. Consequently, we must understand Mt 26:64 as descent—also because the allusion to Dan 7:13 follows that to Ps 110, concerning the session at God's right hand.[1] Does Dan

---

9 [1958], 232—concerning the clouds). Cf. A. Feuillet, *RB*, 60 (1953), 173ff., 321ff.

[1] H. H. Rowley answers that this objection misses the point that the Son of man is not held to stand for the saints as such, but for their *kingdom* or *rule* (*Darius the Mede* [Cardiff, 1935], 63). How then can he answer the argument that the kingdom or rule is *given* to the Son of man and therefore cannot be equated with him?

[2] Cf. C. H. Kraeling, *Anthropos and Son of Man* (New York, 1927), 132f.

[3] W. F. Albright, *From the Stone Age to Christianity*, 290ff.; W. O. E. Oesterley, *The Jews and Judaism during the Greek Period* (London, 1941), 152ff.; Gressmann, *op. cit.*, 343ff.; C. H. Kraeling, *Anthropos and Son of Man*. Cf. features of the Davidic Messiah similar to those of the primordial man: origin in the dim past (Mic 5:2), mysterious birth (Is 7:14; Mic 5:3), kingship over a paradisaic earth (Is 11:6-8; Gen 49:8-12; etc.) (Jenni, in *IDB*, III, p. 361).

[4] Strack-Billerbeck, *op. cit.*, I, 956f. Besides the rabbinical references, see the Targum to Ps 8:5; 80:18; 144:3.

[5] W. Manson, *op. cit.*, 99, 171. Cf. the building of Dan 12:3 on Is 53:11, and Qumran interpretation, on which see F. F. Bruce, *NTS*, 2 (1955/56), 176; *idem, Biblical Exegesis*, 55ff.

7:13 likewise refer to a descent of the Son of man? In Dan 7:9 there is no suggestion that the scene has shifted from the terrestial sphere of the preceding part of the vision. Rather, thrones are set, and the Ancient of days sits on one of them. It is hardly probable that a throne for God would be set in heaven, since that is his usual place of abode. Furthermore, according to verse 22 the Ancient of days "came." It is by far most natural, then, to understand that a throne was placed for God in the terrestial sphere and that he came and sat upon it. Compare the theophany in the terrestial atmosphere in Ezek 1. When therefore the Son of man comes "with the clouds of heaven" to the Ancient of days, we can understand nothing else than that he comes earthward to receive the dominion over the earth which is now to be taken from the beasts and given to him, and to exercise that dominion upon the earth with the saints.[2] Jesus' interpretation of Dan 7:13 as a descent by an eschatological, Messianic figure is not to be rejected.

Since Dan 7 presents a Messianic figure as receiving the eschatological kingdom, it is only natural we should see Messianic significance in the stone which smites the image in Dan 2 and becomes the kingdom of God (Mt 21:44).[3]

The unidentified pierced one over whom the tribes of Israel mourn in Zech 12:10 (Mt 24:30) and the smitten shepherd in Zech 13:7 (Mt 26:31) come in an unquestionably eschatological and Messianic context. In view of the suffering Servant in Is, the Messianic title "my servant the Branch" in Zech 3:8, and Zech's emphasis on Messiah's lowliness and meekness (Zech 9:9), there is

---

[1] See H. K. McArthur, *NTS*, 4 (1958), 156-158; H. P. Owen, *SJT*, 12 (1959), 173f.; Cranfield, *Mk*, 444f. Against Glasson, *The Second Advent*, 13ff., 63ff., 186f.; J. A. T. Robinson, *ET*, 67 (1955/56), 337f.; *idem*, *Jesus and His Coming* (London, 1957), 45, who see both in Dan and in the NT a reference to enthronement in heaven. Robinson would make the expressions in Mt 26:64 synonymously parallel to avoid the difficulty of order. But "sitting" and "coming" simply cannot be equated. E. Schweizer resorts to inverting the order of the expressions (*JBL*, 79 [1960], 120). In a rejoinder to Mc Arthur, Glasson refers the Ps 110-allusion to the individual exaltation of Christ, but the Dan 7-allusion to the collective coming into being of the new people of God—neglecting Jesus' individualizing use of Dan 7:13 (Mt 24:30 par) to describe his descent (*NTS*, 7 [1960], 88-93). Glasson's difficulty in seeing a temporal progression from sitting to coming is imaginary.

[2] For this view, see Dalman, *Words*, 241; Beasley-Murray, *op. cit.*, 90f.

[3] Cf. the Messianic interpretation of Dan 2:45 in *Tanch.* B תרומה § 6 (46b), cited by Strack-Billerbeck, *op. cit.*, I, 877.

no difficulty in supposing these personages were conceived of Messianically and in connection with the suffering Servant.[1] Particular attention should be paid to the appellation "my fellow" in Zech 13:7 and to the calling of the Davidic Messiah "my servant" and "shepherd" in Ezek 37:24.[2] Zech 12:10 is referred to the Josephite Messiah in *Sukka* 52a.[3] It is usually thought that Jesus broadens the reference in Zech 12:10 by including the tribes of the whole earth as well as of Israel. But in view of Mt 23:37-39 (= Lk 13:34 f.),[4] the occasion of the Olivet Discourse (Jesus' statement about the fate of Jerusalem and the Temple), and the special interest displayed in the discourse toward events in Palestine (the abomination of desolation, the flight from Judaea), we may better regard Jesus' reference as identical with Zech's, viz., the repentance of the tribes of Israel throughout the land of Palestine as they see their Messiah returning.[5]

If these OT prophecies have a higher meaning than can be found in historical situations and personages before Jesus and if this full meaning finds realization in him, then—and only then—can the OT be considered anything more than a source-book for the historical background of Christianity. Typological correspondences become nebulous and coincidental, unless supported by detailed fulfilments of individual predictions. Such specific fulfilments are not fragmentary; they are parts of an organic whole.[6] They are also consistent with the original meaning of the OT texts. When we anchor the broad Christian view of the divine purpose guiding OT history toward Jesus Christ in specific fulfilments as well as in general typology, then the remarkable correspondence between OT history and prophecy and the life and ministry of Jesus becomes the kind of kerygmatic argument intended by Jesus and the first evangelist in their use of the OT.

---

[1] Cf. Edghill, *op. cit.*, 234f.

[2] Zech 13:7 appears in the Zadokite work (both MSS: A—vii.20; B—xix. 5-9). Rabin suggests the shepherd was thought to be the Teacher of Righteousness (*The Zadokite Documents*, 30). F. F. Bruce thinks the application was to a ruler considered wicked by the Zadokites (*Biblical Exegesis*, 34). It appears to me the citation puts no emphasis on the identity of the shepherd, but is introduced only because of the smiting-motif.

[3] See Moore, *Judaism*, II, 370.

[4] "O Jerusalem, ... Ye shall not see me henceforth, till ye shall say, Blessed is he that cometh in the name of the Lord."

[5] Γῆ is, of course, used regularly in the LXX for Palestine.

[6] M. Barth, *Theology Today*, 11 (1954), 342-353; Stonehouse, *op. cit.*, 194.

BIBLIOGRAPHY[1]

Books on Quotations of the OT in the NT

Amsler, S. *L'Ancien Testament dans l'église.* Neuchatel, 1960.

Anger, R. *Ratio, qua loci Veteris Testamenti in evangelio Matthaei laudantur, quid valeat ad illustrandam huius evangelii originem, quaeritur.* (Leipziger Programme I-III.) Leipzig, 1861-62.

Böhl, E. *Die alttestamentlichen Citate im NT.* Wien, 1878.

Bonsirven, J. *Exégèse rabbinique et exégèse paulinienne.* Paris, 1939.

Carpzov, J. G. *Critica Sacra Veteris Testamenti.* Leipzig, 1728.

——. *A Defence of the Hebrew Bible.* Translated by M. Marcus. London, 1729.

Chasles, R. *L'Ancien Testament dans le NT.* Paris, 1937.

Clapton, E. *Our Lord's Quotations from the OT.* London, 1922.

Clemen, A. *Der Gebrauch des Alten Testamentes in den neutestamentlichen Schriften.* Gütersloh, 1895.

Credner, K. A. *Beiträge zur Einleitung in die biblischen Schriften.* Bd. II: *Das alttestamentliche Urevangelium.* Halle, 1838.

Davidson, S. *Sacred Hermeneutics.* Edinburgh, 1843. [See Chap. XI, "Quotations from the OT in the New," pp. 334-515.]

Dittmar, W. *Vetus Testamentum in Novo.* Göttingen, 1903.

Dodd, C. H. *According to the Scriptures.* London, 1952.

——. *The OT in the New.* London, 1952.

Döpke, J. C. C. *Hermeneutik der neutestamentlichen Schriftsteller.* Leipzig, 1829.*

Doeve, J. W. *Jewish Hermeneutics in the Synoptic Gospels and Acts.* Te Assen Bij, 1954.

Drusius, J. *Parallela Sacra: hoc est, Locorum Veteris Testamenti cum iis quae in Novo citantur conjuncta Commemoratio, Ebraice et Graece, cum Notis.* Franeck, 1588. [Republished 1616 and in *Critica Sacra,* Vol. VIII, pp. 1262-1326. London, 1660.]*

Ellis, E. E. *Paul's Use of the OT.* Edinburgh, 1957.

Feigel, F. K. *Der Einfluss des Weissagungsbeweises und anderer Motive auf die Leidensgeschichte.* Tübingen, 1910.

Gibson, E. C. S. *The OT in the New.* (The Warburtonian Lectures for 1903-1907.) London, 1907.

Gough, H. *The NT Quotations.* London, 1855.

[Gregory, J. B.] *The Oracles Ascribed to Mt by Papias.* London, 1894.*

Grelot, P. *Sens Chrétien de L'Ancien Testament.* Tournai, 1962.*

Hänel, J. *Der Schriftbegriff Jesu.* (Beiträge zur Förderung christlicher Theologie. 24. Bd., 5./6. Heft.) Gütersloh, 1919.

Harris, J. R. *Testimonies.* With the assistance of V. Burch. 2 vols. Cambridge, 1916-20.

Haupt, E. *Die alttestamentlichen Citate in den vier Evangelien.* Colberg, 1871.

Hody, H. *De Bibliorum Textibus Originalibus.* Oxford, 1705.

Hoffmann, I. *Demonstratio Evangelica.* Tübingen, 1773.

Hofmann, J. Chr. K. *Weissagung und Erfüllung im alten und im neuen Testamente.* 2 vols. Nördlingen, 1841-44.

[1] An asterisk following the entry indicates that the work cited has been unavailable to me.

Hommes, N. J. *Het Testimoniaboek*. Amsterdam, 1935.*
Hühn, E. *Die alttestamentlichen Citate und Reminiscenzen im NT*. Tübingen, 1900.
Hunt, B. P. W. Stather. *Primitive Gospel Sources*. London, 1951.
Johnson, F. *The Quotations of the NT from the Old considered in the Light of General Literature*. London, 1896.
Junius, F. *Sacrorum parallelorum libri III*. Heidelberg, 1588.*
Kähler, M. *Jesus und das Alte Testament*. Gütersloh, 1938.
Kautzsch, A. F. *De Veteris Testamenti locis a Paulo Apostolo allegatis*. Leipzig, 1867.
Kistemaker, S. *The Psalm Citations in the Epistle to the Hebrews*. Amsterdam, 1961.
Larcher, C. *L'Actualite Chretienne de l'Ancien Testament*. Paris, 1962.*
Lindars, B. *NT Apologetic*. Philadelphia, 1961.
Massebieau, E. *Examen des citations de l'Ancien Testament dans l'évangile selon saint Matthieu*. Paris, 1885.
Michel, O. *Paulus und seine Bibel*. (Beiträge zur Förderung christlicher Theologie. 2. Reihe, 18. Bd.) Gütersloh, 1929.
Mounier. *De locis nonnullis Evangeliorum in quibus Veteris Testamenti libri ab Jesu laudantur*. Amsterdam, 1856.*
Oepke, A. *Jesus und das Alte Testament*. Leipzig, 1938.
Owen, H. *The Modes of Quotation Used by the Evangelical Writers Explained and Vindicated*. London, 1789.
Passages cited from the OT by the Writers of the NT, compared with the Original Hebrew and the Septuagint Version. Arranged by the Junior Class in the Theological Seminary, Andover (U.S.A.); and published at their request, under the superintendence of M. Stuart. Andover, Mass., 1827.*
Plooij, D. *Studies in the Testimony Book*. (Verhandelingen der Koninklijke Akademie van Wetenschappen te Amsterdam. Afdeeling Letterkunde. Nieuwe Reeks, Deel XXXII, no. 2.) Amsterdam, 1932.
Randolph, T. *The Prophecies and Other Texts Cited in the NT, Compared with the Hebrew Original and with the Septuagint Version to which are Added Notes*. Oxford, 1782.
Roepe, G. *De Veteris Testamenti Locrum in Apostolorum Libris Allegatione*. 1827.*
Scott, J. *Principles of NT Quotation*. Edinburgh, 1877.
Selwyn, E. C. *The Oracles in the NT*. London, 1912.
Smits, C. *Oud-Testamentische Citaten in het NT*. Deel I: *Synoptische Evangelien*. Malmberg, 1952.
Stendahl, K. *The School of St. Mt and Its Use of the OT*. (Acta Seminarii Neotestamentici Upsaliensis, XX.) Uppsala, 1954.
Surenhusius, G. ספר המשוה *sive* ΒΙΒΛΟΣ ΚΑΤΑΛΛΑΓΗΣ. Amsterdam, 1713.
Tasker, R. V. G. *The OT in the NT*. 2nd ed. London, 1954.
Taylor, C. *The Gospel in the Law*. Cambridge, 1869.
Torrey, C. C. *Documents of the Primitive Church*. New York, 1941. [See "The Biblical Quotations in Mt," pp. 41-90.]
Toy, C. H. *Quotations in the NT*. New York, 1884.
Turpie, D. M. *The NT View of the Old*. London, 1872.
——. *The OT in the New*. Edinburgh, 1868.
Ungern-Sternberg, A. *Der traditionelle alttestamentliche Schriftbeweis "de Christo" und "de Evangelio" in der alten Kirche bis zur Zeit Eusebs von Caesarea*. Halle, 1913.

Whiston, W. *An Essay towards Restoring the True Text of the OT*. London, 1722.*

Articles and Periodical Literature on Quotations Of the OT in the NT

Allen, W. C. "Matthew xii. 19—Isaiah xlii.2.," *ET*, 20 (1908/09), 140f.
——. "The OT Quotations in St. Matthew and St. Mark," *ET*, 12 (1900/01), 187-189, 281-285.
Alting, J. "Parallelismus Testimoniorum Veteris Testamenti Quae in Euangelio suo citat S. Matthaeus," *Operum*, Vol. II. Amsterdam, 1685.
Argyle, A. W. "Scriptural Quotations in Q Material," *ET*, 65 (1953/54), 285f.
Atkinson, B. F. C. "The Textual Background of the Use of the OT by the New," *Journal of the Transactions of the Victoria Institute*, 79 (1947), 39-60.
Ayles, H. H. B. "Our Lord's Refutation of the Sadducees," *The Expositor*, 11, 6th Series (1905), 440-446.
Bacon, B. W. "Jesus' Voice from Heaven," *American Journal of Theology*, 9 (1905), 451-473.
——. "Supplementary Note on the Aorist εὐδόκησα, Mk i.11," *JBL*, 20 (1901), 28-30.
Barret, C. K. "The OT in the Fourth Gospel," *JTS*, 48 (1947), 155-169.
Bates, W. H. "Quotations in the NT from the OT," *BibSac*, 77 (1920), 424-428.
Baumstark, A. "Die Zitate des Mt.-Ev. aus dem Zwölfprophetenbuch," *Biblica*, 37 (1956), 296-313.
Black, M. "The Problem of the OT Quotations in the Gospels," *Journal of the Manchester University Egyptian and Oriental Society*, 23 (1942), 4.
Boman, T. "Das letzte Wort Jesu," *Studia Theologica*, 17 (1963), 103-119.
Braun, H. "Das Alte Testament im Neuen Testament," *ZTK*, 59 (1962), 16-31.
Bruce, F. F. "The Book of Zech and the Passion Narrative," *BJRL*, 43 (1961), 336-353.
Buckler, F. W. " 'Eli, Eli, Lama Sabachthani?' ", *American Journal of Semitic Languages and Literatures*, 55 (1938), 378-391.
Burkitt, F. C. "On St. Mk xv 34 in Cod. Bobiensis," *JTS*, 1 (1900), 278f.
Buse, I. "The Markan Account of the Baptism of Jesus and Is LXIII," *JTS*, 7 (1956), 74f.
Cappellus, L. "Quaestu de Locis Parallelis Veteris et Novi Testamenti," *Critica Sacra*, 444-557. Paris, 1650.
Cerfaux, L. "L'exégèse de l'Ancien Testament par le NT," *Recueil Lucien Cerfaux*, II, 205-217. Gembloux, 1954.
——. "Les sources scripturaires de Mt. XI, 25-30," *Ephemerides Theologicae Lovanienses*, 31 (1955), 331-342.
Chapman, J. "Zacharias, Slain Between the Temple and the Altar," *JTS*, 13 (1912), 398-410.
Coggan, F. D. "Note on the Word ὡσαννά," *ET*, 52 (1940/41), 76f.
Davidson, S. "Quotations from the OT in the New," Chapters XXVIII-XXXII in *An Introduction to the Critical Study and Knowledge of the Holy Scriptures* by T. H. Horne, II, 113-201. 10th ed. London, 1856.
Dibelius, M. "Die alttestamentlichen Motive in der Leidensgeschichte des Petrus- und des Johannes-Evangeliums," *Beihefte zur ZAW*, 33 (1918), 125-150. (Abhandlungen zur Semitischen Religionskunde und Sprachwissenschaft; Wolf Wilhelm Grafen von Baudissin Festschrift.) Giessen, 1918.

Van Dodewaard, J. A. E. "La force évocatrice de la citation," *Biblica*, 36 (1955), 482-491.

Dreyfus, F. "L'argument scripturaire de Jésus en faveur de la résurrection des morts (Marc, XII, 26-27)," *RB*, 66 (1959), 213-224.

——. "Saint Mt et l'Ancien Testament," *La Vie Spirituelle*, 41 (1959), 121-135.

Dupont, J. "L'arrière-fond biblique du récit des tentations de Jésus," *NTS*, 3 (1956/57), 287-304.

——. "L'utilisation apologétique de l'Ancien Testament dans les discours des Actes," *Ephemerides Theologicae Lovanienses*, 29 (1953), 289-327.

Edgar, S. L. "Respect for Context in Quotations from the OT," *NTS*, 9 (1962), 55-62.

Ellis, E. E. "A Note on Pauline Hermeneutics," *NTS*, 2 (1955/56), 131f.

Findlay, J. A. "The Book of Testimonies and the Structure of the First Gospel," *The Expositor*, 20, 8th Series (1920), 388-400.

Fisher, L. R. "Betrayed by Friends," *Interpretation*, 18 (1964), 20-27.

Fitzmyer, J. A. "The Use of Explicit OT Quotations in Qumran Literature and in the NT," *NTS*, 7 (1961), 297-333.

Flusser, D. "Blessed Are the Poor in Spirit," *Israel Exploration Journal*, 10 (1960), 1-13.

Gärtner, B. "The Habakkuk Commentary (DSH) and the Gospel of Mt," *Studia Theologica*, 8 (1954), 1-24.

Gibson, E. C. S. "Our Lord's Use of the OT," *The Expositor*, 1, 2nd Series (1881), 292-304.

Glasson, T. F. "Mk xiii and the Greek OT," *ET*, 69 (1957/58), 213-215.

——. "The Reply to Caiaphas (Mark XIV. 62)," *NTS*, 7 (1960), 88-93.

Gnilka, J. "Mein Gott, mein Gott, warum hast du mich verlassen?", *BZ*, 3 (1959), 294-297.

Gordis, R. "Quotations as a Literary Usage in Biblical, Oriental and Rabbinic Literature," *HUCA*, 22 (1949), 157-219.

Guillaume, A. "Mt. 27, 46 in the Light of the Dead Sea Scroll of Is," *PEQ* (1951), 78-80.

Gundry, R. "למטלים. 1 Q Is a 50, 6 and Mk 14, 65," *Revue de Qumran*, Tome 2, Num. 8 (1960), 559-567.

Haering, T. "Das Alte Testament im Neuen," *ZNW*, 17 (1916), 213-227.

Harris, J. R. "Did Jesus Use Testimonies?", *ET*, 36 (1924/25), 410-413.

——. "A Factor of OT Influence in the NT," *ET*, 37 (1925/26), 6-11.

——. "Traces of Targumism in the NT," *ET*, 32 (1920/21), 373-376.

Jeremias, J. "Die Muttersprache des Evangelisten Mt," *ZNW*, 50 (1959), 270-274.

Johnson, S. E. "The Biblical Quotations in Mt," *HTR*, 36 (1943), 135-153.

Katz, P. "The Quotations from Dt in Heb," *ZNW*, 49 (1958), 213-223.

Kennard, J. S., Jr. " 'Hosanna' and the Purpose of Jesus," *JBL*, 67 (1948), 171-176.

——. "Nazarean and Nazareth," *JBL*, 66 (1947), 79-81.

——. "Was Capernaum the Home of Jesus?", *JBL*, 65 (1946), 131-141.

Kent, Homer A., Jr. "Matthew's Use of the OT," *BibSac*, 121 (1964), 34-43.

Kilpatrick, G. D. "Mt iv.4," *JTS*, 45 (1944), 176.

King, E. G. "St. Paul's Method of Quotation," *The Expositor*, 10, 3rd Series (1889), 233-238.

Klein, G. "Hosanna in der Höhe," *ZNW*, 2 (1901), 345f.

König, E. "The Origin of ζαφθανεί in Cod. D of Mt xxvii. 46 and Mk xv. 34," *ET*, 11 (1899/1900), 237f.

Kraemer, A. [A review of *Het Testimoniaboek* by N. J. Hommes], *Philologische Wochenschrift*, 58 (1938), 73-83.
Lohse, E. "Hosianna," *Nov Test*, 6 (1963), 113-119.
Lyonnet, S. " 'Quoniam Nazaraeus vocabitur,' " *Biblica*, 25 (1944), 196-206.
Manson, T. W. "The Argument from Prophecy," *JTS*, 46 (1945), 129-136.
——. "The OT in the Teaching of Jesus," *BJRL*, 34 (1951/52), 312-332.
Martz, J. "Citations de l'A.T. dans le N.T.," *Dictionnaire Encyclopédique de la Bible*, I, 213f. Paris, 1932.
McArthur, H. K. "Mk XIV.62," *NTS*, 4 (1958), 156-158.
Mead, R. T. "A Dissenting Opinion about Respect for Context in OT Quotations," *NTS*, 10 (1964), 279-289.
Metzger, B. M. "The Formulas Introducing Quotations of Scripture in the NT and the Mishnah," *JBL*, 70 (1951), 297-307.
——. "Scriptural Quotations in Q Material," *ET*, 65 (1953/54), 125.
Nestle, Eb. " 'Between the Temple and the Altar,' " *ET*, 13 (1901/02), 562.
——. "Mk xv.34," *ET*, 9 (1897/98), 521f.
——. "Mt xii. 19-Is xlii.2," *ET*, 20 (1908/09), 92f., 189.
——. "The Quotation in Mt xv.9; Mk vii.7.," *ET*, 11 (1899/1900), 330.
——. "Über Zacharias in Mt 23," *ZNW*, 6 (1905), 198-200.
Nicole, R. "NT Use of the OT," in *Revelation and the Bible*, 137-151. Edited by Carl F. H. Henry. London, 1959.
O'Rourke, J. J. "The Fulfillment Texts in Mt," *CBQ*, 24 (1962), 394-403.
Prigent, P. "Quelques testimonia messianiques," *TZ*, 15 (1959), 419-430.
Rehm, M. "Eli, Eli, lamma sabacthani," *BZ*, 2 (1958), 275-278.
Rembry, J. G. " 'Quoniam Nazaraeus vocabitur' (Mt 2/23)," *Studii Biblici Franciscani Annus*, 12 (1961/62), 46-65.*
Rigaux, B. "ΒΔΕΛΥΓΜΑ ΤΗΣ ΕΡΗΜΩΣΕΩΣ," *Biblica*, 40 (1959), 675-683.
Robinson, J. A. T. "The Second Coming—Mk xiv.62," *ET*, 67 (1955/56), 336-340.
Rose, A. "L'influence des Psaumes sur les annonces et les récits de la passion et de la résurrection dans les évangiles," in *Le Psautier*, 297-356. Edited by R. de Langhe. Louvain, 1962.
Scherer, M. "De l'interpretation de l'Ancien Testament par les auteurs du Nouveau," *Revue de Strasbourg* (or *Revue de Théologie de M. Colani*), IX.*
Schmitz, O. "Das Alte Testament im NT," in *Wort und Geist, Festgabe für Karl Heim*. Berlin, 1934.
Schweizer, E. [Mt 2:23], in *Judentum, Urchristentum, Kirche* (J. Jeremias Festschrift; Berlin, 1960), 90-93.
Scott, T. "A Collection of the Quotations from the OT in the New, with the Septuagint," *The Christian Observer*, Vols. 9 and 10.*
Sherlock, T. "On the Use and Intent of Prophecy in the Several Ages of the World," *The Works of Bishop Sherlock*, IV, iii-131. London, 1830.
Shires, H. M. "The Meaning of the Term 'Nazarene,' " *Anglican Theological Review*, 29 (1947), 19-27.
Sidersky, D. "Les citations de l'Ancien Testament dans les évangiles," in *Actes du Congrès International d'Histoire des Religions* (Paris, 1923), Vol. II. Paris, 1925.
——. "Un passage hébreu dans le NT," *Journal Asiatique*, 3 (1914), 232f.
Smith, C. W. F. "The Horse and the Ass in the Bible," *Anglican Theological Review*, 27 (1945), 86-97.
Smith, H. "Ναζωραῖος κληθήσεται," *JTS*, 28 (1927), 60.
Sparks, H. F. D. [A review of] *The School of St. Mt* by K. Stendahl, *JTS*, 7 (1956), 103-105.

Sparks, "St. Mt's References to Jer," *JTS*, 1 (1950), 155f.
Sperber, A. "NT and Septuagint," *JBL*, 59 (1940), 193-293.
——. "The NT and the Septuagint," *Tarbiz*, 6 (1934/35), 1-29.
Staerk, W. "Die alttestamentlichen Citate bei den Schriftstellern des NT," *ZWT*, 36 (1893), 70-98, 40 (1897), 211-268.
Steele, W. H. "Hosanna," *The Expositor*, 25, 8th Series (1923), 398-400.
Stendahl, K. "Quis et Unde," in *Judentum, Urchristentum, Kirche* (J. Jeremias Festschrift). Berlin, 1960.
Stephenson, T. "The OT Quotations Peculiar to Mt," *JTS*, 20 (1919), 227-229.
Sundberg, A. C., Jr. "On Testimonies," *NovTest*, 3 (1959), 268-281.
Sutcliffe, E. F. "Mt 27^9," *JTS*, 3 (1952), 227f.
Swaeles, R. "L'arrière-fond scripturaire de Matt. XXI. 43 et son lien avec Matt. XXI. 44," *NTS*, 6 (1959), 310-313.
Tholuck. "The Citations of the OT in the New," *BibSac*, 11 (1854), 568-616. [This is a translation by C. A. Aiken of the treatise "The OT in the New," an appendix to the third completely revised edition of the author's commentary on Heb.]
Thomson, J. G. S. S. "Christ and the OT," *ET*, 67 (1955/56), 18-20.
Turner, C. H. "Ο ΥΙΟΣ ΜΟΥ Ο ΑΓΑΠΗΤΟΣ," *JTS*, 27 (1926), 113-129.
Venard, L. "Citations de l'Ancien Testament dans le NT," *Dictionnaire de la Bible, Supplément*, II, 23-51. Paris, 1934.
Weidel, K. "Studien über den Einfluss des Weissagungsbeweises auf die evangelische Geschichte," *Theol. Stud. u. Krit.*, 83 (1910), 83-109, 163-195, 267-286.
Werner, E. " 'Hosanna' in the Gospels," *JBL*, 65 (1946), 97-122.
Wiles, M. F. "The OT in Controversy with the Jews," *SJT*, 8 (1955), 113-126.
Winter, P. "Genesis 1:27 and Jesus' saying on Divorce," *ZAW*, 70 (1958), 260f.
——. "Ṣadoqite Fragments IV 20, 21 and the Exegesis of Gen 1: 27 in late Judaism," *ZAW*, 68 (1956), 71-84, 264.
Wood, C. T. "The Word ὡσαννά in Mt xxi.9," *ET*, 52 (1940/41), 357.
Woods, L. "Manner of Quoting from the OT by the Writers of the New," *The Works of Leonard Woods*, I, 116-133. Boston, 1851.
Wright, A. [A review of] *The Oracles ascribed to Mt by Papias, The Critical Review*, 5 (1895), 11-17.
Zimmermann, F. "The Last Words of Jesus," *JBL*, 66 (1947), 465f.
Zimmern, H. "Nazoräer (Nazarener)," *ZDMG*, 74 (1920), 429-438.
Zolli, E. "Nazarenus Vocabitur," *ZNW*, 49 (1958), 135f.

Unpublished Material on Quotations
Of the OT in the NT

Hirschgärtner. "Examen des citations de l'Ancien Testament dans le Nouveau." Dissertation; Geneva, 1858.*
Karnetzki, M. "Die alttestamentlichen Zitate in der synoptischen Tradition." Dissertation; Tübingen, 1955 [Summary in *TLZ*, 81 (1956), 492f.]
Thomas, K. J. "The Use of the Septuagint in the Epistle to the Hebrews." Dissertation; Manchester, 1959.

AUTHOR INDEX

INDEX OF SCRIPTURE REFERENCES